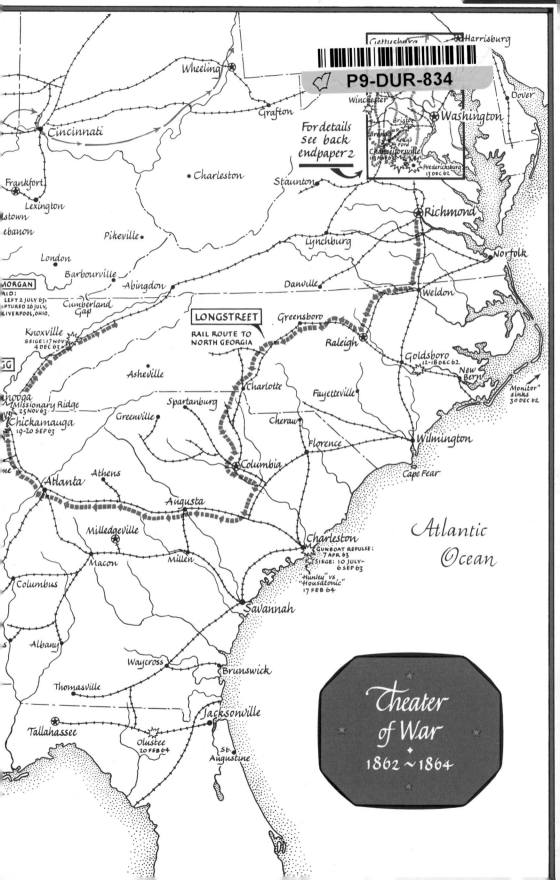

Gettysburg
Harrisburg
Dover
Winchester
Bristoe
Kelly's Ford
Brandy
Washington
Chancellorsville
13 MAY 63
Fredericksburg
13 DEC 62

For details
see back
endpaper 2

Wheeling
Grafton
Cincinnati
Charleston
Staunton
Frankfort
Lexington
Richmond
Lynchburg
Norfolk
stown
ebanon
Pikeville
Danville
Weldon
London
Barbourville
Abingdon
MORGAN
RAID:
LEFT 2 JULY 63;
CAPTURED 26 JULY,
LIVERPOOL, OHIO.
Cumberland
Gap
Greensboro
LONGSTREET
RAIL ROUTE TO
NORTH GEORGIA
Goldsboro
12-18 DEC 62
Knoxville
SEIGE: 17 NOV
4 DEC 63
Raleigh
New
Bern
Asheville
Charlotte
Fayetteville
"Monitor"
sinks
30 DEC 62
GG
nooga
Missionary Ridge
25 NOV 63
Spartanburg
Cheraw
Greenville
Chickamauga
19-20 SEP 63
Florence
Wilmington
me
Columbia
Cape Fear
Atlanta
Athens
Atlantic
Ocean
Augusta
Milledgeville
Charleston
GUNBOAT REPULSE:
7 APR 63
SIEGE: 10 JULY-
6 SEP 63
"Hunley" vs
"Housatonic"
17 FEB 64
Macon
Millen
Columbus
Savannah
Albany
Waycross
Brunswick
Thomasville
Jacksonville
Tallahassee
Olustee
20 FEB 64
St.
Augustine

Theater
of War
◆
1862 ~ 1864

The Civil War
A Narrative

ALL THESE WERE HONOURED IN THEIR GENERATIONS

AND WERE THE GLORY OF THEIR TIMES

THERE BE OF THEM

THAT HAVE LEFT A NAME BEHIND THEM

THAT THEIR PRAISES MIGHT BE REPORTED

AND SOME THERE BE WHICH HAVE NO MEMORIAL

WHO ARE PERISHED AS THOUGH THEY HAD NEVER BEEN

AND ARE BECOME AS THOUGH THEY HAD NEVER BEEN BORN

AND THEIR CHILDREN AFTER THEM

BUT THESE WERE MERCIFUL MEN

WHOSE RIGHTEOUSNESS HATH NOT BEEN FORGOTTEN

WITH THEIR SEED SHALL CONTINUALLY REMAIN

A GOOD INHERITANCE

AND THEIR CHILDREN ARE WITHIN THE COVENANT

THEIR SEED STANDETH FAST

AND THEIR CHILDREN FOR THEIR SAKES

THEIR SEED SHALL REMAIN FOR EVER

AND THEIR GLORY SHALL NOT BE BLOTTED OUT

THEIR BODIES ARE BURIED IN PEACE

BUT THEIR NAME LIVETH FOR EVERMORE

Ecclesiasticus xliv

THE
Civil War
A Narrative

— ★★ —

TULLAHOMA
to MERIDIAN

— ★★ —

Riot and Resurgence

By SHELBY FOOTE

RANDOM HOUSE · NEW YORK

Originally published in slightly different form as
Part 3 of THE CIVIL WAR: A Narrative—Fredericksburg to Meridian
© Copyright, 1963, by Shelby Foote
All rights reserved under International and Pan-American Copyright
Conventions. Published in New York by Random House, Inc., and
simultaneously in Toronto, Canada, by Random House of Canada, Limited
Library of Congress Catalog Card Number: 58–9882
ISBN: 0-307-29028-X
Manufactured in the United States of America
10 9 8 7 6 5 4 3 2 1

CONTENTS

★ ✄ ☆

☆

Tullahoma
to
Meridian

☆

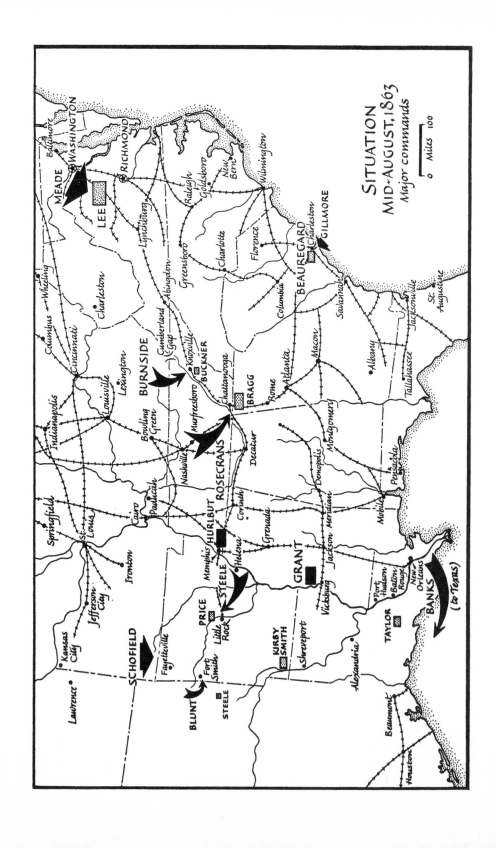

SITUATION
MID·AUGUST, 1863
Major commands

0   Miles   100

Riot and Resurgence

★ ✗ ☆

AS JUNE WORE ON, ROSECRANS AND HIS ARMY
of the Cumberland approached the end of their six-month convalescence from the rigors of Stones River. The narrowness of his escape
from total disaster on that field having convinced him more than ever of
the wisdom of meticulous preparation — which, as he saw it, had made
the hairbreadth difference between victory and defeat — he would no
more respond to prodding now than he had done in the months leading
up to that horrendous New Year's confrontation just short of Murfreesboro. Directly or indirectly, but mostly directly, Lincoln and Stanton
and Halleck all three had tried their hand at getting him to move: to no
avail. He would not budge, though he would sometimes agree blandly,
as if for the sake of prolonging the argument, that an advance was highly
desirable.

Immediately after Chancellorsville, for instance, when Stanton
reported — quite erroneously — that Hooker had inflicted as many
casualties as he suffered, Rosecrans replied: "Thanks for your dispatch. It
relieves our great suspense. What we want is to deal with their armies.
Piece for piece is good when we have the odds. We shall soon be ready
here to try that." So he said. But May went by, and still he would not
budge. "I would not push you to any rashness," Lincoln wrote, "but I
am very anxious that you do your utmost, short of rashness, to keep
Bragg from getting off to help Johnston against Grant." The Ohioan's
answer was both prompt and brief: "Dispatch received. I will attend to
it." But he did not. June came in, and still he would not budge. "If you
can do nothing yourself," Halleck wired, "a portion of your troops
must be sent to Grant's relief." Old Rosy was unperturbed by this threat
of amputation. "The time appears now nearly ripe," he responded, "and
we have begun a movement, which, with God's blessing, will give us
some good results." He omitted, however, a definition of "nearly." June
wore on; he would not budge. By June 16 Lincoln's patience was ex-

hausted, and he had the general-in-chief put a point-blank question to the Middle Tennessee commander: "Is it your intention to make an immediate movement forward? A definite answer, yes or no, is required." Halleck asked for a yes or a no, but Rosecrans gave him both. "In reply to your inquiry," he wired back, "if immediate means tonight or tomorrow, no. If it means as soon as all things are ready, say five days, yes."

At any rate this fixed the jump-off day; Washington settled back to wait for word, June 21, that the Army of the Cumberland was in motion. What came instead, by way of anticlimax on that date, was another wire, so little different in substance from the many received before that the whole sheaf might have been shuffled and refiled, indiscriminate of sequence, with little or no disturbance of its continuity, since in point of fact it had none. Bulky though it was — Old Brains had already complained to Rosecrans of the strain his frequent telegrams had placed on the military budget — the file was not so much a series of pertinent dispatches as it was a loose collection of secondhand maxims designed to strengthen his brief for refusing to expose his troops to bloodshed. "We ought to fight here," he wired, "if we have a strong prospect of winning a decisive battle over the opposing force, and upon this ground I shall act. I shall be careful" he added, "not to risk our last reserve without strong grounds to expect success." It was exasperating, to say the least; for it was becoming increasingly apparent, on evidence supplied by himself, that what Old Rosy was doing was fighting a verbal holding action, not so much against the rebels in his front as against his own superiors in his rear. Lincoln's patience almost snapped again. Three days later, however — on June 24, in a telegram headed barely two hours after midnight — the longed-for word came through: "The army begins to move at 3 o'clock this morning. W. S. Rosecrans, Major General."

The "strong grounds" on which he based his expectation of success were twofold, logistical and tactical, and he had neglected no detail in either category. Logistically he had adopted what might be called a philosophy of abundance. His requisitions, submitted practically without remission, reflected a conviction that there simply could not be too much of anything. As long ago as mid-April, for example, one of his brigadiers had been awed by the sight, at the Murfreesboro depot, of 40,000 cases of hard bread stacked in a single pile, while there were also gathered roundabout, in orderly profusion, such quantities of flour, salt pork, vinegar, and molasses as the brigadier had never seen before; he marveled at the wealth and prodigality of the government he was defending. Nor was food by any means the commander's sole or even main concern. Operating as he would be in a region that called for long supply trains and numerous cavalry to guard them and protect the flanks and front of the infantry line-of-march, he had put in for and received since December 1 no fewer than 18,450 horses and 14,067 mules. Exclusive of culls, this gave him — or should have given him, according to the quartermaster general, when combined with the number shown on hand — a total of 43,023 animals, or about one for every two men in his army. Rosecrans did not consider this one beast too many, especially since he had evacuated some 9000 of them as unserviceable and was complaining even then that over a fourth of those remaining were worn out. So it went; he kept demanding more of everything. The same applied to men. He had, as of mid-June, a total of 87,800 effectives, a considerable preponderance when compared to his estimated total for Bragg of 41,680 of all arms. However, this left out of account the necessary garrisons for Nashville, Donelson, Clarksville, and other such vital places in his rear — including Murfreesboro itself, when move-out time came round — which reduced, or would reduce, his total to 65,137 strictly available for the offensive. That was still a preponderance, but it was scarcely a man too many, as he saw it, to assure him what he called "a strong prospect of winning a decisive battle over the opposing force." Moreover, to this would be added, as he had complained soon after the bloodletting at Stones River, multiple difficulties of terrain. "The country is full of natural passes and fortifications," he informed the impatient Washington authorities, "and demands superior forces to advance with any success."

Lacking what he considered strength enough to assure a victory as the result of any direct confrontation, he had decided to depend instead on guile, and with this approach to the problem he began to perceive that the tricky terrain of which he had complained in January could be employed to his advantage. Bragg had his infantry disposed along the near side of Duck River, two divisions at Shelbyville under Polk and two at Wartrace under Hardee, about twenty miles from Murfreesboro and roughly half that far from Tullahoma, his headquarters and supply base on the Nashville & Chattanooga Railroad leading down across Elk River and the Tennessee, respectively twenty-five and sixty miles in rear of the present line of intrenchments north of the Duck. Just to the front of this line, and occupied by rebel outpost detachments, an almost mountainous ridge, broadening eastward into a high plateau, stood in the path of a direct advance by the superior blue force. Formerly Rosecrans had seen this as a barrier, further complicating the tactical problem Bragg had set for him, but presently he began to conceive of it

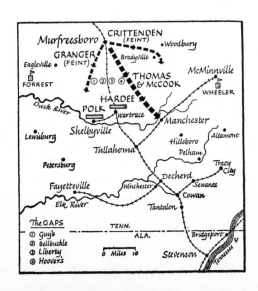

as a convenient screen, behind which he could mass his army for a surprise maneuver designed to turn the graybacks out of the works they had spent the past five months improving. Four main passes, each accommodating a road, pierced the ridge and gave access to the lush valley just beyond. In the center were Bellbuckle Gap, through which the railroad ran, and Liberty Gap, a mile to the east, with a wagon road also leading down to Wartrace. The remaining two gaps, Guy's and Hoover's, were respectively six miles west and east of the railroad, the former accommodating the Shelbyville pike and the latter the macadamized road from Murfreesboro to Manchester, which was sixteen miles east of Wartrace and twelve miles northeast of Tullahoma. It was in this tangled pattern of gaps and roads, so forbidding at first inspection, that Rosecrans found the answer to the problem Bragg had posed him.

He had no intention of advancing due south, through Bellbuckle or Liberty Gap, for a frontal assault on the Confederate intrenchments, which presumably was just what Bragg was hoping he would do. Nor was it any part of his design to launch an isolated attack on either of the rebel corps alone, since their positions were mutually supporting. His plan was, rather, to outflank them, thereby obliging the graybacks to come out into the open for a fight against the odds — or, better yet, to throw them into headlong retreat by threatening their rear, either at Tullahoma, where their supplies were stored, or somewhere else along the sixty brittle miles of railroad leading down past the Alabama line. This could be done, he figured, by forcing one of the outer gaps, Guy's or Hoover's, and swinging wide around the western or eastern flank of the rebel infantry. The western flank was favored by the terrain, which was far more rugged to the east; but it also had the disadvantage of being the more obvious, and therefore expected, approach. Then too, Polk's was the stronger of the two enemy corps, Hardee's having been weakened by detachments sent to Johnston in Mississippi. Rosecrans weighed the alternatives, one against the other, and chose the eastern flank. He would send his main body, the two corps of Thomas and McCook, southeastward through Hoover's Gap, then down the macadamized road to Manchester, from which place he could lunge at Tullahoma, in case the rebels remained in position north of the Duck, or continue his march southeastward for a strike at some point farther down. By way of initial deception, however, he would feint to the west, sending Granger's corps through or around Guy's Gap and down the pike toward Shelbyville, thus encouraging his opponent to believe that it was there the blow would land. Simultaneously — and here was where the deepest guile and subtlety came in — he would feint to the east with Crittenden's corps, through Bradyville toward McMinnville: with the difference that this supplementary feint was intended to be recognized as such, thereby convincing Bragg (who, he knew, took great pride in his ability to "see through" all such tactical deceptions) that the main effort was certainly in the opposite direction. . . . Looking back over the plan, now that he had matured and refined it during months of poring over maps and assembling supplies, meantime resisting impatient and unscientific proddings from above, Old Rosy was delighted with his handiwork. And indeed he had good cause to be pleased by the look of the thing on paper. If he reached the unfordable Tennessee before the rebels did, he would be between them and Chattanooga, his true goal, the capture of which he knew was one of Lincoln's fondest hopes; he could turn on the outnumbered and probably demoralized Bragg, who would be confined by necessity to the north bank of the river, and destroy him at his leisure. Or at its worst, if the Confederates somehow avoided being cut off from a crossing, he still would have driven them, brilliantly and bloodlessly, out of Middle Tennessee.

Secrecy being an all-important element of guile, he played his cards close to his vest. He said nothing of the particulars of his plan to either his subordinates or his superiors when, on June 16, he confided to the latter — prematurely, as it turned out — that he would advance in "say five days." Not even on June 24, in the telegram sent at 2.10 in the morning to announce that the army would be on the march within fifty minutes, did he say in what direction or strength the movement would be made. He was taking no chance on a Washington leak, even at that late hour, though of course his corps and division commanders had been informed of their share in the grand design and told to have their units deployed on schedule. Gordon Granger, with the one division remaining in his reserve corps after heavy detachments for garrison duty at Nashville and other points, began his march down the pike toward Shelbyville, preceded by a full division of cavalry, with instructions to kindle campfires on a broad front every night in order to encourage Polk, and therefore Bragg, to believe that this was the Federal main effort. Crittenden, one of whose three divisions remained on guard at Murfreesboro, began to execute the transparent feint eastward in the direction of McMinnville with the other two, preceded by a brigade of cavalry. George Thomas, whose four-division corps was much the largest in the army, took up the march for Hoover's Gap and Manchester, followed by Alex McCook, who had been told to make a disconcerting attack on Liberty Gap with one of his three divisions, thereby fixing Hardee in position at Wartrace, just beyond the gap, while Thomas circled his flank to threaten his rear. As usual, with Old Rosy in charge, no detail had been neglected. The foot soldiers were massed in their respective assembly areas, all ten divisions of them under carefully briefed commanders, and staff officers checked busily to see that all was as it should be, not only among the combat elements, but also in the rear echelon, including the various supply trains loaded with rations for twelve days. Nothing that could be calculated had been overlooked. Half the beef had been salted, for example, and loaded in wagons for ready distribution, while the other half was on the hoof: self-propelled, so to speak, for speed and ease of transportation.

Whereupon, just as the troops stepped out in the predawn darkness, beginning to weave the network of marches designed to accomplish Bragg's discomfiture, something uncalculated — indeed, incalculable — occurred. What Rosecrans later described as "one of the most extraordinary rains ever known in Tennessee at that period of the year" began to fall; "no Presbyterian rain, either," an Illinois soldier called it, "but a genuine Baptist downpour."

That was only the beginning. Crittenden afterwards maintained that, from this day forward, it "rained incessantly for fifteen days," and reports by lesser commanders bore witness to the difficulties involved. "Rain poured in torrents the entire night"; "Train not up in consequence of difficult traveling"; "Wet weather all day"; "Troops and animals much jaded." There was small comfort in knowing that the rain also fell on the rebels, but the men derived a kind of bitter satisfaction from the knowledge that they could learn to put up with almost anything. "It rained so much and so hard," one declared, "that we ceased to regard it as a matter of any consequence and simply stood up and took it, without attempting to seek shelter or screen ourselves in the least. Why should we, when we were already wet to the skin?" Besides, they had been heartened at the outset, before the fields and secondary roads were churned shin-deep in mud, by reports of a solid achievement that opened the way for the column under Thomas, who had been given the leading role in the present act of the drama Rosecrans was directing. More specifically, the accomplishment had been scored by Colonel John T. Wilder's brigade of Major General J. J. Reynolds' division.

It had been Wilder, a former Indiana industrialist, who surrendered Munfordville to Bragg, together with more than 4000 soldiers and 10 guns, as an incident of the Confederate advance into the Bluegrass region of Kentucky the previous September. The memory of that still rankled, and Wilder and his command, two regiments of fellow Hoosiers and two from Illinois, exchanged soon after their captors released them on parole — though not in time to fight at Perryville — were determined to make the rebels pay for that indignity. Just now they were in an excellent position to do so, for they were the lead element of the column that would deliver the main effort intended to throw Bragg into confusion. Moreover, they were superbly equipped for the work at hand, both in mobility and firepower, partly as a result of efforts by Rosecrans and partly as a result of efforts of their own. Short of cavalry, the army commander had mounted two of his infantry brigades, and one of these was Wilder's, who had also seen to it that his troops were armed with seven-shot Spencer carbines, the first unit in the West to be so accoutered. He had done this by signing a personal note upon which security bankers in his home town of Greensburg had a .vanced funds for purchase of the Spencers, the men having agreed to periodic deductions from their pay in order to reimburse their commander, pending their own reimbursement by the army once the red tape had been cleared away. So armed and mounted, 2000 strong, they left their camps above Murfreesboro at exactly 3 a.m. and by midmorning were herding enemy pickets into the northern mouth of Hoover's Gap, the prompt seizure of which was prerequisite to the success of the whole campaign. Wilder did not hesitate in fear of a trap or ambush, but plunged straight ahead through the three-mile-long pass with all the strength and speed he could muster, his mounted infantry driving the graybacks before them with the considerable help of their rapid-fire weapons. The works at the southern end of the gap were taken in a rush, together with the silk-embroidered colors of the 1st Kentucky Infantry, an elite Confederate outfit. Unlimbering their six guns, the Hoosiers and Prairie Staters broke up a savage counterattack and held the pass alone until the other two brigades of the division came plodding up to reinforce them, swinging their caps and cheering despite the rain. As a result of Wilder's daring and resolution, and at a relatively minor cost of 14 killed and 47 wounded, the way now lay open for an advance by Thomas around Hardee's flank and into his rear.

Bragg personally was not in good shape, either physically or mentally, for resisting the strain his opponent was about to apply as a test of his staunchness and perception. He had weathered the criticisms leveled at him by his chief subordinates, the steady depletion of his army by detachments ordered to Pemberton and Johnston, and the near-fatal illness of his wife, only to undergo a siege of boils which, by his own admission, had culminated in "a general breakdown" of his health by early summer. None of these troubles, particularly the last, had had the effect of sweetening his temper, lengthening his patience, or enabling him to abide the shortcomings of his associates, most of whom he considered unfit for their present duties. Unfortunately, too, these various woes and discomforts had served to increase, if anything, his accustomed savagery of looks and reflexes. "This officer in appearance is the least prepossessing of the Confederate generals," the ubiquitous Colonel Fremantle had recorded in his diary when he visited Bragg that spring, en route from Texas to Richmond. "He is very thin; he stoops; and has a sickly, cadaverous, haggard appearance; rather plain features, bushy black eyebrows which unite in a tuft on the top of his nose, and a stubby, iron-gray beard; but his eyes are bright and piercing. He has the reputation of being a rigid disciplinarian, and of shooting freely for insubordination. I understand he is rather unpopular on this account, and also by reason of his occasional acerbity of manner."

Not that the Tennessee commander lacked grounds for pride in what he and his men had accomplished during their sojourn in the lush

Duck River Valley. After all — though admittedly it was with the determined co-operation of an adversary who resisted all urgings to advance — he had held his ground and managed to feed and refit his badly outnumbered army in the process. "Our transportation is in fine condition," Polk was writing home, "horses and mules all fat, and battery horses and batteries in fine condition. The troops have plenty of clothes and are well shod. We have plenty of food also, and so far as the fields before us are any indication, there never was such a wheat harvest." Moreover, despite the permanent loss of some 6000 men at Murfreesboro and the detachment since of at least that many more, including Breckinridge's whole division, Bragg's mid-June strength of 46,250 effectives (for once in this war, at any rate, a Union commander had underestimated the force arrayed against him) was appreciably greater than it had been before New Year's. Primarily he had accomplished this by rigid enforcement of the conscription laws in the region threatened by a Federal advance, for he knew only too well that this might be his last chance to get at this particular reservoir of manpower, Davis having given him permission beforehand to fall back across the Tennessee as soon as he judged the pressure against his front to be insupportable. Rosecrans, however, for all his underestimation of Bragg's strength, had exerted almost no pressure at all in the past five months; so that Bragg had had ample opportunity to drill and condition his soldiers for the work that lay ahead. This was the sort of thing he did best, and the results had been gratifying. Even Fremantle, a product of the most rigid sort of training, admitted that the citizen soldiers "drilled tolerably well, and an advance in line was remarkably good." That was high praise indeed from an officer of the Coldstream Guards, though he could not repress a shudder on observing that some of the men had removed their jackets because of the heat and marched past the reviewing stand in shirt sleeves. When he expressed a desire to see them "form squares," he was told by his host that they had not been taught this maneuver, since "the country does not admit of cavalry charges, even if the Yankee cavalry had the stomach to attempt it." Similarly, he noted that the absence of the bayonet as a standard piece of equipment was a matter of small concern to the troops, "as they assert that they have never met any Yankee who would wait for that weapon." This last, of course, was far from true — as any stormer of the Hornets Nest or the Round Forest could have testified — but it was a measure of the men's high spirits that they made the claim to the credulous Englishman, who closed the account of his visit by remarking that "the discipline in this army is the strictest in the Confederacy."

In round numbers, 32,000 infantry and artillery were with Polk and Hardee on the Shelbyville-Wartrace line, while 14,000 cavalry were with Wheeler and Forrest, strung out for thirty miles east and west, respectively, with headquarters at McMinnville and Columbia.

These 46,000 effectives, comprising the Army of Tennessee, did not include some 15,000 under Buckner, who was charged with the defense of Knoxville against Burnside. That general, what time he was not fulminating against the Copperheads in his rear, was known to be preparing for an advance by the Army of the Ohio, though he had been crippled even more sorely than Bragg by detachments sent to Mississippi. To help discourage the threat in that direction, and also to continue the harassment of his Middle Tennessee opponent's lines of supply, Bragg had recently agreed to a proposal by John Morgan that he stage another of his famous "rides" into Kentucky with his 2500 Bluegrass troopers. Nettled by the defeats suffered in late March and early April at Milton and Liberty — he had in fact accomplished nothing significant since his spectacular Christmas Raid, hard on the heels of his marriage to Mattie Ready — Morgan had sought permission to extend his field of operations beyond the Ohio River, for the double purpose of carrying the scourge of war into the heartland of the North and restoring the glitter to his somewhat tarnished reputation; but Bragg (unlike Lee, who assented, though with misgivings, to a somewhat similar proposal by Jeb Stuart that same week in Virginia, preliminary to his crossing of the Potomac) had withheld approval of this extension of the raid, not wanting the Kentuckian and his men to be too far away in case Rosecrans lurched into motion in their absence. As it turned out, however, when he received word from his outposts on June 24 that the Federals were indeed in motion, not only on the left and right but also against his center, Morgan was already beyond reach, and Bragg did not discover until some weeks later, along with news of the disastrous consequences, that the freewheeling cavalryman had simply disobeyed the restrictive portion of the orders he had received.

Just now, though, Bragg had troubles enough on his hands, without looking afield for others. Correctly identifying the movements on Bradyville and Guy's Gap as feints, he left Crittenden and Granger to the attention of Forrest and Wheeler, and concentrated instead on opposing with his infantry the more immediate danger to his front. On the 25th he counterattacked at Liberty Gap, which had fallen to McCook the previous evening. Hardee failed to drive the bluecoats from the pass but he did succeed in holding them there, and Bragg, encouraged by this, sent orders for Polk to advance next day through Guy's Gap, then swing east for a descent on the rear of the troops opposing Hardee. Polk, as usual, protested, and Bragg as usual insisted. He reversed himself that night, however, on learning that the column under Thomas was approaching Manchester, still preceded by Wilder's rapid-firing horseback infantry and followed by Crittenden, who had abandoned his feint toward McMinnville and turned south at Bradyville. There was nothing for it now, as Bragg assessed the situation, but to call off the proposed attack on Liberty Gap and fall back on Tullahoma to protect his base and his present flank and rear. This he did with all possible speed, though the going was heavy; Polk left Shelbyville early on the 27th and did not reach Tullahoma, eighteen muddy miles away, until late next afternoon, soon after Hardee completed his march down the railroad in the rain. At any rate Bragg's army now was concentrated, protected by works prepared in advance, and he was determined to give the Yankees battle there.

Once more Rosecrans was unco-operative. Having reached Manchester the day before, June 27, he spent a day replenishing supplies brought forward on the hard-surfaced pike, and then resumed his march, not toward Tullahoma, as Bragg expected, but southeastward as before, toward Hillsboro and Pelham, still threatening the railroad on which his adversary depended for subsistence. At a council of war held on the night of the 28th, when Polk expressed some uneasiness that the Federals would continue their previously successful tactics by circling the right flank, Bragg taunted him by asking: "Then you propose that we shall retreat?" The bishop did indeed. "I do," he said firmly, "and that is my counsel." Hardee was less positive; he thought perhaps protection of the rear could be left to the cavalry while the infantry fought in its present intrenched position, outflanked or not; Rosecrans might gain the Confederate rear only to find the Confederates in his own. Bragg adjourned the council without making any definite decision. He would await developments, he said.

Developments were not long in coming. Granger and McCook had occupied Shelbyville and Wartrace that same day, moving in behind the departed graybacks, and though Rosecrans had no intention of attacking Tullahoma from the north, the presence of these two divisions at the crossings of the Duck was a menace Bragg could not ignore. Meanwhile Thomas, with McCook's other two divisions in support and Crittenden close behind, continued his march from Manchester to Hillsboro, a dozen miles due east of Bragg's right flank, and sent Wilder's hard-riding foot soldiers — already dubbed "The Lightning Brigade" as a result of their rapid seizure of Hoover's Gap on the opening day of the campaign — ahead to Pelham for an independent crossing of Elk River and a strike at the railroad near Decherd or Cowan, twenty miles in rear of the rebel works at Tullahoma. High trestles over gorges along this mountainous stretch of the line presented inviting targets, since the destruction of even one of them would be about as effective, so far as the flow of supplies was concerned, as the destruction of them all. Wilder's men rode fast and hard, anticipating further revenge for the Munfordville indignity. Reaching Decherd on June 28, they attacked a small detachment of rebel guards and drove them from a stockade: only to discover that a railroad might be vulnerable in some ways, yet still be highly defensible in others. No less than six gray regiments of infantry, responding to a telegraphic summons from the guards, arrived suddenly aboard cars from up the line. The blue raiders had barely time to get away on their horses, avoiding capture by the superior force and contenting themselves with the wrecking of an alternate trestle near Winchester, on the branch line to Fayetteville. Next morning, after a fireless bivouac in the brush, they tried the main line again, this time below Cowan, but with similar results; the ultramobile Confederate infantry once more drove them off before they could inflict any serious damage. Wilder fell back toward Pelham, pausing near Sewanee to wreck another trestle on the branch line to Tracy City, then continued his withdrawal, hastened by the interception of information that Forrest was on his trail. Aided by a driving rain, which obliterated his tracks, he eluded his pursuers and rode back into Manchester at noon of the 30th. Though he had failed to carry out his primary assignment, which had been to interrupt traffic on the Nashville & Chattanooga by destroying one of its main-line trestles, he had at any rate demolished one on each of the two branch lines, east and west, and he reported proudly that he had done so without the loss of a single man on the three-day expedition deep in the enemy rear. Thankful for what he had done, rather than critical for what he had not done, both Thomas and Rosecrans praised him highly for his resourcefulness and daring.

So did Bragg, though indirectly, not so much in words as by reaction. Wilder's strike, deep in his rear, plus the presence of Thomas on his flank with eight divisions, convinced him at last that retreat was the wisest policy at this juncture. The two-day wait having gained him time for removal of his stores and heavy equipment, he issued orders on the last night of June for a withdrawal. At Decherd next day he asked his corps commanders for advice: "The question to be decided instantly [is] shall we fight on the Elk or take post at the foot of the mountain at Cowan?" Polk favored Cowan, but Hardee was more explicit. "Let us fight at the mountain," he advised. Bragg did neither. The retreat being under way, he preferred to continue it rather than risk a long-odds battle with the unfordable Tennessee immediately behind him. While the infantry plodded southward under the unrelenting rain, Forrest guarded the rear. On July 3, with Polk and Hardee safely across Sewanee Mountain and out of the unsprung trap Old Rosy had devised, Federal cavalry in heavy numbers forced the pass near Cowan, and as the rear-guard Confederate troopers fell back rapidly through the streets of the town a patriotic lady came out of her house and began reviling them for leaving her and her neighbors to the mercy of the Yankees. "You great big cowardly rascal!" she cried, singling out Forrest himself for attack, not because she recognized him (it presently was made clear that she did not) but simply because he happened to be handy; "why don't you turn and fight like a man instead of running like a cur? I wish old Forrest was here. He'd make you fight!" Old Forrest, as she called him, did not pause for either an introduction or an explanation, though later he joined in the laughter at his expense, declaring that he would rather have faced an enemy battery than that one irate female.

Bragg could find nothing whatever to laugh about in his present situation. He had saved his army, but at the cost of abandoning Middle Tennessee. Moreover, with every horseback mile a torture to his boils, he was nearer than ever to the physical breakdown of which he had spoken earlier, and when a solicitous chaplain remarked from the roadside that he seemed "thoroughly outdone," he replied: "Yes, I am utterly broken down." Nor did he deny that he had been outdone tactically as well. "This is a great disaster," he confided dolefully, leaning from his saddle to whisper the words into the chaplain's ear.

Beyond Cowan he transferred to a railway car for less discomfort and more speed. After pausing at Bridgeport to send a dispatch notifying the Adjutant General of his retreat, he reached Chattanooga early on July 4, at about the same time his telegram reached Richmond, where it served as a forecast of even darker ones that followed at staggered intervals with the staggering information of what had occurred on that same day at Gettysburg, Helena, and Vicksburg. Meantime his army continued its withdrawal. Descending the slopes of the Cumberland Plateau, it entered the lovely Sequatchie Valley, then turned south along the right bank of the Tennessee for a crossing downstream at Bridgeport, just beyond the Alabama line. Here Forrest gave over his rearguard duties to a brigade from Cheatham's division, which was charged with maintaining a temporary bridgehead to discourage pursuit, and crossed the river in the wake of the rest of the army on the night of July 6, just three days short of the anniversary of his crossing northward as the spearhead of the advance into Kentucky. After a year of marching nearly a thousand miles and fighting two great battles, both of which he claimed as victories though both were preludes to retreat, Bragg was back where he started.

Rosecrans was willing to leave him there for the present. At a cost of 570 casualties, including less than a hundred dead and barely a dozen missing, the Federals had captured no fewer than 1634 prisoners — many of them Middle Tennessee conscripts who came into the northern lines of their own accord, wanting no more of the war now that their homeland was no longer being fought for — and had inflicted, despite their role as attackers, about as many wounds as they had suffered. They were proud of themselves and proud of the chief who had planned and supervised the campaign that ended, so far as the foot soldiers were concerned, with Bragg's retreat across the Elk on July 2. On that day, having moved into the abandoned rebel works at Tullahoma, they settled down for the first true rest they had enjoyed since setting off in their predawn marches from Murfreesboro, nine days back. Rain and mud, short rations, and all too little sleep had been their portion all this time; "It would be hard to find a worse set of used-up boys," an Indiana infantryman confessed. But they were well enough rested, a few days later, to cheer heartily at the news of Vicksburg's fall. Tremendously set up by their own recent success in a campaign which even the enemy newspapers were already calling "masterful" and "brilliant," they figured that Chattanooga was next on the list, and they were ready to take it whenever Old Rosy gave the word.

✗ 2 ✗

In Washington, too, there was delight that the campaign had gone so well, although the fact that so much had been accomplished with so little bloodshed seemed rather to validate the opinion, urged for months, that the issue could have been forced much sooner to the same conclusion with a corresponding gain in time. The first discordant note, struck amid the general rejoicing, was sounded by Stanton on July 7 in a telegram informing Rosecrans that Vicksburg had fallen and that the Gettysburg attackers were in full retreat. "Lee's army overthrown; Grant victorious," the Secretary wired. "You and your noble army now have the chance to give the finishing blow to the rebellion. Will you neglect the chance?" Nettled that the goading thus was resumed almost before his weary men had time to catch their breath and scrape the mud from their boots and clothes — not to mention that the taunt preceded any official congratulations for an achievement which even the enemy had begun to refer to as masterful — Rosecrans managed, as was usual in such verbal fencing matches with his superiors, to give as good as, if not better than, he got. "You do not appear to observe the fact that this noble army has driven the rebels from Middle Tennessee," he replied on that same day. "I beg in behalf of this army that the War Department may not overlook so great an event because it is not written in letters of blood." Four days later, in hope of avoiding further prods and nudges of this kind, he listed for Halleck some of the difficulties he faced. These included the necessary replacement of a 350-foot railroad bridge across Duck River, as well as a long trestle south of there, the relaying of several miles of track, both on the main line down to Tullahoma and on the branch line out to Manchester and McMinnville, and the construction of new corduroy roads in order to get his wagon trains across the seas of mud. Then too, he noted, there was the problem of Burnside and his delayed advance on Knoxville, which would not only protect the flank of the Army of the Cumberland when move-out time came round, but would also complicate matters for the enemy on the opposite bank of the Tennessee. In short, Rosecrans wanted it understood by the general-in-chief and those with whom he was in daily contact, meaning Stanton and Lincoln, that "the operations now before us involve a great deal of care, labor, watchfulness, and combined effort, to insure the successful advance through the mountains on Chattanooga."

The result was that Halleck stepped up the prodding. "You must not wait for Johnston to join Bragg," he wired on July 24, "but must move forward immediately.... There is great dissatisfaction felt here at the slowness of your advance. Unless you can move more rapidly, your whole campaign will prove a failure." A confidential letter written that same day put the issue even more bluntly: "The patience of the authorities here has been completely exhausted, and if I had not repeatedly promised to urge you forward, and begged for delay, you would have been removed from your command." This was a familiar threat, and Rosecrans met it much as he had done before. "I say to you frankly," he replied on August 1, "that whenever the Government can replace me by a commander in whom they have more confidence, they ought to do so, and take the responsibility of the result." He followed this with an expanded list of the difficulties in his path, but once more with results quite different from the ones he had hoped to bring about. "Your forces must move forward without further delay," Halleck snapped back at him three days later. "You will daily report the movement of each corps till you cross the Tennessee River." Rosecrans could scarcely believe his eyes. But when he inquired, by return wire, "if your order is intended to take away my discretion as to the time and manner of moving my troops," Old Brains replied that this was precisely his intention: "The orders for the advance of your army, and that its movements be reported daily, are peremptory." On August 6, a Thursday, the Middle Tennessee commander started a dispatch with what seemed a definite commitment — "My arrangements for beginning a continuous movement will be completed and the execution begun by Monday next" — only to proceed at once to enlarge on the difficulties and to request either that the order be modified or else that he be relieved of his command. He may or may not have been bluffing; in any case it did not work. Halleck was relentless. "I have communicated to you the wishes of the Government in plain and unequivocal terms," he replied next day. "The object has been stated, and you have been directed to lose no time in reaching it. The means you are to employ, and the roads you are to follow, are left to your own discretion. If you wish to promptly carry out the wishes of the Government, you will not stop to discuss mere details."

Old Rosy had one string left to his bow: an out-of-channels appeal made early that month to Lincoln, in hopes that he would intervene on the side of the field commander. "General Halleck's dispatches imply that you not only feel solicitude for the advance of this army but dissatisfaction at its supposed inactivity," he had written, thus extending to the Commander in Chief an invitation to step into the argument with a denial that this was so. On August 10 — the "Monday next" which Rosecrans had set as the date on which he would march, though he did not — Lincoln replied at length. "I have not abated in my kind feeling for and confidence in you," the letter began encouragingly, but then went into a review of the anxiety the writer had felt because of the Middle Tennessee general's immobility while Bragg was sending troops to Johnston for the relief of Vicksburg. As strategy, Lincoln added, this "impressed me very strangely, and I think I so stated to the Secretary of War and General Halleck." In the present case, moreover, he had doubts about the wisdom of accumulating such vast amounts of food and equipment as a prelude to the move on Chattanooga. "Does preparation advance at all? Do you not consume supplies as fast as you get them forward? ... Do not misunderstand," he said in closing. "I am not casting blame upon you. I rather think, by great exertion, you can get to East Tennessee. But a very important question is, Can you stay there? I make no order in the case — that I leave to General Halleck and yourself." In other words, he would not intervene. Old Rosy's bow was quite unstrung, even though the President ended his letter with further expression of his personal good will. "And now, be assured that I think of you in all kindness and confidence, and that I am not watching you with an evil eye. Yours very truly, A. Lincoln."

Having lost this ultimate appeal for a delay, Rosecrans finally began his march on August 16. This time, the recuperative halt had lasted not six months, as at Murfreesboro, but six weeks. It was time enough, however, for his purpose. Now as then, once he got moving he moved fast, with much attention to detail and much dependence on deception.

Burnside had begun his march on Knoxville the day before, after similar difficulties with the Washington authorities were brought to a head by a similar direct order for him to get moving, ready or not. In point of fact, despite the impatience of those above him, he had had excellent reasons for delay. First, when he was about to move in early June he was stripped of his veteran IX Corps, which went to Vicksburg under Parke. While waiting for its return he began assembling another, composed of inexperienced garrison troops brought forward from such places as Cincinnati, and sent a mixed brigade of 1500 cavalry and mounted infantry under Colonel William P. Sanders to look into conditions beyond the mountainous bulge of the horizon. Sanders, a thirty-year-old Kentucky-born West Pointer, set out on June 14, and in the course of the next nine days he not only disrupted rebel communications throughout East Tennessee, but also destroyed a number of bridges along the vital Tennessee & Virginia Railroad, including a 1600-foot span across the Holston River. He returned on June 23, elated by his success, which he reported was due in large part to the friendliness of natives whose loyalty to the Union had not been shaken by more than two years of waiting in vain for deliverance from Confederate oppression. Much encouraged, Burnside might have set out then and there with his green corps — thus matching Old Rosy's advance on Tullahoma, which got under way next morning — except that it was at this point that John Hunt Morgan exploded in his rear, necessitating the employment of all his cavalry in a chase through the Copperhead-infested region north of the Ohio, which the raiders crossed near Brandenburg on the night of July 8 after a wild ride northward through Kentucky, capturing blue detachments as they went and provoking alternate reactions of fear and elation in the breasts of the loyal and disloyal in their path.

On July 2, about midway between Nashville and Barbourville, Morgan crossed the upper Cumberland with eleven regiments, 2460 men in all, and a section of rifled guns. Four of his five brothers rode with him, Calvin, Richard, Charlton, and Thomas, and his brother-in-law Colonel Basil Duke commanded the larger of his two brigades; so that the raid was in a sense a family affair. Indeed, in an even more limited sense, it was a private affair. His disobedience of Bragg's orders regarding a crossing of the Ohio, which he had intended from the start, was based on the conviction that no mere "ride," even if the itinerary included Louisville, Frankfort, and Lexington, would accomplish his objective of stopping Rosecrans or Burnside, who would simply let the Bluegrass region look out for itself while they marched south, respectively, through Middle and East Tennessee. On the other hand, a strike into Indiana and Ohio could not so easily be ignored, either by them or by their superiors, for political as well as military reasons. As for the danger, though admittedly it was great, Morgan thought it might not prove so extreme as it appeared. Boldness was sometimes its own best protection, as he had demonstrated often in the past, and this was the epitome of boldness. Once across the Ohio he intended to ride east, through or around Cincinnati, always keeping within reach of the river, which was reported to be seasonally low, for a recrossing into Kentucky whenever the pressure on the north bank grew too great. Or at the worst, if this maneuver proved impractical, he would continue east and north for a juncture with Lee in Pennsylvania and a return by easy stages to his proper theater of the war. This would be an affair not only for the history books and tactics manuals of the future, but also for the extension and enlargement of the legends and songs already being told and sung in celebration of earlier, lesser horseback exploits by Morgan and his "terrible" men: an inheritance, in short, to be handed down to Confederate patriots yet unborn, including the child his young wife was about to bear him down in Tennessee. And so it was; so it became; though not precisely in the form intended.

At least the beginning was propitious, the entry into Kentucky despite the presence of some 10,000 soldiers Burnside had posted along the Cumberland with instructions to prevent just that. The raiders penetrated the screen without encountering anything more substantial than a small detachment of cavalry beyond Burkesville, which they easily brushed aside. Late the following night, however, while taking a rest halt at Columbia, they heard bluecoats on the north bank of the Green preparing earthworks from which to challenge any attempt to cross the bridge. They were five companies of Michigan infantry, and next morning, not wanting to leave them active in his rear, Morgan sent in a demand for their surrender. "On any other day I might," the Federal colonel replied, smiling, "but on the Fourth of July I must have a little brush first." By way of testing his earnestness and the strength of his position, the raiders gave him what he sought: to their regret, for they were repulsed with a loss of 80 killed and wounded, out of less than 600 engaged, having inflicted fewer than 30 enemy casualties, most of whose hurts were superficial. Morgan crossed the river elsewhere, convinced by now that he should have done so in the first place, and pressed on through Campbellsville to camp that night near Lebanon, where he had his second fight next day. Here the challengers were a regiment of Union-loyal Kentuckians, whose colonel replied in the Wolverine vein to a note demanding instant capitulation. "I never surrender without a struggle," he said grimly. This time the attack was made by both Confederate brigades for a quick settlement of the issue, however bloody. After some savage house-to-house fighting, the Federals fell back to the railroad station, where they finally yielded under assault. More than 400 prisoners were taken, along with valuable medical supplies, again at a cost of about 80 casualties for the attackers. But for Morgan personally the price was steeper than any comparison of cold figures could possibly indicate. Tom, the youngest of the brothers with him, was killed in the final volley fired before the white flag went up. The four surviving brothers buried him in the garden of a sympathetic Lebanon preacher, then resumed their ride northward, though with much of the glory and all of the gladness already gone from the raid for them.

In Bardstown on July 6, hoping to throw his pursuers off his trail, Morgan feinted simultaneously north and east by sending fast-riding columns toward Louisville and Harrodsburg, but swung the main body westward through Garnettsville to Brandenburg, where an advance detachment seized two small steamers for crossing the wide Ohio. This was accomplished between noon and midnight, July 8, despite some interference from a prowling Union gunboat that hung around, exchanging shots with the two rebel guns, till it ran out of ammunition. Their crossing completed, the raiders burned the steamers against the Indiana bank and pushed on six miles northward before halting for what little was left of the night. As they approached the town of Corydon next morning they found a sizable body of Hoosier militia drawn up to contest their entrance. Not wanting to take time to go around them, Morgan decided to go through them; which he did, scattering the home guardsmen in the process — they suffered a total of 360 casualties, of whom 345 were listed as missing — but at a cost to himself of 8 men killed and 33 wounded. Nor was that the worst of it. Taking the midday meal at a Corydon hotel, he learned from the innkeeper's daughter that Lee had been whipped six days ago at Gettysburg and was on his way back to Virginia. This meant that Morgan's alternate escape plan, involving a hookup with the invaders in Pennsylvania, was no longer practical, if indeed it had ever been. Apparently undaunted, he pressed on northward, that day and the next, through Palmyra to Salem, just over forty air-line miles from the Ohio and less than twice that far from Indianapolis. The Indiana capital was in a turmoil, its celebration of the great double victory at Gettysburg and Vicksburg brought to an abrupt and woeful end by news that Morgan was over the river with 10,000 horsemen and on his way even now to capture and sack the city. Church and fire bells rang the alarm, and a crowd turned out in front of the Bates House to hear Governor Morton read the latest dispatches. More than 60,000 citizens responded throughout the state to his appeal for militia volunteers, as many as possible of those who were immediately available being posted along the southern outskirts of the capital, toward Martinsville and Franklin, with orders to stop the gray raiders at all costs.

But they were not coming that way after all. Morgan had veered east from Salem on July 10, through Vienna to Lexington, where he allowed himself, if not his companions, the luxury of a night's rest in a hotel — and narrowly avoided, as it turned out, the ignominy of being captured in bed by a detachment of blue troopers who rode up to the building while he slept, then fell back hastily when his orderly gave the alarm, never suspecting the prize that lay within their grasp. Doubling the column to regain the lead, the Kentucky brigadier took up a zigzag course next day, through Paris and Vernon, for a small-hours halt at Dupont. Back in the saddle by dawn of the 12th, he rode that night into Sunman, fifteen miles short of the Indiana-Ohio line, which he crossed next day into Harrison, barely twenty miles from downtown Cincinnati. With Vicksburg lost, Lee defeated, and Bragg in full retreat, his purpose was no longer to cut railroads, wreck supply dumps, or even disrupt communications — except, of course, to the extent that such depredations would serve to confuse his pursuers — but simply to stretch out the expedition and thus prolong the inactivity of Burnside, who could not advance on Knoxville, in conjunction with Rosecrans' advance on Chattanooga, until his cavalry rejoined him. Morgan's proper course, in line with this reduced objective, was to move rapidly, appear suddenly at unexpected points, and then slip away before the superior forces combined against him could involve him in time-consuming fights that would only serve to exhaust his men and horses. Yet there was the rub. In the past ten days he had covered nearly 400 miles, including the crossing of three major rivers, at a cost of some 500 casualties and stragglers. Men and horses were beginning to break down at an alarming rate, just as he was about to call on them for even more strenuous exertions. However, he had no choice in the matter. What had begun as a raid, a foray as of a fox upon a henhouse, had turned into a foxhunt — and, hunting or hunted, Morgan was still the fox. He pressed on, southeastward now, in the direction of Cincinnati and the Ohio, which he was obliged to keep close on his right for a crossing in case he was cornered.

Down to fewer than 2000 men, he rode fast that night through the northeast suburbs of Cincinnati, not wanting to risk their dispersion in the labyrinth of its streets or to expose them to the temptations of its downtown bars and shops, overburdened as some of them were already with plunder they had gathered along the way. He did not call a halt for sleep until the column reached Williamsburg late that afternoon, some two dozen miles beyond the city, having covered no less than ninety miles in the past day and a half. Next morning, July 15, Morgan was feeling confident and expansive as his troopers took up the march. "All our troubles are now over," he told his staff, anticipating a three-day ride by easier stages to the fords upstream from Buffington, which he had had reconnoitered by scouts before he left Tennessee and which had been reported as an excellent point for a crossing back into Kentucky. While he traversed the southern tier of Ohio counties, through or around Locust Grove, Jasper, and Jackson, newspaper editors in his rear recovered sufficiently from their fright to begin crowing. "John Morgan's raid is dying away eastward," the Chicago *Tribune* exulted, "and his force is melting away as it proceeds. Their only care is escape and their chances for that are very slight." This was on July 16, and two days later the editor felt spry enough to manage a verbal sally. "John Morgan is still in Ohio," he wrote, "or rather is in Ohio without being allowed to be still."

It was true; Morgan was still in Ohio, delayed by militiamen quite as determined as the Hoosiers he had encountered on his first day on northern soil. Bypassing Pomeroy that morning, 150 miles east of Cincinnati, he had had to call a halt at Chester, just beyond, to wait for stragglers: with the result that the head of the column did not approach the river above Buffington until well after dark. Here he received his worst shock to date. Swollen by two weeks of rain, the Ohio was on an unseasonal boom, and the fords — if they could be called that, deep as they were — were guarded by 300 enemy infantry who had been brought upstream on transports, together with two guns which they had emplaced on the north bank, covering the approaches to the shallowest of the fords. Moreover, if transports could make it this far upriver, so could gunboats; which was something the general had not counted on. Deciding to wait for daylight before attacking, he gave his men some badly needed sleep, then sent two regiments forward at dawn, only to discover that the bluecoats had abandoned their position in the darkness, tumbling their guns into the river unobserved and leaving the crossing unguarded for most of the night. However, there was no time for crimination or even regret for this lack of vigilance on the part of the scouts; for just then two things happened, both calamitous. A gunboat rounded the lower bend, denying the raiders access to the ford, and heavy firing broke out at the rear of the long gray line of weary men on weary horses. Two heavy columns of Federal cavalry, 5000 strong and well rested, had come up from Pomeroy after an overnight boat ride from downstream and had launched an immediate all-out attack on the raiders, who were wedged in a mile-long valley beside the swollen river, awaiting their turns at a ford they could not use. Morgan reacted with his usual quick intelligence, leading the head of the column out of the unblocked northern end of the narrow valley while the rear guard did what it could to fight off the attackers. But resistance quickly crumpled and the withdrawal became a rout. He was fortunate, under the circumstances, to lose no more than half of his command, including 120 killed or wounded and some 700 captured — Duke and two more of the Morgan brothers, Richard and Charlton, were among the latter — together with both of his guns and such of his wagons as had managed to keep up. One of these belonged to an old Tennessee farmer who had intended to trade for a load of salt at Burkesville, then return to his home on Calf-killer Creek, near Sparta. Unable to turn back for lack of an escort, he had stayed with the column, and now he found himself in far-off Ohio, beside an alien river, with Yankee troopers charging full-tilt at him and shooting as they came. Exhausted though he was, and badly frightened, he delivered extemporaneously one of the great, wistful speeches of the war. "Captain," he said to an officer standing beside him amid the twittering bullets, "I would give my farm in White County, Tennessee, and all the salt in Kentucky, if I had it, to stand once more safe and sound on the banks of Calf-killer Creek."

So would the thousand survivors who got away from Buffington with Morgan have liked to be back on their farms in Tennessee and Kentucky; but that was not to be, at least not soon, except for some 300 who made it across the river that afternoon at Blennerhassett's Island, a few miles below Parkersburg, West Virginia. The ford was deep, the current swift, and a number of riders and their mounts were swept away and drowned. Moreover, the crossing had scarcely begun when the gunboat reappeared from below, guns booming, and slammed the escape hatch shut. In midstream aboard a powerful horse, Morgan himself could have made it across, yet he chose instead to return to the north bank and stay with the remaining 700 to the bitter end of what, from this point on, was not so much a raid as it was a frantic attempt to avoid capture by the greatly superior forces converging from all points of the compass upon the dwindling column of graybacks. Northward they rode, through Eagleport and across the Muskingum River, twisting and turning for six more days, still following the right bank of the Ohio in search of another escape hatch. But there was none; or at any rate there was none that was not blocked. On July 26, down to fewer than 400 now because of the increasing breakdown of their horses, the survivors were brought to bay at Salineville, on Beaver Creek, near New Lisbon, and there — just off the tip of West Virginia's tiny panhandle, less than a hundred miles from Lake Erie and only half that far from Pittsburgh — Morgan and the 364 troopers still with him laid down their arms. In the thirty days since leaving Sparta on June 27, they had ridden more than 700 miles, averaging twenty hours a day in the saddle from the time they crossed the Ohio, and though they met with disaster in the end, they had at least accomplished their primary objective of preventing an early march southward by Burnside, in conjunction with Rosecrans' advance on Tullahoma, which would have made Bragg's retreat across the Tennessee a far more difficult maneuver than the unharassed withdrawal it actually was.

Morgan and his chief lieutenants, captured at Salineville and elsewhere, were brought in triumph back to Cincinnati, where Burnside pronounced them ineligible for parole. Nor was that the worst of it. Acting on misinformation that Abel Streight had been so treated after his capture in Alabama three months earlier, the authorities ordered that the Ohio raiders were to be confined in the State Penitentiary at Columbus for the duration of the war. And there they were lodged before the month was out. "My sleep was very much disturbed," a Kentuckian recorded in his diary, "by the terrible impression made upon my mind by our confinement in such a place." It was, he said, "enough to shock the sensibilities of any refined gentleman." Now that Burnside had his hands on Morgan he was taking no chance whatever of his escaping. All visitors were denied access to the prisoners, even the general's mother, presumably on the suspicion that she might smuggle in a bustle full of hacksaws. Hardest of all for them to bear, however, was the indignity of being dressed in convict clothes and shorn of their hair and beards. This last was the ultimate in inhumanity, according to one of the four reunited Morgan brothers, who had the full horror of war brought home to him by the loss of his mustache and imperial. Presently Governor Tod himself tendered what one of the captives called "a most untimely apology for an outrageous and disgraceful act." The shearing had been an administrative error, the governor explained, but Morgan's brother Charlton expressed a harsher opinion of the action. "The entire world will stamp it as disgraceful to this nation and the present age," he fervently protested.

Pleased with the capture and prompt disposition of the raiders — and encouraged as well, although it scarcely bore out his previous contention that they had been waiting for just such a treacherous chance, by the failure of the Copperheads to come to the aid of these outlaws deep in his rear — Burnside ordered his cavalry to rejoin the three divisions of infantry marking time all this while on the line of the Cumberland, gave them a couple of weeks to rest and get their horses back in shape, and then came forward himself in mid-August to direct in person the maneuver he had devised, under pressure from Washington, for delivering East Tennessee from the grip of the rebels under Buckner. Like Rosecrans, who was to advance simultaneously on his right, he counted heavily on deception to offset the disadvantages of terrain, and in this connection, by way of increasing his opponent's confusion and alarm, he had resolved to make his approach march in four columns. Two were of cavalry, one to advance on the left through Big Creek Gap and the other on the right through Winter's Gap, while the third, made up of two divisions of infantry, marched between them on Kingston, which lay at the confluence of the Clinch and Tennessee rivers, forty miles below Knoxville, the objective of all three columns. The fourth, composed of the remaining infantry division, would move directly on Cumberland Gap, which the Federals had taken in June of 1862 and then been obliged to abandon when Bragg and Kirby Smith outflanked it on their way to Kentucky, a year ago this month, and which was occupied now by a garrison of about 2500 graybacks, well entrenched, heavily armed, and amply supplied with provisions for a siege. Burnside had some 24,000 effectives in all, a comfortable preponderance; but the way was long, the roads steep, and the adversary tricky. Consequently, he planned carefully and gave his full attention to details, substituting pack mules for wagons in his trains, for instance, and mounting the lead regiments of both infantry columns so that they would set a fast pace for the troops who slogged along behind them. Learning at the last minute that his long-lost IX Corps veterans were finally on the way to rejoin him, though sadly decreased by casualties and sickness in the Mississippi lowlands — the two divisions, in fact, were down to about 6000 men between them — he decided not to wait. They could join him later, after they had rested, got the fever out of their bones, and been brought back up to strength. Besides, having planned without them and waited all this time in vain for their return, he preferred to move without them. And once he got moving he moved fast, with a march that matched the mid-November performance of the Army of the Potomac when he shifted it from the upper to the lower Rappahannock by way of preparation for the mid-December nightmare at Fredericksburg, which had haunted him, waking or sleeping, ever since.

This time it was otherwise. Though the two marches were alike in the sense that he encountered no opposition en route, this one differed profoundly in that he encountered none at the end, either. Reaching Kingston on September 1, unchallenged, he entered Knoxville with the infantry main body two days later, to find that the mounted column that had proceeded by way of Winter's Gap had arrived the day before.

Buckner had pulled out, bag and baggage, abandoning everything east of Loudon and west of Morristown, except Cumberland Gap, which the one-division column was attacking from the north. Delighted by his first large-scale victory since Roanoke Island, nineteen months ago, Burnside made a triumphal entrance at the head of the two-division column, September 3, and was hailed by the joyous citizens as their deliverer from oppression; "a rather large man, physically," an observer noted, "about six feet tall, with a large face and a small head, and heavy side-whiskers." These last added considerably to the over-all impression of the general as "an energetic, decided man, frank, manly, and well educated." He was, in brief, what was called a show officer. "Not that he *made* any show," the witness added; "he was naturally that."

Discontent with anything less than the whole loaf, he left two thirds of his infantry and cavalry to maintain his grip on Knoxville and that vital stretch of the only railroad directly connecting the rebel East and West, and set out three days later with the rest for Cumberland Gap, where the garrison still held out. He covered sixty miles of mountainous road in two days and four hours, completing the investment from the south as well as the north, and on the day of his arrival, September 9, forced the unconditional surrender of the 2500 defenders, together with all their equipment and supplies, including fourteen guns. Hearing next day from Rosecrans that Bragg was in full retreat upon Rome, Georgia, Burnside assumed that everything was under control in that direction; he turned his attention eastward instead, intending to complete his occupation of East Tennessee, to and beyond the North Carolina line, and to seize, by way of lagniappe, the important Confederate saltworks near Abingdon, Virginia. After a long season of blight and personal disappointment, he had rediscovered the heady delight of victory, and he was hard after more of the same.

With as little bloodshed — which, in effect, meant none at all — Rosecrans had marched on as rigid a schedule, over terrain no less forbidding, to accomplish as much against more seasoned defenders of an even tougher objective. For him too, once he got started, speed and dexterity were the keynotes. His army completed its crossing of the Tennessee on September 4, the day after Burnside rode into Knoxville, and five days later — September 9, the day Cumberland Gap came back into Union hands — he occupied Chattanooga, long recognized as the gateway to the heartland of the South, whose seizure Lincoln had said a year ago was "fully as important as the taking and holding of Richmond." Not only were many Confederates inclined to agree with this assessment, but they also considered the fall of one to be quite as unlikely as the fall of the other. On the face of it, in fact, the western bastion seemed to them the stronger of the two. Though it lacked the protective genius of Lee, it had its geographical compensations, such as the Tennessee

River to serve as a moat and the surrounding mountains and ridges to serve as ramparts in its defense, both of them the gift of God himself. "I tell you," a high-ranking Deep South officer later told a Federal correspondent, "when your Dutch general Rosencranz commenced his forward movement for the capture of Chattanooga, we laughed him to scorn. We believed that the black brow of Lookout Mountain would frown him out of existence, that he would dash himself to pieces against the many and vast natural barriers that rise all around Chattanooga, and that then the northern people and the government at Washington would perceive how hopeless were their efforts when they came to attack the real South."

In determining a solution to the problem during his six-week halt at Tullahoma and McMinnville, on the northwest side of the Cumberland Plateau, Rosecrans had reached deeper than ever into the bag of tricks that was always part of his military luggage. Bragg had Polk's corps disposed for a close-up defense of the city and Hardee's off to the east, protecting the railroad to Cleveland and beyond, while Wheeler's cavalry guarded the river crossings below and Forrest's those above. The obvious Federal strategy called for a movement toward the left, the better to make contact with Burnside. But this would not only take the army across the Sequatchie River and over Walden's Ridge, away from its railroad supply line back to Nashville; it also had the disadvantage of being expected, with Bragg already half deployed to meet it. The alternative was a move to the right for a crossing downstream, in the vicinity of the new forward supply base at Stevenson, and this was the one Old Rosy chose. It too would have its drawbacks, once he was over the river, since it would give him a longer way to go and three steep ridges to cross before he got to Chattanooga; but the reward would be correspondingly great. That way, with skill and luck, he might trap Bragg's whole army in its city fortress beside the river to the north, much as Grant had trapped Pemberton's at Vicksburg. Or if Bragg grew alert to the danger in his rear and fell back southward, down the line of the Western & Atlantic Railroad to Dalton or Rome, Rosecrans might catch him badly strung out and destroy him. However, if either of these aims was to be accomplished, it was necessary meanwhile to keep his opponent's attention fixed northward or northeastward, for the double purpose of making an undelayed crossing well downstream and a rapid march eastward, across the ridges in Northwest Georgia, to gain the rebel commander's rear before he became aware of what was looming. And here again was where guile and deception came in.

Keeping his main body well back from the river to screen his true intention, he demonstrated upstream with three brigades. Every night they lighted bonfires in rear of all possible crossings, from opposite Chattanooga itself clear up to Washington, a distance of forty miles, and while special details sawed the ends from planks and threw the scraps into creeks flowing into the Tennessee, others pounded round the clock on empty barrels in imitation of shipyard workers, thereby encouraging rebel scouts across the way to report that boats were being constructed for an amphibious assault somewhere along that stretch of the river. On August 21, by way of adding punch to the show, a battery went into action on Stringer's Ridge, directly across from the city, throwing shells into its streets and scoring hits on two steamboats at its wharf, one of which was sunk and the other disabled. Bragg's reaction was to withdraw the brigade from the north-bank bridgehead he had been holding all this time near Bridgeport, fifty miles downstream, and before the week was out a crossing by the mass of the blue army was underway in that vicinity: by Thomas at Bridgeport itself, where pontoons were thrown in replacement of the burned railroad bridge: by McCook, twelve miles below at Caperton's Ferry: and by Crittenden, ten miles above at Shellmound, which was twenty air-line miles due west of Chattanooga and twice that far by river. None of the three met any substantial resistance, so well had the upstream deception served its purpose. Except for Granger's one-division reserve corps, on guard at the Stevenson depot of supplies, and the three detached brigades, which kept making threatening gestures to fix Bragg's attention northward, Rosecrans had his whole army across the Tennessee by September 4, including all his artillery and trains loaded with ammunition enough for two great battles and rations for better than three full weeks, in case he remained that long out of touch with his base on the north bank. The main thing, as he saw it, was to keep moving and move fast. And that he did.

It took some doing, for the terrain was rugged; but Old Rosy had planned for that as well, directing the formation of company-sized details equipped with long ropes for hauling guns and wagons up difficult grades when the mules faltered. Perpendicular to his line of march, the three lofty ridges — actually long, narrow mountains, with deep valleys intervening — were Raccoon Mountain, Lookout Mountain, and Missionary Ridge. Lookout, which extended all the way to the bend of the river just below Chattanooga, was penetrated by only two gaps: Stevens Gap, 18 miles southwest of the city, and Winston Gap, 24 miles farther down. Rosecrans planned to use them both for a fast march eastward, sending Crittenden directly along the railroad, around the sheer north face of the mountain and into the city, which Bragg would probably evacuate when he learned that the other two corps were moving through the passes in his rear — McCook by way of Winston Gap, then around the lower end of Missionary Ridge, toward Alpine and Summerville, and Thomas by way of Stevens Gap, which also pierced Missionary Ridge within a dozen miles of LaFayette — for a blow at his vital and vulnerable rail supply line from Atlanta. Here again there were drawbacks, theoretical ones at any rate. The two outer columns, Crittenden's and McCook's, would be more than forty miles apart, and neither would be within a day's march of Thomas in the center; Bragg might concentrate and strike at any one of the isolated three. But this too had been foreseen and guarded against by sending all but one brigade of the cavalry with McCook — who seemed most susceptible in that regard, being on the remoter flank — while the remaining brigade preceded Crittenden, ready to give warning in case such a threat developed. The main thing was speed, and this assured just that. Rosecrans rode with the trooperless middle column, not only to keep in closer touch with all three of his chief lieutenants, but also to act as a goad to Thomas, who had many admirable qualities but was known to be somewhat lethargic on occasion.

Proud in the knowledge that they were the first Federals to penetrate this region since the beginning of the war, the men reacted with enthusiasm to the march, particularly when they saw spread out before them such vistas as the one unrolled from atop Raccoon Mountain. "Far beyond mortal vision extended one vast panorama of mountains, forests, and rivers," an Illinois veteran later wrote. "The broad Tennessee below us seemed like a ribbon of silver; beyond rose the Cumberlands, which we had crossed. The valley on both sides was alive with the moving armies of the Union, while almost the entire transportation of the army filled the roads and fields along the Tennessee. No one could survey the grand scene on that bright autumn day unmoved, unimpressed with its grandeur and the meaning conveyed by the presence of that mighty host." Presently word came from Crittenden that Bragg had apparently had a similar reaction to the presence of all those bluecoats in his rear; for when the Kentuckian drew near Chattanooga on September 8 he learned that the Confederates were in mid-evacuation, and next morning, as the tail of the gray column disappeared through Rossville Gap and behind the screen of Missionary Ridge, the city fell without the firing of a shot. Rosecrans passed the word to the troops of the central column, who did their best to rock Lookout with their cheers as they slogged through Stevens Gap.

Simultaneously, scores of butternut deserters began to filter into the Union lines with reports of Bragg's demoralization. He was in full flight for Rome or perhaps Atlanta, they declared, quite unmanned by this latest turning movement and in no condition to resist an attack if one could be thrown at him before he got there. Convinced that he had acted wisely in accepting the risk of dispersion for the sake of speed, Old Rosy urged his cheering soldiers forward, intent on giving the panic-stricken rebels what the deserters said would amount to a coup de grâce.

★ ★ ★

Rosecrans was partly right about Bragg, but only up to a point a good way short of the whole truth. The Confederate commander had been outsmarted, and he had fallen back in haste, even in some disorder, to escape the closing jaws of the Federal trap; but that was as far as it went. He was not retreating now, nor was he avoiding a fight. Rather, he was in search of one, although on different terms, having by now devised a trap of his own. As for the butternut scarecrows who had come stumbling into the northern lines, peering nervously over their shoulders and babbling of demoralization in the fleeing press of comrades left behind, Old Rosy would have done well to bear in mind some words one of his young staffers wrote years later: "The Confederate deserter was an institution which has received too little consideration.... He was ubiquitous, willing, and altogether inscrutable. Whether he told the truth or a lie, he was always equally sure to deceive. He was sometimes a real deserter and sometimes a mock deserter. In either case he was sure to be loaded." In the present instance, a considerable number of them were indeed "loaded," being scouts sent forth by Bragg himself, who had chosen them for their ability to be convincing in misrepresentation of the true state of affairs in the army that lay in wait for the exuberant bluecoats, just beyond the last of the screening ridges.

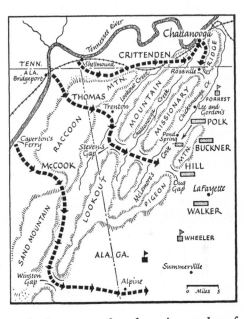

Bragg's present aggressiveness had come only after six weeks of uncertainty and confusion following his retreat across the Tennessee. Hearing from Adjutant General Cooper on August 1 that the government was anxious to reinforce him with most of Johnston's army, on condition that he recross the river for an attack on Rosecrans, he replied next day that he was willing, provided "a fight can be had on equal terms." But three days later he withdrew the offer. "After fully examining all resources," he wired, "I deem them insufficient to justify a movement across the mountains." He meant the Cumberland Plateau, which he had just traversed and which by then was serving Rosecrans as a screen to hide his preparations for pursuit. He did not like having it there at all; he wished it could be abolished. "It is said to be easy to defend a mountainous country," he complained to one of his corps commanders, "but mountains hide your foe from you, while they are full of gaps through which he can pounce upon you at any time. A mountain is like the wall of a house full of rat holes. The rat lies hidden at his hole, ready to pop out when no one is watching. Who can tell what lies hidden behind that wall?" Respectfully, while in this frame of mind, he informed Richmond that he declined to plunge his army into "a country rugged and sterile, with a few mountain roads only by which to reach a river difficult of passage. Thus situated," he explained, "the enemy need only avoid battle for a short time to starve us out." But he added, by way of final encouragement: "Whenever he shall present himself on this side of the mountains the problem will be changed."

On the strength of this last, though disappointed that Bragg was unwilling to take the offensive, the authorities decided to reinforce him anyhow. In point of fact, even aside from the evidence that Joe Johnston seemed determined to do nothing with the troops standing idle in Mississippi all this time, they had no choice; repulses or surrenders at Gettysburg and Vicksburg, Helena and Port Hudson, plus the loss of Middle Tennessee and Morgan's raiders, all within a single month, had caused them to question whether the South could survive another large-scale defeat this soon, particularly one that would swing ajar the gateway to its heartland. Informed of Richmond's decision, Bragg set about reorganizing his army so as to incorporate without delay the new brigades and divisions about to join or rejoin him from various directions. Indeed, reorganization had already begun on a limited scale. Hardee having been detached in mid-July to take over the mutinous remnant of Pemberton's band of parolees awaiting exchange at Demopolis, the irascible and highly competent D. H. Hill, promoted to lieutenant general subject to congressional approval, had come from North Carolina to replace him. Likewise the dapper and experienced, if disgruntled, Tom Hindman arrived in mid-August from the Transmississippi, and a place was made for him by transferring the less distinguished Withers to an administrative post in his native Alabama. Soon afterwards Buckner was ordered to evacuate Knoxville, and having moved southwest to Loudon, where he burned the railroad bridge across the Tennessee, he continued his march to the Hiwassee, less than forty miles from Chattanooga. There he stopped, for the time being, under orders to contest an advance by Burnside, if one developed, and stand ready to join Bragg on short notice if one did not. By that time Breckinridge had arrived with the first of two divisions being sent from Mississippi. He rejoined his old corps, formerly Hardee's, and Major General A. P. Stewart's division was detached from Hill to be combined with Buckner's and thus form a new third corps under the Kentuckian, who was summoned from the Hiwassee, Burnside having turned his attention elsewhere. When W. H. T. Walker joined Bragg with the second of the two divisions from Johnston, another division was organized by detaching and combining brigades from divisions already present, thus providing a fourth corps under his command. Practically overnight — that is, within a ten-day period extending from late August into early September — the Army of Tennessee had grown from two to four corps, each with two divisions, and a total strength of about 55,000 effectives, including cavalry.

Having in these eight infantry divisions 26 brigades with which to oppose 33 brigades in the eleven Federal divisions — considerably better odds, after all, than the ones he had prevailed against at Murfreesboro — Bragg developed, in the course of the reorganization of his expanded army, strong hopes of being able to defeat his adversary in pitched battle. He was not so sure, however, that this was what it would come to here, any more than it had at Tullahoma, where he had been outmaneuvered and given no real chance to defend a position he had been determined not to yield without a fight. In fact, there were signs that it would not. All this time Rosecrans had been demonstrating as if for a crossing well above Chattanooga, a repetition of the strategy that had won him Middle Tennessee, and Bragg had been reacting fretfully. Harvey Hill, for one, was quite unfavorably impressed. The junior lieutenant in Bragg's battery a dozen years ago in Texas — George Thomas, now commanding a blue corps across the way, and John Reynolds, recently killed at Gettysburg, were the other two lieutenants — Hill had looked forward to the reunion at Chattanooga, but was received with none of the warmth he had expected from his chief. "He was silent and reserved and seemed gloomy and despondent," Hill said later of his fellow North Carolinian. "He had grown prematurely old since I saw him last, and showed much nervousness." Moreover, as the newcomer learned from those who had been with the army all along, this was not entirely due to worry about his opponent on the far side of the river. "His relations with his next in command (General Polk) and with some others of his subordinates were known to be not pleasant. His many retreats, too, had alienated the rank and file from him, or at least had taken away that enthusiasm which soldiers feel for the successful general, and which makes them obey his orders without question." Fresh from the East, where he had been impressed by Lee's great daring, always based on sound knowledge of the enemy's dispositions, Hill was shocked by Bragg's apparent ignorance of the enemy's whereabouts and movements, which resulted in his maintaining a supine attitude while waiting for Rosecrans to show his hand. It was Hill to whom he described the Cumberlands as "the wall of a house full of rat holes," and Hill afterwards recorded that he "was most painfully impressed with the feeling that it was to be a haphazard campaign on our part."

However that might be, and it was as yet no more than an impression, it presently developed that Bragg had been quite right to suspect that Old Rosy was groping elbow-deep in his bag of tricks. No sooner was the Confederate reorganization completed than Bragg learned that the Federals were not only over the river, well downstream, but were also far in his rear, crossing Lookout and the other north-south Georgia ridges for a strike at the rail supply line whose loss would mean starvation for the defenders of Chattanooga. Determined not to be trapped as Pemberton had been at Vicksburg, he promptly evacuated the city and fell back southward through Rossville Gap to a position from which to block the continued advance of the three blue columns when they came around and over Missionary Ridge. His left was at LaFayette, two dozen miles from Chattanooga, and his right at Lee & Gordon's Mill, twelve miles north, where the road from Rossville crossed Chickamauga Creek. Walker held the former, Polk the latter, and Hill and Buckner were posted in between, confronting the westward loom of Pigeon Mountain, a crescent-shaped spur of Lookout Mountain which inclosed the lower end of Missionary Ridge and its eastern valley, a cul-de-sac known locally as McLemore's Cove. Bragg saw in this the trap he had been seeking, the trap he had encouraged Rosecrans to enter by sending out loaded deserters to dispel the Ohioan's native caution and hasten his march with the promise of an easy triumph over a demoralized opponent. Wheeler and Forrest, who had been called in and now were operating respectively on the immediate left and right, toward Alpine and Rossville, were instructed to impede the advance of McCook and Crittenden from Winston Gap and Chattanooga. This would leave the balance of the army, some 40,000 infantry and artillery, free to concentrate against Thomas, who had a total of 23,000 effectives, and destroy him there in the fastness of McLemore's Cove; after which the victors would turn on either or both of the remaining enemy columns, still well beyond supporting distance of each other, and administer the same annihilation treatment. Bragg so ordered on the evening of September 9, shortly after receiving from his scouts, civilian as well as military, reports that Thomas's lead division had entered the cove that afternoon and made a sundown camp on upper Chickamauga Creek.

His plan combined the virtues of simplicity and power, and his orders were issued with the coolness of a gambler holding four aces against a splurger whose overconfidence had been nurtured by an inordinate run of luck. While Cleburne's division of Hill's corps attacked due west through Dug Gap, corking the Pigeon Mountain outlet and fixing the bluecoats in position, Hindman's division of Polk's corps would move southwest from Lee & Gordon's Mill, up Chickamauga Creek, sealing the mouth of the cul-de-sac and striking the enemy flank and rear. Basically, the operation was intended to be like that of a meat-grinder, and if Thomas reinforced his lead division in the cove, so much the better; Breckinridge would be in support of Cleburne, Cheatham of Hindman, and the Federal reinforcements would only give them that much more meat to grind. Hindman set out an hour after midnight, September 10, and halted at dawn, four miles short of contact, waiting to hear from Cleburne. He had a long, tense wait. Finally a message came from Hill, protesting that he had not received his orders till after daylight, that Cleburne himself was sick in bed, with four of his best regiments absent on other duties, and that the proposed attack was risky in the first place, since Thomas had probably sent his lead division forward "as a bait to draw us off from below." In short, Cleburne would not be coming; not this morning at any rate. Later in the day, while still maintaining his indecisive position short of contact, Hindman received a message from Bragg, urging him to finish up his work in the cove as quickly as possible, because Crittenden's corps was on the march from Chattanooga by way of Rossville Gap, directly in his rear. This added fright to confusion, and after remaining all night in a position which he judged perilous in the extreme, the veteran of Prairie Grove decided next morning to withdraw the way he had come. By now, though, Bragg had sent Buckner to his support, with orders to force the issue promptly, and Cleburne was through Dug Gap; so Hindman returned southward. But when the two gray forces came together that afternoon in McLemore's Cove there was nothing blue between them. Thomas at last had spotted the danger, despite his lack of cavalry, and withdrawn to the far side of Missionary Ridge.

Bragg was furious, blaming the lost opportunity on Hindman's indecisiveness and Hill's "querulous, insubordinate spirit," while they in turn put the blame on him, claiming that their orders had been permissive rather than peremptory. However, he resolved to try again, in a different direction and with different commanders. Thomas had withdrawn to safety, but Crittenden had not. Polk having retired toward LaFayette at his approach, the Kentuckian had sent one of his three divisions to occupy Lee & Gordon's Mill while the other two moved against Ringgold, a station on the railroad between Chattanooga and Dalton, in accordance with his orders to break the rebel supply line. Learning of this next morning from Forrest, who was patrolling that flank of the army, Bragg directed Polk to return to his former position with his own reunited corps and Walker's, and attack the isolated Federals there at dawn, September 13. "This division crushed and the others are yours," he told him. The bishop protested that Crittenden, taking alarm, had recalled the two divisions from their march on Ringgold and now had his whole corps posted for defense behind the Chickamauga at that point. This was quite true, as it turned out, but Bragg replied that it was no matter; Polk had four divisions to the enemy's three, and he would send Buckner's two to assist him in case they were needed, which seemed unlikely; the attack was to be launched on schedule, as directed. But when he reached the field at 9 o'clock next morning he found Polk on the defensive, still unwilling to advance lest he be swamped. Madder than ever, the terrible-tempered Confederate commander finally got Polk and Walker and Buckner into assault formation by noon and sent them forward — only to discover that Crittenden, after the manner of Thomas two days ago in McLemore's Cove, had escaped the trap by withdrawing undetected beyond Missionary Ridge. In a rage of frustration and regret for the two rare chances he had lost in the past three days, Bragg pulled his whole army once more back to LaFayette, the best position from which to counter a thrust at his vital supply line by any one or all three of the blue columns across the way.

But there was small likelihood of any such thrust by then. The scales having fallen at last from his eyes, Rosecrans was doing all he could to get the three isolated segments of his army back together before they were abolished, one by one, by a rebel army which he now knew was not only not retreating in disorder, but also had been heavily reinforced. And now there followed a three-day interlude during which neither commander knew much of what the other was doing, although the graybacks at least had the physical advantage of standing still while their opponents tramped the dusty hills and valleys that lay between them and concentration. Presently the blue movements took on a new urgency, a new franticness, with the circulation of reports that Bragg was about to be even more substantially reinforced by troops already on the way by rail from Lee in Virginia; three divisions of them, rumor had it, under Longstreet. Old Rosy and his staff began to curse Burnside, who had turned east by now from Knoxville and Cumberland Gap instead of in their direction for the intended hookup: with the result, as they believed, that now it was they who were in grievous danger of being cut off from their base, exposed to the threat of starvation, and swamped by superior numbers, including a whole corps of hard-bitten killers from the far-off eastern theater.

Meanwhile at LaFayette, where the Confederates were recovering from their recent fruitless exertions in McLemore's Cove and near Lee & Gordon's Mill, Harvey Hill marveled at the apparent casualness with which these Westerners, blue and gray alike, accepted the proximity of their adversaries just on the opposite side of the intervening ridge. It was quite unlike what he had known before, back in Virginia under Lee. "When two armies confront each other in the East, they get to work very soon," he remarked to one of his veteran brigadiers. "But here you look at one another for days and weeks at a time." The brigadier, a cockfight enthusiast, laughed. "Oh, we out here have to crow and peck straws awhile before we use our spurs," he said.

All the same, as Hill, observed long afterwards in recording the exchange, "the crowing and pecking straws were now about over." A dozen to twenty miles north of there, above Lee & Gordon's Mill, the woods-choked field of Chickamauga awaited the confrontation that would result, within the week, in what would not only be the greatest battle of the West, but would also be, for the numbers engaged, the bloodiest of the war.

✕ 3 ✕

Reports that Longstreet was en route were true, but once more only up to a point, the difference being that this time the exaggeration was in the opposite direction, serving rather to deepen the blue commander's fears than to heighten his expectations. Old Peter was coming with two, not three divisions; Pickett's was still in no shape for another headlong commitment, and though it too had been detached from Lee, it was left behind to assist in the close-up defense of Richmond when the other two, under McLaws and Law — or Hood, as it turned out — passed through the capital on the first stage of their long ride to Northwest Georgia. The decision to send them to join Bragg had been arrived at during a White House conference in late August and early September, a conference not unlike the one that had preceded the march into Pennsylvania, except that this time the gray-bearded commander of the Army of Northern Virginia carried much less weight in council than he had done before his defeat at Gettysburg, which had been the direct result of the weight he exerted then in overriding the objections of Reagan. Besides, since that and the other early-July reverses in Mississippi, Arkansas, Louisiana, and Middle Tennessee, additional threats to the national existence had developed, including not only the menace to East Tennessee — which was lost while the conference was in progress — but also on the Atlantic seaboard, particularly at Charleston, and in the far-off Transmississippi. These too had served to strengthen the conviction that the country simply could not afford another defeat in the vital central theater, and therefore the decision had been to reinforce Bragg at the expense of all the others, including Lee, who would be left to face the victorious Meade with a greatly reduced force, and Beauregard, who was calling urgently for assistance in resisting an all-out Union amphibious effort to rock and wreck the cradle of secession.

Du Pont's repulse, back in April, had resulted in some sour-grapes talk on the part of Gideon Welles to the effect that Charleston, "a place of no strategic importance," had not been worth taking in the first place; but the failure rankled badly over the span of the next two months, with the result that he decided to try again with a more determined commander. Rear Admiral Andrew H. Foote, apparently recovered from the wound he had suffered while clearing the lower Tennessee and the Cumberland, as well as the Mississippi down to Memphis, was the logical choice for the job and was appointed despite his reluctance to supersede his old friend Samuel Du Pont. He died in New York in late June, however, while on the way to his new post, and the position went instead to Rear Admiral John A. Dahlgren, head of the Bureau of Ordnance, inventor of the bottle-shaped gun that had done so much to give the Union its victories afloat, and an intimate friend of Lincoln's during his command of the Washington Navy Yard in the first two years of the war. Described by a correspondent as "a light complexioned man of perhaps forty years of age," though he was in fact in his mid-fifties, Dahlgren was "slight and of medium height, [with] pale and delicate features. His countenance is exceedingly thoughtful and modest . . . while his eye is inevitably keen, and his thin nostrils expand as he talks, with a look of great enthusiasm." Welles believed this last proceeded from less admirable qualities than those the reporter discerned. "He is intensely ambitious," the Secretary noted in his diary, "and, I fear, too selfish. He has the heroism which proceeds from pride, and would lead him to danger and death; but whether he has the innate, unselfish courage of the genuine sailor and soldier, remains to be seen." Despite these doubts on the part of his superior, based in part on personal observation and in part on the fact that he had never been in action, Dahlgren was given command of the South Atlantic Blockading Squadron, which he took over as Du Pont's successor in early July, together with special instructions covering the employment of his patched-up ironclads to effect the reduction of the South Carolina city, defiant behind the guns and obstructions around and in its harbor.

This time there was no plea from the Department that the army not be allowed to "spoil" the show by having a vital part in it. Rather, the admiral was to work in conjunction with Brigadier General Quincy Gillmore, who had arrived three weeks earlier to assume command of the 15,000 infantrymen, artillerists, and engineers assigned to take the lead in the opening phase of the combined attack. Fort Sumter was seen as the key to control of Charleston harbor, and Gillmore, a thirty-eight-year-old Ohio-born West Pointer — top man in the otherwise undistinguished class of 1849 — had been called in, as a fortifications expert and a master of siege operations, to give an opinion on whether the army could reduce it. He replied that this could best be done by mounting heavy guns on the north end of Morris Island, held at present by the Confederates, and using them to knock the famed pentagonal fort to pieces; after which, as Gillmore saw it, the ironclads would be able to steam in and administer the same treatment to the city itself, on the far side of the harbor, until such time as the white flag went up. His plan approved, he got to work as soon as he arrived in mid-June, and by the time Dahlgren took over from Du Pont he was ready to launch his opening attack from Folly Island, where he had secretly massed a 3000-man assault force, against the adjoining southern end of Morris Island, preparatory to a drive up its narrow four-mile length to Cummings Point, which was less than 1500 yards from Sumter. On July 10, encouraged by a promotion to major general, he sprang a dawn attack which caught the rebels so thoroughly off guard that by noon he had the lower three fourths of the island in his grip. All that remained was Battery Wagner, dead ahead, and Battery Gregg, 1300 yards farther along on Cummings Point. His loss so far had amounted to scarcely more than a hundred men, only fifteen of whom were dead. Wasting no time, he ordered another all-out assault next morning. This too was launched with verve and determination, but with considerably less satisfactory results. The first wave made it up to Wagner's parapet, only to be shattered by heavy volleys of grape and musketry, while the support formations were scattered by high-angle fire from Gregg. Within an hour the attackers lost 49 killed, 167 captured or missing, and 123 wounded, and so far as the repulsed survivors could see, these 339 casualties had been expended without any effect whatever on either the earthwork or its defenders, who kept up a deadly sniping at everything blue that showed above the level of the sandy ground out front.

Undaunted, Gillmore spent a week bringing up another 3500 soldiers and emplacing 41 guns for counterbattery work; then at noon of July 18 he opened fire, which was also the signal for Dahlgren's monitors to close the range and pound both rebel works from the seaward flank. This continued for more than seven hours, and presently Battery Wagner ceased to reply, its cannoneers driven from their guns. Then at 7.30 — the attack hour had been set for twilight so that the defenders would not be able to take careful aim — the Union guns fell silent too, ashore and afloat, and the 6000 Federals started forward on a necessarily narrow front of less than 200 yards. In the lead was a Massachusetts regiment, all-Negro except for its officers, who were mostly Boston bluebloods, including its young colonel, Robert Gould Shaw, whose mother had wept for joy at the sight of her boy leading black men forth to war; "What have I done, that God has been so good to me!" she cried at the grand farewell review staged in Boston in late May. In less than seven weeks, however, it developed that God had not been so good to her after all, unless what she wanted in place of her son was a fine bronze statue on the Common. The 1000-man rebel garrison came out of the bombproof to which it had retired at the height of the cannonade and met the attackers as it had done the week before, with even more spectacular results. Here in the East, on Morris Island just outside Charleston harbor, as formerly in the West, at Milliken's Bend and Port Hudson, Negro troops proved that they could stop bullets and shell fragments as well as white men; but that was about all. When flesh and blood could stand no more, the survivors fell back from the ditch and parapet, black and white alike, and returned to the trenches they had left an hour ago. Casualties had been heavy; 1515 of the attackers had fallen, as compared to 174 of the defenders, and next morning when the latter peered out of their sight slits they saw live and dead men strewn in piles and windrows, their bodies horribly mangled by close-up artillery fire, while detached arms and legs and heads were splattered all about. A brief truce sufficed for removal of the wounded and disposal of the slain, including the twenty-six-year-old Shaw, who had taken a bullet through the heart and was buried in a common grave with his Negro soldiers, nearly half of whom had been lost in the repulse.

Somewhat daunted, but still determined, Gillmore decided to settle down to regular siege operations and take Sumter under fire from where he was, the range being only about 3000 yards. From close up, he would batter Wagner and Gregg into submission, meanwhile bringing eighteen heavy guns to bear in a round-the-clock attempt to breach the fort less than a mile across the water from the inaccessible north end of the island. By mid-August three parallels had been drawn and advanced, preparatory to launching a sudden, swamping rush upon the stubborn earthwork dead ahead, and Sumter was being bombarded at a rate of nearly 5000 shells a week, its brick walls cracking and crumbling under the impact of 300-pound projectiles, the heaviest ever employed by rifled field artillery up to then. Another innovation was the use of calcium lights, which threw the ramparts of Battery Wagner into stark relief and helped to prevent the rebels from making nighttime sorties against the gunners and diggers in their immediate front. Still a third innovation was the establishment in the marshes between Morris and James islands, off to the left and about 8000 yards from downtown Charleston, of an 8-inch Parrott rifle — promptly dubbed the "Swamp Angel" by the engineers who sweated and floundered in the salty mud to place the big gun on its platform — for the purpose of heaving its 200-pound shells, specially filled for the occasion with liquid and solidified Greek Fire, into the city's streets and houses. On August 21 the monster weapon was reported ready, and Gillmore sent a note across the lines demanding the immediate evacuation of Morris Island and Fort Sumter; otherwise, he warned, he would open fire "from batteries already established within easy and effective range of the heart of the city." No answer having been received by midnight, he sent word for the gun to go into action. At 1.30 a.m. the first shell was on the way. The sound of alarm bells and whistles, which reached them faintly across the nearly five miles of marsh and water, told the crew that the percussion-fuzed shell had found its mark, and they followed this with fifteen others, equally accurate, before dawn. At that time Gillmore received a message signed G. T. Beauregard, protesting his barbarity and rejecting his ultimatum that Wagner and Gregg and Sumter be abandoned. "It would appear, sir, that despairing of reducing these works, you now resort to the novel measure of turning your guns against the old men, the women and children, and the hospitals of a sleeping city," the Creole hotly accused his adversary, and he predicted that this "mode of warfare, which I confidently declare to be atrocious and unworthy of any soldier . . . will give you 'a bad eminence' in history, even in the history of this war." Gillmore replied that the city had had forty days' notice, this being the length of time he had been battering at its gates, and despite the added protests of the Spanish and British consuls he ordered the bombardment resumed on August 23. Twenty more incendiary shells were fired, six of which exploded prematurely in the tube with spectacular pyrotechnical effects, and though no member of the crew was hurt by these sudden gushes of flame from the vent and muzzle, the gun itself was probably weakened. At any rate, on the twentieth shot the breech of the piece blew out of its jacket, just behind the vent, and the Swamp Angel ended her brief career of thirty-six rounds, thirty of which had landed squarely on target in the birthplace of secession, whatever "bad eminence" she might have gained for Gillmore in the process.

He made no attempt to replace the ruined cannon, believing as he did that he soon would have possession of Cummings Point, where the ground was firmer and the range to Charleston shorter. By August 26 his sappers were within 200 yards of Battery Wagner, and within another week the distance was half that. All this time, the bombardment of Fort Sumter had continued, with gratifying results. Most of its southern wall was down, and both the western and eastern walls were badly cracked. Practically every casemate had been breached. On the first night in September, when six of the monitors gave the crumbling fort a five-hour pounding, not a shot was fired from the rubble in reply. Gillmore stepped up the action against Wagner. On September 5 he began a relentless 42-hour cannonade during which no less than 3000 shells were rained upon the earthwork, preparatory to the final assault. But when the guns stopped firing in the predawn darkness of September 7, so that the infantry could rush forward and end the 58-day siege — in the course of which the Federals had suffered a total of 2318 casualties and inflicted 641 — it was discovered that the Confederates had evacuated both Wagner and Gregg the night before, despite the constant deluge of metal, and withdrawn in rowboats to James Island. Once more, Beauregard's uncanny sense of timing had not failed him. Advancing to emplace his heaviest guns on Cummings Point, from which he could resume his shelling of the city, Gillmore passed the word to Dahlgren that the army's share of the operation had been accomplished. Morris Island had been occupied entirely and Fort Sumter had been neutralized; now the navy's turn had come to take the lead. Proud Charleston would be brought to its knees if the ironclads would only steam across the harbor and bring it under the muzzles of their guns.

But could they? Dahlgren was far from certain: so little so, in fact, that he was unwilling to make the attempt until Sumter had not only been "neutralized," as the army claimed, but taken. Moreover, he wanted the honor of doing the taking, and he believed he saw how this could be done without exposing his valuable monitors to sudden destruction by a torpedo or by point-blank fire from a gun kept hidden amid the rubble for that purpose. Constant shelling had tumbled the bricks of the south wall down to the water's edge, affording an incline which, though steep and rugged, could be scaled without the delay the use of ladders would involve. If a surprise landing could be accomplished, a storming party would be into the place before its defenders even had time to sound the alarm. So at least the naval commander believed, or reasoned, when he called on September 7 — the same day Morris Island fell to the army — for 500 naval volunteers to make a small-boat landing by the dark of the moon the following night. By way of preamble he sent in a demand for the fort's surrender and received, at second hand, Beauregard's reply: "Tell Admiral Dahlgren to come and take it." That was just what he was preparing to do, and when the officer he had placed in charge of the venture expressed some doubts that it would succeed, Dahlgren scoffed at his fears. "You have only to go and take possession," he assured him. "You will find nothing but a corporal's guard." Accordingly, the volunteers were loaded into some thirty assault boats and towed within half a mile of Sumter before moonrise the next night. No lights were shown and the oars were muffled, but the rebel lookouts spotted them anyhow and gave the alarm, including the firing of rockets, which was the signal for batteries on James and Sullivan's islands to open fire on the waters near the fort. Caught under the resultant two-way barrage, the marines and sailors hurried ashore and were received by the 300-man garrison lying in wait for them with rifles, fire-balls, hand grenades, and brickbats, which combined to make conditions even worse on the beach than on the water. Five of the boats were captured, along with more than a hundred men and thirteen officers. The rest got away as best they could through the ring of fire, bringing their wounded with them. "Nobody hurt on our side," Beauregard reported.

Dahlgren took the check as proof that he had been wise not to risk his iron flotilla in any such challenge to the alert and tricky rebels, but he could not escape the depression that proceeded from the knowledge that he had done no better, so far, than the man he had replaced. The enervating heat, plus long confinement in the poorly ventilated monitors, had impaired his health; moreover, he was often seasick, which caused him to lose caste with his sailors and perhaps with himself as well. Worst of all, though, was the gnawing sense of failure. Victory was the cure, he knew, but he would not risk the alternative, defeat, which in this case would be utterly disastrous, not only to his ships and men, but also to his career. Nothing helped, or even seemed to. "I am better today," he confided in his journal, "but the worst of this place is that one only stops getting weaker. One does not get stronger." Torn between desire and fear, ambition and indecision, he reacted physically to the mental strain. "My debility increases, so that today it is an exertion to sit in a chair. I do not see well. How strange — no pain, but so feeble. It seems like gliding away to death. How easy it seems! Why not, to one whose race is run?" It was scarcely to be expected, with the admiral in this frame of mind, that the navy would press matters beyond the point that had been reached when Morris Island fell. Nor did it. Dahlgren perceived that Sumter had become little more than an infantry outpost, its heaviest guns having been removed in secret to Sullivan's Island during the two-month siege of Battery Wagner; Fort Moultrie was now the real obstacle to a penetration of the harbor, and the only way to close with it was by steaming through the torpedo-infested channel, which was something he was by no means willing to attempt. Meanwhile — illogically, but for lack of anything better in the way of employment for his vessels and their crews — he maintained an intermittent bombardment of Sumter. Formerly a brick masonry fort, it was now a powerful earthwork; the shells it absorbed only served to make it more impervious by stirring up and adding to the rubble any attackers would have to climb and cross, dodging fire-balls and grenades, in order to come to grips with the defenders. He had tried that once, however, and he had no intention of trying it again.

Gillmore at least had the satisfaction of knowing that he had carried out his primary assignment by securing possession of Morris Island, but even if he had had another intermediary objective in mind — which he did not — he would have had no way to get there, shipless as he was, with bottomless marshes on one flank, open sea on the other, and the mine-strewn harbor dead ahead. Like Dahlgren, he contented himself with lobbing projectiles into Sumter, barely 1400 yards away, or into Moultrie, twice that distance across the harbor mouth. By way of diversion he sometimes threw a long-range salvo or two at Charleston, which was about half a mile closer to Cummings Point than it was to the platform that had kept the ill-fated Swamp Angel out of the mud. None of these seemed to accomplish much, however. Sumter merely continued to squat there, defiant and misshapen — "a noble mass of ruins," Beauregard called it, "over which still float our colors" — responding to hits by sending up puffs of brickdust, but otherwise appearing as indifferent as an elephant to flea bites. Moultrie did not even do that much, so far as the Federal spotters could see from a range of 2800 yards, and presently they left off shooting at it. As for Charleston itself, while banks moved their resources from the lower to the upper part of town and hospitals were evacuated in the impact zone, the chief complaint of those citizens who had recovered from their early panic and returned to their homes, keeping tubs of water handy in all the rooms for fighting fires, was that the scream of the Yankee shells disturbed their sleep. They were proud of themselves, proud of their defenders out on the firing line, and proudest of all of Beauregard, their original hero, to whom Congress afterwards tendered a joint resolution of thanks for "a defense which, for the skill, heroism, and tenacity displayed during an attack scarcely paralleled in warfare ... is justly entitled to be pronounced glorious by impartial history and an admiring country."

But that was later. The Richmond conference ended on September 7, a day that seemed more the occasion for alarm than for high-flown congratulations, least of all to Beauregard, since it was then that Morris Island fell and the Charleston commander stepped up his plea for reinforcements, predicting graver disasters unless the odds he faced were shortened. All the statesmen and generals knew, as they studied the situation from their council room in the White House, was that events appeared to be mounting rapidly toward an unwelcome climax — not only down the Atlantic seaboard, but also along the opposite end of the thousand-mile frontier. In that far-western quarter the odds were even longer and the enemy had mounted a two-pronged offensive designed to restore the northern two thirds of Arkansas, including its capital, to the domain of the Union. The Confederacy having been sundered by the loss of Vicksburg and Port Hudson, the Federals seemed to be losing no time in getting to work on the disconnected halves, particularly the one that lay beyond what Lincoln called the "unvexed" Mississippi.

One prong was being driven eastward from Indian Territory, with Fort Smith as its immediate goal, and the other was being driven westward from Helena, whose garrison, flushed by its success in breaking up the Independence Day assault, had been strengthened by the return of Frederick Steele's division, which had gone downriver eight months ago with Sherman and now came back with the names of the many engagements of the Vicksburg campaign proudly stitched to its battle flags. Much to the disgruntlement of Prentiss, who submitted his resignation as a result, command of the inland expedition went to Steele, together with instructions to "break up Price and occupy Little Rock," a hundred crow-flight miles away in the heart of the state. To do this he had two divisions of infantry, totaling only about 6000 effectives — "The sick list is frightful," he reported — plus one division of cavalry, as large as the two of infantry put together, detached from Schofield. This mounted force, led by Brigadier General John W. Davidson, a forty-year-old Virginia-born West Pointer, left Bloomfield, Missouri, and proceeded south down Crowley's Ridge to Clarendon, Arkansas, which it reached on August 8, to be joined nine days later by Steele, who marched his foot soldiers from Helena and took command of the combined 12,000. Shifting his base to De Valls Bluff, a dozen miles northwest, he spent another two weeks making final preparations and then on September 1, in accordance with his instructions, set out for the capital, just under fifty miles due west. By that date the opposite prong — a scratch collection of seven regiments, three composed of Union-loyal Indian volunteers and one of Negroes, all under James Blunt, the former Ohio doctor who had been promoted to major general as a reward for Prairie Grove — had attained its initial objective with a bloodless occupation of Fort Smith, 125 miles from Little Rock and just short of the western border. Back in mid-July, Blunt had prepared the way for this maneuver with an attack on the Confederates to his front at Honey Springs, fifty miles west of his goal, driving them south in disorder and destroying the stores they had collected for subsistence in that barren region of Indian Territory. Commanded by Brigadier General William Steele, a forty-year-old New Yorker and West Pointer who had married South, the rebel force of nine regiments, six of them Indian, was actually larger than Blunt's; but when the action was joined the graybacks found to their dismay that their powder, imported from Europe by way of Texas, had turned to paste in their cartridge boxes. They ran and kept on running. Satisfied merely to have them out of the way for the time being, Blunt did not pursue. He returned instead to the Arkansas River to rest and refit his victorious 3000 multicolored troops, then turned east in late August to occupy Fort Smith on September 1, the day the other Steele started west from De Valls Bluff.

About this time, while events were heading up for the recovery of most of Arkansas, word came of a "raid" some 300 miles to the north, across the Missouri-Kansas line, that provoked more excitement and indignation throughout the country than any that had been staged in the

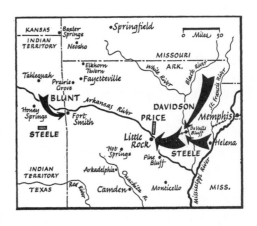

course of the nearly four years since John Brown struck at Harpers Ferry. The difference was that this one, launched against the region where Brown had got his start, was not only a good deal bloodier, and therefore more atrocious, but was also as complete a success as the other had been a failure. Heavy detachments of troops from Schofield to Grant and Steele, well downriver, had emboldened the guerillas lurking in the Missouri brush: particularly Charles Quantrill, who had secured a captain's commission from Richmond and was eager to justify his bars, as well as to pay off old scores from the prewar border troubles, by leading his irregulars on a more daring expedition than any they had attempted up to now. He favored a strike at Lawrence, an old-time abolitionist settlement forty miles beyond the Kansas line. At first his men would not agree, believing that the prize, though fat, would not be worth the risk; but two developments which occurred in rapid succession in mid-August changed their minds, adding a thirst for revenge to their already strong desire for loot. For the past three months the Federal commander of the District of the Border, Brigadier General Thomas Ewing, had been arresting women charged with giving encouragement and assistance to guerillas, many of whom were their sons and brothers and husbands. This had enraged the men in the brush, who, whatever their excesses in other directions, had invariably maintained a hands-off attitude toward the mothers and sisters and wives of their Jayhawk adversaries. The prisoners were confined in certain buildings in Kansas City, and on August 14 one of these, a dilapidated three-story brick affair with a liquor shop on the ground floor, collapsed — as Ewing had been warned it might do — killing four of the women outright and seriously injuring several others. When news of this reached Quantrill's men they promptly reconsidered their chief's proposal for a raid on Lawrence. "We can get more revenge and more money there than anywhere else in the state of Kansas," he told them. Then four days later Ewing announced in a general order that not only would more such arrests be made, but that "the wives and children of known guerillas, and also women who are heads of families and are willfully engaged in aiding guerillas, will be notified . . . to remove out of this district and out of the State of Missouri forthwith." The order was dated August 18; "We could stand no more," a guerilla who had lost a sister in the Kansas City tragedy wrote later. Next day Quantrill set out from Blackwater Creek in Johnson County, headed west for Lawrence with a column of just under 300 bloody-minded men.

The distance was over seventy miles and they made it in two days, riding strapped to their saddles the second night so that they could sleep without falling off their horses. While still in Missouri they encountered a party of 104 mounted Confederate recruits proceeding south under Colonel John D. Holt, who decided to take them along on the raid as a training exercise. These, plus a number of other volunteers picked up in the course of the ride to the border, brought the column to a strength of about 450 men by the time it drew rein at daybreak of August 21 on the outskirts of Lawrence. Three weeks past his twenty-sixth birthday, wearing a gaudy, low-cut guerilla shirt, gray trousers stuffed into cavalry boots, a gold-corded black slouch hat, and four revolvers in his belt, Quantrill assigned each unit its special mission, then led the howling charge that swept from the southeast into the streets of the sleeping town. Long since warned to expect no quarter, the raiders intended to give none. With the exception of a single adult male civilian — the hated Jayhawk chieftain Senator James H. Lane, who was to be taken back to Missouri alive, if possible, for a semi-public hanging — Quantrill's orders called for the killing of "every man big enough to carry a gun." First to fall, in accordance with these instructions, was the Reverend S. S. Snyder, sometimes lieutenant of the 2d Kansas Colored Infantry, shot dead under the cow he was milking in his yard. Next were seventeen recruits encountered in the otherwise deserted camp of the 14th Cavalry, several of them pistoled before they emerged from their blankets. Thus began a three-hour orgy of killing, interspersed with drinks in commandeered saloons and exhibitions of fancy riding. Men were chased and shot down as they ran; others were ⸲ragged from their homes and murdered in front of their wives and children; still others were smothered or roasted alive when the houses in which they hid were set afire. Holt and other less bloodthirsty members of the band managed to protect a few of the fugitives, but not many; Quantrill, who had lived for a time in Lawrence before the war, had prepared a vengeance list beforehand, and all who were on it and in town this morning wère disposed of, except for the man whose name was at its head. Wily Jim Lane took flight in his nightshirt, warned by the first thunder of hooves as the guerillas swept in across the prairie, and hid out undetected in a cornfield until they rode away, leaving 80 new widows and 250 fatherless children weeping in the ruins of the town. Nearly 200 buildings had been wrecked or burned, including all three newspaper offices and most of the business district, for a property loss amounting to about two million dollars. In all, though not one woman was physically harmed, no less than 150 Kansans were killed, fewer than twenty of whom were soldiers and several of whom were scarcely more than boys. Not one of them sold his life dearly, however, for the only casualty the raiders suffered was a former Baptist preacher who got drunk, passed out, and was killed and scalped by an Indian when he was discovered, shortly after his friends had ridden away. His body was dragged through the streets behind a horse by a free Negro until it was stripped naked, and the grieving citizens pelted it with stones by way of revenge.

Loaded with booty, the rest of the guerillas had pulled out southward about 9 o'clock that morning, shortly after lookouts on Mount Oread reported a heavy column of troopers approaching from the north and west, beyond the Kansas River. Setting ambushes to delay his pursuers, who converged from all points of the compass as the news from Lawrence spread across the plains, and swerving aside in the twilight to avoid a blue garrison lying in wait for him at Paola, Quantrill made it back across the Missouri line next morning with nearly all of his command. At this point the order was "Every man for himself," and the raiders faded into the brush by a hundred different trails to resume their various disguises as farmers, parolees, and Union-loyal residents of the scattered towns and hamlets. All who were detected subsequently were executed on the spot, as those had been who were caught up with when their horses went lame or collapsed from exhaustion during the chase across the prairie. "No prisoners have been taken, and none will be," Ewing informed Schofield, and four days after what became known as the Lawrence Massacre he issued, at Jim Lane's insistence, his famous General Order Number 11, directing the forcible removal of all persons, male or female, child or adult, loyal or disloyal, who lived more than a mile from a Federal post in the four Missouri counties south of the Missouri River and adjacent to the border. The time limit was fifteen days from the date of issue, August 25. By mid-September the order had been so effectively enforced that Cass County, which had had a population of 10,000 before the war, was occupied by fewer than 600 civilians; Bates County, directly south, had even less. Moreover, the vengeance-minded 15th Kansas Cavalry, delighted at having been given the assignment of seeing that Ewing's order was obeyed, went through the region so enthusiastically with torch and sword, leaving nothing but chimneys to show where houses and cabins once had stood, that it was known for years thereafter as the Burnt District. Not that Quantrill was deterred. He collected his scattered guerillas, continued his depredations, including attacks on wagon trains and steamboats on the Missouri, and finally withdrew south in early October to winter in Texas with a force of 400 hard-bitten men, most of whom had been with him on the raid that nearly wiped Lawrence from the map.

By then the issue had been settled in central Arkansas, and though Steele had failed to "break up Price," he had succeeded admirably in carrying out the rest of his assignment. In temporary command of the district after Holmes fell sick in late July, Price concentrated his 8000 effectives at Little Rock, squarely between the menacing blue prongs of Blunt and Steele, the former in occupation of Fort Smith, just under 150 miles to the west, and the latter advancing from De Valls Bluff, one third that distance to the east. Bracing to meet the nearer and heavier threat — Blunt had only about 4000 men, while Steele had three times as many — the bulky but agile Missourian intrenched a line three miles in length on the north bank of the Arkansas, protected by swamps in front and anchored to the river below the capital in his rear, access to which was provided by three pontoon bridges. Though he took the precaution of sending his accumulated stores to Arkadelphia, sixty miles southwest, he reported that his troops were "in excellent condition, full of enthusiasm, and eager to meet the enemy." So was he, despite the known disparity in numbers, if the bluecoats would only attack him where he was. But Steele, as it turned out, had a different notion. Maneuvering as if for a frontal assault, he sent Davidson's 6000 troopers on a fast ride south to strike the river well downstream from the Confederate position.

This was begun on September 6, and Price on that same day lost one of his two cavalry brigadiers, not by enemy action, but rather as the result of a quarrel between them. For the past two months Marmaduke had been openly critical of Lucius Walker's failure to support him in the attack at Helena; now as they skirmished with the advancing Federals and the Tennessean gave ground under pressure, the hot-tempered Missourian accused him of outright cowardice. Walker replied, as expected, with a challenge which was promptly accepted, the terms being "pistols at ten paces to fire and advance," and the former Memphis businessman fell mortally wounded at the second fire. The conditions of honor having been satisfied in accordance with the code — which, presumably, was one of those things the South was fighting to preserve as part of its "way of life" — presently, after a period of intense suffering by the loser, the Confederacy had one general less than it had had when the two men took position, ten paces apart, and began to walk toward one another, firing as they advanced.

Within four days of this exchange the South also had one state capital the less. Assisted no doubt by the resultant confusion across the way, Davidson got his horsemen over the river at dawn of September 10, moved them rapidly up the scantly defended right bank toward Little Rock, and after forcing a crossing of Bayou Fourche, five miles below the town, received its formal surrender by the civil authorities shortly after sundown. Price had reacted fast: as indeed he had had need to do, if he was to save his army. Outflanked by the cavalry while Steele kept up the pressure against his front, he withdrew from his north-bank intrenchments, set his pontoons afire to prevent the blue infantry from following in his wake, and put his troops on the march for Arkadelphia, to which point he had prudently removed his stores the week before. There on the south bank of the Ouachita he took up a new position extending fifty miles downstream to Camden, with detachments posted as far east as Monticello, about midway between the latter place and the Federal gunboats prowling unchallenged up and down the Mississippi. Steele did not pursue.

Casualties had been light on both sides in both operations — 137 for Steele, 64 for Price; 75 for Blunt, 181 for Steele — but they were no adequate indication of what had been won and lost in the double-pronged campaign. "If they take Fort Smith, the Indian country is gone," Holmes had remarked in February, and now in September his prediction had been unhappily fulfilled. Similarly, the loss of Little Rock — fourth on the list of fallen capitals, immediately following Jackson, which had been preceded the year before by Baton Rouge and Nashville — extended the Union occupation to include three fourths of Arkansas, a gain for which the victors presumably would have been willing to pay ten or even one hundred times the actual cost.

This too was included in the Richmond assessment of the over-all situation. Although, like Chattanooga and Cumberland Gap, Little Rock had not fallen by the time the White House conference ended on September 7 — it fell three and the others two days later — its loss, like theirs, could be anticipated as a factor to be placed in the enemy balance pan alongside Fort Smith, Knoxville, and Morris Island, all of which passed into Federal possession while the council was considering what could best be attempted to offset the reverses lately suffered at Tullahoma, Gettysburg, Vicksburg, Helena, and Port Hudson. Within that same horrendous span, late June through early September, only two events occurred which might have been considered as adding weight to the South's high-riding opposite pan, one the New York draft riot and the other the Quantrill raid on Lawrence. However, both of these were not only comparatively slight, they were also of doubtful character as assets: especially the latter, which, if claimed, would expose the Confederacy to charges of land piracy, or worse, before the bar of world opinion. In strategic terms, moreover, the outlook was no less clear for being bleak. Rosecrans was over the Tennessee River, and unless Bragg could stop him — as, apparently, he could not — the Army of the Cumberland would be free to march southeast through Georgia to the coast, which would mean that the eastern half of the nation, already severed from the western half by the loss of the Mississippi, would itself be cut in two. In that event, nothing would remain to be governed from Richmond but the Carolinas and so much of Virginia as lay south of the Rappahannock, a political and geographical fragment whose survival was already threatened from the north by the Army of the Potomac, from the west by the troops now in occupation of Knoxville and East Tennessee, and from the east by the amphibious force holding Charleston under siege, all three of which had lately been victorious, to various degrees, under Meade, Burnside, and Gillmore.

Despite the fact that it now had some 20,000 fewer effectives than it had had three months ago when its commander urged a similar course of action under similar circumstances, Davis had warmed at first to Lee's proposal, submitted at the outset of the strategy conference, that the Army of Northern Virginia once more take the offensive against Meade. On the last day of August Lee sent word to Longstreet, who had been left in charge on the Rapidan, to "prepare the army for offensive operations." Old Peter replied that he would of course obey his chief's instructions and had already passed them on to Ewell and A. P. Hill, but "I do not see that we can reasonably hope to accomplish much" by continuing to fight a war of stalemate and attrition. "I am inclined to the opinion that the best opportunity for great results is in Tennessee," he asserted. "If we could hold the defensive here with two corps and send the other to operate in Tennessee with [Bragg's] army, I think that we could accomplish more than by an advance from here." This was written on September 2, the day Burnside's cavalry rode into Knoxville, and two days later Rosecrans completed his crossing of the Tennessee River, posing the intolerable threat of a march through Georgia to the sea. Davis and Seddon — to whom Longstreet had written earlier, by invitation, renewing his pre-Gettysburg claim "that the only hope of reviving the waning cause was through the advantage of interior lines" — reacted with a sudden shift from approval of Lee's proposal to approval of his lieutenant's, except that they preferred that the Virginian himself go west to deliver in person the blow designed to bring Old Rosy to his knees. Lee demurred, asserting that the general already on the scene and familiar with the terrain could do a better job. Davis reluctantly acquiesced, and the final plan to reinforce Bragg from

Virginia, though not to supersede him, was approved. On September 6 Lee sent word for his quartermaster to arrange for transportation by rail to Northwest Georgia for two of Longstreet's divisions. Next morning the Richmond council adjourned, and he returned to Orange. By the following day, September 8, the designated troops were on the move.

Longstreet rode over to headquarters to bid his gray-bearded commander farewell. They talked for a while in the latter's tent and then emerged. Lee said nothing more until the burly Georgian had one foot in the stirrup, prepared to mount. "Now, General, you must beat those people out in the West," he told him. Old Peter took his foot from the stirrup and turned to face his chief. "If I live," he said. "But I would not give a single man of my command for a fruitless victory." This was a rather impolitic thing to say to a commander whose greatest victories had been "fruitless" in the sense that Longstreet meant, but Lee either missed or ignored the implication. He merely repeated that arrangements had been made and orders issued to assure that any success would be exploited. Then he watched the man he called "my old warhorse" mount and ride away, leaving him barely more than 45,000 troops with which to block or parry an advance by an army that lately had whipped him with nearly equal numbers and now had almost twice the strength of his own.

"Never before were so many troops moved over such worn-out railways," a First Corps staff officer later wrote, though not quite accurately, since he left out of account (as most veterans of the eastern theater, together with most eastern-born or -trained historians, were prone to do in matters pertaining to the western theater) Bragg's transfer of his whole army from Tupelo to Chattanooga by way of Mobile the previous year. "Never before were such crazy cars — passenger, baggage, mail, coal, box, platform, all and every sort wobbling on the jumping strap-iron — used for hauling good soldiers," the staffer went on. "But we got there nevertheless." Here too a degree of inaccuracy crept in; for out of a total of 12,000 men in the two divisions, only about 7500 reached the field in time for a share in the fighting that had begun before the first of them arrived. Primarily this was because the fall of Knoxville, just the week before, denied them use of the East Tennessee & Virginia Railroad, which up till then had afforded a direct 550-mile route from Gordonsville to Dalton. As a result, a roundabout route had to be taken — first by way of southern Virginia, then down through both of the Carolinas, and finally across the width of Georgia, with no possibility of using through trains because of the varying gauges of track on the dozen different lines — for a total distance of nearly 1000 miles from Orange Courthouse to Catoosa Station, which was within earshot of the battle they heard raging as they approached the end of their long journey through the heartland.

For the troops themselves — Deep Southerners to a man, except the Texans and Arkansans, now that Pickett's Virginians had been de-tached — the trip had all the elements of a lark, despite the cramped ac-commodations, the thrown-together meals, and the knowledge that pos-sible death and suffering awaited them at its end. Many of the Carolinians and Georgians — South Carolinians, that is; for there were no North Carolinians in Longstreet's corps — passed through home towns they had not visited in two years, and though guards were posted at all the stops to assure that no unauthorized furloughs were taken, it was good to see that the old places were still there, complete with pretty girls who passed out delicacies and blushed at the whoops of admirers. For Hood's men there was an added bonus in the form of their commander, who re-joined them when they passed through Richmond, where he was re-cuperating from his Gettysburg wound. Though his arm was still use-less in a sling, he was unable to resist the impulse to come along when he saw, as he said later, that "my old troops, with whom I had served so long, were thus to be sent forth to another army — quasi, I may say, among strangers." They cheered at the news that he was aboard and was going to Georgia with them. At Weldon, North Carolina, alter-nate routes — one via Raleigh, Charlotte, and Columbia, the other via Goldsboro, Wilmington, and Florence — relieved the strain on the over-worked roads until they combined again at Kingsville, South Carolina, where a matron diarist watched the overloaded trains chuff past in what seemed a never-ending procession. "God bless the gallant fellows," she wrote; "not one man intoxicated, not one rude word did I hear. It was a strange sight. What seemed miles of platform cars, and soldiers rolled in their blankets lying in rows with their heads all covered, fast asleep. In their gray blankets packed in regular order, they looked like swathed mummies. . . . A feeling of awful depression laid hold of me. All those fine fellows going to kill or be killed, but why? A word took to beating about my head like an old song, 'The Unreturning Brave.' When a knot of boyish, laughing young creatures passed, a queer thrill of sympathy shook me. Ah, I know how your homefolks feel. Poor children!"

From Branchville, immediately south of there, the route ex-tended due west, via Augusta, to Atlanta, where it turned northwest and ran the final 125 miles northwest to the unloading point, four miles short of Ringgold and 965 circuitous miles from Orange. McLaws and Hood had four brigades each. Two of the former's and one of the lat-ter's would not reach the field until the action had ended — neither would McLaws himself, who was charged with hurrying the last infantry elements northward from Atlanta; nor would a single piece of the corps artillery with which Alexander, still back in the Carolinas, was bringing up the rear — but the five brigades that did arrive in time were to play a significant part in the battle that was in progress when they got there. Hood arrived on September 18, had his horse unloaded from a boxcar, then mounted, still with his arm in its sling, and rode toward the sound of firing, some half a dozen miles away along the banks of a sluggish, meandering, tree-lined creek whose name he now heard for the first time: Chickamauga, an Indian word that meant "stagnant water" or, more popularly, "River of Death." Before nightfall he and his three brigades had a share, by Bragg's direction, in forcing a crossing of the stream at a place called Reed's Bridge, near which they were joined next day by the two brigades from McLaws' division.

Longstreet reached Catoosa Station the following afternoon, September 19, but found no guide waiting to take him to Bragg or give him news of the battle he could hear raging beyond the western screen of woods. When the horses came up on a later train, he had three of them saddled and set out with two members of his staff to find the headquarters of the Army of Tennessee. He was helped in this, so far as the general direction was concerned, by the rearward drift of the wounded, although none of these unfortunates seemed to know exactly where he could find their commander. Night fell and the three officers continued their ride by moonlight until they were halted by a challenge out of the darkness just ahead: "Who comes there?" "Friends," they replied, promptly but with circumspection, and in the course of the parley that followed they asked the sentry to identify his unit. When he did so by giving the numbers of his brigade and division — Confederate outfits were invariably known by the names of their commanders — they knew they had blundered into the Union lines. "Let us ride down a little way to find a better crossing," Old Peter said, disguising his southern accent, and the still-mounted trio withdrew, unfired on, to continue their search for Bragg. It was barely an hour before midnight when they found him — or, rather, found his camp; for he was asleep in his ambulance by then.

He turned out for a brief conference, in the course of which he outlined, rather sketchily, what had happened up to now in his contest with Rosecrans, now approaching a climax here at Chickamauga, and passed on the orders already issued to the five corps commanders for a dawn attack next morning. Longstreet, though he had never seen the field by daylight, was informed that he would have charge of the left wing, which contained six of the army's eleven divisions, including his own two fragmentary ones that had arrived today and yesterday from Virginia. For whatever it might be worth, Bragg also gave him what he later described as "a map showing prominent topographical features of the ground from the Chickamauga River to Mission Ridge, and beyond to the Lookout Mountain range." Otherwise he was on his own, so far as information was concerned.

✗ 4 ✗

Before the close of the Sunday that presently was dawning — September 20; the sun both rose and set at approximately straight-up 6 o'clock, for this was the week of the autumnal equinox — Old Peter was to discover that he was on his own in other ways as well. He was up and about at first light, correcting the faulty alignment of his wing and alerting his troops for their share in the attack Bragg had ordered to be opened "at day-dawn" on the far right, where Polk was in command, and then to be taken up in sequence by the divisions posted southward along the four-mile line of battle. Sunlight dappled the topmost leaves of the trees, then moved down the branches, but there was no sound of the firing Longstreet had been told to expect from the right as the signal for his own commitment on the left. An hour he waited, then another and another, and still there was no crash of guns from the north or word from headquarters of a postponement or cancellation of the attack. Like Lee at Gettysburg, where the shoe had been on the other foot, the burly Georgian scarcely knew what to make of this, except as an indication that such things were not ordered well in the western army. However, he was not of an excitable or even impatient nature, being rather inclined, as a matter of course, to take things as they came. Besides, whatever its cause, the present delay gave him time to examine and improve his dispositions, to familiarize himself at least to some extent with the heavily wooded terrain, and to learn a good deal more than Bragg had taken the trouble to tell him of what had happened, so far, on this confusing field where the two armies had come together for the fourth of their bloody confrontations, a year and a half after Shiloh, a year after Perryville, and nine months after Murfreesboro, all three of which it gave promise of exceeding, both in fury and in bloodshed, despite the apparent — and indeed, in the light of this indication of suffering to come, quite natural — reluctance of the two forces to resume what had got started here the day before.

Bragg now had on hand all the troops he was going to have for the battle. Each of his five corps had two divisions, except Longstreet's, now under Hood, which had three or anyhow parts of three: Hood's own under Law, McLaws' under Kershaw, and one created the previous week, when two more brigades arrived from Mississippi and were combined with Brigadier General Bushrod Johnson's brigade, detached from Stewart's division of Buckner's corps, to form a new provisional division under his command. Longstreet massed this three-division corps, the bulk of which had come with him from Virginia and comprised his Sunday punch, at the right center of his portion of the line, alongside Hindman's division, which had been detached from Polk the day before. On the left and right, respectively on the outer and interior flanks, were Buckner's two divisions under Preston and Stewart. Exclusive of Wheeler's cavalry, patrolling southward beyond an eastward bend of the creek on which his left was anchored, Old Peter had some 25,000 effectives. Polk had roughly the same number in his wing, exclusive of Forrest's cavalry on his right. Hill's two divisions, under Breckinridge and Cleburne, were on the outer flank, and next to them, massed in depth along the center, were the two divisions of Walker's corps, commanded by Brigadier Generals St John Liddell and States Rights Gist. Cheatham's division was posted on the interior flank, adjoining Longstreet. All eleven of these divisions, six in the left and five in the right wing, had three brigades each, with the exception of Cheatham's, which had five, and Liddell's and Kershaw's, which had two apiece; Polk had 16, Longstreet 17 brigades. Bragg's total of 33 infantry brigades was thus the same as the number Rosecrans had in his eleven divisions, but the average blue division was somewhat larger than the average gray division, with the result that the Federals had some 56,000 infantry and artillery, as compared to the Confederate 50,000. However, this disparity was offset by the fact that Rosecrans had only just over 9000 troopers, while Bragg had nearly 15,000, so that the total for each of the opposing forces was approximately 65,000 of all arms. A further disparity in guns, 170 Federal and 200 Confederate, made little tactical difference on terrain so densely wooded that visibility seldom extended for more than fifty yards in any direction; Chickamauga was by no means an artillery contest. On the other hand, Rosecrans had the decided advantage of commanding an army he had trained and fought as a unit for nearly a year now, whereas a good third of Bragg's had joined him during the past few weeks, including five brigades that had arrived in the past two days and a wing commander who had never seen the field by daylight until dawn of the second day of battle.

Already the effect of this had seemed likely to prove fatal. To judge from the poor showing the Confederates had made in failing to spring the trap on Thomas, nine days ago in McLemore's Cove, and then again on Crittenden, two days later at Lee & Gordon's Mill — both as a result of breakdowns along the unfamiliar chain of command — the evident inability of Bragg's subordinates to work in harmony, either with him or with each other in the execution of carefully laid plans, certainly did not promise well for the outcome of future confrontations, which were unlikely to afford them any such lopsided numerical and tactical advantages as they had twice neglected. Bragg was so put out by this turn of events that he fell back on LaFayette and sulked for three whole days: during which time Rosecrans, thoroughly alarmed though unmolested, got his three divergent columns approximately back together and brought his reserve corps forward from Stevenson to Rossville. Crittenden remained at the foot of Missionary Ridge, near Lee & Gordon's Mill, and Thomas shifted to Pond Spring, midway between Crittenden and his own former post at Stevens Gap, while McCook

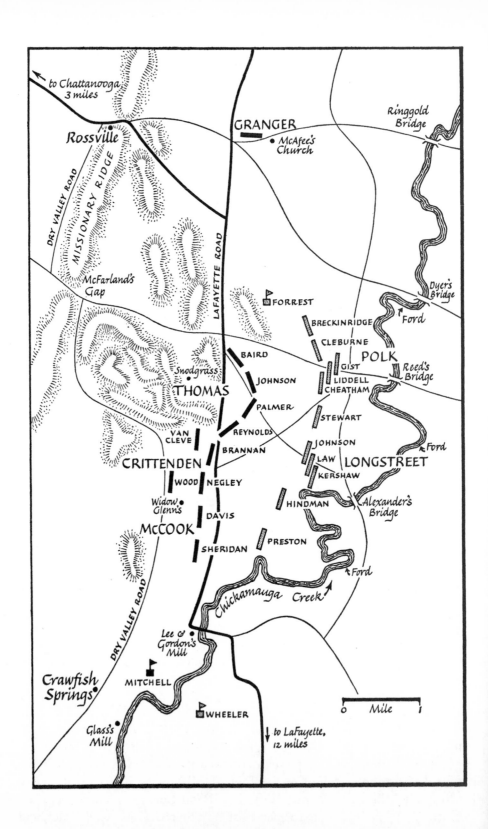

made a long march northward, in rear of Lookout Mountain, to take up the position Thomas had just vacated. By sundown, September 17, all this had been accomplished; Granger, Crittenden, Thomas, and Mc-Cook had their corps respectively in bivouac near Rossville Gap, Lee & Gordon's Mill, Pond Spring, and Stevens Gap, each within about six miles of the next one up or down the line that more or less followed the course of Chickamauga Creek, just east of Missionary Ridge. Rosecrans could draw his first easy breath since his discovery, four days back, that the rebels, far from fleeing in fear and disorder, as they had encouraged him to believe, had been intent on destroying his divided army.

He would have breathed less easily, however, if he had known what his opponent was planning, and had in fact begun to do that day, by way of accomplishing his further discomfiture. Encouraged by word that Longstreet was close at hand with reinforcements from Virginia, Bragg had emerged Achilles-like from his sulk and put his troops in motion, once more with Old Rosy's destruction as his goal. Marching north from LaFayette that morning, he massed his army before nightfall on the east side of Chickamauga Creek, his left at Glass's Mill, a mile above (that is, south of) Lee & Gordon's, and his right near Reed's Bridge, five miles downstream. Polk advised a rapid march on Rossville Gap, the seizure of which would cut the Federals off from their new base at Chattanooga and thus oblige them to attack the Confederates in a position selected in advance; but Bragg had something more ambitious in mind, involving the cul-de-sac in which Thomas had nearly come to grief a week ago tomorrow. According to orders written late that night and issued before daylight, Polk would demonstrate on the left, fixing Crittenden in position, while Buckner and Walker — supported by Hood, who was scheduled to arrive in the course of the day — crossed by fords and bridges, well below, with instructions to "sweep up the Chickamauga, toward Lee & Gordon's Mill." As they approached that point, Polk was to force a crossing and assist in driving the outflanked blue-coats southward into McLemore's Cove for another try at the meat-grinder operation. Wheeler's horsemen would plug the gaps in Pigeon Mountain, preventing a breakout, and Forrest's would guard the outer flank of the two corps — three, if Hood arrived in time — charged with executing the gatelike swing that was designed to throw Crittenden into retreat by bringing them down hard on his flank and rear. Meanwhile, opposite Glass's Mill, Hill would hold the pivot and stand ready to strike at any reinforcements from Thomas, moving north from Pond Spring toward the mouth of the cove, and pack them back into the grinder. The attack was to open in the far right at Reed's Bridge, and the jump-off hour was set for sunrise. Remembering what had happened near here a week ago, when a similar maneuver was attempted on a smaller scale, Bragg closed his field order with an admonition: "The above movements will be executed with the utmost promptness, vigor, and persistence."

Perhaps, after all that had gone wrong before, this was more an expression of hope than an expectation. At any rate he was sorely disappointed. Already nervous about his left — "It is of utmost importance that you close down this way to cover our left flank," he had wired Burnside yesterday, adding (though in vain, as it turned out) "I want all the help we can get promptly" — Rosecrans had taken alarm at sundown reports from scouts that there were rebels on the march in large numbers in the woods across the creek, and he had begun, accordingly, to sidle his army northward in the darkness. Moving Crittenden beyond Lee & Gordon's to cover the Chattanooga-LaFayette road, he advanced Thomas to Crawfish Springs, a hamlet just in rear of Glass's Mill, and McCook to the position Thomas had vacated at Pond Spring. By sunrise, as a result of these three shifts, his four corps — Granger had stayed put at Rossville Gap — were not only more tightly concentrated, the intervals between them having been reduced by half or better, but his left was also about two miles north of where it had been at sunset, when the southern commander made his calculations for an attack which thus was based on faulty or outdated information as to the blue dispositions. Then too, despite the closing admonition, there was the habitual lack of promptness in the movement of the various gray columns, plus what Bragg later referred to, rather charitably, as "the difficulties arising from the bad and narrow country roads," not to mention the stinging opposition of Federal mounted units with their rapid-fire weapons. In any event, though crossings were effected late in the day — by Hood, who arrived with his three brigades about 4 o'clock, and Walker — Buckner, Polk, and Hill were still on the east side of the creek at nightfall, with six of the ten divisions now on the field. Buckner crossed in the darkness, as did one of Polk's divisions; so that by daylight, September 19, Bragg had all of his infantry on the west bank except Hindman's division and the two with Hill. He had scarcely accomplished a fraction of all he intended today, but at any rate he was at last in a position to launch the turning movement he had designed two nights ago.

Or so he thought, still basing his calculations on a belief that the Union left was at Lee & Gordon's Mill. Actually, however, he was even wronger now than he had been the day before. Still concerned about his flank and his lines of supply and communication leading back to Chattanooga, Rosecrans had continued his sidling movement along the road toward Rossville Gap. Again leaving his position to be filled by McCook, Thomas marched across the rear of Crittenden in the darkness and extended the left another two miles north. By dawn, although Negley had not yet vacated Crawfish Springs and Reynolds was still en route, the Union-loyal Virginian's other two divisions, under Brigadier Generals Absalom Baird and J. M. Brannan, were in position at the intersection of the LaFayette Road and the road leading east to Reed's Bridge and west

to McFarland's Gap, two miles south of Rossville. Consequently —
though Bragg not only failed to suspect it, but in fact continued to base
his attack plan on a belief that the reverse was true — the Federal left
extended beyond the Confederate right. As Harvey Hill said later, with
all the wisdom of hindsight, "While our troops had been moving up
the Chickamauga, the Yankees had been moving down, and thus outflanked us."

The first real indication that this was so came in the emphatic
form of an attack that struck and nearly crumpled the northern extremity of the Confederate line before it could begin the movement Bragg
had ordered. Informed at sunup by an outpost colonel that the rebels
had only a single brigade across the creek at Reed's Bridge, directly to
his front, Thomas decided, on the basis of this misinformation, to attack
and abolish it then and there. Brannan's division, advancing eastward,
soon encountered Forrest's cavalry, out on a prowl. Dismounting his
troopers, Forrest skirmished briskly to delay the bluecoats while Walker
was sending Gist to his assistance. Surprised and thrown into sudden retreat when the gray infantry struck, Brannan managed to rally on Baird,
sent forward by Thomas to bolster the line; but not for long. Walker
threw Liddell into the conflict alongside Gist, and the two of them, with
Forrest still tearing at the blue flank, drove the Federals back on their
line of departure, one mile east of the LaFayette Road. Finding himself
with a good deal more of a fight on his hands than he had expected,
Thomas by now had called for reinforcements, and Rosecrans, still concerned about his left, responded promptly by sending Palmer of Crittenden's corps and Johnson of McCook's. The latter got there first and
went in hard, stemming the near rout that had developed. Once more
the line of battle swayed indecisively until the weight of numbers told.
Then the graybacks began to give ground, until they in turn were reinforced by two brigades from Cheatham and the balance was restored.

That was the pattern, here and elsewhere along the four-mile
line today. Always the weight of numbers decided the issue at every
point in what was patently a battle not of generals but of soldiers. ("All
this talk about generalship displayed on either side is sheer nonsense,"
Wilder declared long afterwards, looking back on the Chickamauga
nightmare. "There was no generalship in it. It was a soldier's fight
purely, wherein the only question involved was the question of endurance. The two armies came together like two wild beasts, and each fought
as long as it could stand up in a knock-down and drag-out encounter.
If there had been any high order of generalship displayed, the disasters
to both armies might have been less.") What mainly distinguished the
conflict from the outset was its fury. An Alabamian described the racket
as "one solid, unbroken wave of awe-inspiring sound . . . as if all the fires
of earth and hell had been turned loose in one mighty effort to destroy
each other." Fighting deep in the woods, with visibility strictly limited

to his immediate vicinity, each man seemed to take the struggle as a highly personal matter between him and the blue or butternut figures he saw dodging into and out of sight, around and behind the clumps of brush and trunks of trees. "By the holy St Patrick, Colonel," a Tennessee private replied when told to pick up the flag that had fluttered down when the color-bearer fell, "there's so much good shooting around here I haven't a minute's time to waste fooling with that thing." All such interruptions, or attempts at interruption, were resented, sometimes even by men of rank. Bedford Forrest, for example, flew into a towering rage at an infantry brigadier for distracting him with messages expressing concern for his flanks. When the first of these was brought to him by an aide — "General Forrest, General Ector directed me to say to you that he is uneasy about his right flank" — the cavalryman, who wore a linen duster over his uniform today with his sword and pistol buckled outside, replied laconically: "Tell General Ector that he need not bother about his right flank. I'll take care of it." Presently, though, the staffer was back with word that his chief was uneasy again, this time about his left. Forrest, who was busy directing the fire of a battery of horse artillery, gave a roar of exasperation. "Tell General Ector that by God I am here," he shouted above the din of the guns, "and will take care of his left flank as well as his right!"

He did as he promised, but only by the hardest. All morning, here on the Confederate right, the struggle was touch and go, until the beginning was unrememberable and no end seemed possible. All there was was now, a raging fury. When an owl flew up, startled out of a tree by the battle racket, some crows attacked it in flight between the lines. "Moses, what a country!" a soldier exclaimed as he watched. "The very birds are fighting."

By now it was past midday. Rosecrans came up from Crawfish Spring about 1 o'clock, riding toward the sound of guns, and established headquarters in a small log house belonging to Mrs Eliza Glenn, the widow of a Confederate soldier. Located on a commanding elevation a bit under two miles north of Lee & Gordon's Mill and half a mile west of the road along with his army was deployed, this afforded him an excellent site, just south of the center of his line, from which to give close attention to his right, while the ablest of his corps commanders took charge of the left, which extended to the intersection not quite three miles to the north. Neatly dressed in black trousers, a white vest, and a plain blue coat, Old Rosy was in fine spirits, and with cause; Thomas had gotten the jump on the rebels this morning and seemed to be holding them handily with the reinforcements sent in prompt response to his request. Not even the capture, in the course of an early afternoon skirmish in the woods about a mile due east of headquarters, of some prisoners from Hood's division — conclusive evidence that part at least of Longstreet's corps, with an estimated strength of 17,000 effectives, was already on the scene — served to diminish the confidence displayed in the northern commander's bearing. A reporter, observing the general's flushed cheeks and sparkling eyes, considered him "very handsome," Roman nose and all, as he went over the growing collection of dispatches from subordinates, brought by couriers from all quarters of the field, and studied a rather sketchy map unrolled on the Widow Glenn's parlor table. He was in such good spirits, in fact, that he took the occasion to indulge in one of his favorite pastimes, the interrogation of a prisoner.

The man selected was a Texas captain, taken just now in the skirmish on the far side of the LaFayette Road. Rosecrans invited him to step outside, and the two sat together, apart from the officers of the staff, on a log in the side yard. Whittling as he spoke, the Ohioan conversed pleasantly for a time, then casually inquired about the Confederate dispositions.

"General, it has cost me a great deal of trouble to find your lines," the captain answered. "If you take the same amount of trouble you will find ours."

Smiling, Rosecrans went on whittling and asking questions, but to small avail. The prisoner, though he readily admitted that he was from Bragg's army, could not recall what corps or division he belonged to.

"Captain," Rosecrans said at last, "you don't seem to know much, for a man whose appearance seems to indicate so much intelligence."

Now it was the Texan's turn to smile.

"Well, General," he replied, "if you are not satisfied with my information, I will volunteer some. We are going to whip you most tremendously in this fight."

Soon after the rebel captain had been taken to the rear — alternately reticent and voluble, but about as irksome one way as the other — there was evidence that his parting remark might well turn out to be an accurate prediction. Moreover, the evidence was not only promptly presented; it was also repeated twice in the course of the next four hours, in the form of three extremely savage attacks launched against as many parts of the Federal line by Stewart, Hood, and Cleburne, three of the hardest-hitting commanders in Bragg's army.

So far, except for some minor skirmishing between the lines, there had been no action on the Union right with anything like the violence of the fighting that had continued all this time on the left, where Thomas was engaged with four of the eight blue divisions now on hand. Bragg had sent for Stewart's division of Buckner's corps, intending to throw it into the seesaw battle raging on the Confederate right; but Stewart — a forty-two-year-old Tennessean called "Old Straight" by his men, partly because of his ramrod posture, but mostly because he had taught mathematics at West Point, where he had acquired the nickname, and afterwards at Cumberland University — as he marched downstream through the woods, took a sudden turn to the west at about 2.30, either by design or error, and lunged instead at the enemy center, a mile south of where Bragg had intended to commit him. He struck Van Cleve's division of Crittenden's corps, which had seen no combat so far in the campaign and was unbraced for the shock. Having recently come into line after making their second night march in the past two days, Van Cleve and his men were not only considerably worn but were also as thoroughly confused as the Illinois soldier who later remarked wryly that "the reassembling of his three corps by Rosecrans was a tactical proceeding that even the privates could not make heads or tails of." At any rate, the three brigades broke badly under the impact of a host of screaming rebels, hurled at them from the dense woods in their front. Crittenden himself and Van Cleve, who at fifty-four was the oldest Federal brigadier — a New-Jersey-born Minnesotan and a member of the West Point class of 1831, he had been twenty-five years out of uniform when the war came — did what they could to stay the rout, though with little or no success. Stewart's troops made it up to and across the LaFayette Road to where the Glenn house, its yard crowded with staff orderlies and couriers and their mounts, was in plain view across the rolling landscape. But so, by now, was something else; two somethings else, in fact. Thomas's two remaining divisions under Reynolds and Negley, hard on their way north to join him, were halted in their tracks, still in column and nearly a mile apart, then faced right and thrown without delay into the breach, which Thomas had already begun to narrow by sending Brannan's troops — recovered by now, in part at least, from the mauling they had taken on the left — against its northern lip. As these three blue divisions converged upon his isolated gray one, Stewart fell sullenly back from contact, firing as he went. Half a mile east of the road he called a halt, and there, under cover of the woods he had emerged from, laid down a mass of fire that discouraged pursuit.

Hood was in position on the left of Stewart, due west of Alexander's Bridge. At the height of the uproar to his right front, though he was without orders, he put his two divisions in line abreast, Johnson on the left of Law, and started them forward at about 4 o'clock, by which time the racket up ahead had begun to subside. Tramping westward through the woods and brush, the Texas brigade, on the far right, went past one of Stewart's Tennessee regiments, which had just returned, blown and bloody, from its brief penetration of the Union line. "Rise up, Tennesseans," one of the advancing soldiers called, "and see the Texans go in!" Too weary to reply, let alone stand, Stewart's fought-out infantry lay there panting and watching as Hood's men swept past them, first the skirmishers, then the solid ranks of the main body, the pride of the Army of Northern Virginia, Lee's hard hitters who had shattered many a Yankee line, from Gaines Mill to the Devil's Den. Holding their attack formation as best they could in the heavy woods, these stalwarts broke into the clear near the LaFayette Road, a mile south of where Stewart had crossed it an hour ago, and went with a shout for a blue division drawn up to receive them on the west side of the road, apparently without supports on either flank.

It was Davis, of McCook. His three brigades were struck by the rebel six with predictable results; for though the bluecoats stood for a time, firing nervously but rapidly into the long line of attackers, the limit of their endurance was soon reached. Both overlapped flanks gave way at once, as if on signal, and the center promptly buckled under the strain. Once more, however, as the unstrung Federals fled westward and the Confederates pursued them to within plain view of the Widow Glenn's, yelling for all they were worth, a pair of blue divisions — the last two of the ten that would reach the field today — arrived most opportunely from the south, with all the patness of the cavalry in light fiction. Wood's division of Crittenden's corps was in the lead, coming down from Lee & Gordon's Mill, and now it was the rebels who were outflanked; Johnson had to call a halt to meet the menace to his left, as did Law, beyond him on the right. Davis rallied and led his fugitives back into the fight at about the same time Sheridan's division arrived from Crawfish Springs to tip the balance in favor of the Union. Halted, Johnson had to yield to this new pressure, and Law was obliged to conform: especially when Wilder's Lightning Brigade, still detached from Reynolds and held by Rosecrans in reserve for such emergencies, added the weight of its multishot carbines to the fray. The two butternut divisions fell back to the east side of the road, which then became and remained the dividing line between the Confederate left and the Federal right. Sheridan, in accordance with his instinct for aggression, tried to press matters with a charge, but was repulsed, and Hood settled into a new line about a mile in advance of his old one. On the right, as the men of the Texas brigade retired through the woods, badly cut up by Wilder's rapid-fire weapons in the final stage of their withdrawal, they came back to where they had called on Stewart's blown and bloody Tennesseans to "rise up ... and see the Texans go in." The regiment was still there, fairly well rested from its exertions, and one of its members did not neglect the opportunity thus afforded. "Rise up, Tennesseans," he called, "and see the Texans come out!"

By now it was sunset and the third in this sequence of savage attacks was about to be launched at the far end of the line. Summoned for one more go at the Federal left, where the fighting had slacked as if by common consent though the issue was still in doubt, Cleburne left his position opposite Lee & Gordon's at about the time Stewart's drive on the enemy center was being repulsed and Hood's was getting started against the right. Fording the Chickamauga well above Alexander's Bridge, the use of which would have delayed their march, his men found the spring-fed water icy cold and armpit deep. Wet and chilled, they continued northward through the woods for another four miles to reach their jump-off position just after sundown. Across the way, Thomas now had five divisions, Reynolds having come on to join him while Negley stayed behind to plug the gap created when Van Cleve was driven rearward. "Old Pap," as the solidly built Virginian's soldiers liked to call him, had seen to it that Baird and Johnson, who were posted at the extremity of his line, were braced for the assault he was convinced would be renewed before the day was over, while Palmer, Reynolds, and Brannan, who continued his line southward in that order, were warned to be ready to lend a hand. When the sun went down behind Missionary Ridge and no new attack had developed, they began to tell each other he was wrong; until Cleburne exploded out of the darkling woods, directly in front of Baird and Johnson, and proved him emphatically right. The three gray brigades were in line abreast, covering more than a mile from flank to flank, with Cheatham in close support. Though little could be seen in the gathering darkness, the immediate impression was one of absolute chaos as Cleburne's 5000 screaming men bore down on roughly twice that many defenders in the two blue divisions in their path. They charged with a clatter of musketry so tremendous that they seemed to be trying to make up for the disparity in numbers by the rapidity of their fire. That was in fact the case; Cleburne placed great stock in fast, well-aimed fire, and had drilled his troops relentlessly in rifle tactics, in and out of normal work hours, with just the present effect in mind. An Indiana captain later recorded that the advancing graybacks were "loading and firing in a manner that I believe was never surpassed on any battlefield during the rebellion," and Cleburne himself declared soon afterwards that "for half an hour [the firing] was the heaviest I ever heard."

This time there was no last-minute outside help; unlike Crittenden and McCook, Thomas had to fight with what he had when he was hit. After all, however, what he had was half the army, and though he lost a pair of guns, three stands of colors, some 400 captured men, and nearly a mile of ground on his outer flank, it was enough to stave off disaster. When full darkness put an end to what another Hoosier called "a display of fireworks that one does not like to see more than once in a lifetime," the blue line was severely contracted but unbroken. Baird and Brannan were forced back to the LaFayette Road on the left and right, but the three divisions between them maintained an eastward bulge of about 600 yards at its deepest. Cleburne's men, bedding down wherever they happened to be when the order reached them to stop firing, could hear the Federals hard at work beyond the curtain of night, felling trees to be used in the construction of breastworks along the contracted bulge of their new line. Shivering in their still-wet clothes, for the night was unseasonably cold for September, the listening Confederates knew only too well that they would have to try to overrun those breastworks in the morning.

Back at his campfire near Alexander's Bridge, Bragg was telling his corps commanders — all but Longstreet, who would get his instructions when he arrived near midnight, and Hill, who afterwards explained that he had not been able to locate the command post in the darkness — that the army's objective remained the same as yesterday: "to turn the enemy's left, and by direct attack force him into McLemore's Cove." Kershaw arrived after dark with his two brigades, completing a fast march from the Ringgold railhead, and was sent at once to Hood. By way of final preparation, Breckinridge was ordered to take position on Cleburne's right, extending the gray line northward in an attempt to outflank Thomas, while Hindman made a shorter march to get between Hood and Preston on the left. These three divisions, so far uncommitted, would complete the order of battle for tomorrow's attack, which Polk was scheduled to open at dawn on the far right and which would then be taken up in sequence, corps by corps, all down the line.

Hill would later refer caustically to the disjointed sequence of attacks, in which he himself had taken no part except to detach one of his divisions, as "the sparring of the amateur boxer, not the crushing blows of the trained pugilist," and Bragg in turn would describe the action, so far, as nothing more than "severe skirmishing" engaged in by his various corps and division commanders, for the most part on their own, "while endeavoring to get into line of battle." But no one knew better than Rosecrans, across the way in the Widow Glenn's lamp-lighted parlor, how near a thing it had been for him at times. In addition to the day-long pounding his left had managed to absorb — including the blood-curdling twilight assault by what sounded like tens of thousands of fiends equipped with the latest style rapid-fire weapons — two rebel penetrations, one of his center and one of his right, had surged to within plain view of army headquarters, and of these the second had come so close that he and members of his staff had had to shout at one another in order to be heard above the din.

Some measure of his mounting concern could be seen in a series of telegrams sent to the War Department in the course of the day by Charles Dana, who had arrived from Vicksburg the week before to continue his services as a behind-the-scenes observer for Stanton. "Rosecrans has everything ready to grind up Bragg's flank," he reported from Crawfish Springs that morning, and at 1 p.m. he followed this up — or, rather, he failed to follow it up — with a somewhat less encouraging or at any rate less emphatic message, sent as he left for the scene of the fighting three miles north: "Everything is going well, but the full proportions of the conflict are not yet developed." By 2.30 the telegraph line had been extended to the Glenn house, and Dana kept the operator busy. "Fight continues to rage," he wired. "Decisive victory seems assured." At 3.20 he passed along a report from Thomas "that he is driving rebels, and will force them into Chickamauga tonight." Though the center was being assailed by then, and the right was about to be, Dana was not fazed. "Everything is prosperous. Sheridan is coming up," he announced at 4 o'clock. A near commitment at 4.30 as to the outcome — "I do not yet dare to say our victory is complete, but it seems certain" — was modified in the dispatch that followed at 5.20: "Now appears to be undecided contest, but later reports will enable us to understand more clearly."

So it went; so it had gone all day. Despite his show of heartiness, what he mainly communicated was his confusion in attempting to follow a battle which, as he said, was "fought altogether in a thick forest, invisible to outsiders." In that sense, even the army commander was an outsider. Except for a rearward trickle of reports, most of them about as disconcerted as Dana's to Stanton, no one at headquarters could do much more than guess at what was happening in the smoky woods beyond the LaFayette Road. Rosecrans tried for a time, with the help of Mrs Glenn, to follow the progress of the fight by ear. She would make a guess, when a gun was heard, that it was "nigh out about Reed's Bridge" or "about a mile fornenst John Kelly's house," and he would try to match this information with the place names on the map. But it was a far from satisfactory procedure, for a variety of reasons. The map was a poor one in the first place, and after a while the roar was practically continuous all along the front. A reporter thought he had never witnessed "anything so ridiculous as this scene" between Old Rosy and the widow. Presently, when Stewart's men broke through the Federal center, she had to be removed to a place of greater safety, but Rosecrans, "fairly quivering with excitement," continued to pace back and forth, rubbing his palms rapidly together as the sound of firing swelled and quickened. "Ah! there goes Brannan!" he exclaimed with obvious satisfaction. He might have been right; besides, the noise was about all he had to go on; but it did not seem to the reporter that the general understood the situation any better than the departed countrywoman had done. Still, he kept pacing and exclaiming, perhaps in an attempt to ease the tension on his nerves and keep his spirits up. "Ah — there goes Brannan!" he would say; or, "That's Negley going in!"

Out on the line, when darkness finally put an end to the long day's fighting, the troops had a hard time of it. "How we suffered that night no one knows," a veteran was to recall. "Water could not be found; the rebels had possession of the Chickamauga, and we had to do without. Few of us had blankets and the night was very cold. All looked with anxiety for the coming of the dawn; for although we had given the enemy a rough handling, he had certainly used us very hard."

Under such conditions, despite much loss of sleep both nights before, work on the construction of breastworks was welcome as a means of keeping warm, as well as a diversion from thoughts of tomorrow. For Rosecrans, however, there could be no release from the latter; it was his job. He could take pride in the fact that his line, though obliged to yield an average mile of ground throughout its length today, was not only intact but was also considerably shorter than it had been when this morning's contest opened. Then too, word had come that Halleck at last was doing all he could to speed reinforcements to North Georgia; urgent appeals had gone from Washington to Burnside and Grant, at Knoxville and in Mississippi, directing them to send troops to Chattanooga in all haste, and similar messages had been dispatched to Hurlbut at Memphis, Schofield in Missouri, and John Pope in far-off Minnesota. It was a comfort to Rosecrans to know that in time there would be these supports to fall back on. Meanwhile, though, he had to fight with what he had on hand, and he was by no means sure that this would be enough, since prisoners had been taken from no less than a dozen regiments known to have arrived just yesterday from Virginia. How many others had come or were arriving tonight he did not know, for the captives were nearly as close-mouthed under interrogation as the Texas captain had been this afternoon, but intelligence officers had little trouble identifying these "Virginians" by their standard gray uniforms, which were in natty contrast to the "go-as-you-please" garments worn in the western armies. Occasionally, too, a scrap of information could be extracted by goading the prisoners into anger. "How does Longstreet like the western Yankees?" one was asked in a mocking tone, and he replied with a growl: "You'll get enough of Longstreet before tomorrow night."

This might be nothing more than wishful rebel thinking. On the other hand it might be an informed and accurate prediction. At any rate, whichever it was, Rosecrans decided — as he had done under similar circumstances on New Year's Eve almost nine months ago — that he would do well to call a council of war for the triple purpose of briefing his principal subordinates on the over-all situation, of obtaining their recommendations as to a proper course of action, and of enabling him, at some later date, to shift at least a share of the blame in event of a defeat. Besides, he had a natural fondness for conference discussions, especially late-at-night ones, whether the subject was strategy or religion. The council accordingly convened at headquarters at 11 o'clock that evening. Most of those present, including the three corps commanders, had attended the conference held at the close of the first day's fighting in the last great battle; the difference was in the staff. "Poor Garesché," as Rosecrans had referred to the previous chief of staff after his head was blown off by a cannonball, had been replaced in January by Brigadier General James A. Garfield, a thirty-two-year-old former Ohio schoolteacher, lawyer, lay preacher, and politician, whose warm handclasp seemed to one observer to convey the message, "Vote early. Vote right," and whose death, at the hands of an assassin who voted both early and right and then failed to get the appointment to which he believed this entitled him, would occur exactly eighteen years from today, partly as a direct result of what was going to happen here tomorrow. Big-headed, with pale eyes and a persuasive manner — like Hooker, he was a protégé of Secretary Chase's, and up to now his most notable service in the war had been as a member of the court-martial that convicted Fitz-John Porter — Garfield opened the council by displaying for the assembled generals a map with the positions of all the Union divisions indicated, along with those of the Confederates so far as they were known; after which Rosecrans called for individual opinions as to what was to be done. McCook and Crittenden — the Ohioan, according to an obviously unfriendly fellow officer, had "a weak nose that would do no credit to a baby" and a grin that gave rise to "suspicion that he is either still very green or deficient in the upper story," while the Kentuckian was characterized more briefly as "a good drinker," one of those men, fairly common in the higher echelons of all armies, who "know how to blow their own horns exceedingly well" — had little to contribute in the way of advice, each perhaps being somewhat chagrined by the loss of one of his three divisions, detached that morning to reinforce the left, and somewhat subdued by the near-destruction of one of his remaining two in the course of the afternoon. Not so Thomas, who differed as much from them in outlook, or anyhow in the emphatic expression of his outlook, as he did in appearance. Ponderous and phlegmatic, he was described by another observer as "not scrimped anywhere, and square everywhere — square face, square shoulders, square step; blue eyes with depths in them, withdrawn beneath a pent-house of a brow, features with legible writing on them, and the whole giving the idea of massive solidity, of the right kind of man to 'tie to.' " Though he slept through much of the conference — not only because it was his custom (he had done the same at Stones River) but also because he had spent the last two nights on the march and most of today under heavy attack — he repeated the same words whenever he was called on for a tactical opinion: "I would strengthen the left." But when Rosecrans replied, as he did each time, "Where are we going to take it from?" there was no answer; Thomas would be back asleep by then, propped upright in his chair.

　　At the council held nine months ago in the rain-lashed cabin beside the Nashville pike, the discussion had centered mainly on whether the army should retreat; but here tonight, in the small log house on the field of Chickamauga, the word was used only in connection with the rebels. The decision, committed to paper for distribution as soon as it was reached, was that the Federals would hold their ground. Unless

Bragg withdrew under cover of darkness — there was some conjecture that he might, though it was based more on hope than on tangible evidence, of which there was not a shred that indicated a change in his clear intention to destroy them — they would offer him battle tomorrow, on the same terms as today. At this late hour, in point of fact, that seemed not only the bravest but also the safest thing to do, considering the risk a retreating army would run of being caught, trains and all, strung out on the roads leading back through Rossville and McFarland's gaps to Chattanooga, which was a good ten miles from the Widow Glenn's. There would be minor readjustments, though not of Granger's three-brigade reserve force, which was instructed to remain where it was, covering Rossville Gap and holding that escape hatch open in case of a collapse. To lessen the chances of this last, which would be most likely to occur as a result of a rebel breakthrough, Rosecrans directed that his ten-division line of battle along the LaFayette Road was to be strengthened by further contraction. Thomas would hold his five divisions in their present intrenched position on the left, and McCook would move his two northward to connect with Negley's division, on Thomas's right, while Crittenden withdrew his two for close-up support of the center or a rapid shift in whichever direction they were needed, north or south. When all this had been discussed and agreed on, Garfield put it in writing and read it back, and when this in turn had been approved it was passed to the headquarters clerks for copying. By now it was midnight. While the generals were waiting for the clerks to finish their task, Rosecrans provided coffee for a social interlude, the principal feature of which was a soulful rendition by "the genial, full-stomached McCook," as one reporter called him, of a plaintive ballad entitled "The Hebrew Maiden."

Possibly Thomas slept through this as well; possibly not. In any event, it was 2 o'clock in the morning before he returned to his position on the left, where he found a report awaiting him from Baird, who warned that his division, posted on the flank, could not be extended all the way to the Reed's Bridge road, as ordered, and still be strong enough to hold if it was struck again by anything like the twilight blow that had sent it reeling for more than a mile until darkness ended the fighting. Thomas made a quick inspection by moonlight and arrived at the same conclusion, then sent a message back to headquarters, explaining the trouble and requesting that Negley, who had been halted and thrown in to shore up the crumbling center while on his way to the left that afternoon, be ordered to resume his northward march and rejoin his proper corps, the critical outer flank of which was in danger of being crushed for lack of support or turned for lack of troops to extend it. Rosecrans promptly agreed by return messenger, as he had done to all such specific requests from his senior corps commander; Negley would march at dawn. Reassured, Thomas at last bedded down under a large oak, one of whose protruding roots afforded a pillow for his head, and there resumed the sleep that had been interrupted, if not by McCook's singing, then at any rate by the breakup of the council of war, some time after midnight.

He woke to Sunday's dawn, already impatient for Negley's arrival. The sun came up blood red through the morning haze and the smoke of yesterday's battle, which still hung about the field. "It is ominous," the chief of staff was saying, back at the Widow Glenn's, as he pointed dramatically at the rising sun. "This will indeed be a day of blood." Thomas needed no sign to tell him that, but he was growing increasingly anxious about his unsupported flank, which the army commander had assured him would be reinforced without delay. The sun rose higher. Presently it was a full hour above the land-line, and still Negley had not arrived. Rosecrans himself came riding northward about this time, however, and though his face was drawn and puffy from strain and lack of sleep, he spoke encouragingly as he drew rein from point to point along the line. "Fight today as well as you did yesterday," he told his troops, "and we shall whip them!" This had a somewhat mixed effect. "I did not like the way he looked," a soldier later recalled, "but of course felt cheered, and did not allow myself to think of any such thing as defeat."

✗ 5 ✗

Bragg and his staff were up and mounted before daylight, waiting for the roar of guns that would signal Polk's compliance with his orders, received in person the night before, "to assail the enemy on our extreme right at day-dawn of the 20th." Perhaps by now, after the repeated frustrations of the past two weeks, the Confederate commander might have been expected to accept delay, if not downright disobedience, as more or less standard procedure on the part of his ranking subordinates — particularly Polk and Hill, the wing and corps commanders directly in charge of the troops who would open the attack — but such was not the case. Even if he had learned to expect it, he had by no means learned to take it calmly. Three months later, when he submitted his official account of the battle, his anger was still apparent. "With increasing anxiety and disappointment," he wrote then, "I waited until after sunrise without hearing a gun, and at length dispatched a staff officer to Lieutenant General Polk to ascertain the cause of the delay and urge him to a prompt and speedy movement."

By the time the aide located Polk, delivered the message, and returned, the sun was more than an hour high and Bragg's impatience had been mounting with it. Not a gun had yet been fired, and across the way the Yankees were hard at work improving by daylight the breastworks they had constructed in the darkness. The thought of this was enough to sour a far sweeter disposition than Bragg would ever be able to lay claim to. Moreover, what the staff officer had to report on his return brought his chief's wrath to what might be called full flower. He had found the bishop, he declared, "at a farm house three miles from the line of his troops, about one hour after sunrise, sitting on the gallery reading a newspaper and waiting, as he said, for his breakfast." Hearing this, Bragg did something rare for him. He cursed — "a terrible exclamation," the aide termed the outburst — then rode to Polk's headquarters, intending no doubt to rebuke the wing commander in person, but found that he had just left for the front, remarking as he did so: "Do tell General Bragg that my heart is overflowing with anxiety for the attack. Overflowing with anxiety, sir."

It was close to 8 o'clock by then, better than two hours past the hour scheduled for an advance on the far right, and Bragg learned from one of the bishop's aides, who had remained behind, something of what had caused the mix-up and delay. Hill had not only failed to find army headquarters last night; he had also failed to locate Polk, who in turn had been unable to find him. As a result, unlike Cheatham and Walker, who had reported to headquarters the evening before, Hill had neither received his orders to attack nor been led to suspect that Bragg or anyone else had any such plans in mind for the two divisions on the northern flank. Learning of this for the first time from the courier who returned that morning from an unsuccessful all-night search for Hill, Polk sent orders directly to Breckinridge and Cleburne, bypassing the fugitive corps commander, for them to "move and attack the enemy as soon as you are in position." Hill was with them when the message was delivered, and when they protested that their men were not only not "in position," but had not had time to eat their morning rations, he backed them up with a note in which he blandly informed the wing commander that it would be "an hour or so" before the two divisions would be ready to go forward. It was this reply, received at about 7.30, that had caused the bishop — whose overflowing heart by now outweighed his empty stomach — to interrupt his breakfast on the farmhouse gallery, or perhaps not even wait any longer for it to be served, and set out instead for the front and a conference with Hill.

Bragg got there first, however, apparently by taking a shorter route. Trailed by his staff, he rode up to where Hill had established headquarters between Breckinridge and Cleburne, whose troops had still not been placed in attack formation and were just now being fed. When Bragg inquired testily why he had not attacked at daylight in accordance with last night's order, Hill replied coolly and with obvious satisfaction, as he afterwards recalled, "that I was hearing then for the first time that such an order had been issued and had not known whether we were to be the assailants or the assailed." Bragg's anger and impatience had no discernible effect on him whatever. He would not be hurried. Miffed at having been cast in a role subordinate to that of the other two lieutenant generals, who had been made wing commanders while all he had under him was the corps he had brought onto the field, he was unmistakably determined, in the words of a later observer, "to assert to the limit what authority he retained." Soon Polk arrived, but neither he nor Bragg, scarcely on speaking terms by now with one another, was able to get their fellow North Carolinian to hurry things along; Hill's claim was that he could scarcely be held responsible for not obeying instructions that had not reached him. He took his time, and what was more he saw to it that his two division commanders took theirs as well. The troops were aligned punctiliously under cover of the woods, and all was reported ready, down to the final round in the final cartridge box, before Hill gave the nod that sent Breckinridge forward at 9.30, followed within fifteen minutes by Cleburne on his left, a full four hours past the time Bragg had set for the attack to open on the far right of the army.

Across the way, Rosecrans too had been having his troubles during the long delay, and though he began the day in a frame of mind that seemed cheerful enough for a man who had had but little sleep to ease the built-up tension on his nerves, he completely lost his temper before he returned to headquarters from his early morning ride along his still-contracting line of battle. Greeted by Thomas when he reached the left, he found him in high spirits over his successful resistance to yesterday's frantic rebel attempts to drive him from the field. "Whenever I touched their flanks they broke, General; they broke!" he exclaimed. In point of fact, as the long silence continued on through sunrise and beyond, it had become increasingly apparent that they had learned their lesson; they seemed to want no more of it today. Still, it was strange to see the phlegmatic Virginian display such exuberance, even though it lasted only until he spotted a newsman riding with the staff; whereupon he flushed and withdrew at once into the habitual reserve which he used as a shield between himself and such people. He spoke instead of possible danger to his left. Scouts had reported that the Confederates, out beyond the screening woods and thickets, were continuing to shift in that direction. "You must move up, too, as fast as they do," Rosecrans told him. Thomas agreed, but he also pointed out that this required more troops. There was the rub; Negley had not arrived. Rosecrans assured him that Negley was on the way by now, for he himself had seen to it in the course of his ride north along the line. Thomas was relieved to hear this, though he repeated that he would not consider his flank secure until reinforcements got there to extend and shore it up.

But when the Union commander rode back south, retracing his steps but not stopping now for speeches, he found to his chagrin that the reinforcements he had just assured Thomas were already on their way had not budged from their position in the center, where he had left them an hour ago with orders to march north. However, Negley had an excellent reason for his apparent insubordination. McCook still had not closed the gap created by Crittenden's withdrawal in compliance with last night's instructions, so that if Negley had pulled out in turn, as ordered, he would have left a mile-wide hole in the Federal center; which plainly, at a time when an all-out rebel assault was expected at any minute almost anywhere along the front, would not do. Nettled — as well he might be, for the sun was two hours high by now — Rosecrans hurried rearward and told Crittenden to return Wood's division to the line in place of Negley's, which then could be released to join Thomas, two miles away on the unshored northern flank. Next he rode south in search of McCook, whose slowness was at the root of the present trouble. Finding him, he stressed the need for haste and an early end to the grumbling confusion into which his two divisions had been thrown by a renewal of their sidling movement toward the left. All this time, though only by the hardest, Old Rosy had managed to keep a grip on his temper. But when he returned to the center and found Negley still in position, with Wood nowhere in sight, he lost it entirely. Pausing only long enough to order Negley to send one of his three brigades to Thomas at once, even though no replacements had arrived, he galloped rearward and presently came upon Wood, who was conferring with his staff about the unexpected and still pending movement back into line. "What is the meaning of this, sir?" Rosecrans barked at him. "You have disobeyed my specific orders. By your damnable negligence you are endangering the safety of the entire army, and by God I will not tolerate it! Move your division at once, as I have instructed, or the consequences will not be pleasant for yourself." Wood, a forty-year-old Kentuckian, flushed at being upbraided thus in the presence of his staff, but as a West Pointer, a regular army man, and a veteran of all the army's fights, from Shiloh on, he knew better than to protest. Choking back his resentment, he saluted and put his three brigades in motion.

The lead brigade was just coming into line, at about 9.45, when an uproarious clatter broke out on the far left, fulfilling Thomas's prediction that his would be the flank the rebels would assault. From the sound of it, as heard by Rosecrans at the Widow Glenn's, to which he had returned after venting his spleen in the encounter with Wood, they were putting in all they had.

They were indeed putting in all they had at that end of the line: not all at once, however, as the sudden eruption seemed to indicate by contrast with the silence which it shattered, but rather in a series of divisional attacks, as Bragg had ordered. Breckinridge struck first, on the far right. Though his left brigade came up against the north end of the mile-long curve of breastworks and was involved at once in an unequal fire fight, standing in the open to swap volleys with an adversary under cover, the other two found no such obstacle in their path. Thomas had prolonged his line by shifting one of Johnson's brigades from his center, and the brigade detached in haste from Negley had just arrived to extend the left still farther, but there had not been time enough for felling trees, much less for the heavy task of snaking and staking the trunks into position to fight behind. As a result, the two gray brigades advancing southward down the LaFayette Road met and fought the two blue ones on equal terms, first with a stand-up exchange of volleys, face to face, and then, as the defenders began to waver, with a charge that drove them rearward in a rush. However, Thomas had made good use of the time afforded him by the delaying action. Two more brigades were at hand by then, one from Brannan, which he brought over from his right, and one from Van Cleve, which Rosecrans had sent double-timing to the left when the attack first exploded in that direction. Together they stalled the advance of the jubilant graybacks, and then with the help of the other two brigades, which rallied when the pressure was relieved, drove them back northward, restoring the flank that had crumbled under assault. There was, of course, the danger that they might be reinforced to try again in greater strength; in which case Thomas would be hard put to find reinforcements of his own, for Cleburne's attack had been launched by now, due south of and adjoining Breckinridge, with such persistent savagery that not a man could be spared from the close-up defense of the long line of breastworks in order to meet a new threat to the left. All Thomas could do was continue what he had been doing ever since he reached the field; that is, call on Rosecrans for more troops from the right and center, which had been stripped to less than four divisions, as compared to the more than six already concentrated here.

Events would show that this was rather beside the point, however, for though the old one would continue with much of its original fury all morning, there was not going to be any new end-on threat to the Union left. Bragg had called for a definite series of attacks, beginning on his far right and continuing in sequence down the full length of his line, and neither Polk nor Hill (if, indeed, they were even aware of the Chancellorsville-like opportunity — which apparently they were not) was in any frame of mind to make suggestions, let alone appeals, to a commander who was already in a towering rage because his instructions had not been followed to the letter. Instead, they continued to hammer unrelentingly at the long southward curve of enemy breastworks, encouraged from time to time by reports such as one sent back by Brigadier General Lucius Polk, the bishop's thirty-year-old nephew, whose brigade of Cleburne's division smashed through the Federal outpost works, just in front of the center of the bulge, and drove the blue pickets back on their main line of resistance. Elated, he turned in mid-career to an officer on his staff. "Go back and tell the old general," he said, meaning his uncle, "that we have passed two lines of breastworks; that we have got them on the jump, and I am sure of carrying the main line." By the time this reached the wing commander, who was conferring with Cheatham, the brigade had been repulsed. But that was no part of the report, and Polk was as elated by the message as his nephew had been when he gave it to the aide. "General," he told Cheatham, "move your division and attack at once." The Tennessean, who had massed his five brigades in anticipation of the order, was prompt to comply. "Forward, boys, and give them hell!" he shouted, much as he had done nine months ago at Murfreesboro, and the bishop approved now, as he had then, of the spirit if not of the words his friend had chosen to express it. "Do as General Cheatham says, boys!" he called after the troops as they moved out.

But Cheatham had no greater success than Hill had had before him. His men went up to within easy range of the breastworks, which seemed to burst into flame at their approach, then recoiled, all in one quick involuntary movement like that of a hand testing the heat of a still-hot piece of metal. Walker's two divisions, held in reserve till then, had much the same reaction when they were committed at about 10.45, shortly after Cheatham had been repulsed. By now the entire right wing was engaged, including Forrest's dismounted horsemen, who went in with Breckinridge. "What infantry is that?" Hill asked in the course of a tour of inspection on the right. He had never seen troops like these in the East. "Forrest's cavalry," he was told. Presently, when Forrest himself came riding back to meet him, the North Carolinian removed his hat in salutation. "General Forrest," he said, "I wish to congratulate you and those brave men moving across that field like veteran infantry upon their magnificent behavior. In Virginia I made myself extremely unpopular with the cavalry because I said that so far I had not seen a dead man with spurs on. No one could speak disparagingly of such troops as yours." Whether the Tennessean blushed at this high praise could not be told, for in battle his face always took on the color of heated bronze. "Thank you, General," he replied, then wheeled his horse and with a wave of his hand galloped back into the thick of the fight that had excited Hill's admiration.

At no one point along the Confederate right had the issue been pressed to its extremity by the mass commitment of reserves to achieve a breakthrough. Rather, the pressure had been equally heavy on all points at once, as if what Bragg intended to accomplish was not so much a penetration as a cataclysm, a total collapse of the whole Union left, like that of a dam giving way to an unbearable weight of water. This was in fact what he was after, and at times it seemed to some among the defenders that he was about to get it. "The assaults were repeated with an impetuosity that threatened to overwhelm us," according to John Palmer, whose division was on loan to Thomas from Crittenden. Except on the extended flank, however, where there had been no time to throw up breastworks, casualties had been comparatively light for the Federals, who were protected by the stout log barricade they had constructed overnight and improved during the four daylight hours which Hill's delay had afforded them this morning. It was not so for the attackers; their losses had been heavy everywhere. "The rebs charged in three distinct lines," an Ohio captain wrote, "but each time they charged they were driven back with fearfully decimated ranks." Some measure of the truth of this was shown in the loss of those who led the frantic charges. Breckinridge, Cleburne, and Gist each had a brigade commander killed or mortally wounded in the course of this one hour: Brigadier Generals Ben Hardin Helm, who had married Mary Lincoln's youngest sister and recently succeeded to command of the Orphan Brigade, and James Deshler, who had been exchanged, promoted, and transferred east after his discomfiture by Sherman at Arkansas Post, and Colonel Peyton Colquitt, who had taken over Gist's brigade when that general was put in charge of the division Walker brought from Mississippi. Moreover, another of Breckinridge's brigadiers, Daniel W. Adams, an accident-prone or perhaps merely unlucky Kentucky-born Louisianan who had lost an eye at Shiloh and been severely wounded again at Murfreesboro, was shot from his horse and captured when the attack that crumpled the Union flank was repulsed by reinforcements whose arrival was unmatched by any of his own. It had gone that way, with varying degrees of success, but nowhere with complete success, all along the front of the Confederate right wing. Still, with the evidence of the casualty lists before him, Bragg could scarcely complain of any lack of determination in the fighting, no matter how disappointed he was at the outcome so far of his attempt to smash Old Rosy's left as a prologue to rolling up his entire line and packing it southward into McLemore's Cove for destruction.

By 11 o'clock all five of Polk's divisions had been committed. Now Longstreet's turn had come. Bragg passed the word for Stewart to go in, and in he went, driving hard for the enemy breastworks at the point where they curved back to the LaFayette Road immediately opposite his position on the right of the Confederate left wing.

★ ⋆ ★

There Reynolds was posted, with Brannan on his right, one east and the other west of the road, the latter having pulled his division back about a hundred yards in order to take advantage of the cover afforded by some heavy woods in rear of a cleared field which would have been much harder to defend. Stewart hit them both, attacking with all the fury of yesterday, when he had shattered the blue line half a mile to the south and penetrated to within sight of the Widow Glenn's before he was expelled. Today, though, there were breastworks all along the front, and he achieved nothing like his previous success. He was, in fact, flung back before he made contact, just as most of Polk's attackers had been, and had to be content, like them, with laying down a mass of fire that seemed to have little effect on the defenders beyond obliging them to keep their heads down between shots. There was, however, a good deal more to it than that, even though the result would not be evident for a while. What Stewart mainly accomplished was a further encouragement of Thomas's conviction that Bragg was throwing everything he had at the Union left, and this caused the Virginian to intensify his appeal for still more troops from the right and center, an appeal that had been communicated practically without letup, ever since the first attack exploded on his flank, by a steady procession of couriers who came to headquarters with messages warning that the left would surely be overwhelmed if it was not strengthened promptly.

Rosecrans still was quite as willing to do this as he had been earlier, when he said flatly that Thomas would be sustained in his present position "if he has to be reinforced by the entire army." In point of fact, that was what it was fast coming to by now. Shortly after 10 o'clock, with Van Cleve's remaining brigades already on their way north, McCook had been told to alert his troops for a rapid march to the left "at a moment's warning," and half an hour later the order came, directing him to send two of Sheridan's brigades at once and to follow with the third as soon as the corps front had been contracted enough for Davis to hold it alone. This would put eight divisions on the left, under Thomas, and leave only two on the right, one under Crittenden and one under McCook, but Rosecrans was preparing to send still more in that direction if they were needed. His calculations — "Where are we going to take it from?" — were interrupted at this point, however, by another of Thomas's couriers, a staff captain who, in addition to the accustomed plea for reinforcements, brought alarming news of something he had observed (or failed to observe) in the course of his ride from the left. Passing in rear of Reynolds, he had not seen Brannan's troops in the woods to the south; consequently, he reported "Brannan out of line and Reynolds' right exposed." The same opinion, derived from the same mistake, was expressed in stronger terms by another Thomas aide, who arrived on the heels of the captain and declared excitedly that there was "a chasm in the center," between the divisions of Reynolds and Wood, who had replaced Negley in the position on Brannan's right. Apparently convinced by the independent testimony of two eyewitnesses, Rosecrans did not take time to check on a report which, if true, scarcely allowed time for anything but attempting to repair an extremely dangerous error before it was discovered and exploited by the rebels. Instead, he turned to a staff major — Garfield, he later explained, "was deeply engaged in another matter" — and told him to send an order to Wood at once, correcting the situation. The major did so, heading the message 10.45 a.m.

> Brigadier General Wood, Commanding Division:
>   The general commanding directs that you close up on Reynolds as fast as possible, and support him. Respectfully, &c.
>   FRANK S. BOND, Major and Aide-de-Camp.

Wood received it at 10.55, barely more than an hour after the vigorous dressing-down Old Rosy had given him for slowness in obeying a previous order. This time he did not delay execution, although there was a degree of contradiction in the terms "close up on" and "support." Nor did he take time to find and confer with Crittenden, who had been bypassed as if in emphasis of the need for haste expressed in the phrase, "as fast as possible." McCook happened to be with him, though, when the message was delivered, and on receiving his assurance that Davis would sidle northward to fill the gap that would be left, the Kentuckian promptly began the shift the order seemed to require. There being no way to close on Reynolds without going around Brannan, who was in position on Reynolds' right, Wood did just that. He pulled his division straight back out of line and set out, across Brannan's rear, for the hookup with Reynolds. Riding ahead to scout the route, he encountered Thomas, told him of the order, and asked where his brigades should be posted in compliance. To his surprise, Thomas declared that Reynolds was in no need of support — he and Brannan had just repulsed Stewart without much trouble — but that Baird needed it badly, up at the far end of the line. Wood said that he was willing to go there if Thomas would take the responsibility for changing his instructions, and when the Virginian, duly thankful for a windfall that had plumped a full division of reinforcements into his empty lap, replied that he would gladly do so, Wood rode back to pass the word to his brigade commanders.

That was how it came about that in attempting to fill a gap that did not exist, Rosecrans created one; created, in fact, what Thomas's overexcited aide had referred to, half an hour ago, as "a chasm in the center." The aide had been mistaken then, but his words were now an accurate description of what lay in the path of Longstreet, who was preparing, under cover across the way, to launch an all-out assault directly upon the quarter-mile stretch of breastworks Wood's departure had left unmanned.

Old Peter had followed the progress of the fight with mounting dissatisfaction. Up to now, the piecemeal nature of the attacks had given the battle an all-too-familiar resemblance to Gettysburg, and he wanted no more of that than he could possibly avoid. At 11 o'clock, with Polk's wing unsuccessfully committed, he ventured a suggestion to the army commander, of whom he had seen nothing since the night before, "that my column of attack could probably break the enemy's line if he cared to have it go in." In referring thus to his entire wing as a "column of attack," he was recommending that the attack in echelon, which in alley-fight terms amounted to crowding and shoving and clawing and slapping, be abandoned in favor of a combined assault, which amounted in those same terms to delivering one hard punch with a clenched fist. Just then, however, Stewart moved out alone on direct orders from Bragg, who had thrown caution to the winds — and science, too — by sending word for all the division commanders to go forward on their own in a frantic, headlong, unco-ordinated effort to overrun the Federal defenses. This was altogether too much for Longstreet. Though his admiration for the naked valor of the Confederate infantry was as large as any man's, he had recently seen the South's greatest single bid for victory turned into its worst defeat by a similar act of desperation in Pennsylvania, and he was determined not to have the same thing happen here in his home state if he could help it. He rode to the front at once to restrain Hood, whom he knew to be impetuous, from committing his corps before all three of his divisions, Johnson's and Law's and Kershaw's, were massed to strike as a unit, together with Hindman's on his left.

He got there just in time; Hood already had Johnson deployed, with Law in close support, and was about to take them forward. Longstreet had him wait for Kershaw, who formed a third line behind Law, and for Hindman, who dressed in a double line on Johnson, extending the front southward for a total width of half a mile. With Stewart engaged on Hood's right and Preston held in reserve on Hindman's left, Old Peter thus had four of his six divisions, eleven of his seventeen brigades, and some 16,000 of his 25,000 soldiers massed for the delivery of his clenched-fist blow. This was roughly half again more than he had had for the "charge" on the third day at Gettysburg, and not only were the troops in better condition here in Georgia than the ones had been in Pennsylvania, where four of the nine brigades had been shot to pieces in earlier actions, but they also had less than half as far to go before making contact, as well as excellent concealment during most of their approach. Longstreet apparently had no doubt whatsoever that the attack would be successful. Earlier that morning, speaking with what Hood described as "that confidence which had so often contributed to his extraordinary success," he had assured the tawny-bearded young man "that we would *of course* whip and drive [the Yankees] from the field," and Hood said afterwards: "I could not but exclaim that I was rejoiced to hear him so express himself, as he was the first general I had met since my arrival who talked of victory." However, for all his confidence, Old Peter did not forget the dangers that lurk in military iotas. He saw to it, in person and with the help of his staff, that his preliminary instructions were followed to the letter. Then and only then, shortly before 11.15, he gave the order for the column to go forward, due west through the dense woods that had screened his preparations.

With barely a quarter mile to go before they reached it, Bushrod Johnson's lead brigades crossed the LaFayette Road within ten minutes of receiving Longstreet's nod. As they surged across the dusty road and the open field beyond — the field that Wood had recessed his line to avoid — they encountered galling fire from the left and right, where Hindman and Law were hotly engaged, but almost none from directly ahead. Welcome though this was, they thought it strange until they found out why. Entering the woods on the far side, they scrambled over the deserted breastworks and caught sight, dead ahead and still within easy reach, of the last of Wood's brigades in the act of carrying out the order to "close up on and support" Reynolds. Yelling, the Confederates struck the vulnerable blue column flank and rear, sitting-duck fashion, and, as Johnson described the brief action, "cast the shattered fragments to the right and left." Still on the run, the butternut attackers crashed on through the forest and soon emerged into another clearing, larger than the first, with Missionary Ridge looming westward beyond the tops of intervening trees. Here at last, after their half-mile run, they paused to recover their breath and alignment, and Johnson later communicated something of the elation he and those around him felt, not only at what they had accomplished so far, but also at what lay spread before them, stark against the backdrop of the green slopes of the ridge. "The scene now presented was unspeakably grand," he declared in his report. "The resolute and impetuous charge, the rush of our heavy columns sweeping out from the shadow and gloom of the forest into the open fields flooded with sunlight, the glitter of arms, the onward dash of artillery and mounted men, the retreat of the foe, the shouts of the hosts of our army, the dust, the smoke, the noise of firearms — of whistling balls and grapeshot and of bursting shell — made up a battle scene of unsurpassed grandeur."

There was little time for admiring the view, however, since it included, in addition to the items mentioned, a number of hostile guns in furious action along a low ridge half a mile away, some firing southeast, some northeast, and some due east at him. Hood rode up amid the shellbursts, managing his horse with one hand because the other still hung useless in its sling. "Go ahead," he told Johnson, who was realigning his three brigades, "and keep ahead of everything." The Ohio-born Tennessean did just that. His men had taken a six-gun Federal battery soon after they crossed the road, but this had only sharpened their appetite for more. Resuming the advance, they quickly overran a position from which nine guns were firing, then plunged ahead to seize four more whose crews did not limber them in time for a getaway, as several others managed to do along that ripple of high ground overlooking a scene of moiling confusion in the enemy rear. Here Johnson called a halt at last, having accomplished a mile-deep penetration of the Union center, the destruction or dispersal of a whole brigade of bluecoats, and the capture of nineteen pieces of artillery, all between 11.15 and noon. Bracing his troops for a possible shock, he threw out skirmishers and sent word back to Longstreet of his need for reinforcements in case the enemy launched a counterattack at his isolated division, which had lost about one fourth of its strength in the course of its long advance. Such an attack did not seem likely, though, if he could judge by what he saw from where he stood. The blue army seemed to have come apart at the seams under the impact of that one savage blow, and its fugitives were streaming in disorder up the Dry Valley Road, which curved north and west across their rear, toward Missionary Ridge and the solitary notch that indicated McFarland's Gap and possible deliverance from the terror that had suddenly come on them, less than an hour ago, after a morning of taking it easy while the battle raged at the far end of the line.

Hindman had had much to do with the creation of the blue confusion. Though he encountered a far greater number of Federals in the course of his advance on Johnson's left, and thus was limited to a shallower penetration, this gave him the chance to inflict a far greater number of casualties, and that was what he did. Johnson had struck and shattered a single brigade, but Hindman served two whole divisions in that manner within the same brief span of time, converting McCook's supposed defense of the Union right into the headlong race for safety which Johnson observed with such elation when he called a halt soon afterward on the ridge overlooking the Dry Valley Road, a mile beyond the point where he had pierced the enemy center. Much as the unmanned breastworks in his front had facilitated the Tennessean's breakthrough, so did the Arkansan have the good fortune to find both Sheridan and Davis in motion when he hit them. The former, in compliance with his orders to reinforce the left, was marching north across the latter's rear, and the latter was sidling in the same direction, under instructions to close the gap created by Wood's abrupt departure, when they were assailed by Hindman's yelling graybacks, who came swarming out of the woods before the pickets along the LaFayette Road had time to do more than get off a few wild shots by way of sounding the alarm. Davis's men scattered rearward in a panic that soon infected Sheridan's two lead brigades, whose ranks were overrun by the fugitives as a prelude to being struck by their pursuers, with the result that the two divisions were mingled in flight. "McCook's corps was wiped off the field without any attempt at real resistance," an Illinois colonel later testified, adding that he had seen artillerists cut the traces and abandon their guns in order to make a faster getaway, while others on foot, including some who might otherwise have been willing to stand their ground, were swept along by the mob, "like flecks of foam upon a river." McCook himself was one of those flecks, and Sheridan and Davis were two more; but Brigadier

General William H. Lytle was not. Commanding Sheridan's third brigade, which had been left behind as a covering force southeast of the Widow Glenn's, he ordered a countercharge in an attempt to stem the rout, but fell at the first rebel volley and died soon after his men ran off and left him, the only Union general, out of thirty of that rank on the field, to be killed or captured or even touched by metal in this bloodiest of all the western battles.

One check there was, and a bloody one at that, though not from McCook or either of his two division commanders. Detached from Reynolds, the Lightning Brigade was still posted in support of the Union right, and when Hindman routed the foot soldiers there, capturing guns and colors on the run, Wilder brought his mounted troops in hard on the rebel flank and opened fire with his repeaters. That tore it. The southernmost gray brigade lost its momentum, then collapsed in a rush as frantic as any on the other side, falling back all the way to the LaFayette Road and beyond. On the alert for some such reverse, however, Longstreet promptly threw in a brigade from Preston's reserve division, restored the line with the help of the rallied brigade, and forced the mounted bluecoats westward in the wake of their companions, who had not paused to take advantage of this respite, but had used it rather to increase their lead in the race for McFarland's Gap. Struck by an exploding shell, the Glenn house was afire by now, burning briskly under the noonday sun, with no sign of Rosecrans or his staff. Hindman called a halt, put his cannoneers to work shelling the throng of fugitives to the north and west on the Dry Valley Road, and began to reckon the fruits of his triumph, which were rich. He had taken 17 guns, ten of them abandoned, 1100 prisoners, including three full colonels, 1400 small arms, together with 165,000 rounds of ammunition, and five stands of colors, all within less than an hour and against a force considerably larger than his own.

Law and Kershaw had made similar gains, along with the infliction of a similar disruption, against much stiffer resistance by the defenders of the Union center. Watching Johnson's cheering soldiers hurdle the unmanned breastworks in their front, Law saw that they were taking cruel punishment from the bluecoats on their northern flank as they poured through the gap; so with soldierly instinct he obliqued his three brigades to the right, intending to accomplish a double purpose, first of relieving the pressure on Johnson, by drawing at least a part of the fire, and then of widening the gap by dislodging Brannan, whose own flank had been exposed by Wood's departure. Both of these objectives were attained in rapid order. Turning from the breakthrough on their right to meet this sudden menace to their front, the Federals divided their fire and wavered in the face of what seemed to them a limited choice of falling back or being ground between two rebel millstones. They chose the former course, and chose it with an individual urgency in direct ratio to each regiment's proximity to the threatened flank. Brannan's line swung gatelike, hinged on its left at the juncture with Reynolds, who held firm despite a renewal of Stewart's attack. Now it was Law's troops who were hurdling unmanned breastworks. Moreover, just as Johnson had found one of Wood's brigades defenseless in his path, so now did Law find one of Van Cleve's in that predicament as a result of having been delayed in setting off on its march to reinforce Thomas. It too was struck and shattered, quite as abruptly as the other had been: except that this time there was retribution. Hearing the uproar in its rear, which signified the destruction of its companion brigade, Wood's middle brigade was halted by its commander, Colonel Charles G. Harker, New Jersey-born, only five years out of West Point, and at twenty-five a veteran of all the western battles from Shiloh on. He faced his men about and launched a savage counterattack, not at Johnson, who had pressed on westward out of reach, but at Law, who had just knocked Brannan's gate ajar and shattered Van Cleve's sitting-duck brigade. Boldness paid off for the youthful colonel. Not only was Law stopped in his tracks by Harker's unexpected lunge, but the Texas brigade on the open flank was driven rearward in what for a time had the makings of a large-scale repulse.

Returning from his hurried conference with Johnson, midway of that general's exuberant advance, Hood arrived to find his old brigade in full retreat. This was a rare sight at any time, despite the reverse that had ended its brief penetration of the enemy line the day before, but it was particularly unwelcome in this apparent hour of victory. Blond and gigantic, though his useless arm prevented him from gesturing with his sword by way of emphasis, he rode among the fleeing Texans, exhorting them to stand their ground. They stopped in time to catch him as he toppled from the saddle, shot through the upper thigh by a rifle bullet that shattered the bone and necessitated a field amputation that would leave him barely enough of a stump to accommodate an artificial leg. As he fell he muttered incongruously, repeating in shock what he had said a few minutes ago to Johnson: "Go ahead, and keep ahead of everything." These were thought at the time to be his dying words, a fitting valedictory to battle — such wounds were all too often fatal — but that was not to be the case, and besides he had the satisfaction, as he was being taken away on a stretcher, of knowing that the line had been restored by Kershaw. Bringing up his two brigades at the critical moment of the corps commander's fall, the South Carolinian not only stemmed the incipient rout; he also resumed the advance, driving the resurgent bluecoats west and north with the help of the rallied Texans, who were eager now to get revenge for what had been done to them and their beloved Hood.

At this point, some time after noon, Longstreet rode up from the south, where he had repaired a similar reverse by sending in one of Preston's brigades to shore up Hindman's collapsed flank, and expressed great

satisfaction at finding that all three elements of his clenched-fist blow —
Hindman on the left, Johnson in the center, and Law and Kershaw on
the right — had succeeded admirably, so far, in fulfilling his prediction that "we would of course whip and drive [the Yankees] from the
field." Up to now, this only applied to about one third of the blue army,
including two complete divisions and portions of three others, but Old
Peter believed he had solved the problem of how best to press the issue
to its desired conclusion: "As our right wing had failed of the progress
anticipated, and had become fixed by the firm holding of the enemy's
left, we could find no practicable field for our work except by a change
of the order of battle from [a] wheel to the left, to a swing to the
right." Instead of pivoting on Preston, as originally intended, he proposed to pivot on Stewart, in the opposite direction. In other words,
Bragg's plan was not only to be abandoned; it was to be reversed. Pursuit of the remnant of the Union right, in flight for McFarland's Gap
across the way, could be left to Wheeler, whose troopers, after exchanging
shots all morning with enemy vedettes across the creek below Lee &
Gordon's, had just forced a crossing at Glass's Mill and driven the Federal horsemen southward, away from the battle which was then approaching its climax three miles north. Couriers were sent at once to
have him take up the chase of the fugitives on the Dry Valley Road,
which passed through nearby Crawfish Springs, while the gray infantry
turned sharp right to complete — with the aid of Polk's wing, which
would have little to do but keep up the pressure it had been applying for
better than three hours now, although without conspicuous success —
the destruction of the remaining two thirds of the blue army. Law and
Kershaw had faced in that direction already, drawn by the retirement of
Brannan's right, but instructions had to be sent to Johnson and Hindman, as well as to Preston, who was still holding the abandoned pivot,
to form their three divisions on the left of Law and Kershaw, along a
new east-west line from which Longstreet intended to launch one last
clenched-fist blow that would result in a knockout victory over an adversary who presumably was groggy from the effects of the punch just
landed in his midriff.

However desirable it might have been, there was no question of
an immediate jump-off. Preparations involving a right-angle variation in
the direction of attack for an entire wing of the army, as well as changes
in the posting of practically all of the elements that composed it, would
of course take time, since they would require not only a great deal of
shifting of units, large and small, over considerable distances — Preston,
the extreme example, had nearly three miles to go before his troops
would be in position — but also a prerequisite restoration of control
within the five divisions themselves, most of which had been severely
disorganized by the mingling of regiments and brigades in the course of
their furious breakthrough and their long advance over difficult terrain.

Besides, Old Peter had never been one to begrudge time spent in preparation for the delivery of an assault, particularly in a situation such as the one that now obtained, with a good six hours of daylight still remaining and a single, well-co-ordinated effort being counted on to accomplish the objective. Orders had to be drawn up and distributed before they could be obeyed, and limber chests and cartridge boxes had to be refilled. Nor did he believe in neglecting the inner man; stomachs needed refilling, too, and that included his own. Before leaving on a tour of inspection, he directed that a lunch be spread for him to eat on his return. Dodging snipers, he reconnoitered the new defensive line the Federals had established, perpendicular to their old one along the LaFayette Road, along the irregular slopes of an eastern spur of Missionary Ridge; Snodgrass Hill was its name, according to Bushrod Johnson, whom he encountered in the course of his ride along the front. The Tennessean pointed out what he believed was "the key of the battle," a point where the bluecoats clustered thickly on the wooded slope ahead. Longstreet looked at it carefully. "It was a key, but a rough one," he said later. For the present, he instructed Buckner to establish a twelve-gun battery at the junction of the two wings, explaining that this would give him the advantage of enfilade fire down both segments of the Union line: the old one extending north, which had resisted Polk's attacks all day, and the new one extending west, which he himself was about to test for the first time. Now as before, he seemed to have little doubt as to the outcome. "They have fought their last man, and *he* is running," he said jovially, despite the evidence he had just seen to the contrary, when he returned to headquarters and sat down to his lunch of Nassau bacon and Georgia sweet potatoes. The former was an all-too-familiar item on the diet of all Confederates, East and West; "nausea bacon," it was sometimes called; but not the latter — anyhow not in the theater in which Old Peter had done all his fighting up to now. "We were not accustomed to potatoes of any kind in Virginia," he would remark more than thirty years later, still remembering the meal, "and thought we had a luxury."

There were two interruptions, both of them drastic though only the first was violent. It came in the form of a shell that burst in the woods nearby, one of whose jagged splinters ripped through a book a mounted courier was reading and struck a staff colonel, knocking him from his place at the table and to the ground, where he lay gasping as if in the throes of death. Startled, his fellow staffers leaped up to staunch the expected flow of blood, but they could not find the wound. Reacting with his usual calm, Longstreet saw that the gasping was caused by a large bite of sweet potato, which had become lodged in the colonel's windpipe when the iron fragment grazed him, and "suggested that it would be well to first relieve him of the potato and give him a chance to breathe. This done, he revived," the general recalled; "his breath came freer, and he was soon on his feet." That was the first interruption. The second came soon after the other officers rejoined their chief at the table, and if it was less violent it was also a good deal more alarming in the end. It came in the form of a message from Bragg, from whom the commander of the left wing had heard nothing since the night before, requesting his attendance at a conference a short distance in rear of the new mile-long line that was being formed in the woods to the west of the LaFayette Road. Longstreet promptly rode to meet him amid the wreckage of what had been the Union right, and after giving him a brief description of the rout that had resulted in the capture of some forty guns, together with thousands of small arms and prisoners and no less than two square miles of ground, explained his decision to wheel right instead of left, as originally instructed, in order to complete the destruction of what remained of the blue army.

Bragg did not seem to share his lieutenant's enthusiasm, and when the latter went on to suggest that the left wing be reinforced from the right, which would have little more to do than hold its ground once the attack was resumed on the south, the North Carolinian broke in testily: "There is not a man in the right wing who has any fight in him." Taken aback, Longstreet at last saw what the trouble was. Bragg was miffed because his design for herding the bluecoats into McLemore's Cove had gone astray; or as the Georgian later put it, "He was disturbed by the failure of his plan and the severe repulse of his right wing, and was little prepared to hear suggestions from subordinates for other moves or progressive work." In other words, if he could not win in just the way he wanted, he did not care about winning at all, or anyhow he wanted no personal share in such a victory. So at any rate it seemed. This fairly incredible impression was strengthened, moreover, by the manner in which Bragg brought the conference to a close. "If anything happens, communicate with me at Reed's Bridge," he said curtly, and he turned his horse and rode in that direction, which would place him well in rear of the stalled right, as far as possible from the scene of the critical attack about to be launched by Longstreet on the left.

Old Peter scarcely knew what to make of his chief's reaction. "From accounts of his former operations, I was prepared for halting work," he afterwards wrote, understating the case in an attempt to bring in a touch of humor that was altogether lacking at the time, "but this, when the battle was at its tide and in partial success, was a little surprising." However, as he returned to his new-drawn line to give the signal that would launch the assault designed to complete his half-won triumph, he soon recovered his aplomb, if not his accustomed heartiness. "There was nothing for the left wing to do but work along as best it could," he said.

Thus Bragg, in effect, removed himself from management of the battle, but only after his opponent had removed himself, in fact and person, not only from the battle but also from the field on which it was being fought. Whether out of petulance or panic, each of the two leaders reacted in accordance with his nature and his lights, for while the southern commander appeared to doubt that the contest was half won, Rosecrans had not seemed to question the evidence that it was considerably more than half lost. Not that he was a coward: Rich Mountain, Iuka, Corinth, and above all Stones River were sufficient refutation of the charge, and moreover his gloomy assessment was shared by those around him. With the exception of Lytle, whose sudden death was taken as confirmation of the majority opinion, no one with stars on his shoulders and a close-up look at the proportions of the rebel breakthrough failed to share the abrupt and general conviction that all was lost. Not only the army commander, but also his chief of staff, two of his three corps commanders, and four of his ten division commanders — in short, every man in charge of anything larger than a brigade on that quarter of the field — agreed that in the present instance, with the choice narrowed to flight or death or capture, discretion was the better part of valor. Practically of one accord, they all turned tail and ran and their troops ran with them, flecks of foam on the blue stream rushing northward up the Dry Valley Road and westward through McFarland's Gap, eager to put the bulletproof mass of Missionary Ridge between themselves and their screaming gray pursuers.

Soon after getting off the order to Wood, Rosecrans had ridden to the right, accompanied by Dana and Garfield and several other members of his staff, intending to hurry the sidling movement that would thicken the thinned center. He was sitting his horse directly in rear of Davis, whose division was in motion, when Longstreet's attack exploded dead ahead and to the immediate left front. Dana, who was badly in need of sleep, had dismounted for a nap in the grass; the first he knew of the impending breakthrough was when he was awakened by what he afterwards called "the most infernal noise I ever heard." Startled — "Never in any battle had I witnessed such a discharge of cannon and musketry" — he looked up and saw something that alarmed him even more. Old Rosy was crossing himself. "Hello!" he thought. "If the general is crossing himself, we are in a desperate situation." Sure enough, when he looked around he "saw our lines break and melt away like leaves before the wind. . . . The whole right of the army had apparently been routed." Rosecrans by then had reached the same conclusion, for he turned to his staff and said in a voice surprisingly calm amid the confusion of the headlong rush which Dana would compare to melting leaves: "If you care to live any longer, get away from here." His advice was so quickly taken that Dana did not even attempt a description of the dispersal or employ a single additional metaphor, mixed or otherwise. He simply remarked that "the headquarters around me disappeared."

Others "disappeared" as rapidly, even though they were out of earshot of their chief's advice. McCook's third great battle was also his third rout, and the greatest of the three. Like Davis and Sheridan, he made a brief attempt to stem the tide, then took off rearward, a leader in the race for safety, and those of his men who had not already bolted were quick to follow his example. Crittenden, too, was a part of the crush, but strictly on an individual basis. He had no troops left under him anyhow, the last of his three divisions having been detached to Thomas by midmorning, though Van Cleve himself was swept from the field with the remnant of the brigade that was wrecked by Law. Similarly, Negley became a fugitive when he led his rear brigade off on a tangent, then found his way to the left blocked by Johnson's mile-deep penetration of the center. A few among the responsible commanders, such as Wilder, maintained control of their units, but they were the exception. "Many of the officers of all ranks," according to another Indiana colonel, "showed by their wild commands and still wilder actions that they had completely lost their heads and were as badly demoralized as the private soldiers."

One among the exceptions was a young officer from McCook's staff, who managed to skirt the confusion and get through to Thomas on the left. The Virginian told him to return the way he had come and bring up Davis and Sheridan to support his dangling right. He made it back to the Dry Valley Road, and as he rode westward alongside it — for the road itself was jammed with fugitives crowding it shoulder-to-shoulder and raising a waist-high cloud of dust — he appealed to various officers in the fleeing column, but to small avail. Although the rebel pursuit had broken off by now, they either would not believe him when he said so, or else they could not see in this any reason for slowing the pace of their retreat. "See Jeff, Colonel," they told him, or "See Phil." Appeals to the men themselves were even less successful. "We'll talk to you, my son, when we get to the Ohio River!" one veteran replied, much to the amusement of his fellow trudgers. Finally, in McFarland's Gap, the young staffer overtook Davis and Sheridan, and though the former expressed a doubtful willingness to give the thing a try, the latter wanted nothing further to do with the mismanaged contest he had just put behind him. "He had lost faith," the colonel observed as he pushed on to gain the head of the column, up toward Rossville.

There where the road forked, one branch leading northwest to Chattanooga, the other east through Rossville Gap, then south to the field on whose opposite flank the scramble had begun — the distance in each case was about four miles — Rosecrans and the remnant of his staff drew rein to breathe their horses. By now the battle racket had died down, screened by the loom of Missionary Ridge, and though by dismounting and putting their ears to the ground they could hear the rattle of small arms, which signified that Thomas was still in action with at least a part of his command, the lack of any rumble from his guns seemed to indicate that the left wing had not fared much better than the right. If this was so, the thing to do was establish a straggler line on the outskirts of Chattanooga, where the two sundered portions of the army could be reunited and rallied for a last-ditch stand with the deep-running Tennessee River at its back. For his own part, Old Rosy was determined to return to the field and share with whatever troops were left the final stages of their withdrawal, leaving to his chief of staff the task of bringing the fugitives to a halt and putting them into a new defensive position before the gray wave of attackers swept over them again. However, when he turned to Garfield and began to tell him all that would have to be done — the selection of proper ground, the assignment of units to their places in line, the opening of new channels of supply and communication, and much else — the chief of staff, confused by the complexity of what he termed "the great responsibility," made a suggestion: "I can go to General Thomas and report the situation to you much better than I can give those orders." Rosecrans thought this over briefly, then reluctantly agreed. "Well," he said, "go and tell General Thomas my precautions to hold the Dry Valley Road and secure our commissary stores and artillery. [Tell him] to report the situation to me and to use his discretion as to continuing the fight on the ground we occupy at the close of the afternoon or retiring to a position in the rear near Rossville."

So while Garfield set out eastward on a ride that would take him in time to the White House — though not for long; the assassin's bullet would find him before he had been four months in office — Rosecrans took the left-hand fork that led to Chattanooga. But now the shock set in. The nearer he drew to the city the more depressed he became, as if some sort of ratio obtained between his distance from the battlefield and his realization of the enormity of his position as a commander who had deserted his army in its bloodiest hour of crisis. When he pulled rein at last, about 3.30, in front of the three-story residence where departmental headquarters had been established eleven days ago, he was so exhausted in body and broken in spirit that he had to be assisted to dismount. "The officers who helped him into the house did not soon forget the terrible look of the brave man, stunned by sudden calamity," an observer remarked, and added: "In later years I used occasionally to meet Rosecrans, and always felt that I could see the shadow of Chickamauga upon his noble face."

Dana arrived immediately behind him, having become separated from the others in what he called "the helter-skelter of the rear." That he too was much depressed by what he had seen, though his depression took a different form, was obvious from the wire he got off to Stanton at 4 o'clock, as soon as he had had time to catch his breath. "My report today is of deplorable importance," he informed the Secretary. "Chickamauga is as fatal a name in our history as Bull Run." Still badly shaken,

he described the onslaught of the rebels, which was unlike anything he
had seen at Vicksburg, his one previous experience of war. "They came
through with resistless impulse, composed of brigades formed in divisions. Before them our soldiers turned and fled. It was wholesale panic.
Vain were all attempts to rally them." He was as uncertain of what would
happen next as he was of the army's losses up to now, but he ventured a
guess or two in both directions. "Davis and Sheridan are said to be coming off at the head of a couple of regiments in order, and Wilder's brigade
marches out unbroken. Thomas, too, is coming down the Rossville road
with an organized command, but all the rest is confusion. Our wounded
are all left behind, some 6000 in number. We have lost heavily in killed
today. The total of our killed, wounded, and prisoners can hardly be
less than 20,000, and may be much more. . . . Enemy not yet arrived before Chattanooga. Preparations making to resist his entrance for a time."

★ ★ ★

Some of this was useful to the Washington authorities as an estimate of the situation resulting from the sudden turn of fortune — surprisingly so, in light of the fact that it amounted to little more than guess-
work by a rattled nonprofessional who had seen only a portion of the
field — but much of it was about as inaccurate as might have been expected. This last applied in particular to the reference to Thomas. Not
only was he not "coming down the Rossville road," as Dana claimed,
but even as the telegrapher clicked away at the doleful message composed in haste and panic, the Virginian was fighting hard, resisting the
combined assaults of both Confederate wings in a climactic struggle to
maintain the integrity of the position he had held all morning against
one. In the end — that is, before nightfall — his skill and determination
in continuing this odds-on fight with what remained of the blue force
after its commander had fled with a full third of the troops who had
composed it at the outset, would win him the name by which he would
be known thereafter: "The Rock of Chickamauga."

Indeed, there was much about him that was rocklike, not alone in
the sense of being "the right kind of man to tie to," but also in appearance, especially when viewed from up close. According to a soldier observer, his "full rounded, powerful form," six feet in height and well
over two hundred pounds in weight, "gradually expands upon you, as a
mountain which you approach." Moreover, in addition to sheer bulk, he
gave an impression of doggedness and imperturbability. "This army
doesn't retreat," he had said in a similar crisis at Stones River, despite the
evidence to the contrary, and it was obvious from his manner that the
same thing applied here, so far at least as concerned the two thirds of the
army still on the field and in his charge. Brannan's gatelike swing had
ended on the rising ground in his left rear; there he posted his division,
extending his right westward along the convenient eastern spur of Mis-

sionary Ridge. Single brigades
from the variously shattered and
scattered commands of Wood,
Van Cleve, and Negley, combined with those of Brannan,
provided the equivalent of two
divisions for the defense of this
new line, and Thomas reinforced it further by detaching
one brigade each from Johnson
and Palmer, who stood at the
bulging center of the north-
south line confronting Polk.
The east-west position was one
of great natural strength, heavily
wooded and uphill for attackers,

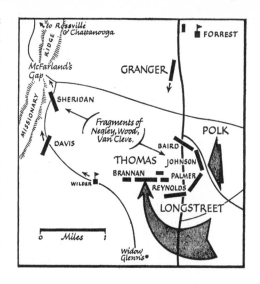

but whether or not it could be held against as savage a fighter as Longstreet would depend in the final analysis on the troops who occupied it.
Thoroughly aware of this, as he also was of the fact that they had already
backpedaled once today under pressure from the same gray veterans
who were massing now for a follow-up assault, Thomas moved among
them in an attempt to stiffen their resolution for what he knew was coming. "This hill must be held and I trust you to do it," he told Harker,
who replied: "We will hold it or die here." Thomas rode on, and presently came to one of Harker's regimental commanders, Colonel Emerson
Opdycke. "This point must be held," he told him. The Ohio colonel
agreed. "We will hold this ground," he said, "or go to heaven from it."
Opdycke's men nodded approval of his words, but whether they really
meant it remained to be seen.

They meant it. About 2 o'clock, while Longstreet was returning
from his unprofitable conference with Bragg, Kershaw assaulted the left
of the new Federal position with the demidivision composed of his own
South Carolina brigade and Barksdale's Mississippians, now under Brigadier General Ben G. Humphreys. "Ranks followed ranks in close order,
moving briskly and bravely against us," a defender later wrote. These
were the men who had taken the Wheat Field and the Peach Orchard,
eighty days ago at Gettysburg, and they were determined to do as well
this afternoon at Chickamauga. They did not; not yet, at any rate. Harker's troops, together with those in Brannan's left brigade and the brigade from Palmer, under Brigadier General William Hazen, fired their
rifles with such steadiness and precision that the gray ranks faltered,
withered, and fell back. Kershaw, who had thought one hard rap would
cause the bluecoats to continue their withdrawal, was unwilling to admit
that this had been disproved so quickly. After a pause for realignment he
again sent his two brigades forward against the Union there. The result

was the same. They surged up the slope, then fell back down it, having taken losses quite as heavy as before. Still unconvinced, he tried a third assault, and suffered a third repulse. Such uphill work was about as exhausting as it was bloody. One regimental commander reported that his men were "panting like dogs tired out in the chase." In the course of the last charge, he would recall, he had seen a fifteen-year-old soldier lagging behind and weeping, and when he told him that this was no time for hanging back out of fear, the boy explained that his trouble was not fright but exasperation. "That aint it, Colonel," he wailed between sobs. "I'm so damned tired I can't keep up with my company." Convinced at last, and perceiving that even his full-grown men were winded, Kershaw called a halt at the base of the hill to watch for some sign that the Federals were weakening their left to meet the attack that was being launched by now against their right by Johnson and Hindman, off at the far end of the line.

Thomas might well have weakened his embattled left to reinforce his threatened right, outnumbered and overlapped as it was by the two butternut divisions being massed in the woods below, except that he received unexpected help at just this critical juncture. All morning, up near McAfee's Church, which was two miles east of Rossville and about twice that distance from the hilly spur where Brannan staged his rally, Gordon Granger had fretted because his one-division Reserve Corps, charged with guarding the Rossville Gap in case it was needed as an escape hatch, was being kept from the battle he could hear raging to the south. About 11 o'clock — an hour and a half after Polk began his delayed attack and shortly before Longstreet scored the breakthrough that threw Davis and Sheridan off the field and swung Brannan out of his place in the disintegrating center of the Union line — he and his chief of staff climbed a haystack in an attempt to see something of what was going on. All they saw, far down the LaFayette Road, was a boiling cloud of dust and smoke with the fitful yellow flash of batteries mixed in at its base, but Granger soon arrived at a decision. "I am going to Thomas, orders or no orders!" he declared, snapping his glasses back in their case. The staffer was more cautious. "And if you go," he warned, "it may bring disaster to the army and you to a court martial." Granger was a career man, West Point '45, and normally an avoider of such risks; but not now. "There's nothing in our front but ragtag, bobtail cavalry," he said. "Don't you see Bragg is piling his whole army on Thomas? I am going to his assistance." And with that he climbed down off the haystack and ordered Steedman to prepare to march at once with two of his brigades, leaving the third behind to continue holding the Rossville escape hatch open in the event of a collapse by the main body, which he would soon be joining, four miles south.

Within half an hour the march was under way. Granger's remark that Bragg was "piling his whole army on Thomas" had been in error at the time he made it; Longstreet had not yet gone in. But now that the remaining half of the Confederate force had been committed, with the resultant abolition of the Federal right, the statement was in the rapid process of becoming quite literally true; so that Granger's decision, though based in part on an erroneous assumption, turned out to be militarily sound; Thomas was indeed in need of help, and it was fortunate for him that Granger began his four-mile march before the need existed, let alone before it became acute. Even so, there were delays. About noon, a mile down the LaFayette Road, the lead brigade was taken under fire by a pair of batteries in position on the flank. Steedman was obliged to go from column of march into line of battle, facing east to meet this threat from what turned out to be a sizable detachment of Forrest's men. Blue skirmishers, moving against the guns, caused the rebel troopers to give ground; yet when the skirmishers returned the graybacks followed, resuming their harassing tactics. Finally, in exasperation — for he was a short-tempered man at best — Granger sent for the third brigade to come down from McAfee's Church and hold the troublesome horsemen off while he took up his march, southwest now across the fields and through the woods in order to approach the nearly beleaguered Thomas from the rear. A mile short of the blue flank the second delay occurred; but it was brief, consisting of nothing more than a short wait for part of Negley's division to get out of the way, which it soon did, being hard on the go for Rossville and deliverance from chaos. The two columns passed each other, one headed into and the other out of the battle, and Granger rode ahead to report that his two brigades were close at hand.

He was a hard-mannered regular, originally from upper New York State, a veteran of Mexico and the Indian wars, shaggy in looks, brusque in speech, and not much liked — either by his troops, who resented a strictness that sometimes prescribed horsewhipping for minor camp offenses, or by his fellow officers, who found him uncongenial — but Thomas had seldom been as glad to see anyone as he was to see Granger, whom he greeted with a handshake and a smile that was all the broader because he had thought the column approaching his rear was hostile. That would indeed have been the final straw; for Kershaw's attack was in full career on his left by now, and Hindman and Johnson were massing their divisions for an advance on the right, which they overlapped. When they began to move forward, out of the woods and onto an intervening ridge, Granger saw the problem at a glance. "Those men must be driven back," he said. Thomas agreed. "Can you do it?" he asked. Granger nodded grimly. "Yes," he said. "My men are fresh, and they are just the fellows for that work. They are raw troops and they don't know any better than to charge up there."

Whether the basis for their conduct was ignorance, sheer heroism, or a combination of both, the men of the reserve corps were indeed "the fellows for that work." Steedman, who was forty-seven, Pennsylvania born, a former printer, Texas revolutionist, and Ohio legislator — "a great, hearty man, broad-breasted [and] broad-shouldered," whose face, according to an admirer, was "written all over with sturdy sense and stout courage" — brought them up on the double and committed them with no more delay that it took to tell a staff officer to see that his name was spelled correctly in the obituaries. Leading the charge on horseback, he saw his green troops waver at their first sight of the enemy up ahead; whereupon he grabbed the regimental colors from an Illinois bearer alongside him and waved the rippling silk to draw their attention. "Go back, boys, go back," he roared, "but the flag can't go with you!" They did not go back; they went forward, still with Steedman in the lead, but now on foot; for the rippling blue of the colors had attracted the attention of the rebels, too, with the result that his horse had been shot from under him. Badly shaken by the fall, the general got up and hobbled forward, still brandishing the flag and roaring, "Follow me!" Ahead, the graybacks gave ground before such fury and determination, then rallied and counterattacked. However, the bluecoats had the ridge by then and held it, though at the cost of losing one fifth of their number within their first twenty minutes of combat. And that was only the beginning; they would lose as many more in the next three hours. In fact, of the 3700 men in the two brigades, nearly half — 1788 — would be casualties by sundown.

Steep though the price was, the gain was great. Not only had they shored up and prolonged Brannan's overlapped western flank; they also had brought with them from McAfee's Church a hard-hitting battery of three-inch rifles, which added the weight of their metal to the blue resistance, and no less than 95,000 rounds of small-arms ammunition. This last was in particular demand, because the army's main ordnance supply train had been involved in McCook's collapse and flight, and Thomas's soldiers were burning up what they had on hand at a fearful rate; an Ohio regiment of 535 men, for example, would expend nearly 45,000 rounds of rifle ammunition before the day was over. In the face of such fiery opposition — an average expenditure of better than 80 rounds per man, including casualties — it was no wonder that Longstreet pronounced Johnson's "key of the battle," by which the Tennessean meant the hilly spur along whose slopes the east-west Union line was drawn, "a rough one."

Returning from his conference with the disgruntled Bragg, Old Peter arrived to find Kershaw checked on the right and Johnson and Hindman just going in on the left. Like them, he had thought it probable that a determined nudge would persuade the bluecoats to continue their retreat, but when the second attack was repulsed — disclosing, as he said later, that the defenders were "full of fight, even to the aggressive" — he knew he was in for trouble. Hindman, who had been struck in the neck by a fragment of shell but declined to quit the field, agreed with this revised assessment, subsequently reporting that while he "never saw Confederate soldiers fight better," he had "never known Federal troops to fight so well." However, Longstreet wasted no time on regret that Kershaw had jumped the gun, committing his two brigades before the six at the far end of the line were ready, or that Johnson, conversely, had not swept around the open flank before Granger arrived to brace it. Instead, he sent word for them to keep up the pressure on the two extremities while Preston was massing his three brigades, only one of which had seen any action so far in the battle, for an assault on the blue center. Then at last, with Law coming in on Kershaw's left and Stewart on his right, the second of Old Peter's clenched-fist blows would dispose of what had survived the devastation of the first.

Shortly before 4 o'clock, Preston — "genial, gallant, lovable William Preston," Longstreet called the forty-six-year-old Kentuckian, whom he met for the first time this afternoon — got his troops in position, two brigades advanced in echelon and one held in reserve, and sent them forward against the center of Brannan's line. By now the defenders had improvised breastworks from stones and fallen trees, anything at all that would stop a bullet, so that when the attackers emerged from the woods at the foot of the slope they were met by heavy, well-aimed fire directed confidently at them from the crest ahead. They did not stop or attempt to return this fire until they were within eighty yards of the flame-stabbed smoke that obscured the enemy position. There they halted, exposed as they were, and engaged in a deadly exchange of volleys with the sheltered bluecoats for nearly an hour. "Only new troops could accomplish such a wonderful feat," a general who opposed them declared; which perhaps was true (Hood's Texans, for example, prided themselves on knowing when to stand and when to run, and in point of fact had chosen the latter course twice already on this same field, today and yesterday) except that it left out of account the determined example of the officers who led them. The two brigades were commanded by a pair of Alabamians, Brigadier General Archibald Gracie and Colonel John H. Kelly, both of whom had had considerable experience under fire. New York born — he had distinguished kinsmen in the Union ranks — Gracie was thirty, a graduate of Heidelberg and West Point and a merchant in Mobile before secession returned him to the profession for which he had been trained, while Kelly was only twenty-three, having left West Point as a cadet to go with his native state when the war began. Both had risen fast and far, but strictly on ability, beginning respectively as an infantry captain and an artillery lieutenant; Kelly, who had soldiers under him better than twice his age, had commanded a battalion at Shiloh, a regiment at Perryville and Murfreesboro, and now a brigade at Chickamauga, which would earn him a wreath for his three

stars and make him the youngest general in the army. So led, Preston's
two committed brigades stood their ground and took their punishment,
losing 1054 of their 2879 effectives in the process, but fixing the Federals in position while the divisions on their left and right were heartened by their example and Breckinridge finally got the twelve-gun battery posted near the junction of the two wings. Even Polk, across the
way, came alive at last in response to the sustained uproar of the volleys
Gracie's and Kelly's men were exchanging with their opponents, and
sent word for his division commanders to match the pressure, there on
the east, that Longstreet was exerting from the south.

No one knew better than Thomas, wedged as it were between
anvil and sledge, that once the Confederates achieved this concert of action, east and south, the issue could not long remain in doubt. Moreover,
though the two armies had begun the day with equal numbers and
though each would suffer casualties of about one third its total strength
before the battle ended, another third of the blue army had fled the field
by early afternoon, which left Thomas with only about one third of the
original Union force, as compared to Bragg's two thirds; in short, after
succeeding by default to the command, the Virginian faced odds of
roughly two to one, with the additional disadvantage of being pressed
from two directions, in each of which the enemy strength was about
equal to both Federal wings combined. He knew that under these circumstances he would have to withdraw eventually, but he hoped to prolong
the struggle until he could do so under cover of darkness. As late as 4
o'clock, when Garfield arrived with his absent chief's suggestion for "retiring to a position in the rear," Thomas declined even to consider a retreat by daylight. "It will ruin the army to withdraw it now," he said.
"This position must be held until night." Before another hour had
passed, however, with Preston clawing at him from below and the
other rebel divisions of both wings increasing the tempo of their action
and inching closer to his lines, he saw that to attempt a much longer delay would be to risk a breakthrough which would be even more costly
to him than a daylight disengagement, dangerous though such a maneuver was said to be in all the tactics manuals. Accordingly, about 5
o'clock, while the sun was still an hour high, he settled on a plan for
withdrawal, first on the left, where the pressure was less severe, and
then on the right. The divisions along the north-south line would pull
out in reverse order, first Reynolds, then Palmer, then Johnson, each
passing in rear of the unit on its left; Baird would be last and would
serve as rear guard on the march to McFarland's Gap and Rossville,
where a new line of battle would be formed to discourage pursuit beyond that point. Similarly, Brannan and Steedman, together with the brigades that had been used to reinforce them, would fall back in sequence
from the east-west line, following the same route to comparative safety.

Or so at any rate Thomas hoped, knowing full well that the execution of the orders designed to bring this about would be difficult at best.

Reynolds began the movement at 5.30, and for the next two hours, from broad daylight into darkness, the battle raged with a new intensity, a new sense of urgency, as various units of both armies, obliged by the attendant confusion to operate more or less on their own, attempted on the one hand to achieve, and on the other to forestall, deliverance from slaughter. Thomas had improvised well, but in a situation so fluid that orders no longer applied by the time they were issued, let alone received, success or failure depended almost entirely on the naked valor of his infantry and the ability of his subordinate commanders to maintain control of troops who, after all, were running for their lives. In this regard, Reynolds was outstanding. Marching north on the LaFayette Road, in rear of the other three divisions, he reached the extreme left to find that Liddell had outflanked Baird and was about to strike the Union line end-on. Instead of turning west for McFarland's Gap, as ordered, the Kentucky-born Hoosier launched a savage counterattack that drove the would-be flankers back and kept open the path of retreat for the other three divisions, who were themselves under mounting pressure from Breckinridge and Cleburne. Though they lost heavily in the withdrawal, being obliged to abandon their wounded along with their dead, the four divisions managed to effect a disengagement by moving rapidly westward, outstripping their pursuers in the race for Missionary Ridge, behind which the sun had set by now. Brannan and Steedman had a harder time of it: particularly the former, who was required to hold his ground while the latter began his withdrawal in the wake of the left-wing divisions which had passed across his rear. When Steedman pulled back, Hindman's and Johnson's men boiled over the ridge in close pursuit, and Preston committed his third brigade, which plunged through the newly opened breach and then turned right to fall on Brannan's unprotected flank. Three regiments were captured in one swoop, two from Michigan and one from Ohio, and the battle abruptly disintegrated, here on the right as it had on the left, into a race. That Brannan's survivors won it was due in large part to a pair of Indiana regiments from Reynolds' division. Coming upon a broken-down ammunition wagon, abandoned by a teamster who had fled with his mules in the earlier rout, the Hoosiers filled their empty cartridge boxes and countermarched, under direct orders from Thomas himself, to serve as rear guard and cover the final stage of the retreat. This they did, checking the butternut pursuers with volleys fired blind in the gathering darkness; after which they once more faced about and took up their westward march, the last blue troops to leave the field.

In some ways, though, the hardest part of the battle still lay before them; for they marched now, down the dark valley from McFarland's Gap to Rossville, with the taste of defeat bitter in their mouths and a great weariness in their limbs. Perryville and Stones River had been bad enough, but the fact that they had remained in control of both those fields when the smoke lifted had given their generals and journalists the basis for a claim to victory. Not so here. This was absolute, unarguable defeat, and as such it was depressing beyond anything they had ever known. "Weary, worn, tired and hungry," a captain in a veteran regiment later wrote, "we sullenly dragged ourselves along, feeling a shame and disgrace that had never been experienced by the Old Sixth before." Those who fell out of the column because of wounds or exhaustion were left to their own inadequate devices by those who had the strength to keep going. Behind them, beyond the intervening ridge, they could hear the rebels celebrating their triumph with loud yells. Another officer in the retreating column, First Lieutenant Ambrose Bierce, a topographical engineer with Hazen, thought the sound "the ugliest any mortal ever heard." Presently, however, there was a stretch of road well down the valley "across which that horrible yell did not prolong itself," he added, "and through that we finally retired in profound silence and dejection, unmolested."

Back on the field of Chickamauga, their spirits lifted by the release of tension, the Confederates kept yelling, despite an almost equal physical weariness, long after their adversaries were out of earshot. As Longstreet put it, "The Army of Tennessee knew how to enjoy its first grand victory," beginning at the moment when the two wings came together, there on the reverse slopes of the hilly spur from which the Yankees had just been driven, and continuing into the night with "a tremendous swell of heroic harmony that seemed almost to lift from their roots the great trees of the forest." Harvey Hill declared years later that the cheers "were such as I had never heard before, and shall not hear again." In point of fact, along strictly practical lines, the victors had more to whoop about than anyone yet knew. Afterwards, when the field had been gleaned, Bragg would report the capture of more than 8000 prisoners, 51 guns, and 23,281 small arms, together with 2381 rounds of artillery ammunition and 135,000 rifle cartridges. The multipaged scavenger list, certified by the chief of ordnance, would include such items as 35 pounds of picket rope, 365 shoulder straps, and 3 damaged copper bugles, as well as "wagons, ambulances, and teams, medicines, hospital stores, &c., in large quantities." It was, in brief, the largest haul ever made by either side on a single field of battle. For the present, however, all the exultant graybacks knew was that they had scored a triumph of considerable proportions, and they did not delay their celebration to wait for the particulars of its scope.

Nor did others who were not there to see for themselves. After the recent and apparently interminable sequence of knee-buckling reverses, soldiers and civilians throughout the nation were elated by the news from North Georgia, which seemed to them to bear out earlier predictions that the northern armies would find what true resistance meant when they approached the southern heartland. "The effects of this great victory will be electrical," a Richmond clerk recorded in his diary. "The whole South will be filled again with patriotic fervor, and in the North there will be a corresponding depression.... Surely the Government of the United States must now see the impossibility of subjugating the Southern people, spread over such a vast expanse of territory, and the European governments ought now to interpose and put an end to this cruel waste of blood and treasure."

★ ★ ★

In war, as in love — indeed, as in all such areas of so-called human endeavor — expectation tended to outrun execution, particularly when the latter was given a head start in the race, and nowhere did this apply more lamentably, at any rate from the Richmond point of view, than in the wake of Chickamauga, probably the greatest and certainly the bloodiest of all the battles won by the South in its fight for the independence it believed to be its birthright. Harvey Hill said later that he had "never seen the Federal dead lie so thickly on the ground, save in front of the sunken wall at Fredericksburg." In point of fact, though Hill may not have seen them on his quarter of the field, the Confederate dead lay even thicker; but in any case, now that the Yankees were on the run, he and the other two lieutenant generals, commanding the two wings, were altogether in favor of a rapid and slashing pursuit of the beaten foe. Though Longstreet called a halt in the dusk that followed his second breakthrough, it was for the same purpose as the halt that had followed his first at midday; namely, to consolidate his forces for the delivery of another heavy blow. "As it was almost dark," he afterwards reported, "I ordered my line to remain as it was, ammunition boxes to be filled, stragglers to be collected, and everything [placed] in readiness for the pursuit in the morning." Polk, perhaps aware that he had done less to win the victory up to now, prepared to do more by sending out scouts to look into the possibility of continuing the slaughter of the vanished enemy. Later, when the scouts returned to report that the bluecoats had not slacked their headlong retreat, the bishop rode to headquarters and informed Bragg — whom he roused from bed, much as Old Peter had done at about the same hour the night before — "that the enemy was routed and flying precipitately from the field, and that then was the opportunity to finish the work by the capture or destruction of [Rosecrans'] army, by prompt pursuit, before he had time to reorganize or throw up defenses at Chattanooga." So an aide who rode with him testified: adding, however, that "Bragg could not be induced to look at it in that light, and refused to believe that we had won a victory."

It was true that the commanding general had received no formal

notification of the outcome of the battle, but only because this had
seemed to his subordinates a highly superfluous gesture. ("It did not occur to me on the night of the 20th to send Bragg word of our complete
success," Longstreet explained years later. "I thought that the loud
huzzas that spread over the field just at dark were a sufficient assurance
and notice to anyone within five miles of us.") On the other hand, if
what he wanted was an eyewitness who could testify to the behavior of
the Federals after they reached the far side of Missionary Ridge — beyond which, conceivably, they might rally and lie in wait for him to
commit some act of rashness — that too was available, soon after first
light next morning, in the form of a Confederate private who had been
captured the previous day, then escaped amid the confusion of the blue
retreat, and made his way back to his outfit before dawn. When he told
his captain of what he had seen across the way — for instance, that the
Unionists were abandoning their wounded as they slogged northward,
intent on nothing but their flight from fury — he was taken at once to
repeat his story, first to his regimental and brigade commanders, then to
Bragg himself. The stern-faced general heard him out, but was doubtful,
if not of the soldier's capacity for accurate observation, then at any rate
of his judgment on such a complicated matter. "Do you know what a retreat looks like?" he asked sharply, fixing the witness with a baleful
glare. Irked by his commander's mistrust, the man replied with words
that endeared him to his comrades, then and thereafter, when they were
repeated, as they often were, around campfires and at future veteran
gatherings. "I ought to, General," he said; "I've been with you during
your whole campaign."

Whatever effect this may have had on the irascible general's disposition, a look at the field by daylight quickly convinced him that his
army was in no condition for the pursuit his chief subordinates were
urging him to undertake. The dead of both sides, stiffened by now in
agonized postures, and the wounded, many of them with their hurts
yet untended, seemed to outnumber the unhit survivors, and while this
was true in the case of a dozen regiments under Longstreet — who afterwards computed his losses at 44 percent — it was of course an exaggeration in the main, proceeding from shock at the grisly scene. The fact was
that the two armies had suffered a combined total of nearly 35,000
casualties, and most of them were Bragg's. Though the Federals had
some 2500 more men killed and missing than the Confederates (6414, as
compared to 3780) the latter had about 5000 more wounded (9756 in
blue, 14,674 in gray) so that the butcher's bill, North and South, came to
16,170 and 18,454 respectively. The combined total of 34,624 was exceeded only by the three-day slaughter at Gettysburg and by the week-
long series of five battles known collectively as the Seven Days, in both
of which considerably larger numbers of troops had been engaged. In
all the other battles of the war so far — including Chancellorsville,

which lasted one day longer and also involved about 50,000 more troops — the losses had been less than at Chickamauga, where they were greater by about 10,000 than at Shiloh, Second Manassas, or Murfreesboro, the three next bloodiest two-day confrontations. These statistics could not yet be broken down in any such manner, being as yet unknown, but they were suggested plainly enough by a tour of the field and a talk with unit commanders along the way. Nine Confederate generals had been killed or wounded, as compared to only one in the Federal ranks, and the loss of artillery horses, as a result of fighting at such close quarters, had been so heavy as to cripple that vital arm. "In one place down in the woods," a soldier wrote of a walk he took that morning, "I counted sixteen big artillery horses lying in one heap. A little way off was another heap of twelve more. And that was the way it was all through there." Without horses, Bragg could not haul his guns, and without guns he did not believe that his men could force Rossville Gap or assault the prepared defenses between there and Chattanooga. "How can I?" he replied to urgings that he press northward without delay. "Here is two-fifths of my army left on the field, and my artillery is without horses." He still felt that way about it, some weeks later, when he touched on the matter in his official report of the campaign. "Any immediate pursuit by our infantry and artillery would have been fruitless," he declared, "as it was not deemed practicable with our weak and exhausted force to assail the enemy, now more than double our numbers, behind his intrenchments."

One who did not feel that way about it, then or later, was Bedford Forrest. Early that morning, pressing forward on his own with 400 troopers, the Tennessean charged an outpost detachment of Federals who fired one volley and fled so rapidly that their lookouts had no time to desend from an observation platform they had constructed in the top of a tree on the crest of Missionary Ridge. Forrest's horse had been struck, a large artery severed in its neck, but the general staunched the spurt of blood by thrusting a finger into the bullet hole and thus gave chase. Pulling rein at last beneath the improvised tower atop the ridge, he withdrew his finger and dismounted before the animal collapsed, then summoned his prisoners down from their high perch, questioned them sharply, and climbed up to see for himself what he could see. That he could see a great deal — including the blue army, feverishly active in his front, and the gray army, immobile in his rear — was shown by a dispatch he dictated to a staff officer on the ground:

> We are in a mile of Rossville. Have been on the point of Missionary Ridge. Can see Chattanooga and everything around. The enemy's trains are leaving, going around the point of Lookout Mountain.
> The prisoners captured report two pontoons thrown across [the Tennesee River] for the purpose of retreating.
> I think they are evacuating as hard as they can go.

They are cutting timber down to obstruct our passage.
I think we ought to press forward as rapidly as possible.

The message was addressed to Polk, commander of the nearer wing, and ended with the words, "Please forward to Genl Bragg." Anticipating the response he believed this information would provoke, Forrest continued his policy of "keeping up the scare" by penetrating to within three miles of Chattanooga from the south, meanwhile shifting his guns northward along the ridge to engage the batteries posted in close defense of the town below. All this time, according to one of his troopers, the general was "almost beside himself at the delay." Finally he learned that the infantry would not be coming as he had advised; Bragg was holding it east of Missionary Ridge and near the railroad, shifting Polk to Chickamauga Station and army headquarters to Ringgold Bridge, while Longstreet remained in position to police the field and wait for McLaws, who arrived in the late afternoon with the rest of his division. Nettled by what seemed to him flagrant neglect of an opportunity gained at the cost of much suffering and bloodshed, Forrest rode back to protest in person, only to be told that the army could not move far from the railroad because of its critical lack of supplies. "General Bragg, we can get all the supplies our army needs in Chattanooga," he replied. But this too was rejected: Bragg's mind was quite made up. Forrest returned to his men, exasperated and outdone. "What does he fight battles for?" he fumed.

That was Monday. On Tuesday, unmolested even by Forrest, whose handful of troopers had been recalled, Rosecrans completed the concentration of his army within the Chattanooga defenses, and Bragg ordered the occupation of Missionary Ridge and Lookout Mountain, as well as the establishment of a line of posts across the valley that lay between them. By Wednesday, September 23, the date of the autumnal equinox, all of these abandoned points had been seized, and the Federal works, which rose and thickened hour by hour as shovels flashed along the intrenched perimeter, were under long-range fire from the surrounding heights. Three courses of action — or, rather, two of action and one of inaction — were open to the Confederates. 1.) They could attempt to turn the bluecoats out of their position by crossing the river above or below the town, thus gaining their rear and breaking their tenuous supply line. 2.) They could leave a small force to observe the enemy trapped in Chattanooga, and move with the greater part of the army against Burnside, who would then be obliged to evacuate Knoxville or fight against long odds. 3.) They could concentrate on the present investment, hoping to starve the defenders into surrender. Longstreet favored a combination of the first two — "The hunt was up and on the go," he afterwards explained, "when any move toward [the enemy's] rear was safe, and a speedy one encouraging of great results" — but Bragg, much to Old Peter's disgust and over his vigorous objections, chose the third.

This was by no means as impractical as Longstreet seemed to think. By extending his left to include the crest of Raccoon Mountain, Bragg denied his adversary use of the rail and wagon roads not only on the south but also on the immediate north bank of the Tennessee, which lay well within reach of his high-sited batteries, and thus obliged Rosecrans to haul supplies from Stevenson and Bridgeport by a roundabout and barren route, first across the bridgeless Sequatchie River, then up and over Walden's Ridge, and finally down to the steamboat landing opposite Chattanooga, a distance of some sixty tortuous miles which would become increasingly difficult when the fall rains set in and the mud deepened. Unwilling to leave the harassment entirely to the elements, Bragg on September 30, one week after getting his infantry and artillery into their interdictory positions, ordered Wheeler over the river on a raid. The diminutive Alabamian crossed next morning near Muscle Shoals with 4000 cavalry and eight guns, and on the following day he intercepted a train of 400 heavily loaded wagons at Anderson's Crossroads, deep in the Sequatchie Valley. After burning the wagons and sabering the mules, he moved north to McMinnville, then west to Shelbyville, both of which he captured, together with their supply depots, which he destroyed. By now, though, the rains had come in earnest and he was involved in a running fight with superior blue forces that converged upon him from all directions. Repulsed at Murfreesboro, he turned back south, losing four of his guns and more than a thousand of his men before he recrossed the Tennessee near Rogersville on October 9. Despite his considerable success in the execution of his mission — a Union observer afterwards declared that the disruptive and destructive strike was nearly fatal to the army besieged in Chattanooga — the cost had been high, and Wheeler did not suggest that he attempt another such raid, deep in the enemy rear. Nor did Bragg require one of him, apparently being content to watch and wait.

The fact was, he had troubles enough with his own supply lines, unmolested though they were, without concerning himself unduly about those across the way. No matter how hungry the bluecoats might be getting, down in the town, his own troops were convinced that they themselves were hungrier on the heights. "In all the history of the war," a Tennessee infantryman was to write, "I cannot remember of more privation and hardships than we went through at Missionary Ridge. . . . The soldiers were starved and almost naked, and covered all over with lice and camp itch and filth and dirt. The men looked sick, hollow-eyed, and heart-broken, living principally upon parched corn which had been picked out of the mud and dirt under the feet of officers' horses." There was, as usual, much bitterness over Bragg's apparent reluctance to gather the fruits of a victory they had won, but this time it was intensified by resentment of his attempts to shift the blame to other shoulders than his own. Within two days of the battle, with the army at last on the march, Polk had received a stiff note demanding an explanation of why his attack had been delayed on the morning of the 20th, and when his reply reached headquarters on the last day of September, Bragg pronounced it "unsatisfactory" and relieved the bishop of his command. Hindman received the same treatment for his conduct earlier that month at McLemore's Cove, dispite his acknowledged contribution to the triumph that followed ten days later. Hill too came under fire from the army chieftain, who complained of his former lieutenant's "critical, captious, and dictatorial manner," as well as of his "want of prompt conformity to orders," and recommended to Richmond that he be suspended, like the others, from duty with the Army of Tennessee.

All three were incensed: particularly the two lieutenant generals, who in point of fact had taken care to register their protests beforehand, after a secret meeting on September 26 with Longstreet, who outranked them both. Intent on doing to Bragg what he was about to do to them — that is, accomplish his removal — they urged Old Peter to join them, in his semi-independent capacity, in complaining to Richmond of their commander's "palpable weakness and mismanagement manifested in the conduct of the military operations of this army." Polk wrote privately to his friend the President along these lines, though not in time to forestall the blow which he described as "part of [Bragg's] long-cherished purpose to avenge himself on me for the relief and support I have given him in the past. . . . The truth is, General Bragg has made a failure, notwithstanding the success of the battle, and he wants a scapegoat." Figuratively, but with dignity, the bishop gathered his robes about him for the train ride to Atlanta, where he was sent to await the disposition of his case. "I feel a lofty contempt for his puny effort to inflict injury upon a man who has dry-nursed him for the whole period of his connection with him, and has kept him from ruining the cause of the country by the sacrifice of its armies." So he complained in private, after the blow fell. But Longstreet had already made a stronger statement to the Secretary of War, adopting Prayer Book phraseology to add weight to his words. "Our chief has done but one thing that he ought to have done since I joined his army," Old Peter informed Seddon on the day of his meeting with Polk and Hill. "That was to order the attack upon the 20th. All other things that he has done he ought not to have done. I am convinced that nothing but the hand of God can save us or help us as long as we have our present commander."

Such was the unhappy state of affairs in the Army of Tennessee, the men hungry and disgruntled and the generals bitterly resentful, on the morrow of what Longstreet, in his letter to Richmond, called "the most complete victory of the war — except, perhaps, the first Manassas," he added, remembering past glory and gladder times.

Beyond the semicircular rim of earthworks, down in the town and off at the far end of the chain of command leading back to Washington, a scapegoat hunt was also under way. McCook and Crittenden had already been relieved, ostensibly for flight in time of danger, yet it had not escaped notice that the winner in the headlong race for safety was the man who consented to their removal. Stanton, for one, observed caustically that the two corps commanders had "made pretty good time away from the fight, but Rosecrans beat them both."

Moreover, the reverse had come in sudden and sharp contrast to expectations Old Rosy himself had aroused. "The army is in excellent condition and spirits," he had telegraphed soon after darkness ended the first day's fighting, "and by the blessing of Providence the defeat of the enemy will be total tomorrow." Lincoln did not like the sound of this, finding it reminiscent of Joe Hooker, and when he learned next evening that the army had been routed, he claimed to have foreseen such a turn of events. "Well, Rosecrans has been whipped, as I feared," he said. "I have feared it for several days. I believe I feel trouble in the air before it comes." Nor was the general's immediate reaction of a kind to encourage hope that he would make an early recovery from the setback. "We have met with a serious disaster," he notified Halleck soon after he reached Chattanooga; "extent not yet ascertained. Enemy overwhelmed us, drove our right, pierced our center, and scattered troops there." Despite his own gloom, which was heavy, Lincoln tried to lift the Ohioan's. "Be of good cheer," he wired him late that night. "We have unabated confidence in you and in your soldiers and officers. . . . We shall do our utmost to assist you. Send us your present posting." But the general, in his reply the following morning, gave no indication that he would attempt to stay in the town he had fallen back on. In fact, he expressed some doubt that he could do so, even if he tried: "Our loss is heavy and our troops worn down. . . . We have no certainty of holding our position here." Such irresolution was disturbing in a commander. What was more, when the President asked him next day to "relieve my anxiety as to the position and condition of your army," Rosecrans replied in effect that his faith was not so much in himself or his army as it was in Providence. "We are about 30,000 brave and determined men," he wired; "but our fate is in the hands of God, in whom I hope."

Lincoln soon emerged from his gloom. The important thing, as he saw it, was not that Rosecrans had been whipped at Chickamauga, but that he still held Chattanooga. As long as he did so, he could keep the Confederates out of Tennessee and also deny them use of one of their most important railroads. "If he can only maintain this position,

without [doing anything] more," the President told Halleck, "the rebellion can only eke out a short and feeble existence, as an animal sometimes may with a thorn in its vitals." By now, after three days' rest and
no pursuit, Rosecrans had recovered a measure of his resolution. "We
hold this point, and cannot be dislodged except by very superior numbers," he wired on September 23, although he made it clear that this depended on "having all reinforcements you can send hurried up." Lincoln had been doing his best in this respect, instructing Halleck to order
troops to Chattanooga from Vicksburg and Memphis, while he himself
undertook to prod Burnside into marching fast from Knoxville. When
Burnside replied that he was just then closing in on Jonesboro, which lay
in the opposite direction, the President lost his temper. "Damn Jonesboro," he said testily, and returned to his efforts to get the ruff-
whiskered general to swing west. This proved so difficult, however, that
he decided in the end to leave him where he was, covering Knoxville;
Rosecrans would have to be reinforced from elsewhere. And that same
night, September 23, Lincoln met with Stanton, Halleck, Chase, and
Seward, together with several lesser War Department officials, in an attempt to determine just where such reinforcements could be found.

Stanton, having heard that evening from Dana that the Army of
the Cumberland, outnumbered, dejected, and under fire from the heights
inclosing Chattanooga on the south and east, could not hold out for
more than a couple of weeks unless it was promptly and substantially reinforced, had called the midnight conference to suggest a solution to
the problem. Since Burnside apparently could not be budged, and since
the troops ordered from Vicksburg and Memphis would have to make
a slow overland march for lack of any means of transportation, the
Secretary proposed that Rosecrans be sent a sizable portion of the Army
of the Potomac, which could make the trip by rail. Lincoln and Halleck objected that this would prevent Meade from taking the offensive,
but Stanton replied: "There is no reason to expect General Meade will
attack Lee, although greatly superior in force, and his great numbers
where they are are useless. In five days 30,000 could be put with Rosecrans." The President doubted this last, offering to bet that no such number of men could even be brought to Washington within that span of time.
Still, it was clear that something had to be done, and when Seward and
Chase sided with their fellow cabinet member Lincoln allowed himself
to be persuaded. Unless Meade intended to launch an immediate offensive, two of his corps would be detached at once and sent to Chattanooga. These would be Howard's and Slocum's, and they would be commanded by Joe Hooker, who was conveniently at hand and unemployed.
Aside from this reduction of the force proposed and this choice of a
leader, which rather galled him, Stanton was given full charge of the
transfer operation, with instructions to arrange it as he saw fit. He flew
into action without delay. The meeting broke up at about 2 o'clock in

the morning, and at 2.30 he got off a wire to Meade, directing him to
have the two corps ready to load aboard northbound trains by nightfall,
and another to Dana, informing him that the reinforcements would be
sent. "[We] will have them in Nashville in five or six days from today,"
he declared, "with orders to push on immediately wherever General
Rosecrans wants them."

Telegrams were also sent — in fact had been sent beforehand, so
confident was the Secretary that the council would approve his plan —
to officials of three of the several railroads involved, requesting them to
"come to Washington as quickly as you can." By noon of the 24th they
were in Stanton's office, poring over maps and working out the logistical
details required for transporting four divisions, together with their guns
and wagons, from the eastern to the western theater, 1200 circuitous
miles across the intervening Alleghenies. Four changes of cars were
necessary, two at unbridged crossings of the Ohio, near Wheeling and
Louisville, and two more at Washington and Indianapolis, where there
were no connecting tracks between the roads that must be used. Hooker
was authorized to commandeer all the cars, locomotives, plants, and
equipment that he deemed necessary, but no such action had to be taken,
so complete was the co-operation of all the lines. Before sundown of
the following day, just forty-four hours after Dana's warning reached
the War Department, the first trainload of soldiers pulled into Washington from Culpeper, the point of origin down in Virginia. By the morning
of the 27th, two days later, 12,600 men, together with 33 cars of field
artillery and 21 of baggage, had passed through the capital, and at 10
o'clock that evening Stanton wired former Assistant Secretary Thomas
A. Scott, who had returned to his prewar duties with the Pennsylvania Railroad and was posted at Louisville to regulate the operation
west of the mountains: "The whole force, except 3300 of the XII Corps,
is now moving." Within another two days Scott reported trains pulling
regularly out of Louisville, and at 10.30 the following night — September 30 — the first eastern troops reached Bridgeport, precisely on the
schedule announced at the outset, six days back. By October 2, nearly
20,000 men, 10 six-gun batteries with their horses and ammunition, and
100 carloads of baggage had arrived at the Tennessee railhead. "Your
work is most brilliant," Stanton wired Scott. "A thousand thanks. It is a
great achievement."

It was indeed a great achievement, this swiftest of all the mass
movements of troops in history, and most of the credit belonged to the
Secretary of War, who had worked feverishly and efficiently to accomplish what many, including the Commander in Chief, had said could
not be done. Under his direction, the North had given its answer to the
South's strategic advantage of occupying the interior lines; for though
the Confederates had stolen a march and thereby managed, in Forrest's
phrase, to "get there first with the most men," the Federals had promptly

upped the ante by moving farther and faster with still more. In the final stages of the operation, Wheeler's raiders delayed some of the supply trains by tearing up sections of track, but all got through safely in the end. "You may justly claim the merit of having saved Chattanooga," Hooker wired Stanton on October 11, after posting his four divisions to prevent a rebel crossing below the town and a descent on the hungry garrison's rear. The Secretary was pleased to hear so, just as he had been pleased the week before at the evidence that he had been right in rejecting doleful objections that Lee would attack if Meade's army was weakened by any substantial detachment of troops to Rosecrans. " 'All quiet on the Potomac,' " he had informed the Chattanooga quartermaster on October 4. "Nothing to disturb autumnal slumbers. . . . All public interest is now concentrated on the Tennessee."

Bragg's complaint that the Federals had "more than double our numbers" was untrue in regard to the time he made it his excuse for not rapidly following up the advantage gained at Chickamauga. In fact, when McLaws arrived — with two of his own and one of Hood's brigades, plus the First Corps artillery, which soon was posted atop Lookout Mountain — the Confederates became numerically superior. But now that Hooker had crossed the Alleghenies with nearly 20,000 reinforcements, the situation was reversed. It was the besiegers who were outnumbered. This novel condition, rarely paralleled in military annals, was about to become more novel still; Sherman was on the way from Vicksburg, via Memphis, with another five divisions. Even when he reached Chattanooga, the Army of the Cumberland would not have "more than double" the number of troops in the Army of Tennessee, but it already had a considerable preponderance without him. Although there was still the menace of starvation — an Illinois private was complaining, tall-tale style, that since Chickamauga he and his comrades had eaten "but two meals a day, and one cracker for each meal" — Rosecrans at least could relax his fears that Bragg was going to drive him into the river with a sudden, downhill infantry assault. The rebels lacked the strength, and no one knew this better than their chief. A graver danger, so far as the northern commander was personally concerned, lurked at the far end of the telegraph wires linking his headquarters to those of his superiors in Washington. This applied in particular to the headquarters of the Secretary of War, whose original mistrust of his fellow Ohioan was being confirmed almost daily in the confidential reports he received from Dana, his special emissary on the scene.

Immediately after the battle, the former Brook Farmer had been glad to "testify to the conspicuous and steady gallantry of Rosecrans on the field"; he put the blame for the defeat on "that dangerous blunderhead McCook" and on Crittenden, whom he considered derelict and incompetent. Before the month was out, however, he had begun to sour on Old Rosy. "He abounds in friendliness and approbativeness," Dana wired on the 27th, "[but] is greatly lacking in firmness and steadiness of will. He is a temporizing man. . . . If it be decided to change the chief commander" — there had been no intimation that such a thing was being considered; Dana brought it up of his own accord — "I would take the liberty of suggesting that some Western general of high rank and great prestige, like Grant, for instance, would be preferable as his successor." Three days later he favored Thomas for the post, saying: "Should there be a change in the chief command, there is no other man whose appointment would be so welcome to this army." As for the present leader, Dana informed Stanton "that the soldiers have lost their attachment for [him] since he failed them in the battle, and that they do not now cheer him until they are ordered to do so." In the course of the next two weeks, the first two in October, the Assistant Secretary's conviction became even more pronounced in this regard. "I have never seen a public man possessing talent with less administrative power, less clearness and steadiness in difficulty, and greater practical incapacity than General Rosecrans. He has inventive fertility and knowledge, but he has no strength of will and no concentration of purpose. His mind scatters; there is no system in the use of his busy days and restless nights. . . . Under the present circumstances I consider this army to be very unsafe in his hands." Thus Dana, on the 12th. Six days later, after passing along a report that the soldiers were shouting "Crackers!" at staff officers who moved along them to inspect the fortifications, he added the finishing touches to his word portrait of a man in control of nothing, least of all himself: "Amid all this, the practical incapacity of the general commanding is astonishing, and it often seems difficult to believe him of sound mind. His imbecility appears to be contagious. . . . If the army is finally obliged to retreat, the probability is that it will fall back like a rabble, leaving its artillery, and protected only by the river behind it."

He might have spared himself and the telegrapher the labor of composing and transmitting this last in his series of depositions as to the general's unfitness for command; for by now, although he would not find it out until the following day, the purpose he intended had been achieved. Stanton had been passing his dispatches along to the Commander in Chief, who had found in them a ready confirmation of his own worst suspicions. Despite this, and because he had not yet decided on a replacement, Lincoln had continued his efforts to stiffen Old Rosy's resolution. On October 12, for instance, while Dana was observing the "scattered" condition of the Ohioan's mind, Lincoln wired: "You and Burnside now have [the enemy] by the throat, and he must break your hold or perish." Rosecrans replied that afternoon, complaining that the corn was ripe on the rebel side of the Tennessee, while "our side is barren." Nevertheless, and in spite of this evidence of divine displeasure, he closed by remarking, much as before, that "we must put our trust in God, who never fails those who truly trust." Commendable though such faith was, particularly after all the Job-like strain that had been placed on it of late, the President would have preferred to see it balanced by a measure of self-reliance. And not only did this quality appear to be totally lacking in the commander of the army now holed up in Chattanooga, but it had begun to seem to Lincoln that ever since Chickamauga, as he told his secretary, Rosecrans had been acting "confused and stunned, like a duck hit on the head."

Ridicule by the President was often the prelude to a general's dismissal, and this was no exception; Rosecrans was about to go, as Buell and McClellan had gone before him. But there was still the question of a successor to be settled before he went. Dana's recommendation of Thomas appealed to Lincoln, who had said of the Virginian shortly after the battle that earned him the sobriquet, "The Rock of Chickamauga": "It is doubtful whether his heroism and skill, exhibited last Sunday afternoon, has ever been surpassed in the world." Stanton felt much the same way about him. "It is not my fault that he was not in chief command months ago," he replied to Dana's observation that there was "no other man whose appointment would be so welcome to this army." However, there was also Grant, who had been comparatively idle since the fall of Vicksburg, fifteen weeks ago. This was plainly a waste the nation could ill afford. What was most desirable was some arrangement that would employ the full abilities of both, and it took Lincoln until mid-October to arrive at a solution that did just that.

The Center Gives

★ ✗ ☆

FOR GRANT, THE THREE-MONTH PERIOD THAT
followed the fall of Vicksburg — more specifically, the ninety days
that elapsed between Sherman's recapture of Jackson in mid-July and
Lincoln's mid-October solution to the western command problem —
had been a time of strain not unlike the one that followed Shiloh and the
occupation of Corinth the year before, in which his counsel was rejected
and he felt himself to be more or less a supernumerary in the conduct
of the war. Now as then, he saw his army dismembered and dispersed,
its various segments dispatched to critical theaters, while he himself was
confined with the mere remnant to the quiet backwater which he had
created along his particular stretch of the Mississippi. He did not consider submitting his resignation, as he had done before, but he suffered,
as the result of a horseback accident midway of this season of frustration, an injury which for a term seemed likely to produce the same effect by removing him entirely from the scene, flat on his back on a
stretcher. It was indeed a period of tension, of strain of the kind he had
always borne least well, and it was attended, as all such times had been
for him, by rumors of his drinking, which was said to be his only relief
from the boredom that invariably descended when there was no fighting
to be done and his wife was not around.

Not, of course, that he and the troops who remained with him
had been completely idle all this time. While Herron was conducting his
foray up the Yazoo, which had cost Porter the *De Kalb*, and Sherman
was closing in on Jackson, the price of which was to run him just over
1100 casualties, Grant sent one of McPherson's brigades down to
Natchez to look into a report that there was heavy rebel traffic there in
goods moving to and from the otherwise cut-off Transmississippi.
Brigadier General T. E. G. Ransom, who commanded the expedition,
found the report to be altogether true. Moreover, by sending mounted
pursuers east and west he made the simultaneous capture of a wagon

train bound for Alexandria with half a million rounds of rifle and artillery ammunition and a drove of 5000 Texas cattle bound for Alabama, both of which had crossed the river the day before, headed in opposite directions. This was a sizable haul, achieved without the loss of a man, and one month later, at nearly as cheap a price, Grant made a considerably larger one at Grenada, the railroad junction south of the Yalobusha where the Confederates had collected most of the rolling stock of the Mississippi Central, trapped there since May by Johnson's precipitate burning of the bridge across the Pearl when he evacuated Jackson. The raid was two-pronged, one cavalry column sent south from Memphis by Hurlbut while another was sent north by Sherman. On August 17 they converged upon the junction, which so far had resisted all efforts to take it — including Grant's, back in December — and after a brief skirmish with the outnumbered garrison, which fled to avoid capture, went to work on the huge conglomeration of engines and cars "so closely packed as to make a small town of themselves." An elated trooper described them so, and afterwards the official tally listed no fewer than 57 locomotives and more than 400 freight and passenger cars wrecked and burned, together with depot buildings and machine shops containing a wealth of commissary and ordnance supplies. The total bill of destruction was set at $4,000,000, which made the raid one of the most profitable of the war. Presently, however, this figure had to be scaled down a bit. Learning that the Confederates had returned to Grenada in the wake of the departed bluecoats and were frugally carting away the precious locomotive driving wheels, removed from the rubble and ashes, Hurlbut advised in his report that, next time they went out on such a venture, the raiders use sledges to crack off the flanges of the wheels and thus render them unsalvageable.

Both Natchez and Grenada were satisfactory accomplishments, so far as they went, but after all they were only raids. Grant wanted something more: something comparable, in its influence on the outcome of the war, to the recent reduction of Vicksburg and the attendant opening of the Mississippi: something, in short, that would knock the flanges off the whole Confederate machine. Banks had suggested, soon after the fall of Port Hudson, an operation against Mobile, and so had Sherman, who proposed that the coastal city be taken as prelude to an advance up the Alabama River to Selma and beyond, threatening Bragg's rear while Rosecrans, who had maneuvered his adversary back across the Tennessee, brought pressure against his front. Grant approved and passed the word to Halleck. "It seems to me now that Mobile should be captured," he wired on July 18, "the expedition starting from some point on Lake Pontchartrain." Halleck replied that the plan had merit, but added characteristically that it would not do to hurry. "I think it will be best to clean up a little," he advised. "Johnston should be disposed of; also Price, Marmaduke, &c., so as to hold the line of the Arkansas River . . .

[and] assist General Banks in cleaning out Western Louisiana. When these things are accomplished there will be a large available force to operate either on Mobile or Texas." Just when this would be he did not say. Banks meanwhile had continued to recommend the same objective, though with no better success, and on the last day of the month he left New Orleans aboard a fast packet to confer with Grant at Vicksburg, which he reached the following morning. After putting their heads together both generals continued to urge Halleck to order the reduction of the Confederacy's only remaining Gulf port east of the Mississippi. "I can send the necessary force," Grant offered. Whereupon the general-in-chief suddenly cut the ground from under their feet by flatly rejecting the Mobile proposal in favor of an all-out effort against coastal Texas. "There are important reasons why our flag should be restored to some part of Texas with the least possible delay," he wired on August 6. He did not say what those reasons were, but three days later Lincoln himself got in touch with Grant on the matter. "I see by a dispatch of yours that you incline strongly toward an expedition against Mobile," he wrote. "This would appear tempting to me also, were it not that, in view of recent events in Mexico, I am greatly impressed with the importance of re-establishing the national authority in Western Texas as soon as possible."

Personally considerate though this was, it was not very enlightening; nor was Halleck's explanation, which he made in a covering letter to Banks, that the decision in favor of a Lone Star expedition had been "of a diplomatic rather than of a military character, and resulted from some European complications, or, more properly speaking, was intended to prevent such complications." In point of fact, the matter was more complex than anyone outside the State Department knew, including Old Brains himself, who was a student of international affairs. Benito Juárez, elected head of the Mexican government in the spring of 1861, coincident with the crisis over Sumter, had announced at the time of First Bull Run a two-year suspension of payments to foreign creditors for debts contracted by his predecessor; in response to which Spain, France, and England concluded a convention looking toward a forcible joint collection of their claims and sent some 10,000 troops to Mexico by way of proof that they meant business. By May of the following year, in the period between Shiloh and the Seven Days, while Stonewall Jackson was on the rampage in the Shenandoah Valley, England and Spain had obtained satisfaction from Juárez on the debt, and they withdrew their soldiers. France did not; Napoleon III, attracted by Mexico's wealth and weakness, had plans designed to rival in the New World those of his illustrious uncle in the Old. He stepped up his demands, including insistence on indemnity and payment of certain shady claims advanced by Swiss-French bankers, rapidly increased his occupation force to 35,000 men, and began a march inland from Vera Cruz and Tampico, which was resisted fitfully and ineffectually by guerillas operating much as they had done against Cortez and Winfield Scott, over the same route of conquest. In June of 1863, with Lee on the march for Pennsylvania and Vicksburg under siege, Mexico City fell to the invaders and a pro-French government was set up.

Such was the situation Lincoln faced when Banks and Grant proposed the Mobile expedition the following month. Entirely aside from the violation of the Monroe Doctrine, which he was willing to overlook until the present larger troubles on his hands were cleared away, he knew only too well the pro-Confederate sympathies Napoleon embraced for his own reasons. If foreign intervention came, as the Emperor had been urging for the past two years, Lincoln wanted to be ready to defend the line of the Rio Grande against the imperial forces now in occupation of the capital to the south. That, in brief, was why Mobile had gone by the board; he wanted Union troops in Texas, where none now were, and he did not believe that Banks and Grant were strong enough to accomplish both objectives at the same time. Banks was down to about 12,000 men, the enlistment period of no fewer than twenty-two of his nine-month regiments having expired since the fall of Port Hudson, and the borrowed segments of the army Grant commanded in the taking of Vicksburg were needed now by the generals who had lent them—Burnside in East Tennessee, for instance, Prentiss in Northeast Arkansas, and Schofield in guerilla-torn Missouri — as well as by Rosecrans, who claimed that a farther advance against Bragg was dependent, among other things, on reinforcements being sent him from the army lying idle in Mississippi. "On this matter," Halleck summed up in a wire to Banks on August 12, "we have no choice, but must carry out the views of the Government."

Grant was disappointed, having been convinced that the taking of Mobile, followed by a drive northward into the Confederate heartland to dispose of Bragg and put the squeeze on Lee, would have shortened the war by months — or even years, if that was what it came to — but he accepted the rejection of his counsel in good part, aware that the command decision was based on considerations beyond his ken. In any event there was little he could do about it now, even if the decision were reversed. The dismemberment of his army had begun, and it proceeded with such rapidity that within one month, mid-August to mid-September, his strength was reduced from better than five corps to less than two. Parke's IX Corps left first, dispatched to Burnside, who was marking time in Kentucky. Then Steele's division of Sherman's XV Corps was sent to Helena for the offensive against Price, followed by J. E. Smith's division of McPherson's XVII Corps. Washburn's XVI Corps also returned upriver, one division continuing on to strengthen Schofield in Missouri, while the other two debarked at Memphis to rejoin Hurlbut. Meantime, in order to beef up Banks for the top-priority Texas undertaking, Ord's XIII Corps, with Herron's division attached, proceeded downriver to New Orleans, the staging area for the drive that was intended to secure the line of the Rio Grande against Napoleon's new world dream of conquest and expansion. All that remained by then at Vicksburg were the two reduced corps of Sherman and McPherson. They were quite enough, however, in consideration of the fact that there was practically nothing left for them to do. And now there began for Grant, who was otherwise unemployed, what might be called a social interlude, a time of unfamiliar relaxation and apparent gladness, though it ended all too abruptly with the general confined to a bed of pain in a New Orleans hotel room.

He had a good deal to be glad about at the outset, both for his own sake and his friends'. His appointment as a regular army major general had lifted him almost to Halleck's level as one of the only two men of that rank on active duty. Nor had the government delayed approval of his suggestion that Sherman and McPherson be made regular brigadiers, the reward that had gone to Meade for Gettysburg. Thanks to him, moreover, seven of his colonels now wore stars on their shoulder straps, and so did Rawlins, who was jumped from lieutenant colonel to brigadier general at his chief's solicitation. "He comes the nearest being indispensable to me of any officer in the service," Grant had said of his fellow townsman in the letter of recommendation, and he added, though he must have been aware that this was spreading it rather thick: "I can safely say that he would make a good corps commander." In addition to official recognition, which included the unprecedented You-were-right-I-was-wrong letter from the President, he soon was given cause to know how much his latest victory had raised him in the public's estimation. On August 26 he attended in Memphis the first of many banquets that would be tendered in his honor over the course of the next twenty years. In front of his place at table in the Gayoso House there was a pyramid inscribed with the names of all his battles, beginning with Belmont, and he was presented to the two hundred guests with the toast, "Your Grant and my Grant," in which his reopening of the Mississippi to commerce was compared to the exploits of two other heroes much admired along the river that ran past Memphis, Hernando de Soto and Robert Fulton. He responded with an attractively awkward speech of two brief sentences, thanking the citizens for their kindness and promising to do all he could for their prosperity, then sat down amid loud, prolonged applause. Three days later, after stopping off at Vicksburg for a quick inspection of headquarters, he was in Natchez, where he found the wealthy planters entirely co-operative in their concern for the survival of their fine mansions on the bluff. Proceeding downriver to pay Banks a return visit, he reached New Orleans on September 2.

Banks knew how to entertain a guest; moreover he had all the resources of a high-living Creole society at his disposal. Two days later he staged a grand review at nearby Carrollton in honor of his visitor, who, mounted on a spirited charger procured for him on this occasion as a tribute to his horsemanship, watched Ord's veterans swing past with the names of their and his recent upriver victories on their banners. It was a stirring moment for them and him, a last reunion before they set off for new fields; but the day was grievously marred before it ended. Returning from the suburb to the heart of the city, Grant's borrowed mount shied at a hissing locomotive and, bolting, collided with a carriage that was coming from the opposite direction. Horse and rider went down hard. The animal rose from the cobblestones unassisted, but not Grant, who had suffered a badly dislocated hip, as well as a possible fracture of the skull, and was unconscious; in which condition he was carried on a litter to the nearby St Charles Hotel. Almost at once the story that he had been drinking began to make the rounds, gathering details as it went. Years later William Franklin, who had been transferred from the East to command a corps on the Texas expedition, testified in private that he "*saw* Grant tumble from his horse drunk." It even began to be said that the fall had occurred in the course of the review, which had been brought thereby to an unceremonious end, and that the general had been knocked out not so much by the blow on his head as by the whiskey in his stomach. Grant knew nothing of this at the time, nor indeed of anything else. In fact, the first he knew of having been hurt was when he regained consciousness, somewhat later, to find "several doctors" hovering over him. "My leg was swollen from the knee to the thigh," he afterwards wrote, "and the swelling, almost to the point of bursting, extended along the body up to the armpit. The pain was almost beyond endurance. I lay at the hotel something over a week without being able to turn myself in bed."

★ ★ ★

While Grant was laid up, confined to a world of pain whose limits were described by the four walls of his hotel room, Banks opened the campaign designed to carry out the instructions of his superiors to restore the flag of the Union "to some part of Texas with the least possible delay." As it turned out, however, he encountered something worse than delay in the execution of his plans, the first results of which were about as abruptly disastrous as his fellow general's fall on horseback, drunk or sober.

Halleck had advised an amphibious movement "up Red River to Alexandria, Natchitoches, or Shreveport, and the military occupation of northern Texas. . . . Nevertheless," he added, "your choice is left unrestricted." Banks replied with numerous logistical objections, not the least of which was that the Red was nearly dry at this season of the year. He favored a sudden descent on the coast, specifically at Sabine Pass, to be followed by an overland march on Galveston and other points beyond.

Accordingly, having been given his choice, he ordered Franklin to load a reinforced division onto transports and proceed to Sabine Pass, where he would rendezvous with a four-gunboat assault force. The rebel defenses were said to be weak, despite the reverse the navy had suffered here in January; once these had been subdued by the warships, Franklin was to put his troops ashore and move inland to the Texas & New Orleans Railroad, linking Houston and Beaumont and Orange, and there await the arrival of the balance of his corps, which by then would have been brought forward by the unloaded transports. It was all worked out in careful detail, and on September 7, three days after Grant's accident, Franklin arrived before the pass and was joined that evening by the gunboat flotilla under Lieutenant Frederick Crocker, U.S.N. Fort Griffin, the rebel work protecting Sabine City, mounted half a dozen light guns and was garrisoned by less than fifty men; Crocker attacked it the following afternoon, having six times the number of heavier guns in his four warships. The engagement was brief and decisive. Within half an hour one gunboat was hit in the boiler, losing all her steam, and a few minutes later a second ran aground in the shallow bay and was given the same treatment by the marksmen in the fort. Both vessels struck their colors, surrendering with their crews of about 300 men, including 50 killed or wounded and the luckless lieutenant in command, while the third retired out of range with the fourth, which had not engaged. Still aboard the transports with his soldiers, whom the navy was unable to put ashore, Franklin felt there was nothing to do but turn around and go back to New Orleans, and that was what he did, reporting a total loss of six men, who had been aboard the surrendered gunboats as observers, together with 200,000 rations thrown overboard to lighten a grounded transport and 200 mules served likewise when the steamer on which they were loaded lost her stack in a heavy sea on the way home.

So feeble had the attack been that Magruder at first could not believe it was anything more than a feint, designed to distract his attention from the main effort somewhere else along the coast. When no such blow was delivered in the course of the next few days, Prince John contented himself with what had been accomplished; a "brilliant victory," he called the fight, a "gallant achievement," and finally, in an excess of pride at what his gunners had done in the face of long odds, "the most extraordinary feat of the war." Congress eventually passed a resolution of thanks, "eminently due, and hereby cordially given," to the two officers and the 41 men of the garrison who had stood to their outranged guns and outfought the Yankee warships.

On the other hand, Banks assigned the reason for the failure to the "ignorance" of the naval officers involved; one of his chief regrets, no doubt, was that Farragut was not around to blister them a bit, having returned to New York for badly overdue repairs to his flagship *Hartford* in the Brooklyn Navy Yard. In any case, on Franklin's return the Massachusetts general decided that the line of advance up the Red to North-east Texas, suggested previously by Old Brains, was probably the best invasion route after all, and he informed Lincoln that while the army was "preparing itself" for the execution of this larger plan, which would have to be delayed until rain had swelled the river, he would continue his efforts to move in directly from the Gulf against the Lone Star beaches — or, anyhow, some beach; for he left himself plenty of latitude as to just where he would strike next time, merely remarking that he proposed "to attempt a lodgment upon some point on the coast from the mouth of the Mississippi to the Rio Grande."

By then the year was well into October, and two other Federal commanders in the Transmississippi region, James Blunt and John Scho-field, had unexpected problems on their hands in the departments of the Frontier and Missouri. William Steele and Pap Price had been driven from Fort Smith and Little Rock, the former deep into Indian Territory and the latter beyond the line of the Arkansas. Schofield could breathe easier; so he thought — until Jo Shelby came riding northward, all the way to the Missouri River, and Quantrill, while crossing the southeast corner of Kansas on his way to winter in Texas, gave Blunt an oppor-tune demonstration that he had a talent for something more than mur-dering civilians in or under their beds.

From Arkadelphia, where he ended his retreat in mid-September, Price launched Shelby on a raid into his home state, hoping thus to dis-courage Schofield from reinforcing Fred Steele for a follow-up push from the Arkansas River to the Ouachita. Three months short of his thirty-third birthday, the Missouri cavalryman was still a colonel despite outstanding service in practically every major engagement fought in the region since Wilson's Creek; even now he was nursing an unhealed wound he had suffered in his sword arm during the Helena repulse, twelve weeks ago. Though, like Jeb Stuart, he took his nickname from his initials and wore a foot-long plume on his hat, there was a hard, practical core to his daring, a concentration more on results than on ef-fect, which afterwards caused Alfred Pleasonton, who rode for three years against Stuart before transferring to the far western theater — al-though it perhaps should be noted in passing that he never came up against Forrest — to say flatly, after a year of fighting there as well, that "Shelby was the best cavalry general of the South." Part of the evidence in support of this contention was put on record during the present raid, which lasted longer and covered a greater distance than any under-taken by any body of horsemen from either army in the whole course of the war, including Morgan's famous raid into Ohio, which ended in dis-aster, whereas Shelby returned with a stronger force than he had had at the outset. He set out with 600 troopers on September 22, passing next day through Caddo Gap, forty miles northwest of Arkadelphia, and five days later crossed the Arkansas River a hundred miles above Little Rock, midway between Clarksville and Fort Smith. Riding north through Huntsville and Bentonville, he crossed the state line to reach Neosho on October 4 and promptly forced the surrender of 400 Union cavalry who had holed up in the stout brick courthouse, former capitol of the short-lived Confederate-allied Republic of Missouri, which the bluecoats had converted into a fort and were determined to hold, at any rate until the rebel cannon started knocking it to pieces. Along with the men, the victors took their horses, their fine Sharps rifles and navy revolvers, and their clothes, which were used as an effective disguise, so far at least as they went round, by the former gray-clad raiders. Next day the ride north continued, still with the stockily built and heavily bearded colonel in the lead.

His goal was Jefferson City; he had it in mind to raise the Stars and Bars over the statehouse, not only as a sign that Missouri was by no means "conquered," but also as a gesture to discourage the Union high command from detaching troops from here to exploit its recent gains in Arkansas or to shore up Rosecrans, who had been whipped two weeks ago at Chickamauga and now was under siege in Chattanooga; in furtherance of which intention Shelby sent out parties, left and right of his line of march, to cut telegraph wires, burn installations and depots of supply, attack outlying strong points, and in general spread confusion as to his strength and destination. On north he rode, through Sarcoxie and Bowers Mill, Greenfield and Stockton, Humansville and Warsaw, to Tipton on the Missouri Pacific, which he struck on October 10. Jefferson City was less than forty miles away, due east on the railroad, but his enemies were thoroughly aroused by now, expecting him to move in that direction. Instead, after tearing up track on both sides of Tipton, burning the depot, and setting fire to a large yard of freight cars, he pressed on north to Booneville, where he was greeted next day by the mayor and a delegation of citizens who came out to assure him of their southern loyalty and ask that he spare their property. This he did, except for the new $400,000 bridge across the nearby Lamine River, which he wrecked. "Now the broad bosom of the grand old Missouri lay unveiled before us in the red beams of the autumn sun," his adjutant later wrote, "and the men, forgetting all their privations and dangers, broke out in one long, loud, proud hurrah." The hurrah could indeed have been a loud one, for Shelby's strength had grown by now to more than a thousand troopers by the addition of recruits who had flocked to join him on the way. Moreover, the column was lengthened by three hundred captured wagons, drawn not by mules or draft horses, but by the hundreds of cavalry mounts he had taken in the series of surrenders that had marked his line of march, surrenders or flights which had netted him no fewer than forty stands of colors and ten "forts" of one kind or another. If the blue-clad graybacks cheered themselves hoarse with pride as they stood on the south bank of the wide Missouri, just under four hundred air-line miles from the nearest Confederate outpost, it was not without reason.

Their problem now was escape from the greatly superior Federal columns rapidly converging on them from the south and east and north. Shelby led them west along the south bank of the Missouri, in the direction of his prewar home at Waverly. Before they got there, however, they had their one full-scale engagement of the raid, October 13 near Arrow Rock, where the enemy columns finally brought them to bay, outnumbered five to one. Splitting his command in two, Shelby dismounted the larger half and fought a savage defensive action in which he lost about one hundred men while the smaller half made a mounted getaway by punching a hole in the line of the attackers; whereupon he remounted the remainder and did the same at another point, taking a different escape route to confuse and split his pursuers. On through Waverly he rode that night, still accompanied by his train, which he had brought out with him. At nearby Hawkins Mill, however, he was later to report, "finding my wagons troublesome, and having no ammunition left except what the men could carry, I sunk them in the Missouri River, where they were safe from all capture." This done he turned south. Bypassing Lexington, Harrisonville, and Butler to skirt the Burnt District, he reached Carthage on October 17 and turned east next day through Sarcoxie, which he had visited two weeks before, on his way north. Laying ambushes all the while to delay pursuers, he re-entered Arkansas on October 19 and was joined next day on the Little Osage River by the smaller force that had split off at Arrow Rock a week ago. From the Little Osage he moved by what he called "easy stages" to Clarksville, where he recrossed the Arkansas River on October 26 and made his way south through the Ouachita Mountains to Washington. There at last he called a halt, November 3, forty miles southwest of his starting point at Arkadelphia. In the forty-one days he had been gone he had covered a distance of 1500 miles, an average of better than thirty-six miles a day, and though he had suffered a total loss of about 150 killed and wounded, he had also picked up 800 recruits along the way, so that he returned with twice the number of men he had had when he set out. He listed his gains — 600 Federals killed or wounded, 500 captured and paroled; 6000 horses and mules taken, together with 300 wagons, 1200 small arms, and 40 stands of colors; $1,000,000 in U. S. Army supplies destroyed, plus $800,000 in public property — then laconically closed his report, which was addressed to Price's adjutant: "Hoping this may prove satisfactory, I remain, major, very respectfully, your obedient servant, Jo. O. Shelby, Colonel." Highly pleased — as well it might be; for there was also substance to his claim that the raid had kept 10,000 Missouri bluecoats from being sent to assist in raising the siege at Chattanooga — the government promoted him to brigadier the following month.

Quantrill by now was calling himself a colonel, too, and had even

acquired a uniform in which he had his picture taken wearing three stars
on the collar, a long-necked young man with hooded eyes, a smooth
round jaw, and a smile as faint as Mona Lisa's. But the government —
much to its credit, most historians were to say — declined to sanction
his self-promotion, even after he scored a second victory in Kansas,
one far more impressive, militarily, than the first, which he had scored
six weeks before at Lawrence. While Shelby was preparing to set out
from Arkadelphia, Quantrill was reassembling his guerillas on familiar
Blackwater Creek, intending to take them to Texas for the winter. In
early October the two columns passed each other, east and west of Carthage, Shelby and his 600 going north, Quantrill with about 400 going
south, neither aware of the other's presence, some twenty miles away.
On October 6, when the former passed through Warsaw, the latter drew
near Fort Baxter, down in the southeast corner of Kansas at Baxter
Springs, which was held by two companies of Wisconsin cavalry and
one of Kansas infantry. Quantrill decided to take it. While the attack
was in progress, however, he learned that a train of ten wagons was approaching from the north, attended by two more companies of Wisconsin and Kansas troops; so he pulled back half his men, and went to take
that too. His luck was in. The train and troops were the baggage and escort of James Blunt, lately appointed commander of the District of the
Frontier, on his way to establish headquarters at Fort Baxter. When Blunt
saw the horsemen in line across the road ahead, he assumed they were an
honor guard sent out from the fort to meet him. He halted to have his
escort dress its ranks, then proceeded at a dignified pace to receive the
salute of the waiting line of horsemen.

He received instead a blast of fire at sixty yards, followed
promptly by a screaming charge that threw his hundred-man escort first
into milling confusion and then, when they recognized what they were
up against — the guerillas, having been warned to expect no quarter,
certainly would extend none — into headlong flight. This last availed all
but a handful of them nothing; 79 of the hundred were quickly run
down and killed, including Major Henry Curtis, Blunt's adjutant and the
son of the former department commander. Blunt himself made his escape, though he was nearly unhorsed in taking a jump across a ravine.
Thrown from his saddle and onto his horse's neck by the rebound, he
clung there and rode in that unorthodox position for a mile or more, out-
distancing his pursuers, who turned back to attend to the business of dis-
patching the prisoners and the wounded. Quantrill called off the attack
on the fort — its garrison had suffered 19 casualties to bring the Federal
total to 98, as compared to 6 for the guerillas — and proceeded to rifle
the abandoned wagons. Included in the loot was all of Blunt's official
correspondence, his dress sword, two stands of colors, and several demi-
johns of whiskey. Quantrill was so pleased with his exploit that he even
took a drink or two, something none of his companions had seen him do

before. Presently he became talkative, which was also quite unusual. "By God," he boasted as he staggered about, "Shelby couldn't whip Blunt; neither could Marmaduke; but *I* whipped him." He went on south to Texas, as he had intended when he left Johnson County the week before, and Blunt was removed not long thereafter from the command he had so recently acquired.

But Holmes and Price, reduced by sickness and desertion to a force of 7000, had not been greatly helped by either Shelby or Quantrill; Steele still threatened from Little Rock, and though he had not been reinforced, he outnumbered them two to one. On October 25, the day before Shelby recrossed the Arkansas River on his way back from Missouri, Holmes ordered a withdrawal of the troops left at Pine Bluff, thus loosening his last tenuous grasp on the south bank of that stream in order to prepare for what Kirby Smith believed was threatening, deep in his rear: Banks had begun another ascent of the Teche and the Atchafalaya, which could take him at last to the Red and into Texas. Once this happened, Smith's command, already cut off from the powder mills and ironworks of the East, would be cut off from the flow of goods coming in through Mexico. "The Fabian policy is now our true policy," he declared, and he advised that if further retreat became necessary, Holmes could move "by Monticello, along Bayou Bartholomew to Monroe, through a country abundant in supplies."

★　★　★

Grant by then had left for other fields. In mid-September, after ten days of confinement to the New Orleans hotel room, unable even to sit up in bed, he had himself carried aboard a steamboat bound for Vicksburg, and there, although as he said later he "remained unable to move for some time afterwards," he was reunited with his wife and their four children, who came down to join him in a pleasant, well-shaded house which his staff had commandeered for him on the bluff overlooking the river. Under these circumstances, satisfying as they were to his uxorious nature, his convalescence was so comparatively rapid that within a month he was hobbling about on crutches.

McPherson kept bachelor quarters in town, boarding with a family in which, according to Sherman, there were "several interesting young ladies." Not that his fellow Ohioan had neglected his own comfort. Like Grant, Sherman had his family with him — it too included four children — camped in a fine old grove of oaks beside the Big Black River, near the house from whose gallery, several weeks ago, the dozen weeping women had reviled him for the death of one of their husbands at Bull Run. He had been discomfited then, but that was all behind him now, together with his doubts about the war and his share in it. Grant had given his restless spirit a sense of direction and dedication; he could even abide the present idleness, feeling that he and his troops had earned a decent period of rest. "The time passed very agreeably," he would recall years later, "diversified only by little events of not much significance." That he was in favor of vigorous efforts at an early date, however, was shown in a letter he wrote Halleck on September 17 — the day after Grant's return from New Orleans — in response to one from the general-in-chief requesting his opinions as to "the question of reconstruction in Louisiana, Mississippi, and Arkansas. . . . Write me your views fully," Halleck urged him, "as I may wish to use them with the President."

Never one to require much encouragement for an exposition of his views, the red-haired general replied with a letter that was to fill eight close-spaced pages in his memoirs. He had done considerable thinking along these lines, based on his experiences in the region before and during the war, and if by "reconstruction" Halleck meant a revival of "any civil government in which the local people have much say," then Sherman was against it. "I know them well, and the very impulses of their nature," he declared, "and to deal with the inhabitants of that part of the South which borders on the great river, we must recognize the classes into which they have divided themselves." First, there were the planters. "They are educated, wealthy, and easily approached. . . . I know we can manage this class, but only by *action*," by "pure military rule." Second were "the smaller farmers, mechanics, merchants, and laborers. . . . The southern politicians, who understand this class, use them as the French do their masses — seemingly consult their prejudices, while they make their orders and enforce them. We should do the same." Third, there were "the Union men of the South. I must confess that I have little respect for this class. . . . I account them as nothing in this great game of war." Fourth and last, he narrowed his sights on "the young bloods of the South: sons of planters, lawyers-about-town, good billiard players and sportsmen, men who never did work and never will. War suits them, and the rascals are brave, fine riders, bold to rashness, and dangerous subjects in every sense. They care not a sou for niggers, land, or any thing." His solution to the problem they posed as "the most dangerous set of men that this war has turned loose upon the world" was easily stated: "These men must all be killed or employed by us before we can hope for peace." Just how they were to be employed by the government they were fighting Sherman did not say, but having sketched the various classes to be dealt with, he proceeded to give his prescription for victory over them all. "I would banish all minor questions, assert the broad doctrine that as a nation the United States has the right, and also the physical power, to penetrate to every part of our national domain, and that we will do it — that we will do it in our own time and in our own way; that it makes no difference whether it be in one year, or two, or ten, or twenty; that we will remove and destroy every obstacle, if need be, take every life, every acre of land, every particle of property, everything that to us seems proper; that we will not cease till the end is attained; that all who do not aid us are enemies, and that we will not account to them for our acts." Lest there be any misunderstanding, he summed up what he meant. "I would not coax them, or even meet them half way, but make them so sick of war that generations would pass away before they would again appeal to it. . . . The only government needed or deserved by the States of Louisiana, Arkansas, and Mississippi now exists in Grant's army." He closed by asking Halleck to "excuse so long a letter," but in sending it to Grant for forwarding to Washington, he appended a note in which he added: "I would make this war as severe as possible, and show no symptoms of tiring till the South begs for mercy. . . . The South has done her worst, and now is the time for us to pile on our blows thick and fast."

Halleck presently wired that Lincoln had read the letter and wanted to see it published, but Sherman declined, preferring "not to be drawn into any newspaper controversy" such as the one two years ago, in which he had been pronounced insane. "If I covet any public reputation," he replied, "it is as a silent actor. I dislike to see my name in print." Anyhow, by then he was on the move again; his troops had "slung the knapsack for new fields," and he himself had experienced a personal tragedy as deep as any he was ever to know in a long life.

Rosecrans had been whipped at Chickamauga while Sherman's letter was on its way north, and before it got to Washington the wires were humming with calls for reinforcements to relieve Old Rosy's cooped-up army. On September 23 Grant passed the word for Sherman to leave at once for Memphis with two divisions, picking up en route the division McPherson had recently sent to Helena, and move toward Chattanooga via Corinth on the Memphis & Charleston Railroad, which he was to repair as he went, thus providing a new supply line. Drums rolled in the camps on the Big Black; for the next four days the roads to Vicksburg were crowded with columns filing onto transports at the wharf. The steamer *Atlantic* was the last to leave, and on it rode Sherman and his family. He was showing the two girls and the two boys his old camp as the boat passed Young's Point, when he noticed that nine-year-old Willy, his first-born son and namesake — "that child on whose future I based all the ambition I ever had" — was pale and feverish. Regimental surgeons, summoned from below deck, diagnosed the trouble as typhoid and warned that it might be fatal. It was. Taken ashore at Memphis, the boy died in the Gayoso House, where Grant's banquet had been staged five weeks ago. Sherman was disconsolate, though he kept busy attending to details involved in the eastward movement while his wife and the three remaining children went on north to St Louis with the dead boy in a sealed metallic casket. "Sleeping, waking, everywhere I see poor Willy," he wrote her, and he added: "I will try to make poor Willy's memory the cure for the defects which have sullied my character — all that is captious, eccentric and wrong."

His grief seemed rather to deepen than to lift. A week after his son's death he was asking, "Why was I not killed at Vicksburg and left Willy to grow up and care for you?" By that time, though, his troops were all in motion, some by rail and some on foot, and on October 11 he started for Corinth aboard a train that carried his staff and a battalion of regulars. At Collierville, twenty miles out of Memphis, the train and depot, which had been turned into a blockhouse and surrounded by shallow trenches, were attacked by rebel cavalry under Chalmers, an old Shiloh adversary, whose strength he estimated at 3000. He himself had fewer than 600 and no guns, whereas the raiders had four. To gain time, he received and after some discussion declined a flag-of-truce demand for unconditional surrender, meanwhile disposing his few troops for defense and sending a wire for hurry-up assistance. The fight that followed lasted four hours, at the end of which time the rebels withdrew to avoid contact with a division marching eastward in response to the wire that, after the manner of light fiction, had got through just before the line was cut. Though it had not really been much of a fight, as such things went at this stage of the war — he had lost 14 killed, 42 wounded, and 54 captured, while Chalmers had lost 3 killed and 48 wounded — Sherman was tremendously set up. Five staff horses had been taken, including his favorite mare Dolly, and the graybacks had also confiscated his second-best uniform, but these seemed a small price to pay for the recovery of his accustomed spirits. He had escaped from gloom.

By October 16 he had his entire corps — increased to five divisions by the addition of two from Hurlbut — past Corinth, and three days later the head of the column reached Eastport to find a fleet of transports awaiting its arrival, loaded with provisions and guarded by two of Porter's gunboats. The establishment of this supply route on the Tennessee enabled Sherman to abandon the railroad west of there, but he still had 161 miles of track to rebuild and maintain, in accordance with Halleck's orders, from Iuka to Stevenson. This too he took in stride; for he was again in what he liked to call "high feather." He encouraged his men to live off the country, having decided that the best way to keep raiders out of Kentucky was to cut an arid swath across northern Mississippi and Alabama. The men took to the notion handily, not only because it agreed with their own, but also because their appetites had sharpened with the advent of early fall weather and days of working on the railroad. Sherman could scarcely contain his delight at their performance. "I never saw such greedy rascals after chicken and fresh meat," he exulted in a letter home. "I don't believe I will draw anything for them but salt. I don't know but it would be a good plan to march my army back and forth from Florence and Stevenson to make a belt of devastation between the enemy and our country."

"My army," he said, and truly; for by that time Lincoln's solution of the western command problem had been announced. On October 10, the day before Sherman left Memphis to make his spirit-restoring defense of the Collierville blockhouse, Grant received at Vicksburg a badly delayed order from Halleck directing him to report without delay to Cairo for instructions. The order, dated October 3, had taken a full week to reach him. He left at once, though he was still on crutches, and stopped off at Columbus, Kentucky, six days later — the guerilla-cut telegraph line had been restored to that point by then, only one day short of two weeks after the date on Halleck's order — to report that he was on his way upriver. Perhaps he wondered if he was to be disciplined for not keeping in touch and going off to New Orleans, as he had been after Donelson for not keeping in touch and going off to Nashville, though he could not see that he deserved any more blame in the present instance than he had deserved then. At any rate he was not much enlightened when he reached Cairo next morning, October 17, and was handed a wire directing him to proceed at once to the Galt House in Louisville, where he would receive further instructions from an officer of the War Department. He boarded a train that would take him there by way of Indianapolis. But that afternoon, as the train was pulling out of the station at the latter place, an attendant came hurrying out and flagged it to a halt. Behind him, bustling up the platform on short legs, came the Secretary of War, Edwin M. Stanton himself, whom Grant had never met. He swung aboard the last car, wheezing asthmatically, and worked his way forward, as the train gathered speed, to the car occupied by the general and his staff. "How are you, General Grant?" he said, grasping the hand of Dr Edward Kittoe, the staff surgeon. "I knew you at sight from your pictures."

This was quickly straightened out; Kittoe did not look much like his chief anyhow, though he wore a beard and a campaign hat and was also from Galena. After the amenities, exchanged while the train rocked on toward Louisville, Stanton presented Grant with two copies of a War Department order dated October 16, both of which had the same opening paragraph:

> By direction of the President of the United States, the Departments of the Ohio, of the Cumberland, and of the Tennessee, will constitute the Military Division of the Mississippi. Major General U. S. Grant, United States Army, is placed in command of the Military Division of the Mississippi, with his headquarters in the field.

In brief, this was Lincoln's unifying solution to the western command problem. With the exception of the troops in East Louisiana under Banks, who outranked him, Grant was put in charge of all the Union forces between the Allegheny Mountains and the Mississippi River. That was all there was to one of the copies of the order, but the other had an added paragraph, relieving Rosecrans from duty with the Army of the Cumberland and appointing Thomas in his place. The choice was left to Grant, who had no fondness for Old Rosy; "I chose the latter," he remarked dryly, some years afterward. Sherman of course would succeed to command of the Army of the Tennessee, and Burnside would continue, at least for the present, as head of the Army of the Ohio.

At Louisville, which they reached that night, Grant and the Secretary spent the following day together at the Galt House discussing the military outlook, mostly from the Washington point of view. That evening — by which time, the general said later, "all matters of discussion seemed exhausted" — Grant and his wife, who had come from Vicksburg with him by boat and train, left the hotel to call on relatives, while Stanton retired to his room with an attack of asthma. It had been decided to defer issuance of the War Department order until the general and his staff had had time to attend to various preparatory details. Presently, however, a messenger arrived with the latest dispatch from Dana, announcing that Rosecrans intended to evacuate Chattanooga and predicting utter disaster as a result. Highly agitated, Stanton sent bellboys and staff officers to all parts of the city in a frantic search for Grant. None of them could find him until about 11 o'clock, when they all found him at once. As he returned to the hotel from his call on relatives, it seemed to him that "every person [I] met was a messenger from the Secretary, apparently partaking of his impatience to see me." Upstairs, he found Stanton pacing about in his dressing gown and clutching the fatal dispatch, which he insisted called for immediate action to prevent the loss of Chattanooga and the annihilation of the troops besieged there. Grant agreed, and at once sent two dispatches of his own: one informing Rosecrans that he was relieved of command, the other instructing Thomas to hold onto Chattanooga "at all hazards." Thomas replied promptly with a message that indicated how aptly he had been characterized as the Rock of Chickamauga. "We will hold the town till we starve," he told Grant.

ꭓ 2 ꭓ

" 'All quiet on the Potomac.' Nothing to disturb autumnal slumbers," Stanton had wired the Chattanooga quartermaster on October 4, proud of his management of the transfer west of two corps from the army down in Virginia, which apparently had been accomplished under Lee's very nose without his knowledge, or at any rate without provoking a reaction on his part. Three days later, however, Meade's signalmen intercepted wigwag messages indicating that the rebels were preparing for some sort of movement in their camps beyond the Rapidan, and two days after that, on October 9, word came from the cavalry outposts that Lee was on the march, heading west and north around Meade's flank, much as he had done when he maneuvered bold John Pope out of a similar position, fourteen months ago, and brought him to grief on the plains of Manassas. Presently things were anything but quiet on the Potomac, deep in the Federal rear; for Meade was headed in that direction, too, and the indications were that there was going to be a Third Bull Run.

Lee had been wanting to take the offensive ever since his return from Pennsylvania. "If General Meade does not move, I wish to attack him," he told Davis in late August. The detachment of Longstreet soon afterward had seemed to rule this out, however, since it reduced Lee's strength to less than 50,000, whereas the Federals had nearly twice that number in his immediate front. Also there was the problem of his health, a recurrence of the rheumatic malady that had racked him in early spring. Then had come the news of Chickamauga, which was like a tonic to him. "My whole heart and soul have been with you and your brave corps in your late battle," he wrote Old Peter. "It was natural to hear of Longstreet and Hill charging side by side, and pleasing to find the armies of the East and West vying with each other in valor and devotion to their country. A complete and glorious victory must ensue under such circumstances. . . . Finish the work before you, my dear general, and return to me. I want you badly and you cannot get back too soon." Glorious the victory had been, but he presently learned that it was a long way from complete, which meant that the detached third of his army would not be rejoining him anything like as soon as he had hoped. Then came a second tonic-like report. Two of Meade's corps had been sent west to reinforce Rosecrans, with the result that the odds against Lee were reduced from two-to-one to only a bit worse than eight-to-five. He had taken the offensive against longer odds in the past, and now he prepared to do so again, not only for the same reasons — to relieve the pressure on Richmond, to break up enemy plans in their formative stage, and to provide himself with more room for maneuver — but also by much the same method. What he had in mind, when reports of the Union reduction were confirmed in early October, was a repetition of the tactics he had employed against Pope in a similar confrontation on this same ground; that is, a march around the enemy flank, then a knockout blow delivered as the blue mass drew back to avoid encirclement.

Once he had decided he moved quickly. On October 9 the two

corps of the Army of Northern Virginia began their march up the south bank of the Rapidan, westward beyond the Union right, then north across the river. The last time Lee had done this, just over a year ago, he had also had only two corps in his army. Longstreet and Jackson had led them then; now it was Ewell and A. P. Hill, two very different men. Another difference was in Lee himself. He had ridden Traveller then; now he rode in a wagon, so crippled by rheumatism that he could not mount a horse.

Stuart's cavalry had been organized into two divisions, one under Wade Hampton and the other under Fitzhugh Lee, both of whom were promoted to major general. Hampton was still recuperating from his Gettysburg wounds; Stuart led his division himself, covering the right flank of the infantry on the march, and left Fitz Lee to guard the river crossings while the rest of the army moved upstream. After two days of swinging wide around Cedar Mountain — rich with memories for A. P. Hill, not only because he was a native of the region and had spent his boyhood in these parts, but also because it was here that he had saved Jackson from defeat in early August, a year ago — the gray column entered Culpeper from the southwest on the 11th. Meade had had his headquarters here, and three of his corps had been concentrated in the vicinity, with the other two advanced southward to the north bank of the Rapidan. Now he was gone, and his five corps were gone with him. Like Pope, he was falling back across the Rappahannock to avoid being trapped in the constricting apex of the V described by the confluence of the rivers. Beyond Culpeper, however, Stuart came upon the cavalry rear guard, drawn up at Brandy Station to fight a delaying action on the field where most of the troopers of both armies had fought so savagely four months before. In the resultant skirmish, which he called Second Brandy, Jeb had the satisfaction of driving the enemy horsemen back across the Rappahannock, only failing to bag the lot, he declared, because Fitz Lee did not arrive in time after splashing across the unguarded Rapidan fords. At any rate, he felt that the question of superior abilities, which some claimed had not been decided by the contest here in June, was definitely settled in his favor by the outcome of this second fight on the same ground. Elated though he was, he did not fail to show that he had learned from his mistakes on the recent march into Pennsylvania. Not that he admitted that he had made any; he did not, then or now or later; but he kept in close touch with the commanding general, sending a constant stream of couriers to report both his own and the enemy's position. "Thank you," Lee said to the latest in the series, who had ridden back to inform him that the blue cavalry was being driven eastward. "Tell General Stuart to continue to press them back toward the river. But tell him, too," he added, "to spare his horses — to spare his horses. It is not necessary to send so many messages." Turning to Ewell, whom he was accompanying today, he said of this staff officer and another who had reported a few minutes earlier: "I think these two young gentlemen make *eight* messengers sent me by General Stuart."

He was in excellent spirits, partly because of this evidence that his chief of cavalry had profited from experience; for whatever profited Stuart also profited Lee, who depended heavily on his former cadet for the information by which he shaped his plans. Then too, the pains in his back had let up enough to permit him to enter Culpeper on his horse instead of on the prosaic seat of a wagon, and though he preferred things simple for the most part, he also liked to see them done in style. Moreover, there had been an exchange which he had enjoyed in the course of the welcome extended by the old men and cripples and women and children who turned out to cheer the army that had delivered them from this latest spell of Federal occupation. Not, it seemed, that the occupation had been entirely unpleasant for everyone concerned. At the height of the celebration, one indignant housewife struck a discordant note by informing the general that certain young ladies of the town had accepted invitations to attend band concerts at John Sedgwick's headquarters, and there, according to reports, they had given every sign of enjoying not only the Yankee music, but also the attentions of the blue-coated staff officers who were their escorts. Lee heard the superpatriot out, then looked sternly around at several girls whose blushes proved their guilt of this near-treason. "I know General Sedgwick very well," he replied at last, replacing his look of mock severity with a smile. "It is just like him to be so kindly and considerate, and to have his band there to entertain them. So, young ladies, if the music is good, go and hear it as often as you can, and enjoy yourselves. You will find that General Sedgwick will have none but agreeable gentlemen about him."

Whatever effect these words had on the woman who lodged the complaint — and whose fate, after the general's departure, can only be guessed at — they served, by their vindication of youth, to heighten the gaiety of the occasion. Nor was Culpeper the only scene of rejoicing for deliverance. Bragg's great victory in North Georgia, Lee's northward march, the repulse of the Union flotilla at Sabine Pass, the apparent disinclination of the Federals to follow up their Vicksburg conquest, Beauregard's continuing staunchness under amphibious assault: all were hailed in the Richmond *Whig* on this same October 11, under the heading "The Prospect," as evidence that the South, whose resilience after admittedly heavy setbacks had now been demonstrated to all the world, could never be defeated by her present adversary. "As the campaigning season of the third year of the war approaches its close," the editor summed up, "the principal army of the enemy, bruised, bleeding, and alarmed, is engaged with all its might [at Chattanooga] digging into the earth for safety. The second largest force, the once Grand Army of the Potomac, is fleeing before the advancing corps of General Lee. The third, under Banks, a portion of which has just been severely chastised by a handful of men, is vaguely and feebly attempting some movement against Texas. The fourth, under Grant, has ceased to be an army of offense. The fifth, under Gillmore, with a number of ironclads to aid him, lays futile siege to Charleston. Nowhere else have they anything more than garrisons or raiding forces. At all points the Confederate forces are able to defy them."

Lee had it in mind to brighten his share of the prospect still further by intercepting Meade's withdrawal up the Orange & Alexandria Railroad. He could not divide his army, as he had done against Pope, using half of it to fix the enemy in place while the other half swung wide for a strike at the rear; he lacked both the transport and the strength, and besides, with the bluecoats already in motion, there wasn't time. But he could attempt a shorter turning movement via Warrenton, along the turnpike paralleling the railroad to the east, in hope of forcing Meade to halt and fight in a position that would afford the pursuers the chance, despite the disparity in numbers, to inflict what the dead Stonewall had called "a terrible wound." Accordingly, the Culpeper pause was a brief one; Little Powell had time for no more than a quick look at his home town as he passed through in the wake of Ewell, who in turn pushed his men hard to close the gap between them and the cavalry up ahead, beyond Brandy and the Rappahannock crossings. Stuart skirmished with the blue rear guard all the rest of that day and the next, banging away with his guns and gathering stragglers as he went. Lee, still riding with Ewell, reached Warrenton on the 13th to receive a report from Jeb that the Federals were still at Warrenton Junction, due east on the main line, burning stores. There seemed an excellent chance of cutting them off, somewhere up the line: perhaps at Bristoe Station, where Jackson had landed with such explosive effect that other time. Next morning Hill's lean marchers took the lead. Remembering the rewards of that other strike, they put their best foot forward, if for no other reason than the hope of getting it shod. Shoes, warm clothes, food, and victory: all these lay before them, fifteen miles away at Bristoe, if they could only arrive in time to forestall a Yankee getaway.

As they marched their hopes were heightened by the evidence that Meade, though clearly on the run, had no great head start in the race. "We found the campfires of the enemy still burning," one of Hill's men would recall. "Guns, knapsacks, blankets, etc. strewn along the road showed that the enemy was moving in rapid retreat, and prisoners sent in every few minutes confirmed our opinion that they were fleeing in haste." Another of the marchers, cheered at the outset because he had eaten a whole pot of boiled cabbage for breakfast — perhaps by way of distending his stomach for the feast he hoped to enjoy before nightfall — recorded the satisfaction he and his comrades felt at reliving the glad August days of 1862, when they had tramped these roads with the same goal ahead. "We all entered now fully into the spirit of the movement," he declared. "We were convinced that Meade was unwilling to face us, and we therefore anticipated a pleasant affair, if we should succeed in catching him." Little Powell, it was observed, had put on his red wool hunting shirt, as he generally did at the prospect of a fight, and that seemed highly appropriate today, on a march which the first soldier said "was almost like boys chasing a hare."

Meade had been prodded, these past three months since his re-crossing of the Potomac, more by the superiors in his rear than by the rebels in his front. Lincoln was giving Halleck strategy lectures, and Old Brains was passing them along with interlinear comments which, to Meade at least, were about as exasperating as they were banal. As a result he had become more snappish than ever. Staff officers quailed nowadays at his glance. If Lee had caught him somewhat off balance in his reaction to the sudden advance across the Rapidan, it was small wonder.

Back in September, for instance, when he asked what the government wanted him to do — he could drive Lee back on Richmond, he said, but he failed to see the advantage in this, since he lacked the strength to mount a siege — Halleck referred the question to the President, who replied that Meade "should move upon Lee at once in the manner of general attack, leaving to developments whether he will make it a real attack." The general-in-chief rephrased and expanded this. "The main objects," he told Meade, "are to threaten Lee's position, to ascertain more certainly the condition of affairs in his army, and, if possible, to cut off some portion of it by a sudden raid." Then he, like Lincoln, stressed that these were suggestions, not orders. Meade replied that this last was precisely the trouble, so far as he was concerned. He saw no profit to be gained from the proposed endeavor, whereas he discerned in it the possibility of a good deal of profitless bloodshed, and he was therefore "reluctant to run the risks involved without the positive sanction of the government." Lincoln remained unwilling to accept the responsibility it seemed to him the general was trying to unload; "I am not prepared to order or even advise an advance in this case," he told Halleck. But he added that he saw in the present impasse "matter for very serious consideration in another aspect." If Lee's 60,000 could neutralize Meade's 90,000, he went on, why could not Meade, at that same two-three ratio, detach 50,000 men to be used elsewhere to advantage while he neutralized Lee's 60,000 with his remaining 40,000? "Having practically come to the mere defensive," Lincoln wrote, "it seems to be no economy at all to employ twice as many men for that object as are needed." And having come so far in the way of observation, he went further: "To avoid misunderstanding, let me say that to attempt to fight the enemy slowly back into his intrenchments at Richmond, and there to capture him, is an idea I have been trying to repudiate for quite a year. My judgment is so clear against it that I would scarcely allow the attempt to be made if the general in command should desire to make it. My last attempt upon Richmond was to get McClellan, when he was nearer there than the enemy was, to run in ahead of him. Since then I have constantly desired the Army of the Potomac to make Lee's army, and not Richmond, its objective point. If our army cannot fall upon the enemy and hurt him where he is, it is plain to me it can gain nothing by attempting to follow him over a succession of intrenched lines into a fortified city."

Meade perceived that he had fallen among lawyers, men who could do with logic and figures what they liked. Moreover the President, in his conclusion with regard to the unwisdom of driving Lee back into the Richmond defenses, had merely returned to the point Meade himself had made at the outset, except that now the latter found it somehow used against him. The technique was fairly familiar, even to a man who had never served on a jury, but it was no less exasperating for that, and Meade was determined that if he was to go the way of McDowell and McClellan, of Pope and McClellan again, of Burnside and Hooker, he would at least make the trip to the scrap heap under his own power. In the absence of orders or "sanction" from above, he would accept the consequences of his own decisions and no others, least of all those of which he disapproved; he would fall, if fall he must, by following his own conscience. Thus, by a reaction like that of a man alone in dangerous country — which Virginia certainly was — his natural caution was enlarged. In point of fact, he believed he had reasons to doubt not only the intentions of those above him, but also the present temper of the weapon they had placed in his hands three months ago and had recently diminished by two-sevenths. Of the five corps still with him, only two were led by the generals who had taken them to Gettysburg, and these were Sykes and Sedgwick, neither of whom had been seriously engaged in that grim struggle. Of the other three, the badly shot-up commands of Reynolds and Sickles were now under Newton and French, who had shown little in the way of ability during or since the return from Pennsylvania, and Warren, who had replaced the irreplaceable Hancock, was essentially a staff man, untested in the exercise of his new, larger duties. This too was part of what lay behind Meade's remarks, both to his wife in home letters and to trusted members of his staff in private conversations, that he disliked the burden of command so much he wished the government would relieve him.

So when Lee came probing around his right, October 9 and 10, though he knew that Lincoln and Halleck would not approve, he did as Pope had done: pulled out of the constricting V to get his army onto open ground that would permit maneuver. Unlike Pope, however, he did not stop behind the Rappahannock to wait for an explosion deep in his rear. Instead, he kept moving up the Orange & Alexandria Railroad — bringing his rear with him, so to speak. His aim was basically the same as

Lee's: the infliction of some "terrible wound," if Lee and Providence afforded him the opportunity. Meanwhile he took care to see that he afforded none to an adversary whose considerable fame had been earned at the expense of men who either had been negligent in that respect or else had been overeager in the other. He kept his five corps well closed up, within easy supporting distance of one another as they withdrew northeast along the railroad.

Not all who were with him approved of his cautious tactics; a volunteer aide, for example, considered them about as effective as trying "to catch a sea gull with a pinch of salt"; but Meade was watching and waiting, from Rappahannock Station through Warrenton Junction, for the chance he had in mind. Then suddenly on October 14, just up the line at Bristoe Station, he got it. The opportunity was brief, scarcely more indeed than half an hour from start to finish, but he made the most of it while it lasted. Or anyhow the untried Warren did.

Approaching Bristoe from the west at high noon, after a rapid march of fifteen miles, Hill saw northeastward, beyond Broad Run and out of reach, heavy columns of the enemy slogging toward Manassas Junction, a scant four miles away. He had not won the race. But neither had he lost it, he saw next; not entirely. What appeared to be the last corps in the Federal army was only about half over the run, crossing at a ford just north of the little town on the railroad, which came in arrow-straight from the southwest, diagonal to the Confederate line of march. The uncrossed half of the blue corps, jammed in a mass on the near bank of the stream while its various components awaited their turn at the ford, seemed to Little Powell to be his for the taking, provided he moved promptly. This he did. Ordering Heth, whose division was in the lead, to go immediately from march to attack formation, he put two of his batteries into action and sent word for Anderson, whose division was in column behind Heth's, to come forward on the double and reinforce the attack. Fire from the guns did more to hasten than to impede the crossing, however, and Hill told Heth, though he had only two of his four brigades in line by now, to attack at once lest the bluecoats get away. Heth obeyed, but as his men started forward he caught a glint of bayonets to their right front, behind the railroad embankment. When he reported this to Hill, asking whether he would not do better to halt for a reconnaissance, Hill told him to keep going: Anderson would be arriving soon to cover his flank. So the two brigades went on. It presently developed, however, that what they were going on to was by no means the quick victory their commander had intended, but rather a sudden and bloody repulse at the hands of veterans who had stood fast on Cemetery Ridge, fifteen weeks ago tomorrow, to serve Pickett in much the same fashion, except that here the defenders had the added and rare advantage of surprise.

They made the most of it. Behind the embankment, diagonal to the advancing line, was the II Corps under Warren, the former chief of engineers, who, demonstrating here at Bristoe as sharp an eye for terrain as he had shown in saving Little Round Top, had set for the unsuspecting rebels what a later observer called "as fine a trap as could have been devised by a month's engineering." His — not Sykes's, as Hill had supposed from a hurried look at the crowded ford and the heavy blue columns already beyond Broad Run — was the last of the five Federal corps, and when he saw the situation up ahead he improvised the trap that now was sprung. As the two gray brigades came abreast of the three cached divisions, the bluecoats opened fire with devastating effect. Back up the slope, Little Powell watched in dismay as his troops, reacting with soldierly but misguided instinct, wheeled right to charge the embankment wreathed in smoke from the enfilading blasts of musketry. This new attempt, by two stunned brigades against three confident divisions, could have but one outcome. The survivors who came stumbling back were pitifully few, for many of the startled graybacks chose surrender, preferring to remain with their fallen comrades rather than try to make the return journey up the bullet-torn slope they had just descended. Elated, the Federals made a quick sortie that netted them five pieces of artillery and two stands of colors, which they took with them when they drew off, unmolested, across the run. The worst loss to the Confederates, though, was men. Both brigade commanders were shot down, along with nearly 1400 killed or wounded and another 450 captured. The total thus was close to 1900 casualties, as compared to a Union total of about 300, only fifty of whom were killed. In the particular, the results were even sadder from the southern point of view. A North Carolina regiment on the exposed flank lost 290 of its 416 enlisted men, or just under seventy percent, plus all but three of its 36 officers. Here too fell Carnot Posey, who was struck in the thigh by a fragment of shell when he brought up his Mississippi brigade near the close of the action. The wound, though ugly, was not thought to be grave, but infection set in and he died one month later.

Indignation swept through the gray army when the rest of it arrived in the course of the afternoon and learned of what had happened at midday, down in the shallow valley of Broad Run. No segment of the Army of Northern Virginia had suffered such a one-sided defeat since Mechanicsville, which had also been the result of Little Powell's impetuosity. "There was no earthly excuse for it," a member of Lee's staff declared, "as all our troops were well in hand, and much stronger than the enemy." One North Carolinian, still angered years later by the sudden and useless loss of so many of his friends, said flatly: "A worse managed affair than this . . . did not take place during the war." Hill's only reply to such critics was included in the report he submitted within two weeks. "I am convinced that I made the attack too hastily," he wrote, "and at the same time that a delay of half an hour, and there would have been no enemy to attack. In that event I believe I should equally have blamed myself for not attacking at once." Seddon and Davis both endorsed the report. "The disaster at Bristoe Station seems due to a gallant but over-hasty pressing on of the enemy," the former observed, while the latter added: "There was a want of vigilance." These comments stung the thin-skinned Virginian, but worse by far had been Lee's rebuke next morning when Hill conducted him over the field, where the dead still lay in attitudes of pained surprise, and explained what had occurred. Lee said little, knowing as he did that his auburn-haired lieutenant's high-strung impetuosity, demonstrated in battle after battle — but most profitably at Sharpsburg, of which he himself had written: "And then A. P. Hill came up" — had gained the army far more than it cost.

"Well, well, General," he remarked at last, "bury these poor men and let us say no more about it."

He was distracted by the possibility of much heavier bloodshed, four miles up the line, where so much blood had been shed twice already. It seemed to him that Meade, encouraged by Warren's coup the day before, would call a halt and prepare to fight a Third Manassas. That was very much what Lee himself wanted, despite the disparity in numbers, and when someone expressed regret that so historic a field should be widely known by the unromantic name "Bull Run," he replied that with the blessings of God they would "make it another Cowpens." Others had a different reason for wanting to push on at once to the famed junction. According to one of Stuart's men, "We were looking forward to Manassas with vivid recollections of the rich haul we had made there just prior to the second battle of Manassas, and everybody was saying, 'We'll get plenty when we get to Manassas.'" As it turned out, though, Meade wanted no part of a third fight on that unlucky ground. He marched rapidly beyond it, without even a rest halt for his army. There was no battle, and there was no "rich haul" either. "We were there before we knew it," the hungry trooper wrote. "Everything was changed. There was not a building anywhere. The soil, enriched by debris from former camps, had grown a rich crop of weeds that came halfway up the sides of our horses, and the only way we recognized the place was by our horses stumbling over the railroad tracks."

This dreary vista was repeated all around. "Never have I witnessed as sad a picture as Prince William County now presents," a young staff colonel noted in a letter home. " 'Tis desolation made desolate indeed. As far as the eye can reach on every side, there is one vast, barren wilderness; not a fence, not an acre cultivated, not a living object visible, and but for here and there a standing chimney, on the ruins of what was once a handsome and happy home, one would imagine that man was

never here and that the country was an entirely new one,
without any virtue except its
vast extent." Under such circumstances, with an inadequate
wagon train and the railroad
inoperable because the Federals
had blown the larger bridges as
they slogged northward, for Lee
to remain where he was meant
starvation for his men and horses.
Nor could he attack, except at a
prohibitive disadvantage; Meade
had taken a position of great natural strength, which he promptly

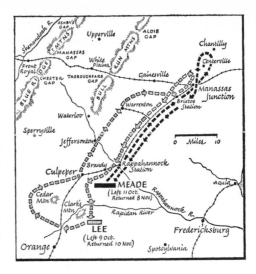

improved with intrenchments, along the Centerville-Chantilly ridge.
Lee was confident he could turn him out of this, but that would be to
drive him back on Washington with its 50,000-man garrison and its
589 guns (Richmond, by contrast, had just over 5000 men in its defenses and 42 guns); which plainly would not do, even if the poorly
shod and thinly clad Confederates had been in any condition for pursuit, now that the weather was turning colder, along the rocky pikes of
Fairfax County. Next day, October 16, a heavy rain seemed more or
less to settle the question of any movement, in any direction whatever,
by drenching the roads and fields, swelling the unbridged streams, and
confining the southern commander to his tent with an attack of what
was diagnosed as lumbago. His decision, reached before the downpour
stopped that night, was to withdraw as he had come, back down the
railroad, completing the destruction his opponent had begun. The march
south got under way next morning, despite the mud. Stuart, assigned
the task of covering the rear, did so with such zest and skill that he won
another of those handy and sometimes laugh-provoking victories by
which he justified his plume and his fox-hunt manner.

Meade did not pursue, except with his cavalry, and he soon had
cause to regret that he had done even that much. Stuart withdrew by
way of Gainesville, down the Warrenton pike, Fitz Lee by way of Bristoe, down the railroad; the arrangement was that the two would combine if either was faced with more than he could handle. Pressed by
superior numbers of blue troopers — Pleasonton had three divisions, under Buford, Gregg, and Kilpatrick — Jeb fell back across Broad Run
on the night of the 18th and, sending word for Fitz to reinforce him,
took up a position on the south bank to contest a crossing at Buckland
Mills. He was having little trouble doing this next morning, banging
away with his guns at the bridge he had purposely left intact as a challenge, when a courier arrived with a suggestion from Fitz Lee, who had

heard the firing and ridden ahead to assess the situation. If Stuart would fall back down the turnpike, pretending flight in order to draw the Yankees pellmell after him, the courier explained, Fitz would be able to surprise them when they came abreast of a hiding place he would select for that purpose, some distance south, behind one of the low ridges adjoining the pike; whereupon Jeb could turn and charge them, converting the blue confusion into a rout. Stuart liked the notion and proceeded at once to put it into effect. The bluecoats — Judson Kilpatrick's division, with Custer's brigade in the lead — snapped eagerly at the bait, pounding across the run in close pursuit of the fleeing graybacks, who led them on a five-mile chase to Chestnut Hill. At that point, only two miles short of Warrenton, the "chase" ended. Hearing Fitz Lee's guns bark suddenly from ambush, Jeb's horsemen whirled their mounts and charged the head of the now halted and badly rattled column in their rear. There followed another five-mile pursuit — much like the first, except that it was in the opposite direction and was not a mock chase, as the other had been, but a true flight for life — all the way back to Buckland Mills, where Stuart finally called a halt, laughing as he watched the Federals scamper across to the north bank of Broad Run. He had captured something over two hundred of them, along with several ambulances, Custer's headquarters wagon, and a good deal of dropped equipment. One regret he had, however, and this was that Kilpatrick had not kept his artillery near the front, as prescribed by the tactics manual; in which case, Jeb was convinced, "it would undoubtedly have fallen into our hands."

Lee congratulated his chief of cavalry, along with his nephew Fitz, for achieving "this handsome success" — an action known thereafter to Confederates as the "Buckland Races" — though he was also prompt to deny the permission sought by Stuart, in his elation at the outcome of the ruse, to undertake a raid behind Meade's lines while the blue troopers were trying to pull themselves together. In truth, Jeb and his men had done quite enough in the past ten days. Not only did the Buckland farce help to restore the army's morale, damaged five days ago by the Bristoe fiasco, but at a cost of 408 casualties, most of them only slightly injured, he had inflicted 1251 on the enemy cavalry, all but about three hundred of them killed or captured, and had assisted in the taking of some 600 infantry prisoners, mostly stragglers encountered during the movement north. Meade's losses totaled 2292, which was only a bit lower than Lee's for the same period, including those suffered at Bristoe. Except for that unfortunate engagement, the gray army could congratulate itself on another highly successful, if necessarily brief, campaign. With no more than 48,402 effectives, as compared to Meade's 80,789, Lee had maneuvered his adversary into a sixty-mile withdrawal, from the Rapidan to beyond Bull Run. And now, though he himself was obliged to withdraw in turn for lack of subsistence, he did what he could to insure that the inevitable Union follow-up would be a slow one. Meade had burned only the bridges on the Orange & Alexandria; now Lee burned the crossties, too, and warped the rails beyond salvation by piling them atop the burning ties. The Federals, unable to feed themselves without the use of the railroad now that the autumnal rains were turning the roads to quagmires, would advance no faster than their work gangs could lay track. Recrossing the Rappahannock, Lee called a halt and gave his men some badly needed rest while waiting for the blue army to arrive.

This took even longer than he had supposed it would do: not only because of the thorough job the blue and butternut wreckers had done on the Orange & Alexandria, but also because the Federal commander was involved again in a distractive telegraphic skirmish with the authorities in his rear. The President had been distressed by what seemed to him the supine attitude of Meade in falling back under pressure from Lee's inferior force, and this distress was increased on October 15, when the general, announcing Warren's repulse of the rebels at Bristoe Station, passed along information gleaned from prisoners "that Hill's and Ewell's corps, reinforced to a reported strength of 80,000, are advancing on me, their plan being to secure the Bull Run field in advance of me." He supposed, he said, that Lee would "turn me again, probably by the right . . . in which case I shall either fall on him or retire nearer Washington." Lincoln presumed from past performances that Meade would certainly choose the latter course, and when it did not come to that, since Lee advanced no farther than Bull Run, he took this as evidence that the Confederates were by no means as strong as the prisoners had claimed. Irked by what seemed to him a superfluity of caution, he risked a near commitment. "If Gen. Meade can now attack [Lee] on a field no worse than equal for us," he wrote Halleck next day, "and will do so with all the skill and courage which he, his officers, and men possess, the honor will be his if he succeeds, and the blame may be mine if he fails." Perhaps Meade noted the "may" in the copy Halleck sent him that same day, or perhaps he recalled that other such letters had preceded other downfalls. In any event, since neither of his superiors was willing to put the suggestion in the form of a direct order, he chose rather to continue the policy he had been following all along. Besides, he protested, this policy was no different from the one being urged on him. "It has been my intention to attack the enemy, if I can find him on a field no more than equal for us," he replied. "I have only delayed doing so from the difficulty of ascertaining his exact position, and the fear that in endeavoring to do so my communications might be jeopardized."

It seemed to Halleck that what Meade was in fear of jeopardizing was his reputation. Accordingly, with the encouragement of their Commander in Chief, he decided to crack down harder, apparently in the be-lief that more pressure from above might stiffen the reluctant general's backbone. Two days later, on October 18, Meade reported that Lee was again in motion, and though he did not know what the Virginian had in mind, he thought he might be headed for the Shenandoah Valley, as he had done after Chancellorsville. Halleck replied that this might be so, but he added tauntingly: "If Lee has turned his back on you to cross the mountains, he certainly has seriously exposed himself to your blows, un-less his army can move two miles to your one." By evening, moreover, the general-in-chief had decided there was nothing to the report. "Lee is unquestionably bullying you," he wired. "If you cannot ascertain his movements, I certainly cannot. If you pursue and fight him, I think you will find out where he is. I know of no other way." Sooner or later, all subordinates — even the placid Grant — bridled under this kind of treat-ment from Old Brains, and the short-tempered Meade was by no means an exception. "If you have any orders to give me, I am prepared to re-ceive and obey them," he shot back, "but I must insist on being spared the infliction of such truisms in the guise of opinions as you have re-cently honored me with, particularly as they were not asked for." By way of emphasis he added: "I take this occasion to repeat what I have before stated, that if my course, based on my own judgment, does not meet with approval, I ought to be, and I desire to be, relieved from command." This was his trump card, never played without overriding effect; for who was there in the Army of the Potomac to replace him? ("What can I do, with such generals as we have?" Lincoln had asked, some weeks ago, in response to urgings that the Pennsylvanian be re-lieved. "Who among them is any better than Meade?") Snail-like, Hal-leck pulled his horns in — as, in fact, it was his custom to do whenever they encountered resistance. "If I have repeated truisms," he wired the general next morning, "it has not been to give offense, but to give you the wishes of the government. If, in conveying these wishes, I have used words which were unpleasing, I sincerely regret it." Now it was Meade's turn to be high-handed. "Your explanation of your intentions is ac-cepted," he replied, "and I thank you for it."

Privately, however — when he found out, as he presently did, that the Confederates were not headed for the Valley but were with-drawing as they had come, back down the railroad — he admitted that Lee had indeed bullied him, though he did not use that word. He per-ceived now that it had never been his adversary's real intention to come between him and Washington at all, as he had supposed, but simply to maneuver him rearward, sixty miles or more, and thus forestall a con-tinued Union advance during the brief period of good weather that re-mained. Lee's had been "a deep game," Meade wrote his wife on October 21, "and I am free to admit that in the playing of it he has got the advantage of me." Accordingly, after his cavalry failed to intercept or indeed scarcely even trouble the retiring enemy, he put his repair gangs to work on the wrecked supply line and followed with his infantry. The advance was necessarily slow, being regulated to the speed with which the rails were laid and the bridges reconstructed. There was even time for a quick visit to the capital, at Halleck's urging, for a conference with the President. This was held on October 23, and Meade reported to his wife that he found Lincoln kind and considerate, though obviously disappointed that he had not got a battle out of Lee. At one point, though, the talk shifted to Gettysburg and the touchy subject of the pursuit of the rebels to the Potomac. "Do you know, General, what your attitude toward Lee for a week after the battle reminded me of?" Lincoln asked, and when Meade replied, "No, Mr President, what is it?" Lincoln said: "I'll be hanged if I could think of anything else than an old woman trying to shoo her geese across a creek."

For once, Meade kept his temper under control, but he was glad to return next day to his army, away from the Washington atmosphere. Though the advance was proceeding about as fast as could be expected with the railroad as thoroughly smashed as it was, he dispensed with none of his previous caution, wanting no part of a battle on such terms as he believed Lee (not Lincoln) would be willing to offer him. Finally, by the end of the month, he was back on the Rappahannock, whose crossings he found defended. He had been reinforced to a strength of 84,321 effectives, whereas Lee was down to 45,614 as a result of sickness brought on by exposing his thin-clad veterans to cold and rainy weather on the march. Unaware that the odds had lengthened again to almost two-to-one, Meade took a long look at the rebel defenses and, finding them formidable — Lee's soldiers had apparently been as hard at work as his own, but with shovels rather than sledges — proposed on November 2 a change of base downstream to Fredericksburg, which he said would not only put him back on the direct route to Richmond, but would also avoid the need for crossing a second river immediately after the first.

Lincoln was prompt to disapprove. He had been willing to have the army fight a Third Bull Run, but it seemed to him only a little short of madness to invite a Second Fredericksburg. So Meade looked harder than ever at what faced him here on the upper Rappahannock, where, if anywhere, he would have to do his fighting.

Despite the nearly two-to-one odds his army faced in its risky position within the constricting V of the rivers, Lee awaited Meade's advance with confidence and as much patience as his ingrained preference for the offensive would permit. "If I could only get some shoes and clothes for the men," he said, "I would save him the trouble." In electing to stand on the line of the Rappahannock — shown in the past to be highly vulnerable at Kelly's Ford, where the south bank was lower than the north — he had evolved a novel system of defense. Massing his troops in depth near the danger point, he prepared to contest a crossing there only after the blue infantry had moved beyond the effective range of its artillery on the dominant north bank, and in furtherance of this plan (patterned, so far, after the one he had used with such success at Fredericksburg, just short of eleven months ago) he maintained at Rappahannock Station, five miles upstream, a bridgehead on the far side of the river, fortified against assault by the labor-saving expedient of turning the old Federal works so that they faced north instead of south. A pontoon bridge near the site of the wrecked railroad span, safely beyond the reach of enemy batteries, made possible a quick withdrawal or reinforcement of the troops who, by their presence, were in a position to divide Meade's forces or attack him flank and rear in case he massed them for a downstream crossing. Ewell's corps guarded all these points, with Early in occupation of the tête-de-pont, Rodes in rear of Kelly's Ford, and Johnson in reserve; Hill's was upstream, beyond Rappahannock Station. For more than two weeks, October 20 to November 5, Lee waited in his Brandy headquarters for Meade's arrival. On the latter date his outpost scouts sent word that blue reconnaissance patrols were probing at various points along the river, and two days later the whole Union army was reported to be approaching in two main columns, one headed for the north-bank bridgehead, the other for Kelly's Ford.

This report, which was just what he had expected and planned for, reached him about noon. After notifying Hill to be on the alert for orders to reinforce Ewell, he rode from Brandy to Early's headquarters near the south end of the pontoon bridge affording access to the works on the north bank. When Early explained that he was sending another of his brigades to join the one already across the river, Lee approved but he also took the precaution of ordering Hill to shift his right division over to the railroad so that it would be available as an additional reserve. Similarly, when he learned a bit later that the bluecoats had crossed in force at Kelly's Ford, he instructed Edward Johnson to move in closer support of Rodes. Old Jubal went over to the north bank late in the afternoon and returned to report that the Yankees had made so little impression there that one of his brigade commanders had assured him that, if need be, he could hold the position against the whole Federal army. Dusk came down, and presently, in the gathering darkness beyond the river, Lee and Early saw muzzle flashes winking close to the works on the north bank. A south wind carried the noise away, and anyhow the pinkish yellow flashes soon went out. Convinced that this brief twilight action had been no more than a demonstration, probably to cover the advance on Kelly's Ford — in any event, no enemy had ever made a night attack on his infantry in a fortified position — Lee rode back to Brandy under the growing light of the stars, well satisfied with the results so far of the reception he had planned for Meade along the Rappahannock.

Unwelcome news awaited him at headquarters, in the form of a dispatch from Ewell. The greater part of two regiments assigned by Rodes to picket duty at Kelly's Ford had been gobbled up by the Federals, who then had laid a pontoon bridge and were sending substantial reinforcements across to the south bank. A loss of 349 veterans was not to be taken lightly, but aside from this the situation was about what Lee had expected. The thing to do now was make threatening gestures from within the bridgehead, which should serve to hold a major portion of Meade's force on the north bank, and shift two divisions of Hill's corps eastward to strengthen Rodes and Johnson for an all-out fight in rear of Kelly's Ford. That was the preconceived plan, whereby Lee intended to fall on a segment of the blue army, as he had done so often in the past, with the greater part of his own. Before this could be ordered, however, still worse news — indeed, almost incredible news — arrived from Early. Massing heavily at close range in the darkness before moonrise, the Federals had stormed and overrun the north-bank intrenchments, killing or capturing all of the troops in the two Confederate brigades except about six hundred who had swum the river or run the gauntlet over the pontoon bridge. The loss would come to 1674 men: and with them, of course, went the bridgehead itself, upon which the plan for Meade's discomfiture depended. Nor was it only the offensive that had been wrecked. Obviously the army could not remain in its present position after daylight, exposed on a shallow extended front with the Rapidan in its rear. Lee was upset but he kept his poise, thankful at any rate that Early had set the floating bridge afire to prevent a crossing by the bluecoats now in occupation of Rappahannock Station. Orders went out for Hill to retire by crossing the railroad between Culpeper and Brandy, while Ewell fell back toward Germanna Ford, contesting if necessary the advance of the blue force from Kelly's. For two days the movement continued. On November 9, when the bluecoats drew near, both corps halted and formed for battle, still within the V, but when Meade did not press the issue Lee resumed his withdrawal and crossed the Rapidan next morning. The army was back in the position it had left, marching west and north around the enemy right, a month ago yesterday.

The blue-clad veterans were elated; their 461 casualties amounted to less than a fourth of the number they had inflicted. French had moved with speed and precision on the left, seizing Kelly's Ford before the rebel pickets even had time to scamper rearward out of reach, and Uncle John Sedgwick, on the right with his own and Sykes's corps, had performed brilliantly, improvising tactics which resulted in the capture not only of the fortified tête-de-pont, supposed impregnable by its defenders, but also of the largest haul of prisoners ever secured by the army in one fell, offensive swoop. Meade's stock rose accordingly with the men in the ranks, who began to say that Bobby Lee had better look to his laurels, though there was presently some grumbling that the coup had not been followed by another, equally vigorous and even more profitable, while the rebs were on the run. Conversely, there was chagrin in the Confederate ranks. The double blow had cost a total of 2033 men: more, even, than Bristoe Station and in some ways even worse than that fiasco, which at least had not been followed by an ignominious retreat. Now it was Ewell's turn to be excoriated, as Hill had been three weeks before. "It is absolutely sickening," one of his young staff officers, a holdover from Stonewall's day, lamented. "I feel personally disgraced . . . as does everyone in the command. Oh, how each day is proving the inestimable value of General Jackson to us!" Early and Rodes were both intensely humiliated, and though Lee did not berate them or their corps commander, any more than he had berated Little Powell in a similar situation, neither did he attempt to reduce their burden of guilt by assigning any share of the blame to the men who had been captured and were now on their way to prison camps in the North. Quite the contrary, in fact; for he observed in his report to Richmond that "the courage and good conduct of the troops engaged have been too often tried to admit of question."

Both the elation on the one hand and the chagrin on the other were soon replaced by a sort of mutual boredom on both sides of the familiar Rapidan, where the two armies returned to their old occupation of staring at one another from the now leafless woods on its opposite banks — what time, that is, they were not engaged in the informal and illegal exchange of coffee, tobacco, and laugh-provoking insults. If there was less food on the south bank, there was perhaps more homesickness on the north, the majority of the soldiers there having come a longer way to save the Union than their adversaries had come to save the Confederacy. Presently there was rain and more rain, chill and dripping, which served to increase the discomfort, as well as the boredom, despite the snug huts put up as a sign that the armies had gone into winter quarters. A northern colonel, a staff volunteer, spoke for both sides in giving his reaction to his surroundings. "The life here is miserably lazy," he wrote home; "hardly an order to carry, and the horses all eating their heads off. . . . If one could only be at home, till one was *wanted*, and then be on the spot. But this is everywhere the way of war; lie still and lie still; then up and maneuver and march hard; then a big battle; and then a lot more lie still."

✕ 3 ✕

Rosecrans was relieved on the day of the Buckland Races, exactly one month after the opening day of Chickamauga, whose loss had resulted first in his retreat, then in his besiegement, and finally in his removal from command. Grant left Louisville by rail next morning, October 20, spent the night in Nashville, and went on the following day to Stevenson, Alabama, for an early evening conference with Rosecrans, who had left Chattanooga the day before, promptly on receipt of Grant's wire, because he had not wanted to encourage by his presence any demonstrations of regret at his departure from the army he would have commanded for a full year if he had lasted one week longer. It was untrue that he had intended to evacuate the beleaguered town, as Dana had told Stanton he had it in mind to do; in point of fact, he had been hard at work for the past ten days with his chief of engineers on plans for solving the acute supply problem as a prelude to resuming the offensive. Moreover, though he disliked Grant and knew quite well that Grant returned the feeling, his devotion to their common cause enabled him not only to share with the incoming general, who had just ordered his removal, his recently worked-out plans for lifting the siege, but even to do so cordially. "He came into my car," Grant subsequently wrote, "and we held a brief interview, in which he described very clearly the situation at Chattanooga, and made some excellent suggestions as to what should be done. My only wonder was that he had not carried them out."

After the conference, Old Rosy took up his journey north and Grant proceeded to Bridgeport, where he spent the night. Next morning, with his crutches strapped to the saddle like a brace of carbines — for he still could not manage afoot without them — he began the sixty-mile horseback trek up the Sequatchie Valley and over Walden's Ridge, made necessary by the long-range rebel guns on Raccoon Mountain commanding the direct approach to Chattanooga, which was less than half the roundabout distance the army trains were obliged to travel if they were to maintain a trickle of supplies for the hungry bluecoats cooped up in the town. At Jasper, ten miles out, the party stopped for a visit with Oliver Howard, who had established his corps headquarters there soon after his arrival from Virginia two weeks before. In the course of their talk Howard saw Grant looking intently at an empty whiskey bottle on a nearby table. "I never drink," the one-armed general said hastily, anxious lest his reputation for sobriety be doubted by his new commander, whatever shortcomings the latter himself might have in that regard. "Neither do I," Grant replied, straight-faced, as he rose and hobbled out on his crutches to be lifted back onto his horse. Beyond Jasper — particularly around Anderson's Crossroads, the half-way point, where Wheeler had wrought such havoc twenty days ago — he began, like Browning's Childe Roland, to get an oppressive firsthand notion of the difficulties in store for him ahead. Rain had turned low-lying stretches of the road into knee-deep bogs, and other stretches along hillsides had been made almost impassable by washouts; the crippled general had to be carried over the worst of these, which were too unsafe to cross on horseback. Ten thousand mules and horses had died by now, either by rebel bayonets or from starvation, and a great many of their carcasses were strewn along the roadway, offensive alike to eye and nose and conscience, especially for a man who loved animals as much as Grant did. Perhaps not even the field of Shiloh, with its grisly two-day harvest still upon it, offended him more than what he encountered in the course of the present two-day ride up that quiet valley and over that barren ridge, which he descended late on October 23 to regain the north bank of the Tennessee, immediately opposite the town that was his goal.

In some ways Chattanooga itself was worse; for there, in addition to more dead and dying horses, you saw the faces of the soldiers, which showed the effects not only of their hunger — "One of the regiments of our brigade," a Kansas infantryman was to testify, "caught, killed, and ate a dog that wandered into camp" — but also the dejection proceeding from their month-old defeat at Chickamauga and the apparent hopelessness of their present tactical situation, ringed as they were by the rebel victors on all the surrounding heights. Grant crossed the river just before dark, riding carefully over the pontoon bridge, and went at once to see Thomas, who had promised four days ago to "hold the town till we starve." This was something quite different, Grant now discerned, from saying that the army would be able to live there, let alone come out of the place victorious. "I appreciated the force of this dispatch . . . when I witnessed the condition of affairs which prompted it," he afterwards declared. The night was cold and rainy. He could see the campfires of the Confederates, gleaming like stars against the outer darkness, above and on three sides of him, as if he stood in the pit of a darkened amphitheater, peering up and out, east and west and south.

Chattanooga was said to be an Indian word meaning "mountains looking at each other," and next morning Grant perceived the aptness of the name. He saw on the left the long reach of Missionary Ridge, a solid wall that threw its shadow over the town until the sun broke clear of its rim, and on the right the cumulous bulge of Raccoon Mountain. Dead ahead, though, was the dominant feature of this forbidding panorama. Its summit 1200 feet above the surface of the river at its base, Lookout Mountain rose, a Union correspondent had remarked, "like an everlasting thunder storm that will never pass over." Seen as Grant saw it now, wreathed in mist, the journalist continued, "it looms up . . . and recedes, but when the sun shines strongly out it draws so near as to startle you." Grant was to see it that way too, in time, but for the present what impressed him most were the guns posted high on the slopes and peaks and ridges, all trained on the blue army here below. With the help of glasses he could even see the cannoneers lounging about in careless attitudes, as if to emphasize by their idleness the advantage they enjoyed. "I suppose," he said years later, "they looked upon the garrison of Chattanooga as prisoners of war, feeding or starving themselves, and thought it would be inhuman to kill any of them except in self-defense."

With two thirds of his practically useless cavalry sent away, Thomas had about 45,000 effectives in his Army of the Cumberland, and though nothing had yet been done to relieve the most pressing of their problems — the hunger that came from trying to live on quarter-rations — Dana at least had been quick to inform Stanton, on the day of Grant's arrival "wet, dirty, and well," that "the change at headquarters here [under Thomas] is already strikingly perceptible. Order prevails instead of universal chaos." For one thing, there had been a complete reorganization, a top-to-bottom shake-up, in the course of which regiments were consolidated, brigades re-formed, and divisions redistributed. Formerly there had been eleven of these last; now there were six, assigned three each to two instead of the previous four corps. Palmer had succeeded Thomas, and Granger had been placed at the head of a new corps formed by combining his own with those of the departed Crittenden and McCook. Sheridan, Wood, and Brigadier General Charles Cruft, Palmer's successor, commanded the three divisions under Palmer; Johnson, Davis, and Baird the three under Granger. The other five division commanders had been disposed of or employed in various ways; Negley was sent North, ostensibly for his health, while Steedman and Van Cleve were made post commanders of Chattanooga and Murfreesboro, and Reynolds and Brannan were respectively appointed to be chiefs of staff and artillery, directly under Thomas. Grant approved of all these arrangements, some of which had been effected by Rosecrans, but as he examined the tactical situation confronting the reorganized army — including the alarming discovery that there was not enough ammunition for one hard day of fighting — he found it altogether bleak. "It looked, indeed, as if but two courses were open," he afterwards remarked: "one to starve, the other to surrender or be captured."

Not only did the Confederates have the tactical advantage of gazing down on their opponents with something of the complacency of marksmen contemplating fish in a rain barrel; they also had a numerical advantage. Bragg had close to 70,000 veterans on those heights and in the intervening valleys. This would be considerably overmatched, of course, when and if the Federal reinforcements arrived. Hooker was already standing by, near Bridgeport, with some 16,000 effectives — exclusive, that is, of service personnel — in the four divisions he had brought from the Army of the Potomac, while Sherman was working his way east along the Memphis & Charleston Railroad with another 20,000 in the five divisions of his Army of the Tennessee, and Burnside

had about 25,000 around Knoxville in the four divisions of his Army
of the Ohio. This gave a total of well over 100,000 men in the four
commands. Even without Burnside, who now definitely was not coming — though he was strategically useful where he was, as a bait or a
menace, hovering eastward off Bragg's flank — the combination of
Thomas, Hooker, and Sherman would give Grant nearly half again as
many troops as stood in the ranks of his gray besiegers. First, though, he
must get them into Chattanooga, and before he could do that he would
have to find a way to feed them when they got there, since otherwise
they would only increase the number of hungry mouths and speed the
garrison's already rapid progress toward starvation. That was what it
came to every time, no matter how many angles the problem was seen
from: the question of how to open a new supply line, supplementing or
replacing the inadequate, carcass-littered one that led back over Walden's Ridge and down the Sequatchie Valley to the railhead depots
bulging with food and ammunition at Stevenson and Bridgeport.

The answer came out of a conference with Thomas and his chief
engineer, W. F. Smith, who had served in the same capacity under Rosecrans. This was that same "Baldy" Smith who had led a corps at Fredericksburg but had been transferred out of the Virginia army — as a result,
it was said, of his inability to get along with Hooker any better than he
had with Burnside — and had commanded the Pennsylvania militia that
stood off Jeb Stuart at Carlisle during the Gettysburg campaign, after
which he had been given his present assignment with the army down in
Tennessee. A Vermont-born West Pointer, short and portly, thirty-
nine years old and described by a fellow staffer as having "a light-brown
imperial and shaggy mustache, a round, military head, and the look of a
German officer, altogether," Smith was still a brigadier, despite the lofty
posts he had filled, because Congress refused to confirm his promotion
on grounds that he had been deeply involved in the machinations against
Burnside: as indeed he had, for he was by nature contentious, ever quick
to spot and carp at the shortcomings of his superiors. Grant had not
seen him since their Academy days, twenty years before, but he was
greatly taken with him on brief reacquaintance, mainly because Smith
had arrived, on his own and in conferences with Rosecrans, at what he
believed was the answer to the question of how to open a new and
better supply line back to Bridgeport. It was based of course on geography, but it was also based on daring. The Tennessee River, which flowed
due west past Chattanooga, turned abruptly south just beyond the town,
then swung back north as if by rebound from the foot of Lookout
Mountain. Two miles upstream, on the western side of the point of land
inclosed by this narrow bend — Moccasin Point, it was called, from its
resemblance, when seen from above, to an Indian shoe — was Brown's
Ferry, an excellent site for a crossing because it was beyond the reach
of all but the longest-range guns on Lookout and only a mile from the

pontoon bridge already in use north of the town. From Brown's Ferry
the river flowed on north, then turned south again, around the long
northwestern spur of Raccoon Mountain, to describe a second and
longer bend, along whose base a road led westward through Cummings
Gap to another Tennessee cross-
ing known as Kelley's Ferry,
and from there along the right
bank of the river down to
Bridgeport.

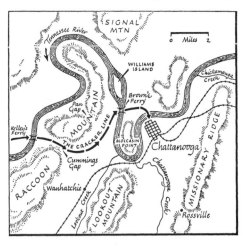

Here then was the ideal
route: save for one drawback.
The rebels held it. They had
guns emplaced on Raccoon
Mountain and pickets advanced
to the river itself, squarely
athwart the coveted approaches
to the gap through which the
road connecting the two ferries
ran. But Smith had the answer to this as well, a tactical solution employing the principles of speed and stealth to achieve surprise and, with surprise, success. Crossing at Bridgeport, a force from Hooker would follow
the railroad east around the south flank of the mountain, then move north
under cover of darkness, still following the railroad through Wauhatchie, to close upon Brown's Ferry from the rear. Meanwhile, and also
under cover of darkness, a force from Thomas would advance on the
same point in two columns, one marching overland, first across the pontoon bridge at Chattanooga, then west across the narrow base of Moccasin Point, and the other floating noiselessly downriver in pontoon
boats, past the sheer north face of Lookout, to spearhead the crossing at Brown's Ferry, capture the gray outpost there, and hold on
while the boats were being anchored and floored over by an engineer
detachment so that the column approaching by land could cross as reinforcements; whereupon the two forces, one from Hooker and one
from Thomas, would combine for mop-up operations, opening Cummings Gap to clear the road leading west to Kelley's Ferry and dislodging the enemy guns on Raccoon Mountain. Once this was done, the new
supply route — half the length of the old one over Walden's Ridge, and a
good deal less than half as tortuous — would be securely in Federal
hands; the troops in Chattanooga could go back on full rations, refill
their cartridge boxes and limber chests, and prepare to deal with the
graybacks still on Lookout Mountain and Missionary Ridge.

Grant liked the sound of this — particularly the notion of the silent run past Lookout, reminiscent as it was of the maneuver that opened
the final phase of the Vicksburg campaign — afterwards saying of
Smith: "He explained the situation of the two armies and the topography

of the country so plainly that I could see it without an inspection." All the same, on the day after his arrival he rode out with Thomas and his chief engineer, back to the north bank of the Tennessee and across the base of Moccasin Point for a look at the lay of the land around Brown's Ferry. In the course of this reconnaissance Smith also showed him the work going on at a sawmill he had established for getting out the lumber needed for building the pontoons and flooring the bridge they would support after serving as transports and assault boats. Fifty of these had already been knocked together and caulked, and the workmen were also busy on an improvised steamboat, powered, as the sawmill itself was, by an engine commandeered from a nearby cotton gin. This last, Smith said, would be used for hauling supplies, once the river had been opened to traffic below the ferry. He seemed to have thought of everything. Grant was so impressed by the thoroughness and ingenuity of these preparations that as soon as he got back to Chattanooga that evening he not only issued orders for the plan to be adopted; he also directed that it was to begin within two days. Hooker was instructed to leave one division behind to guard the railroad back toward Nashville and to cross with the other three at Bridgeport on October 26, marching fast through Wauhatchie to approach Brown's Ferry from the south. Thomas was told to move the following morning, before daylight, thus allowing Hooker time to come within reach of their common objective. Grant further stipulated that Smith was to be in direct charge of the two-pronged approach from Chattanooga, later explaining that the staff engineer "had been so instrumental in preparing for the move, and so clear in his judgment about the manner of making it, that I deemed it but just to him that he should have command of the troops detailed to execute the design."

His trust was not misplaced; there was no better example, in the whole course of the war, of what the combination of careful planning, ingenuity, and great daring could accomplish under intelligent leadership. Hooker crossed on schedule at Bridgeport, leaving Slocum and one of his divisions behind to guard the Nashville & Chattanooga Railroad against saboteurs and raiders, and proceeded eastward along the Memphis & Charleston with Slocum's other division and Howard's two, a force of about 11,000 effectives. That night Smith set out across Moccasin Point with two brigades of infantry and a battalion of engineers, numbering in all about 3500 men, and at 3 o'clock the following morning, October 27, a selected group of 1500 others, who had been loaded aboard the improvised fleet of sixty pontoon-transports, cast off and started downstream from the Chattanooga wharves, two dozen men and one officer in each boat. The current was strong; there was no need for oars, except to steer with, during the nearly circuitous six-mile run. Screened by a light mist, they hugged the right bank and made the trip in just two hours, undetected by rebel lookouts despite the frantic cries of one unfortunate soldier who fell overboard and was left to drown, as he had been warned beforehand would be done if he got careless. Reaching Brown's Ferry at 5 o'clock, half an hour before dawn, the troops in the first boats swarmed ashore and captured the drowsy pickets, while oarsmen in the unloaded transports began their task of ferrying Smith's overland marchers across from the right bank, where they had waited all this time under cover of the brush and darkness.

One dispersed brigade of Confederates — for, as it turned out, this was all the force the enemy had west of Lookout Mountain — attempted to assault the beachhead in the gray dawn, but was quickly thrown into retreat by the superior blue force, which then proceeded to fortify and intrench a defensive perimeter while the engineers went hard to work on the bridge. By midmorning the pontoons had been moored and floored; reinforcements from Thomas could march across in almost any numbers Smith or Grant decided might be needed. Few would be, apparently, for those graybacks who had not been captured at the time of the landing, or knocked out during the quick repulse that followed, had withdrawn eastward across Lookout Valley, leaving Raccoon Mountain and Cummings Gap in Federal hands. Moreover, dispatches sent forward that afternoon by Hooker announced that he was approaching Wauhatchie and would arrive in person the next day. This he did, together with two of his divisions, the third having been posted as a rear guard at Wauhatchie. And now for the first time, here on the south bank of the Tennessee River, near Brown's Ferry, Union soldiers of the East and West shook hands and congratulated each other on the success of their combined operation, by which a new supply route into besieged Chattanooga was about to be opened; "The Cracker Line," they dubbed it.

Hooker had had no share in anything so obviously exciting as a six-mile run downriver through misty darkness. But the fact was, he and his troops had had perhaps the most nerve-racking time of all, if only because of the duration of the strain; and in the end they did the only real fighting involved in the operation. As he marched eastward by daylight on his first and second days away from Bridgeport, Lookout Mountain loomed nearer and taller with every mile. Rebels up there in untold numbers were watching him, alone so to speak in their own back yard, and he knew it. He counted himself fortunate when he reached Wauhatchie without being attacked, and he took the precaution of dropping John Geary's division off at that point, as a safeguard for his rear, while he continued his march north with Howard's two divisions under von Steinwehr and Carl Schurz. Presently, though, on the night of the day he made contact with Smith at Brown's Ferry — October 28 — Fighting Joe had cause to believe that what he had thought was a precautious act had in fact been an extremely rash one that might cost him no less than one third of the force he had brought across the Tennessee, and possibly much more. A sudden midnight booming of guns, loud not only at the ferry but also in the town across the way, informed him that Geary was under assault in his isolated position, three miles off. What was worse, if the attack was in sufficient force it might be launched for the purpose of overwhelming the bridgehead, in which case there would be nothing for Howard's men to do but retreat with Smith's across the river and into Chattanooga, where they would have to share the hungry garrison's meager rations and thus hasten its progress toward starvation or surrender. Determined to do what he could to avert such a fate, along with further damage to the reputation he had been given a chance to retrieve in a new theater, Hooker put Schurz on the march to reinforce the embattled Geary, the flashes of whose guns were playing fitfully on the southern horizon despite the brightness of a moon only two nights past the full, and alerted Steinwehr to stand ready to come, too, if he was needed.

The trouble, as it turned out, was by no means as serious as he had feared: not only because Geary's men gave an excellent account of themselves in defending the position at Wauhatchie, but also because the Confederates — four brigades from the absent Hood's division — became confused in their first attempt at a night attack and were unable to co-ordinate their efforts. Though the soldiers on both sides had traveled a thousand miles or more from Virginia to come to grips here in the darkness near the Tennessee-Georgia line, neither could distinguish the presence of the other except by the flashes of the shots they fired. In this sort of situation the advantage lay with the defenders, who remained in one place and at least knew where they themselves were, whereas the attackers did not even know that much for a good part of the time. Moreover, the element of surprise was by no means altogether with the latter. Geary's teamsters, for example, became frightened by the uproar and deserted their picketed mules; whereupon the mules, left to their own devices in the flame-stabbed pandemonium, broke loose from their tethers and stampeded toward the rebels, who in turn became frightened, thinking a cavalry charge had been launched at them, and stampeded too. (Just as Southerners liked to celebrate such affairs as the Buckland Races with rollicking verses, generally in parody of something at once hackneyed and heroic, so did an anonymous Ohio infantryman immortalize this "Charge of the Mule Brigade":

> *Half a mile, half a mile,*
> *Half a mile onward,*
> *Right toward the Georgia troops*
> *Broke the two hundred.*
> *"Forward, the Mule Brigade;*
> *Charge for the rebs!" they neighed.*

> *Straight for the Georgia troops*
> *Broke the two hundred.*

Five stanzas later came the envoy:

> *When can their glory fade?*
> *O the wild charge they made!*
> *All the world wondered.*
> *Honor the charge they made;*
> *Honor the Mule Brigade,*
> *Long-eared two hundred.)*

In any event — aside, that is, from the disconcerting, not to say unnerving effect on the graybacks of having some two hundred fear-crazed mules come bearing down on them out of the clattering darkness — Schurz came up soon to even the odds, and the confused engagement broke off about as suddenly as it had begun. By 4 o'clock, two hours before sunrise, the Confederates had withdrawn across Lookout Creek, leaving the field to the men who had held it in the first place, and Bragg made no further attempt to interfere with the opening of the new Federal supply line. At a cost of well under five hundred casualties — 420 for Hooker, 37 for Smith — Grant had inflicted perhaps twice as many, including the prisoners taken at Brown's Ferry and picked up later on Raccoon Mountain, and had delivered the Chattanooga garrison from the grim threat of starvation, the most urgent of the several problems he had found waiting for him on his arrival, five days back. On October 30, exactly one week after he rode into town, "wet, dirty, and well," the little steamboat Smith had built tied up at Kelley's Ferry, completing a run from Bridgeport with a cargo of 40,000 rations for the troops at the opposite end of Cummings Gap. According to an officer aboard her, an orderly sent on horseback to announce the steamer's arrival returned to report "that the news went through the camps faster than his horse, and the soldiers were jubilant and cheering, 'The Cracker Line's open. Full rations, boys! Three cheers for the Cracker Line,' as if we had won another victory; and we had."

So far as Grant himself was concerned, the issue had been decided as soon as the pontoon bridge was thrown and the bridgehead secured at Brown's Ferry. His mind had moved on to other matters, even before the night action at Wauhatchie seemed for a moment to threaten the loss of what had been won. "The question of supplies may now be regarded as settled," he wired Halleck that evening, four hours before Geary came under attack. "If the rebels give us one week more time I think all danger of losing territory now held by us will have passed away, and preparations may commence for offensive operations."

✗ 4 ✗

Pleased though he was by the prospect, as he saw it from his Chattanooga headquarters now that the Cracker Line was open, Grant would
have felt even more encouraged if he somehow had been able to sit in on
the councils across the way, on Lookout Mountain and Missionary
Ridge, and thus acquire firsthand knowledge of the bitterness that had
prevailed for the past month in the camps of his adversaries. Bragg's dissatisfaction with several of his ranking lieutenants for their shortcomings
during the weeks that preceded Chickamauga — willful ineptitudes, as
he saw it, which had cost him the opportunity to destroy the Federal
army piecemeal, in McLemore's Cove and elsewhere — was matched, if
not exceeded, by their dissatisfaction with his failure, as they saw it, to
gather the fruits of their great victory during the weeks that followed.
Resentment bred dissension; dissension provoked criminations; recrim-
inations led to open breaks. Polk and Hindman had departed and Harvey
Hill was about to follow, relieved of duty by the army commander;
while still another top subordinate — more nearly indispensable, some
would say, than all the rest combined — had left under his own power.
This was Forrest.

His contention that "we ought to press forward as rapidly as possible" having been ignored on the morning after the battle, the Tennessee
cavalryman was sent northwest with his division, four days later, to head
off or delay a supposed Union advance from Knoxville. No such threat
existed, but Forrest did encounter enemy cavalry hovering in that direction and drove them helter-skelter across the Hiwassee, then through
Athens and Sweetwater, slashing at their flanks and rear, to Loudon,
where the survivors managed to get beyond his reach by crossing the
Tennessee, eighty miles above Chattanooga and less than half that far
from Knoxville. Having determined that no bluecoats were advancing
from the latter place, he was on his way back across the Hiwassee,
September 28, when he received a dispatch signed by an assistant adjutant
on Bragg's staff. "The general commanding desires that you will without
delay turn over the troops of your command previously ordered to Major General Wheeler." There was no explanation, no mention of the raid
that Wheeler was about to make on the Federal supply line: just the
peremptory order to "turn over the troops of your command." Forrest
complied, of course, but then, having done so, dictated and sent through
channels a fiery protest. "Bragg never got such a letter as that before
from a brigadier," he told the staffer who took it down. A couple of
days later, during an interview with the army commander, he was assured that he would get his men back as soon as they returned from over
the river, and he was granted, in the interim, a ten-day leave to go to
La Grange, Georgia, to see his wife for the first time since his visit to
Memphis to recuperate from his Shiloh wound, a year and a half ago.

While he was at La Grange, sixty miles southwest of Atlanta, he received an army order issued just after his interview with Bragg, assigning Wheeler "to the command of all the cavalry in the Army of Tennessee." Since his oath — taken in early February, after the Donelson repulse and their near duel — that he would never again serve under Wheeler was well known at headquarters, this amounted to a permanent separation of Forrest and the troopers he had raised on his own and seasoned, shortly afterward, on his December strike at Grant's supply lines in West Tennessee. Moreover, he took the order as a personal affront and he reacted in a characteristically direct manner. Interrupting his leave, he went at once to see the commanding general, accompanied by his staff surgeon as a witness.

Bragg received him in his tent on Missionary Ridge, rising and offering his hand as the Tennessean entered. Forrest declined it. "I am not here to pass civilities or compliments with you, but on other business," he said, and he launched without further preamble into a heated denunciation, which he punctuated by stabbing in Bragg's direction with a rigid index finger: "I have stood your meanness as long as I intend to. You have played the part of a damned scoundrel, and are a coward, and if you were any part of a man I would slap your jaws and force you to resent it. You may as well not issue any more orders to me, for I will not obey them ... and I say to you that if you ever again try to interfere with me or cross my path it will be at the peril of your life." And having thus attended to what he had called his "other business," he turned abruptly and stalked out of the tent. "Well, you are in for it now," his doctor companion said as they rode away. Forrest disagreed. "He'll never say a word about it; he'll be the last man to mention it. Mark my words, he'll take no action in the matter. I will ask to be relieved and transferred to a different field, and he will not oppose it."

Forrest was right in his prediction; Bragg neither took official notice of the incident nor disapproved the cavalryman's request for transfer, which was submitted within the week. He was wrong, though, in his interpretation of his superior's motives. Braxton Bragg was no coward; he was afraid of no man alive, not even Bedford Forrest. Rather, he was willing to overlook the personal affront — as the hot-tempered Tennessean, with far less provocation, had not been — for the good of their common cause. He knew and valued Forrest's abilities, up to a point, and by not pressing charges for insubordination — which would certainly have stuck — he saved his services for the country. Partly, no doubt, this was because he saw him as primarily a raider, not only a nonprofessional but an "irregular," and as such less subject to discipline for irregularities, even ones so violent as this. Others of higher rank in his army were less direct in their denunciations, but he exercised no such forbearance where they were concerned. Polk and Hindman and Hill, for instance; these he saw as regulars, and he treated them as such, writing directly to the Commander in Chief of their "want of prompt conformity to orders," as well as of their "having taken steps to procure my removal in a manner both unmilitary and un-officerlike."

He had particular reference to Hill in this, and he was right. In fact, there existed in the upper echelon of his army a cabal whose purpose was just that, to "procure [his] removal," and to do so by much the same method he himself had been employing; that is, by complaining individually and collectively to the President and the Secretary of War. Davis had received by now Polk's letter stigmatizing Bragg for "palpable weakness and mismanagement," and had also read Longstreet's note to Seddon, protesting "that nothing but the hand of God can save us or help us as long as we have our present commander." These he sought to deal with indirectly, on October 3, by explaining at some length to Bragg why he had recommended that the charges against the departed Polk not be pressed. "It was with the view of avoiding a controversy, which could not heal the injury sustained and which I feared would entail further evil," he wrote, adding that to persist would involve a full-scale investigation, "with all the crimination and recrimination there to be produced. . . . I fervently pray that you may judge correctly," he said in closing, "as I am well assured you will act purely for the public welfare." He hoped that this appeal to Bragg for a reduction of the pressure from above would serve to lessen the tension elsewhere along the chain of command; but he received a document, two days later, which showed that tension to be even greater than he had supposed. It came in the form of a round robin, a petition addressed to the President and signed by a number of general officers, including Hill and Buckner. While admitting "that the proceeding is unusual among military men," the petitioners contended that "the extraordinary condition of affairs in this army, the magnitude of the interests at stake, and a sense of the responsibilities under which they rest to Your Excellency and to the Republic, render this proceeding, in their judgment, a matter of solemn duty, from which, as patriots, they cannot shrink."

Their grounds for concern were stated at some length. "Two weeks ago this army, elated by a great victory which promised to be the most fruitful of the war, was in readiness to pursue the defeated enemy. That enemy, driven in confusion from the field, was fleeing in disorder and panic-stricken. . . . Today, after having been twelve days in line of battle in that enemy's front, within cannon range of his position, the Army of Tennessee has seen a new Sebastopol rise steadily before its view. The beaten enemy, recovering behind its formidable works from the effects of his defeat, is understood to be already receiving reinforcements, while heavy additions to his strength are rapidly approaching him. Whatever may have been accomplished heretofore, it is certain that the fruits of the victory of the Chickamauga have now escaped our grasp. The Army of Tennessee, stricken with a complete paralysis, will in a few days' time be thrown strictly on the defensive, and may deem itself fortunate if it escapes from its present position without disaster." Having thus stated the problem, the generals then went on to propose a solution that was at once tactful and explicit. "In addition to reinforcements, your petitioners would deem it a dereliction of the sacred duty they owe the country if they did not further ask that Your Excellency assign to the command of this army an officer who will inspire the army and the country with undivided confidence. Without entering into a criticism of the merits of our present commander, your petitioners regard it as a sufficient reason, without assigning others, to urge his being relieved, because, in their opinion, the condition of his health totally unfits him for the command of an army in the field."

Authorship of the document was afterwards disputed. Some said Buckner wrote it, others Hill. Bragg, for one, believed he recognized the hand of the latter in the phrasing, but Hill denied this; "Polk got it up," he said. Whoever wrote it, Davis decided that what it called for — particularly in a closing sentence: "Your petitioners cannot withhold from Your Excellency the expression of the fact that, as it now exists, they can render you no assurance of the success which Your Excellency may reasonably expect" — was another presidential journey west. "I leave in the morning for General Bragg's headquarters," he wired Lee, who was preparing to cross the Rapidan that week, "and hope to be serviceable in harmonizing some of the difficulties existing there."

He left Richmond aboard a special train, October 6, accompanied by two military aides, Colonels William P. Johnston and Custis Lee — sons of Albert Sidney Johnston and R. E. Lee — his young secretary, Burton Harrison, and the still-disconsolate John Pemberton, for whom no commensurate employment had been found in the nearly three months since his formal release from parole. Personally this saddened Davis almost as much as it did the unhappy Pennsylvanian, whom he admired for his firmness under adversity. But the truth was, there was much of sadness all around them as they traveled through the heartland of the South, in the faces of the people in their shabby towns and on their neglected farms, in the condition of the roadbeds and the cars, and even in the itinerary the presidential party was obliged to follow. The Confederacy's shrinking fortunes were reflected all too plainly in the fact that this second western journey was necessarily far more roundabout than the first had been in December, when Davis had gone directly to Chattanooga by way of Knoxville. Now the compass-boxing route led south through Charlotte and Columbia, then westward to Atlanta, and finally north, through Marietta and Dalton, to Chickamauga Station. That other time, moreover, he had extended his trip to include what he called "the further West," but this would not be possible now, the area thus referred to having fallen, like Knoxville and Chattanooga itself, under Federal occupation. Reaching Bragg's headquarters on Missionary

Ridge, October 9, he conferred in private with the general, who un-
burdened himself of a great many woes by placing the blame for them on
his subordinates; regretfully declined the proffered services of Pemberton as a replacement for Polk, though he was still unwilling to restore
the latter to duty; and, in conclusion, submitted his resignation as commander of the Army of Tennessee. This Davis refused, not wanting to
disparage the abilities of the only man under whom a Confederate army
had won a substantial victory since the death of Stonewall Jackson, back
in May. That evening he presided over a council of war attended by
Bragg and his corps commanders, Longstreet, Hill, Buckner, and
Cheatham, who had taken over from Polk, pending the outcome of the
bishop's current set-to with his chief. After what Davis later described
as "a discussion of various programmes, mingled with retrospective remarks on the events attending and succeeding the battle of Chickamauga" — in the course of which he continued his efforts "to be serviceable in harmonizing some of the difficulties" — he inquired whether
anyone had any further suggestions. Whereupon Longstreet spoke up.
Bragg, he said, "could be of greater service elsewhere than at the head of
the Army of Tennessee."

An embarrassing silence followed: embarrassing at any rate to
Bragg, who looked neither left nor right, as well as to Davis, who after
all had come here to compose differences, not to create scenes that would
enlarge them. After a time, however, he asked the other generals how
they felt about the matter, and all replied that they agreed with what
had just been said — particularly Hill, who seemed to relish the opportunity this afforded for an airing of his views. Bragg sat immobile
through the painful scene, his dark-browed face expressionless. Without
giving any opinion of his own, Davis at last adjourned the council. But
next day, when he sounded Longstreet on his willingness to accept the
command in place of Bragg, the Georgian declined. "In my judgment,"
he explained later, "our last opportunity was gone when we failed to follow the success at Chickamauga, and capture or disperse the Union
army, and it could not be just to the service or myself to call me to a position of such responsibility." He had, however, a suggestion: Joseph E.
Johnston. Davis bridled at the name, which Longstreet said "only served
to increase his displeasure, and his severe rebuke." This in turn caused
Old Peter to tender his resignation, but Davis, as he said, "was not
minded to accept that solution to the premise." At the close of the interview, Longstreet afterwards wrote, "the President walked as far as the
gate, gave me his hand in his usual warm grasp, and dismissed me with
his gracious smile; but a bitter look lurking about its margin, and the
ground-swell, admonished me that the clouds were gathering about
headquarters of the First Corps even faster than those that told the doom
of the Southern cause."

If Davis was pained, if a bitter look did lurk in fact about the margin of his smile, it was small wonder; for he was being required to deal with a problem which came more and more to seem insoluble. Though Bragg's subordinates, or former subordinates, all agreed that he should be removed, none of those who were qualified was willing to take his place. First Longstreet, then Hardee, on being questioned, replied that they did not want the larger responsibility, while Polk and Hill, Buckner and Cheatham, either through demonstrated shortcomings in the case of the former pair or lack of experience in the latter, were plainly unqualified. Lee had been suggested, but had made it clear that he preferred to remain in Virginia, where there could be no doubt he was needed. Joe Johnston, on the other hand, had once been offered the command and once been ordered to it, and both times had refused, protesting that Bragg was the best man for the post. Besides, if past performance was any indication of what could be expected from a general, to appoint Johnston would be to abandon all hope of an aggressive campaign against the cooped-up Federals. . . . Davis thought the matter over for three days, and then on October 13 announced his decision in the form of a note to Bragg: "Regretting that the expectations which induced the assignment of that gallant officer to this army have not been realized, you are authorized to relieve Lieutenant General D. H. Hill from further duty with your command." It had been obvious from the outset that one of the two North Carolinians would have to go. Now Davis had made his choice. Bragg would remain as commander of the army, and Hill — an accomplished hater, with a sharp tongue he was never slow to use on all who crossed him, including now the President — would return to his home state.

In addition to concerning himself with this command decision, in which Bragg emerged the winner more by default than by virtue of his claim, Davis also inspected the defenses, reviewed the troops, and held strategy conferences for the purpose of learning what course of action the generals thought the army now should take. Basically, Bragg was in favor of doing nothing more than holding what he had; that is, of keeping the Federals penned up in the town until starvation obliged them to surrender. He felt sure that this would be the outcome, and he said so, not only now but later, in his report. "Possessed of the shortest road to the depot of the enemy, and the one by which reinforcements must reach him," he would still maintain in late December, "we held him at our mercy, and his destruction was only a question of time." When Davis expressed dissatisfaction with his apparent lack of aggressiveness, Bragg came up with an alternate plan, suggested to him earlier that week in a letter from Beauregard, who, as was often the case when he had time on his hands — Gillmore and Dahlgren were lying idle just then, licking the wounds they had suffered in the course of their recent and nearly fruitless exertions, outside and just inside Charleston harbor — had turned his mind to grand-scale operations. In Virginia and elsewhere the

Confederates should hold strictly to the defensive, he said, so that Bragg could be reinforced by 35,000 troops, mainly from Lee, in order to cross the Tennessee, flank the bluecoats out of Chattanooga, and crush them in an all-out showdown battle; after which, he went on, Bragg could assist Lee in administering the same treatment to Meade, just outside Washington. He suggested, though, that the source of the plan be kept secret, lest the President be prejudiced against it in advance by his known dislike of its originator. "What I desire is our success," Old Bory wrote. "I care not who gets the credit." So Bragg at this point, being pressed for aggressive notions, offered the program as his own, expanding it slightly by proposing that a crossing be made well upstream for a descent on the Federal rear by way of Walden's Ridge. Davis listened with interest, Bragg informed Beauregard, finding merit in the suggestion; he "admitted its worth and was inclined to adopt it, only" — here was the catch; here the Creole's spirits took a drop — "he could not reduce General Lee's army." That disposed of the scheme Bragg advanced as his own, and the true author's hopes went glimmering.

Longstreet too had an alternate plan, however, which was not greatly different except that it involved no reinforcements and called for a move in the opposite direction. He proposed a change of base to Rome, for added security, and a crossing in force at Bridgeport; a move, he said, "that would cut the enemy's rearward line, interrupt his supply train, put us between his army at Chattanooga and the reinforcements moving to join him, and force him to precipitate battle or retreat." Davis liked the sound of this much better, largely because it had the virtue of economy in attempting the same purpose. Besides, he knew only too well the danger inherent in waiting idly outside the town while Yankee ingenuity went to work on the very problems for which it was best suited. Bragg concurring, albeit with hesitation, the President hopefully ordered the adoption of Old Peter's proposal and adjourned the conference.

So far, he had not addressed the troops. In fact he had declined to do so on his arrival five days ago, when he was welcomed at Chickamauga Station by a crowd of soldiers who called for a speech as he mounted his horse for the ride to army headquarters. "Man never spoke as you did on the field of Chickamauga," Davis told them, lifting his hat in return salute, "and in your presence I dare not speak. Yours is the voice that will win the independence of your country and strike terror to the heart of a ruthless foe." Now that he had toured their camps, however, and had seen for himself how rife the discontent was, he changed his mind and did what he had said he dared not do. Referring to the men before him as "defenders of the heart of our territory," he assured them that "your movements have been the object of intensest anxiety. The hopes of our cause greatly depend upon you, and happy it is that all can securely rely upon your achieving whatever, under the blessing of Providence, human power can effect." This said, he returned to his primary task of pouring oil on troubled waters, speaking not only to the troops themselves, but also to their officers, particularly those of lofty rank. "When the war shall have ended," he declared, "the highest meed of praise will be due, and probably given, to him who has claimed least for himself in proportion to the service he has rendered, and the bitterest self-reproach which may hereafter haunt the memory of anyone will be to him who has allowed selfish aspiration to prevail over the desire for the public good. . . . He who sows the seeds of discontent and distrust prepares for the harvest of slaughter and defeat. To zeal you have added gallantry; to gallantry, energy; to energy, fortitude. Crown these with harmony, due subordination, and cheerful support of lawful authority, that the measure of your duty may be full." He ended with a prayer "that our Heavenly Father may cover you with the shield of his protection in the hours of battle, and endow you with the virtues which will close your trials in victory complete."

These words were spoken on October 14, the date of A. P. Hill's sudden and bloody repulse at Bristoe Station. Davis stayed on for three more days, continuing his efforts to promote "harmony, due subordination, and cheerful support of lawful authority" at all levels in the strife-torn Army of Tennessee; then on October 17 — the date Stanton overtook Grant at Indianapolis — ended his eight-day visit by reboarding the train to continue his journey south for an inspection of the Mobile defenses. As he left he was assured by Bragg that Longstreet's plan for a crossing of the Tennessee on the Federal right at Bridgeport would be undertaken as soon as the troops could be gotten ready to advance.

Two days later, after inspecting a cannon foundry and other manufacturing installations at Selma, Alabama, he addressed a large crowd from his hotel balcony, asserting that if the "non-conscripts" would volunteer for garrison duty, and thus release more regular troops for service in the field, "we can crush Rosecrans and be ready with the return of spring to drive the enemy from our borders. The defeat of Rosecrans," he added, swept along by the enthusiasm his words had aroused — and unaware, of course, that Rosecrans would be relieved that day by a wire from Grant in Louisville — "will practically end the war." From Selma he proceeded to Demopolis, where he crossed the Tombigbee River and continued west across the Mississippi line to Meridian for a visit with his septuagenarian brother at nearby Lauderdale Springs. The war had been hard on Joseph Davis. Formerly one of the state's wealthiest planters, he had had to move twice already to escape the advancing Federals, not counting refugee stops along the way, and now his wife lay dying in a dilapidated house, having conserved her ebbing strength for one last glimpse of "Brother Jeff." The weary President was distressed by what he saw here, for to him it represented what was likely to happen to all his people, kin and un-kin, if the South failed in its bid for independence. Nevertheless he managed, in the course of his stay in Meridian, to work out a solution to another thorny problem of command. On October 23 — while Grant rode south down Walden's Ridge to enter Chattanooga before nightfall — he wired instructions for Bragg and Johnston, in their now separate departments, to have Polk and Hardee swap jobs and commanders, the latter to take charge of the former's corps in the Army of Tennessee, while the bishop took over the Georgian's duties at the camp for recruitment and instruction near Demopolis. This done, Davis left next morning for Mobile. After a tour of inspection with Major General Dabney H. Maury, commander of the city's defenses, he returned to the Battle House and spoke as he had done at Selma the week before, emphasizing that "those who remain at home, not less than those in arms, have their duties to perform. Each of all can encourage the spirit which can bring success," he told his listeners, adding that "men using the opportunities given by war to make fortunes will be detested by their posterity." A local reporter, impressed by the Chief Executive's "remarkably clear enunciation," observed that, though he spoke "without the slightest apparent effort, his words penetrated far down the street and were heard distinctly by most of the vast crowd gathered on the occasion."

Davis remained in Mobile over Sunday, October 25 — cheered by news of the Buckland Races, which Stuart had staged on Monday, but disappointed by Bragg's report that rain had delayed his preparations for a crossing at Bridgeport, as well as by the returns from Ohio's second-Tuesday elections, held just under two weeks ago, which showed that Lincoln's hard-war candidates had defeated Vallandigham and his Golden Circle friends — then left the following day for Montgomery, where he had arranged to have Forrest board the train for a conference en route to Atlanta. Valuing the Tennessean's abilities, the Commander in Chief not only approved his transfer to North Mississippi, where he would have authority "to raise and organize as many troops for the Confederate service as he finds practicable," but also directed that Bragg send the cavalryman a two-battalion cadre of his veteran troopers, plus Morton's battery, and recommended to Congress his promotion to major general. Forrest left the train at Atlanta, pleased to be taking up new duties as an independent commander in a region he knew well; but for his erstwhile traveling companion there was disturbing news from the Chattanooga theater. While Bragg had been waiting for the weather to clear before he moved against the enemy right, the Federals, with no apparent concern for mud and rain, had anticipated him in that direction by crossing the river themselves. Aggressive as always, Davis saw in this a chance for offensive action. "It is reported here that the enemy are crossing at Bridgeport," he wired Bragg on the 29th. "If so it may give you the opportunity to beat the detachment moving up to reinforce Rosecrans as was contemplated. . . . You will be able to anticipate him, and strike with the advantage of fighting him in detail." It had become increasingly evident, though, that weather was a pretense; that Bragg was favoring his preference for the defensive, despite a presidential warning, repeated today, that "the period most favorable for actual operations is rapidly passing away, and the consideration of supplies presses upon you the necessity to recover as much as you can of the country before you." Anxious that something be done at once, in Middle or East Tennessee, to justify Longstreet's prolonged absence from Virginia — where Lee was facing grievous odds, having fallen back to the line of the Rappahannock, and might need him at any moment — Davis added: "In this connection it has occurred to me that if the operations on your left should be delayed, or not be of prime importance, that you might advantageously assign General Longstreet with his two divisions to the task of expelling Burnside and thus place him in position, according to circumstances, to hasten or delay his return to the army of General Lee."

Much might come of either of these suggestions: the destruction of the blue column that had ventured across the river, within easy reach of the Confederate left, or the expulsion of Burnside from Knoxville and East Tennessee, far upstream on the right, "to recover that country and re-establish communications with Virginia." But for the present, with whatever patience he could muster while waiting for Bragg to make up his mind and move in one direction or the other, Davis resumed his journey back to the capital by way of Savannah and Charleston, neither of which he had visited since the outbreak of the war. He was welcomed to the former place on Halloween with an exuberant torchlight procession, followed by a reception at the Masonic Hall. A young matron who stood in line for a handshake wrote her soldier brother that she and her friends "were much pleased with the affability of the President. He has a good, mild, pleasant face," she added, "and, altogether, looks like a President of our struggling country *should* look — careworn and thoughtful, and firm, and quiet."

His affability came under a strain next morning, however, when Bragg announced the failure of the attempted counterstroke on his left, three nights ago at Wauhatchie, and placed the blame on Old Peter for having used an inadequate force ineptly. "The result related is a bitter disappointment," Davis replied, "as my expectations were sanguine that the enemy, by throwing across the Tennessee his force at Bridgeport, had ensured the success of the operation suggested by General Longstreet, and confided to his execution." In any case, the way was still open for an advance around the Federal right, and he hoped it would be taken, though he was obliged as always to leave the final decision to the commander on the scene. As for himself, he faced an ordeal of his own the following day in Charleston, where Beauregard was in command and the Rhetts had been attacking him, almost without remission, for the past two years in their *Mercury*. As his train drew near the station, November 2, he heard the booming of guns being fired in his honor, and when the presidential car lurched to a stop beside the platform a welcoming committee came aboard. In the lead were Beauregard, his aide and amanuensis Colonel Thomas Jordan, and Robert Barnwell Rhett, a colonel too. As a later observer put it, Davis must have "wondered how the visit would turn out when the first three hands raised in salute to him belonged to three enemies." Perhaps it was this that threw him off his stride for the first time in the course of the autumn journey he had undertaken in the hope of harmonizing discord. At any rate, inadvertently or on purpose, here today in South Carolina he did his office, his country, and his cause the worst disservice he had done since he sent the curt, slashing note in reply to Joe Johnston's six-page letter of protest at being ranked behind Lee and the other Johnston, more than two years ago in Virginia. What made it worse in this case was that he not only passed up an easy chance to heal, he actually widened a dangerous rift, and he did so with nearly as curt a slash as he had used before, except that this time the technique involved omission.

Not that the citizens themselves were cold or unfriendly. "The streets along the line of procession were thronged with people anxious to get a look at the President," a *Courier* reporter wrote. "The men cheered and the ladies waved their handkerchiefs in token of recognition." Proud of their resistance to Du Pont's and Dahlgren's iron fleet, as well as of their standing up to Gillmore's long-range shelling — which had recently begun anew, after a respite of about a month — they were pleased that the Chief Executive had come to praise their valor and share their danger. Flags were draped across the fronts of homes and buildings, and garlands of laurel stretched from the city hall to the courthouse, supporting a large banner that bid him welcome. This was Davis's first Charleston visit since the spring of 1850, when he had accompanied the body of John C. Calhoun from Washington to its grave in St Philip's churchyard, and he recalled that sad occasion when he spoke today from the portico of the city hall. In saluting the defenders of Sumter, he had special praise for the fort's commander, Major Stephen Elliott, and predicted that if the Federals ever took the city they would find no more than a "mass of rubbish," so determined were its people in their choice of whether to "leave it a heap of ruins or a prey for Yankee spoils." ("Ruins! Ruins!" the crowd shouted.) "Let us trust to our commanding general, to those having the charge and responsibilities of our affairs," Davis said, with a sidelong glance at Beauregard, and he added a note of caution, as he had done in all his speeches this past month: "It is by united effort, by fraternal feeling, by harmonious co-operation, by casting away all personal considerations ... that our success is to be achieved. He who would now seek to drag down him who is struggling, if not a traitor, is first cousin to one; for he is striking the most deadly blows that can be [struck]. He who would attempt to promote his own personal ends ... is not worthy of the Confederate liberty for which we are fighting." In closing, he thanked the people and assured them of his prayers "for each and all, and above all for the sacred soil of Charleston."

At the reception held afterwards in the council chamber, people inquired of one another whether they had noticed that the President, after singling out Major Elliott for praise, not only had failed to congratulate Beauregard for his skillful defense of the city by land and water, but also had not mentioned him by name. Indeed, except for that one sidelong reference to "our commanding general," when the crowd was advised to put its trust in those in charge, Old Bory might as well not have been in Charleston at all, so far as Davis was concerned. Most of those present had noted this omission, which could scarcely have been anything but intentional, it seemed to them, on the part of a man as attentive to the amenities as the President normally was. Certainly Beauregard himself had felt the slight, and it was observed that he did not attend a dinner given that evening in Davis's honor by former governor William Aiken in his house on Wragg's Square. In point of fact, the general had already declined an invitation two days earlier. "It would afford me much pleasure to dine with you," he had told Aiken, "but candor requires me to inform you that my relations with the President being strictly official, I cannot participate in any act of politeness which might make him suppose otherwise." However, even if he had accepted earlier, he most likely would not have attended a dinner honoring a man who had just given him what amounted to a cut direct. Hard on the heels of the brief reference to him in the speech, moreover, had come the allusion to complainers as cousins to traitors, and this perhaps infuriated the Creole worst of all, touching him as it did where he was tender. Unburdening his feelings to a friend, he protested that Davis had "done more than if he had thrust a fratricidal dagger into my heart! he has *killed* my *enthusiasm* for our holy cause! ... May God forgive him," he added; "I fear I shall not have charity enough to pardon him."

Although Davis saw little or nothing of the general out of hours, according to a friendly diarist he spent a pleasant week as the former governor's house guest, "Beauregard, Rhetts, Jordan to the contrary notwithstanding. . . . Mr Aiken's perfect old Carolina style of living delighted him," the diarist noted, not only because of "those old greyhaired darkies and their automatic, noiseless perfection of training," but also because it afforded him the leisure, while resting from the rigors of his journey, to hear firsthand accounts of the unsuccessful but persistent siege-in-progress. Gillmore had resumed his bombardment from Cummings Point a week ago, on October 26, and while at first it had been as furious as before, it presently slacked off to an intermittent shelling. An occasional big incendiary projectile was flung at Charleston, but mostly he concentrated his attention on Sumter, chipping away at the upper casemates until it began to seem to observers that the fort, daily reduced in height as debris from the ramparts slid down the outer walls, was sinking slowly beneath the choppy surface of the harbor. The defenders were on the alert for another small-boat assault, but none was attempted; Gillmore and Dahlgren, it was said, were unwilling to risk a recurrence of the previous fiasco, though each kept insisting that the other should try his hand at reducing the ugly thing. To the Confederates, however, the squat, battered pentagon was a symbol of their long-odds resistance, and as such it took on a strange beauty. An engineer captain wrote home of the feelings aroused by the sight of its rugged outline against the night sky, lanterns gleaming in unseen hands as work crews piled sandbags on the rubble, sentinels huddled for warmth over small fires in the casemates. "That ruin is beautiful," he declared, and added: "But it is more than this, it is emblematic also. . . . Is it not in some respects an image of the human soul, once ruined by the fall, yet with gleams of beauty and energetic striving after strength, surrounded by dangers and watching, against its foes?"

Nor, as might have been expected with the resourceful Beauregard in charge, had the garrison's efforts been limited entirely to the defensive. Using money donated for the purpose by Charlestonians, the general had had designed and built a cigar-shaped torpedo boat, twenty feet long and five feet wide, powered by a small engine and equipped with a ten-foot spar that had at its bulbous tip a 75-pound charge of powder, primed to explode when one of its four percussion nipples came in contact with anything solid, such as the iron side of a ship. Manned by a crew of four — captain and pilot, engineer and fireman — she was christened *David* and sent forth after sunset, October 5, to try her luck on the blockading squadron just across the bar. Her chosen Goliath was the outsized *New Ironsides,* the Yankee flagship that had escaped destruction back in April when the boiler-torpedo, over which Du Pont unwittingly stopped her during his attack, failed to detonate. Undetected by enemy lookouts, the *David* made contact with her spar-tip charge six feet below the *Ironsides'* waterline, but the resultant explosion threw up a great column of water that doused the little vessel's fires when it came down and nearly swamped her. As she drifted powerless out to sea, the jolted bluejackets on the ironclad's deck opened on her with a heavy fire of musketry and grape, prompting all four of her crew to go over the side. Two of these were picked up by the Federals, the captain as he paddled about in the darkness and the fireman when he was found clinging next morning to the *Ironsides'* rudder; they were clapped in irons and later sent North by Dahlgren to be tried for employing a weapon not sanctioned by civilized nations. Nothing came of that, however; they presently were exchanged, for the captain and a seaman from a captured Union gunboat, and sent back to Charleston. The other two had been there all along. Returning to the half-swamped *David* after the firing stopped, the pilot found that the engineer had been clinging to her all this time because he could not swim. They relighted her fires with a bull's-eye lantern and, eluding searchers on all sides, steamed back into the harbor before dawn. As for the *New Ironsides*, she had not been seriously damaged, the main force of the underwater explosion having fortunately been absorbed by one of her inner bulkheads. After a trip down to Port Royal for repairs to a few leaky seams, she soon returned to duty with the squadron — though from this time on, it was observed, her crew was quick to sound the alarm and open fire whenever a drifting log or a floating patch of seaweed, or less comically an incautious friendly longboat, happened near her in the dark.

Firsthand knowledge of such events as this brief sortie by the *David*, even though it failed in its purpose, and of such reactions to destruction as those of the engineer captain to the ruins of Sumter, even though no response could be made to the diurnal pounding, served to strengthen Davis's conviction that the South could never be subdued, no matter how much of its apparently limitless wealth and strength the North expended and exerted in its attempt to bring her to her knees; Charleston, for him, was proof enough that the unconquerable spirit of his people could never be humbled, despite the odds and the malignity, as it seemed to him, with which they were brought to bear. He stayed through November 8 — his fifth Sunday away from the national capital and his wife and children — then returned the following day to the Old Dominion. Lee, he learned on arrival, was falling back across the Rapidan, having suffered a double reversal two nights ago at Kelly's Ford and Rappahannock Bridge. Davis did not doubt that the Virginian would be able to hold this new river line, whatever had happened along the old one; his confidence in Lee was complete. His concern was more for what might happen around Chattanooga, for he now was informed that Bragg, while continuing to maintain that the weather prevented a strike at the newly opened Federal supply line on his immediate left, had been quick to adopt the suggestion that Longstreet be sent against Burnside, far off on his right, thereby reducing his army by one fourth.

On the face of it, that did not seem too risky, considering the great natural strength of his position, but others as well as Davis saw the danger in that direction, not only to Bragg but also to the authority that had backed him in the recent intramural crisis. Davis had everywhere been "received with cheers" on his journey, a War Department diarist observed. "His austerity and inflexibility have been relaxed, and he has made popular speeches wherever he has gone. . . . The press, a portion rather, praises the President for his carefulness in making a tour of the armies and forts south of us; but as he retained Bragg in command, how soon the tune would change if Bragg should meet with a disaster!" No one understood this better than Davis, who still believed that the best defense against a Federal assault, even upon so impregnable a position as the one held by the Army of Tennessee, would be for Bragg to knock the enemy in his immediate front off balance with an offensive of his own, and this seemed all the more the proper course now that it was known that the man in command at Chattanooga was Grant, who had made the worst sort of trouble for the Confederacy almost everywhere he had been sent, so far in the war. Accordingly, two days after his return to Richmond, being still immersed in a mass of paperwork collected in his absence, Davis had Custis Lee send Bragg a reminder of this point of view. "His Excellency regrets that the weather and condition of the roads have suspended the movement [on your left]," Lee wired, "but hopes that such obstacles to your plans will not long obstruct them. He feels assured that you will not allow the enemy to get up all his reinforcements before striking him, if it can be avoided." The President, Lee added, stressing by repetition the danger in delay, "does not deem it necessary to call your attention to the importance of doing whatever is to be done before the enemy can collect his forces, as the longer the time given him for this purpose, the greater will be the disparity in numbers."

★   ★   ★

Unlike Davis, who twice in the past eleven months had visited every Confederate state east of the Mississippi except Florida and Louisiana, addressing crowds along the way and calling for national unity in them all, Lincoln in two and one half years — aside, that is, from four quick trips on army business: once to confer with Winfield Scott at West Point, twice to see McClellan, on the James and the Antietam, and once to visit with Joe Hooker on the Rappahannock line — had been no farther than a carriage ride from the White House. He had made no speeches on any of the exceptional occasions, being strictly concerned with military affairs, and for the most part even the citizens of Washington had not known he was gone until after he returned. This was not to say that he had not concerned himself with national unity or that he had made no appeals to the people in his efforts to achieve it; he had indeed, and repeatedly, in messages to Congress, in proclamations, and in public and private letters to individuals and institutions. One of the most successful of these had been his late-August letter to James Conkling, ostensibly an expression of regret that he was unable to attend a rally of "unconditional Union men" in his home town of Springfield, but actually a stump speech to be delivered by proxy at the meeting. John Murray Forbes, a prominent Boston businessman, had been so impressed with the arguments therein advanced in support of the government's views on the Negro question — "a plain letter to plain people," he called it — that he wrote directly to Lincoln in mid-September, suggesting that he also set the public mind aright on what Forbes considered the true issue of the war. "Our friends abroad see it," he declared; "John Bright and his glorious band of European republicans see that we are fighting for Democracy, or (to get rid of the technical name) for liberal institutions. ... My suggestion then is that you should seize an early opportunity, and any subsequent chance, to teach your great audience of plain people that the war is not North against South, but the *People* against the *Aristocrats*. If you can place this in the same strong light that you have the Negro question, you will settle it in men's minds as you have that."

Lincoln filed the letter in his desk and in his mind, and seven weeks later, on November 2, acting on the suggestion that he "seize an early opportunity," accepted an invitation to attend the dedication of a new cemetery at Gettysburg for the men who had fallen there in the July battle. The date, November 19, was less than three weeks off, and the reason for this lateness on the part of the committee was that he had been an afterthought, its original intention having been to emphasize the states, which were sharing the expenses of the project, not the nation. Besides, even after the thought occurred that it might be a good idea to invite the President, some doubt had been expressed "as to his ability to speak upon such a grave and solemn occasion." However, since the principal speaker, the distinguished orator Edward Everett of Massachusetts, had been chosen six weeks earlier, it was decided — as Lincoln was told in a covering letter, stressing that the ceremonies would "doubtless be very imposing and solemnly impressive" — to ask him to attend in a rather minor capacity: "It is the desire that after the oration, you, as Chief Executive of the nation, formally set apart these grounds to their sacred use by a few appropriate remarks." Duly admonished to be on his good behavior, to avoid both length and levity, Lincoln accepted the invitation, along with these implied conditions, on the day it was received.

He had not intended to crack any jokes in the first place, at least not at the ceremony itself, though in point of fact he was in higher spirits nowadays than he had been for months. For one thing, the military outlook — badly blurred by the effects of the heavy body blow Bragg landed at Chickamauga in mid-September — had improved greatly in the past ten days: specifically since October 23, when Grant rode into Chattanooga and set to work in his characteristic fashion, opening the Cracker Line and sustaining it with a victory in the night action at Wauhatchie, all within a week of his arrival, then wound up by notifying Halleck that "preparations may commence for offensive operations." If Banks had been thwarted so far in his designs on coastal Texas, that might be taken as a temporary setback, amply balanced in the far-western theater by Steele's success, on the heels of his Little Rock triumph, in driving the rebels out of Pine Bluff on October 25. Similarly, in the eastern theater, though Gillmore and Dahlgren had made but a small impression down in Charleston harbor, the news from close at hand in Virginia was considerably improved. Lee was on the backtrack from Manassas, presumably chastened by his repulse at Bristoe Station, and Meade was moving south again, rebuilding the wrecked railroad as he went. Lincoln now felt a good deal kindlier toward the Pennsylvanian than he had done in the weeks immediately following Gettysburg. If Meade had much of the exasperating caution that had characterized McClellan in the presence of the enemy, at least he was no blusterer like Pope or blunderer like Burnside, and despite his unfortunate snapping-turtle disposition he did not seem to come unglued under pressure, as McDowell and Hooker had tended to do and done. All in all, though it was evident that he was not the killer-arithmetician his Commander in Chief was seeking, the impression was that he would do till the real thing came along, and this estimate was heightened within another week, when he overtook Lee on the line of the Rappahannock, administered a double dose of what he had given him earlier at Bristoe, and drove him back across the Rapidan. "The signs look better," Lincoln had said in closing his letter to Conkling in late August. Now in November, reviewing the over-all military situation that had been disrupted by Chickamauga and readjusted since, he might have amended this to: "The signs look even better."

But it was on the political front that the news was best of all. Last year's congressional elections had been a bitter pill to swallow, but in choking it down, the Administration had learned much that could be applied in the future. For one thing, there was the matter of names. "Republican" having come to be something of an epithet in certain sections of the country, the decision was made to run this year's pro-Lincoln candidates under the banner of the National Union Party, thus to attract the votes of "loyal" Democrats. For another, with the enthusiastic co-operation of Stanton in the War Department, there were uses to which the army could be put: especially in doubtful states, where whole regiments could be furloughed home to cast their ballots, while individual squads and platoons could be assigned to maintain order at the polls and assist the local authorities in administering oaths of loyalty, past as well as present, required in several border states before a citizen could enter a voting booth. New England had gone solidly Republican in the spring. Then in August, with the help of considerable maneuvering along the lines described above, the President was pleased to note that his native Kentucky had "gone very strongly right." Tennessee followed suit, and so, presently, did all but one of the rest of the states that held elections in the fall. Only in New Jersey, where the organization was weak, did the "unconditional Unionists" lose ground. Everywhere else the outcome exceeded party expectations, particularly in Pennsylvania, Massachusetts, New York, and Maryland, in all of which the situation had been judged to be no better than touch-and-go. Ohio, where Vallandigham was opposed by John Brough in the race for governor, balloted on October 13; Lincoln said that he felt more anxious than he had done three years ago, when he himself had run. He need not have worried. With the help of 41,000 soldier votes, as compared to 2000 for Vallandigham, Brough won by a majority of 100,000. "Glory to God in the highest," Lincoln wired; "Ohio has saved the Nation." Four days later, having got this worry out of the way, he celebrated substantially by issuing another call for "300,000 more." The states were to raise whatever number of troops they could by volunteering, then complete their quotas by drafting men "to reinforce our victorious armies in the field," as the proclamation put it, "and bring our needful military operations to a prosperous end, thus closing forever the fountains of sedition and civil war."

News that the President would appear at Gettysburg reached the papers soon after his acceptance of the tardy invitation, and their reactions varied from bland to indignant, hostile editors protesting that a ceremony intended to honor fallen heroes was no proper occasion for what could only be a partisan appeal. Certain prominent Republicans, on the other hand, professed to believe it was no great matter, one way or the other, since Lincoln was by now a political cipher anyhow, a "dead card" in the party deck. "Let the dead bury the dead," Thaddeus Stevens quipped when asked for an opinion on what was about to happen just outside the little college town where he once had practiced law and still owned property. Lincoln held to his intention to attend the ceremonies, despite the quips and adverse comments in and out of print. He was, he remarked in another connection this week, not much upset by anything said about him, especially in the papers. "These comments constitute a fair specimen of what has occurred to me through life. I have endured a great deal of ridicule without much malice, and have received a great deal of kindness not quite free from ridicule. I am used to it." Meanwhile, in the scant period between the tendering of the invitation and the date for his departure, there was not much time for composing his thoughts, let alone for setting them down on paper. In addition to the usual encroachments by job- and favor-seekers, there was the wedding of Chase's sprightly daughter Kate to wealthy young Senator William Sprague of Rhode Island, the most brilliant social affair to be held in Washington in the nearly three years since the Southerners left the District; there was an urgent visit by the high-powered New York politician Thurlow Weed, who came with a plan for ending the war by means of a ninety-day armistice, a scheme that had to be heard in full and then rejected tactfully, lest Weed be offended into an enmity the cause could not afford; there was the necessity for day-to-day work on the annual year-end message to Congress, which it would not do to put off till the last minute, though the last minute was in fact about at hand already. All this there was, and more, much more: with the result that by the time the departure date came round, November 18, Lincoln had done little more than jot down a few notes on what he intended to say next day in Pennsylvania. Worst of all, in the way of distraction, Tad was sick with some feverish ailment the doctors could not identify, and Mrs Lincoln was near hysterics, remembering Willie's death, under similar circumstances, twenty months ago in this same house. But Lincoln did not let even this interfere with his plans and promise. The four-car special, carrying the President and three of his cabinet members — Seward, Blair, and Usher; the others had declined, pleading the press of business — his two secretaries, officers of the army and navy, his friend Ward Lamon, and the French and Italian ministers, left the capital around noon. Lincoln sat for a time with the others in a drawing room at the back of the rear coach, swapping stories for an hour or so, and then, as the train approached Hanover Junction, excused himself to retire to the privacy of his compartment at the other end of the car. "Gentlemen, this is all very pleasant," he said, "but the people will expect me to say something to them tomorrow, and I must give the matter some thought."

Arriving at sundown, he went to the home of Judge David Wills, on the town square, where he and Everett and Governor Curtin would spend the night. The streets and all the available beds were crowded, visitors having come pouring in for tomorrow's ceremonies, notables and nondescripts alike, many of them with no place to sleep and most of them apparently past caring. Accompanied by a band, a large group roamed about in the early dark to serenade the visiting dignitaries, including the President. He came out at last and gave them one of those brief speeches, the burden of which was that he had nothing to say. "In my position it is somewhat important that I should not say foolish things," he began. "— If you can help it!" a voice called up, and Lincoln took his cue from that: "It very often happens that the only way to help it is to say nothing at all. Believing that is my present condition this evening, I must beg you to excuse me from addressing you further." Unsatisfied, the crowd proceeded next door and called for Seward, who did better by them, though this still was evidently far from enough, since they serenaded five more speakers before calling it a night. Lincoln by then had completed the working draft of tomorrow's address and gone to bed, greatly relieved by a wire from Stanton passing along a message from Mrs Lincoln that Tad was much improved.

By morning the crowd had swelled to 15,000, most of whom were on the prowl about the town in search of breakfast or about the surrounding fields in search of relics, an oyster-colored minnie ball, a tarnished button, a fragment of shell that might or might not have killed a man. In any event, whatever disappointments there were for the hungry, the pickings were good for the souvenir hunters, for it was later calculated that 569 tons of ammunition had been expended in the course of the three-day battle. Coffins were much in evidence, too, though the work of reinterring the dead — at $1.59 a body — had been suspended for the solemn occasion now at hand. At 10 o'clock the procession began to form on the square, marshaled by Lamon and led by the President on horseback. An hour later it began to move, in what one witness referred to as "an orphanly sort of way," toward Cemetery Hill, where the ceremonies would be held. Lincoln sat erect at first, wearing a black suit, a high silk hat, and white gloves, but presently he slumped in the saddle, arms limp and head bent forward in deep thought, while behind him rode or walked the governors of six of the eighteen participating states, several generals, including Doubleday and Gibbon, and a number of congressmen, as well as the officials who had come up with him on the train. Within fifteen or twenty minutes these various dignitaries had taken their places on the crowded platform, and after a wait for Everett, who was late, the proceedings opened at noon with a prayer by the House chaplain, following which the principal speaker was introduced. "Mr President," he said with a bow, tall and white-haired, just under seventy years of age, a former governor of Massachusetts, minister to England for John Tyler, president of Harvard, successor to Daniel Webster as Secretary of State under Millard Fillmore, and in 1860 John Bell's running mate on the Constitutional Union ticket, which had carried Virginia, Kentucky, and Tennessee. "Mr Everett," Lincoln replied, and the orator launched forthwith into his address.

"Standing beneath this serene sky," with "the mighty Alleghenies dimly towering" before him, Everett raised his "poor voice to break the eloquent silence of God and Nature." He did so for two hours by the clock, having informed the committee beforehand that the occasion was "not to be dismissed with a few sentimental or patriotic commonplaces." Nor was it. He outlined the beginning of the war, reviewed the furious three-day action here, discussed and denounced the doctrine of state sovereignty, lacing his eloquence with historical and classical allusions, and came at last to a quotation from Pericles: "The whole earth is the sepulchre of illustrious men." Recognizing the advent of the peroration because he had been given advance proofs of the address, Lincoln took from his coat pocket a fair copy he had made of his own speech that morning, put on his steel-bowed spectacles, and read it through while Everett drew to a close, head back-flung, and pronounced the final sentence in a voice that had not faltered once in the whole two hours: "Down to the latest period of recorded time, in the glorious annals of our common country there will be no brighter page than that which relates the Battles of Gettysburg." Amid prolonged applause he took his seat, and after the Baltimore Glee Club had sung an ode composed for the occasion, Lamon pronounced the words: "The President of the United States." Lincoln rose, and as a photographer began setting up his tripod and camera in front of the rostrum, delivered — in what a reporter called "a sharp, unmusical treble voice," but with what John Hay considered "more grace than is his wont" — the "few appropriate remarks" which the committee had said it desired of him "after the oration."

"Fourscore and seven years ago our fathers brought forth upon this continent a new nation, conceived in liberty and dedicated to the proposition that all men are created equal. Now we are engaged in a great civil war, testing whether that nation, or any nation so conceived and so dedicated, can long endure. We are met on a great battlefield of that war. We are met to dedicate a portion of it as the final resting place of those who here gave their lives that that nation might live. It is altogether fitting and proper that we should do this. But in a larger sense we cannot dedicate, we cannot consecrate, we cannot hallow this ground. The brave men, living and dead, who struggled here, have consecrated it far above our poor power to add or detract." A polite scattering of applause was overridden at this point as Lincoln continued. "The world will little note, nor long remember, what we say here, but it can never forget what they did here. It is for us, the living, rather, to be dedicated here to the unfinished work that they have thus far so nobly carried on. It is rather for us to be here dedicated to the great task remaining before us, that from these honored dead we take increased devotion to that cause for which they here gave the last full measure of devotion; that we here highly resolve that these dead shall not have died in vain; that the nation shall, under God, have a new birth of freedom; and that government of the people, by the people, for the people, shall not perish from the earth."

He finished before the crowd, a good part of whose attention had been fixed on the photographer anyhow, realized that he was fairly launched on what he had to say. In reaction to what a later observer described as the "almost shocking brevity" of the speech, especially by contrast with the one that went before, the applause was delayed, then scattered and barely polite. Moreover, the photographer missed his picture. Before he had time to adjust his tripod and uncap the lens, Lincoln had said "of the people, by the people, for the people" and sat down, leaving the artist with a feeling that he had been robbed. Apparently many of those present felt the same, agreeing in advance with what the Chicago *Times* would say tomorrow about the President's performance here today: "The cheek of every American must tingle with shame as he reads the silly, flat and dishwatery utterances of the man who has to be pointed out to intelligent foreigners as the President of the United States." In fact, as he resumed his seat alongside his friend Lamon and heard the perfunctory spatter of applause whose brevity matched his own, the speaker himself was taken with a feeling of regret that he had not measured up to what had been expected of him. Recalling a word used on the prairie in reference to a plow that would not clean itself while shearing through wet soil, he said gloomily: "Lamon, that speech won't *scour*. It is a flat failure and the people are disappointed."

In time — for not all editors were as scathing as the one in his home state; a Massachusetts paper, for example, printed the address in full and remarked that it was "deep in feeling, compact in thought and expression, and tasteful and elegant in every word and comma" — Lincoln revised not only his opinion of what he called "my little speech," but also the text itself, improving on what a Cincinnati editor had already described as "the right thing in the right place, and a perfect thing in every respect." When Everett remarked in a letter next day, "I should be glad if I could flatter myself that I came as near the central idea of the occasion, in two hours, as you did in two minutes," he replied: "In our respective parts yesterday, you could not have been excused to make a short address, nor I a long one. I am pleased to know that, in your judgment, the little I did say was not entirely a failure." Subsequently, when the orator asked for a copy of the speech, Lincoln gladly sent him one incorporating certain workshop changes. The second "We are met" became "We have come"; "a portion of it" became "a portion of that field"; "resting place of" became "resting place for"; "the unfinished work that they have thus far so nobly carried on" became "the unfinished work which they who fought here have thus far so nobly advanced"; "the nation shall, under God," became "this nation, under God, shall." Two later drafts he also made as presentation copies, with only two additional changes, one in the first sentence, where "upon" was shortened to "on," and one in the last, where "here" was dropped from the phrase "they here gave." The final draft — only two words longer than the one he had part-read, part-improvised at the Gettysburg ceremony, though he had altered, to one degree or another, half of its ten sentences — would be memorized in the future by millions of American school children, including those of the South, despite his claim that a victory by their forebears, in their war for independence, would have meant the end of government by and for the people. That speech did indeed scour, even in dark and bloody ground.

After the ceremonies on Cemetery Hill, Lincoln returned to the Wills house for lunch, after which he held an unscheduled reception, shaking hands for about an hour, then went to a patriotic rally at the Presbyterian church, where he listened to an address by the new lieutenant governor of Ohio. Finally at 6.30 he boarded the train for Washington. Much of the time that afternoon he had seemed gloomy and listless, and now on the train he gave way to weariness and malaise, lying stretched out on one of the side seats in the drawing room, a wet towel folded across his eyes and forehead. Back in the capital by midnight, he found good news awaiting him at the White House: Tad had been up and about today, apparently as well as if he had never been sick at all. Presently it developed however that the first family still had an invalid on its hands, only this time the member who fell ill was the President himself and the doctors had no trouble identifying the ailment. It was varioloid, a mild form of smallpox. Placed in isolation by order of his physician, Lincoln for once was free of the importunities of the office-seekers who normally hemmed him in.

"There is one thing good about this," he said with a somewhat rueful smile. "I now have something I can give everybody."

⚔ 5 ⚔

When Grant learned on November 5 that Bragg had detached Longstreet's two divisions the day before to send them and Wheeler's cavalry
against Burnside, thus reducing the strength of the besiegers of Chattanooga by one fourth, he fairly ached to attack him, then and there, despite the semicircular frown of all those guns on all those heights. Indeed,
there seemed to be sore need for haste: not only because the Confederates had rail transportation as far as Loudon, two thirds of the way to
Knoxville — which meant that Old Peter might be able to return
within a week or ten days, including the time it would take him to defeat and capture the bluecoats there or drive them from the region they
had held for two months now, thereby reopening the Tennessee & Virginia Railroad for the use of such reinforcements as the Richmond government might take the notion to send him or Bragg on an overnight
ride from Lynchburg — but also because Lincoln, who was known to be
touchy about East Tennessee and the protection of its Union-loyal residents, might be tempted for political reasons to disrupt the plans of the
commander of the newly created Military Division of the Mississippi.
Sure enough, as Grant said later, the Washington authorities no sooner
heard of Longstreet's departure from his immediate front than they became "more than ever anxious for the safety of Burnside's army, and
plied me with dispatches faster than ever, urging that something should
be done for his relief."

He was altogether willing, but he could not see that sending part
of his army to Knoxville, at this stage of the campaign, would do anything more than add to Burnside's supply problem, which was nearly as
grievous as his own had been on his arrival, two weeks back. What he
had in mind, instead, was to attack Bragg's right. If successful, this would
break his grip on Chattanooga by dislodging him from Missionary Ridge,
and even if it failed it would be likely, if it was pressed with vigor, to
alarm him into recalling Longstreet. In either case, as Grant saw it,
Burnside would be relieved far more effectively than by the addition of
several thousand hungry mouths to his command. On November 7,
however, when he suggested the attack to Thomas, whose troops would
have to make it, he was told that the thing could not be done. The
Cracker Line had been open barely a week, and though the men were already back on full rations, no replacements for the starved artillery
horses had yet come through. The few survivors, wobbly as they were,
were not enough to move the guns out of the parks, according to
Thomas, much less to pull them forward in support of the advancing infantry, and without them the attack was bound to fail. Unwilling to let
it go at that, Grant proposed that mules or officers' mounts be used to
haul the pieces, but the Virginian explained that the former, though su-
perb in draft, were undependable under fire, while the latter would not

work in traces and lacked the heft required of gun teams anyhow. Regretfully, in the light of this, the general whose arm was infantry felt obliged to defer to the old-line artilleryman. "Nothing was left to be done," he afterwards observed, "but to answer Washington dispatches as best I could; urge Sherman forward, although he was making every effort to get forward, and encourage Burnside to hold on, assuring him that in a short time he should be relieved."

His red-haired successor in command of the Army of the Tennessee was indeed making every effort to get forward, for he had received at Iuka ten days ago an order delivered by "a dirty, black-haired individual with mixed dress and strange demeanor" — thus Sherman later described the messenger — who had left Chattanooga on the day after Grant's arrival and paddled a canoe down the Tennessee, over treacherous Muscle Shoals, to find him. The instructions were for him to leave the railroad work to one division and press on at once with the other four to Bridgeport, where he would be in position to block an attempt by Bragg to turn the Federal right, disrupt the new supply line, and flank the defenders out of Chattanooga. (Though it might have been inferred from this that Grant had been reading his opponent's mail, he did not actually know that Bragg — or, more properly speaking, Longstreet — had any such plan in mind. It just had seemed to him wise to forestall so logical a move on the part of an adversary reputed to be as bold as he was tricky.) Furthermore, as an added logistical precaution, Grant directed Sherman to abandon work on the Memphis & Charleston, west of Decatur, so that the division left behind could concentrate on repairing the Tennessee & Alabama, which ran north of there, through Columbia, to Nashville, and thus provide him with two lines connecting his railhead supply base at Stevenson with his main depot back at the capital. That way, he would not only have a spare all-weather line in case raiders broke through to the Nashville & Chattanooga; he would also be able to keep up his stocks of ammunition and food when the opportunity came for him to forward supplies to Burnside, who at present had no rail connection with the outside world.... This was a large order, for the line north of Decatur had been thoroughly wrecked by cavalry and saboteurs, but the commander of the division assigned to the task was Brigadier General Grenville M. Dodge. A capable soldier, with a wound and a promotion dating from Pea Ridge to prove it, the thirty-two-year-old New Englander was also an experienced railroad builder, civil engineer, and surveyor; "Level Eye," the Indians had dubbed him, watching him at work out on the plains before the war. Grant figured that if anyone could do the job it was Dodge, and his confidence was not misplaced. Working without a base of supplies from which to draw either rations or equipment, without skilled labor of any kind, except such as he could find in the ranks of his 8000-man division, and with nothing but axes, picks, and spades for tools, he completed the job within forty days, although it required the rebuilding of no fewer than 182 bridges and about as many culverts while re-laying 102 miles of track northward across the lowlands and uplands of North Alabama and Middle Tennessee. His troops would get none of the glory in the campaign that now was about to open in earnest, but no division in any of the three blue armies involved worked harder or deserved more credit for the outcome.

But that was still in the future. For the present, Sherman pushed on eastward, crossing the Tennessee at Eastport to reach Florence by November 1, at which point, after three weeks on the go, he was about midway between Memphis and Chattanooga. To avoid the delay that would be involved in ferrying four divisions across Elk River, wide and bridgeless this far down, he marched up its north bank for a crossing by the bridge near Decherd, then followed the railroad down to Stevenson. He reached Bridgeport in advance of his troops on the night of November 13 to find a dispatch awaiting him from Grant, urging him to hurry ahead to Chattanooga for a conference. This he did the following day, proceeding via the Cracker Line, and rode into town that evening to be greeted by the superior he had not seen since he left him on crutches at Vicksburg in September. He was pleased to see that by now the crutches had been discarded; but when they rode out together next morning on a tour of inspection, finding himself confronted by the awesome loom of Lookout Mountain on the south, while to the east, against the long, shadowy backdrop of Missionary Ridge, "rebel sentinels, in a continuous chain, were walking their posts in plain view, not a thousand yards off," Sherman was amazed. He had been told what to expect, but what he saw came as such a shock to him that he involuntarily exclaimed: "Why, General Grant, you are besieged!" Grant nodded. "It's too true," he said. And then he told him what he had in mind to do about it.

Thomas's troops, he said — according to Sherman's recollection of the briefing — "had been so demoralized by the Battle of Chickamauga that he feared they could not be got out of their trenches to assume the offensive." That was where Sherman came into the picture; "he wanted my troops to hurry up, to take the offensive *first*; after which, he had no doubt the Cumberland army would fight well." The attack was to be launched against Bragg's extreme right, Grant explained: specifically against the northern end of Missionary Ridge, which he had reconnoitered and found unfortified. After crossing at Brown's Ferry, Sherman would press on under cover of darkness and throw a pontoon bridge across the Tennessee four miles above Chattanooga, just below the mouth of Chickamauga Creek, for a surprise assault designed to strike the enemy ridge end-on and then sweep down it from the north, dislodging rebels as he went; Thomas meanwhile would fix them in position by threatening from the west, and Hooker would stand ready with his Easterners to lend a hand in whatever direction he was needed. Sherman liked the sound of this, particularly his assignment to the leading role, but said that he would prefer to take a look at the terrain by daylight. So he and Grant, accompanied by Baldy Smith, crossed over to the north bank of the river, then up it to a hill overlooking the scene of the proposed attack on the opposite bank. He studied it as carefully as distance allowed, then returned before dark, well pleased by what he had seen. There was, however, a need for haste; Longstreet had been gone for better than ten days now and might get back before Sherman's men were in position, in which case they would encounter that much more resistance. Accordingly, the Ohioan did not spend another night in Chattanooga, but returned instead to Bridgeport, again by way of the Cracker Line, to brief his four division commanders on the plan of attack and see that they got their troops on the march without delay.

He had hoped to have them in jump-off position within five days; that is, by November 20 for a dawn attack next morning; but, as he explained later, "the condition of the roads was such, and the bridge at Brown's so frail, that it was not until the 23d that we got three of my divisions behind the hills near the point indicated above Chattanooga for crossing the river."

He need not have fretted about those three lost days. They gained him much, as the thing turned out, and Grant as well. In fact, if he had been delayed one day longer, he not only would have profited still more; he would have been spared the considerable mortification he was to suffer two days later at the hands of Pat Cleburne, who in that case would not have been there. For Bragg had decided, only the day before Sherman got into his jump-off position unobserved, to double the strength of Longstreet's 11,000-man infantry column by detaching another two divisions from the lines around Chattanooga to join him for the suppression of Burnside, under siege by then at Knoxville, and one of the two was Cleburne's.

Old Peter had protested his own detachment in the first place, on the double grounds that he would not be strong enough to deal quickly with Burnside and that his departure would leave the main body, strung out along six miles of line, dangerously exposed to an assault by Grant, who already had been reinforced by Hooker and presumably would soon be joined as well by the even larger force marching eastward under Sherman. But Bragg, with what Longstreet described as a "sardonic smile," declined either to cancel or strengthen the movement against Knoxville, and "intimated that further talk was out of order." He had his reasons: largely personal ones, apparently, dating from the conference three weeks ago, at which the Georgian had volunteered the opinion that the Army of Tennessee would benefit from a change of commanders. Informing Davis, who had suggested the detachment in his letter two days earlier from Atlanta, that "the Virginia troops will move in the direction indicated as soon as practicable," Bragg had added: "This will be a great relief to me." That was on the last day of October, and four days later, despite his protest, Longstreet was detached. He took with him the divisions of McLaws and Hood — the latter now under Brigadier General Micah Jenkins, who was senior to Law and had superseded him on his arrival after Chickamauga — Alexander's artillery, and Wheeler's three brigades of cavalry. This gave him a total of about 15,000 effectives of all arms. His assignment was "to destroy or capture Burnside's army," which in turn had just over 25,000 troops in occupation of East Tennessee.

It was Longstreet's belief that his best chance for success, under the circumstances, lay in striking before his adversary had time to concentrate his forces. But that turned out to be impossible, for a variety of reasons. Not the least of these was that he lacked the means of moving his pontoons except on flatcars, which meant that he had to cross the Holston River at Loudon, where the railroad ended because the bridge was out, rather than at some point closer than thirty air-line miles from his objective. To add to his woes, not only did the trains run badly off schedule, but he found no rations on hand when he reached Sweetwater, as he had been assured they would be, and had to mark time there while they were being brought in from the country roundabout. "The delay that occurs is one that might have been prevented," he wired Bragg on November 11, "but not by myself. . . . As soon as I find a probability of moving without almost certain starvation, I shall move, provided the troops are up." Bragg retaliated in kind. "Transportation in abundance was on the road and subject to your orders," he shot back next day. "I regret it has not been energetically used. The means being furnished, you were expected to handle your own troops, and I cannot understand your constant applications for me to furnish them." Old Peter pushed forward on his own, crossing at Loudon on the 13th, but reviewing the situation years later he remarked: "It began to look more like a campaign against Longstreet than against Burnside."

In point of fact, although their methods differed sharply, the blue commander to his front was no less skillful an opponent than the gray one in his rear. Warned by Grant that a heavy detachment was headed in his direction, Burnside was not only on the alert for an attack; he was also mindful of his instructions to keep the enemy from returning to Chattanooga as long as possible. "Sherman's advance has reached Bridgeport," Grant wired on the day after the rebels crossed the Holston. "If you can hold Longstreet in check until he gets up, or by skirmishing and falling back can avoid serious loss to yourself and gain time, I will be able to force the enemy back from here and place a force between Longstreet and Bragg that must inevitably make the former take to the mountain passes by every available road." Accordingly, Burnside did not seriously contest the Confederate advance. Abandoning Kingston, he called his scattered forces in from all points except Cumberland Gap, thus keeping that escape hatch open in the event of a disaster, and aside from a brief delaying action at Campbell Station on the 14th, about midway between Loudon and Knoxville, did not risk a sudden termination of the contest, either by a victory or a defeat. He had some 20,000 soldiers with him; more, he knew, than were in the column advancing on him. But it was not a battle he was after. It was time.

He got it, too. Arriving before Knoxville on November 17, Longstreet found the bluecoats skillfully disposed and well dug in. "We went to work, therefore," he afterwards reported, "to make our way forward by gradual and less hazardous measures, at the same time making examinations of the enemy's entire position." For the better part of a week this continued, his caution enlarged by the knowledge that Burnside had more men inside the place than he himself had outside. Then on November 23 he received a message Bragg had written the day before, informing him that "nearly 11,000 reinforcements are now moving to your assistance." Old Peter was to go ahead and defeat Burnside now, "if practicable"; otherwise he could wait for the additional strength already on the way. Having looked the situation over carefully for the past six days, without finding a single chink in the Federal armor, Longstreet decided that the "practicable" thing to do was wait a couple more.

Bragg's decision to add weight to the blow aimed at Knoxville, seeking thereby to hasten the return of the detachment by giving it the strength to settle the issue there without additional delay, was based in part on a growing suspicion that Old Peter had been right, after all, when he warned of the danger involved in any prolonged weakening of the force in occupation of the six-mile line of intrenchments drawn around two sides of Chattanooga. Longstreet had been gone for nearly three weeks now, and all sorts of things had been happening down in the town, indicative of the fact that the blue commander had something violent in mind. Moreover, Sherman had reached Bridgeport the week before, then suddenly, after crossing at Brown's Ferry, had disappeared as mysteriously as if the earth had swallowed up all four of his divisions. Bragg inferred that the Ohioan must have marched over Walden's Ridge: in which case he was probably headed for Knoxville, with the intention not only of raising the siege but also of swamping the already outnumbered Longstreet. If this was so, the thing to do was beat him to the punch, using the speed made possible by the railroad, and settle the issue before he got there. Accordingly, having reorganized what was left of his army into two large corps of four divisions apiece — one under Hardee, who had replaced Polk, and one under Breckinridge, who had replaced Hill — Bragg decided to dispatch one division from each, Cleburne from Hardee, Buckner from Breckinridge, and send them to Knoxville at once. He no sooner reached this decision than he acted on it. Buckner being absent sick, and Preston having been called to Richmond, his troops were placed under Bushrod Johnson, who pulled them out of line on November 22 and shifted them rearward to Chickamauga Station, where they boarded the cars for a fast ride to Loudon and a march beyond the Holston. Cleburne followed next day to wait for the return of the cars that had carried Johnson up the line.

Consolidation of Walker's two small divisions had reduced the army's total from eleven to ten divisions, and of these, with Johnson and Cleburne gone, Bragg now had a scant half dozen, containing fewer than 40,000 effectives of all arms. Hardee held the left of the semicircular line, with Stevenson posted on the crest of Lookout and eastward across the valley as far as Chattanooga Creek, Walker across the rest of the valley, and Cheatham on his right, occupying the south end of the line on Missionary Ridge, the rest of which was held by Breckinridge, with Stewart adjoining Cheatham and the other two divisions — Breckinridge's own and Hindman's, respectively under William Bate and Patton Anderson, the senior brigadiers — disposed along the northern extension of the ridge, but not all the way to the end overlooking the confluence of Chickamauga Creek and the Tennessee River, where the ground was so rough that Bragg had decided a few outpost pickets would suffice to hold it. The fact was, he had need to conserve his forces, especially since the latest of his two considerable detachments. Sidling left and right to fill the gaps created by the departure of Johnson and Cleburne, the troops disposed in three lines down the western face of the ridge were a good two lateral yards apart, not even within touching distance of each other. Admittedly this was a dangerous situation, but their chief depended on the natural strength of the position to compensate for what he lacked in numbers.

However, on the afternoon of the day Cleburne pulled back to follow Johnson up to Knoxville, Bragg was given cause to believe that his judgment was about to be challenged in the stiffest kind of way. Grant advanced a large body of troops — apparently Thomas's whole army — due east from Chattanooga, as if he intended to have an all-out try at breaking the thin-spread center of the rebel line. Though the mass of bluecoats called a halt about midway across the plain and began to intrench a new line just beyond range of the batteries on Missionary Ridge, Bragg was alarmed into recalling Cleburne, whose men were loading onto the cars when the summons reached him. Early next morning, November 24, the southern commander received a still greater shock in the form of a dispatch from an outpost on the right. Four blue divisions were crossing the Tennessee River immediately below the mouth of Chickamauga Creek, apparently for an assault on the practically undefended north end of the ridge. It was Sherman, the dispatch added, and Bragg knew at last that the Ohioan had not gone off to Knoxville, as he had supposed, but rather had gone into hiding behind the hills above Chattanooga, massing for the attack now being launched.

Hastily, he passed the word for Cleburne, whose troops had returned overnight from Chickamauga Station, to double-time his division northward and repulse if he could the four-division assault which, if successful, would flank the Confederates off the ridge their commander had believed to be impregnable: until now.

★　★　★

As was his custom when confronted with delays, long or short — including the four-month delay above Vicksburg, early this year — Grant used the three days, spent waiting for Sherman to get into position, to polish up the plan he had designed for Bragg's discomfort, improvising variations which he believed would make it at once more certain and complete. Such strain as there was, and admittedly there was much, was not so much on his own account as on Burnside's, and perhaps less on Burnside's account than on the reaction of the Washington authorities to the news that Knoxville was besieged, cut off from telegraphic communication with the outside world. "The President, the Secretary of War, and General Halleck were in an agony of suspense," Grant afterward recalled. "My own suspense was also great, but more endurable," he added, "because I was where I could do something to relieve the situation."

What he specifically had in mind to do, as he had told Burnside the week before, was to "place a force between Longstreet and Bragg" by throwing the latter into retreat and cutting the rail supply line in his rear, thus obliging Old Peter to raise his siege and "take to the mountain passes by every road" in search of food. At that time he had intended to leave the real work to Sherman and his Army of the Tennessee, with the Cumberland and Potomac troops more or less standing by to lend such help as might be needed. Thomas, for instance, was to menace but not attack the enemy center, while Hooker — reduced to a single division by the subtraction of Howard's two, which crossed at Brown's Ferry to be available as a reserve for the forces north and east of Chattanooga — stood guard at the foot of Lookout Valley, below Wauhatchie, to prevent a rebel counterstroke from there. But now, as he waited for Sherman to come up, Grant perceived that if Fighting Joe were strengthened a bit he might take the offensive on the right, against Lookout itself, and thus discourage Bragg from reinforcing his assailed right from his otherwise unmolested left. Accordingly, Thomas was ordered to send Cruft's division from Granger's corps to Hooker, and when Sherman's rear division, under Osterhaus, was kept from crossing by a breakdown of the pontoon bridge at Brown's Ferry, it too was sent to Hooker and replaced by another from Thomas, under Davis, who was detached from Palmer's corps. Thomas thus was reduced from six to four divisions, while Sherman still had four, Hooker three, and Howard two. Such a distribution seemed ideal, considering the assignments of the three commanders and the fact that the last was available as a reinforcement for the first.

These thirteen blue divisions, containing in all about 75,000 effectives, were to be employed by Grant in the following manner against the 43,000 effectives in Bragg's seven divisions. Sherman's effort on the left was still to be the main one, his orders being "to secure the heights on the northern extremity [of Missionary Ridge] to about the railroad tunnel before the enemy can concentrate against him," then drive southward down the crest, dislodging graybacks as he went. To assist in this, Thomas would menace the rebel center, fixing the defenders in position, and Howard would hold his corps "in readiness to act either with [Thomas] or with Sherman." Hooker meanwhile would deliver a secondary attack on the far right, and if successful — although this seemed unlikely, considering the difficulties of terrain on that quarter of the field — was to cross Lookout Mountain and Chattanooga Valley for a descent on Rossville, where he would turn sharp left and, matching Sherman's effort from the opposite direction, sweep northward up Missionary Ridge; at which point in the proceedings, with the rebel army clamped firmly between the two attackers north and south, Thomas's feint against the center might be converted into a true assault that would mean the end of Bragg.

One possible source of difficulty was a growing bitterness between the Federal armies, especially those of the East and West. "The

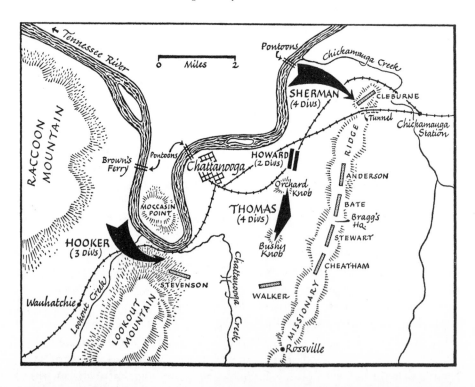

Potomac men and ours never meet without some very hard talk," one of Sherman's veterans wrote home. Westerners jeered at Easterners as paper-collar soldiers. "Bull Run!" they hooted, as if they themselves had never been whipped in battle. Resentful of the fact that the "Virginians," as they sometimes referred to these transfers from the eastern theater, had always had first call on new equipment and such luxuries as the quartermaster afforded, they would remark as they slogged past Hooker's bivouacs: "Fall back on your straw and fresh butter," and they would add, looking rearward over their shoulders: "What elegant corpses they'll make in those fine clothes!" After this would come the ultimate insult, delivered *sotto voce* from the roadside as the Easterners minced by: "All quiet on the Potomac." The latter in turn were disdainful, looking down their noses at the western soldiers, who preferred Confederate-style blanket rolls to knapsacks, walked with the long, loose-jointed stride of plowmen, and paid their officers little deference. "Except for the color of their uniforms, they looked exactly like the rebels," a New Yorker observed with unconcealed distaste. Individual confrontations were likely to produce at least a verbal skirmish. One of Blair's men, for example, wandering over for a look at Slocum's camps, was surprised to see the corps insignia — a five-pointed star — sewn or glued or stenciled onto practically everything in sight, from the flat crowns of forage caps to the tailgates of wagons. "Are you all brigadier generals?" he inquired, in real or feigned amazement. An Easterner explained that this was their corps badge, and asked: "What's yours?" The Westerner bristled. No such device had been known out here before, but he was unwilling to be outdone. "Badge, is it?" he snorted. For emphasis, he slapped the leather ammunition pouch he wore on his belt, just over his liver. "There, by Jesus! Forty rounds in the cartridge box and twenty in the pocket." In time, that would become his own XV Corps insignia — a cartridge box inscribed "Forty Rounds" — but tempers were not sweetened by such exchanges, in which neither antagonist took any care to disguise his low opinion of the other as a dude or a backwoodsman.

Nor were matters improved when the men of the three armies learned of their respective assignments in Grant's plan for lifting the siege of Chattanooga. This applied in particular to members of the Army of the Cumberland, whose role it was to stand on the defensive, merely bristling, while the other two armies "rescued" them by attacking on the left and right. Perhaps, too, they had heard by now of Grant's expressed concern that "they could not be got out of their trenches to assume the offensive." On top of all this, Thomas himself was hopping mad: not at Grant, though doubtless he masked some resentment he must have felt in that direction, but at Bragg, whose headquarters were plainly visible on the crest of the ridge across the way. A letter had arrived from the North for a Confederate officer, and Thomas, having determined that it was harmless from the security point of view, sent it through the lines with a note attached, requesting his one-time battery commander to pass it along. The letter came back promptly, with a curt indorsement on the note: "Respectfully returned to General Thomas. General Bragg declines to have any intercourse with a man who has betrayed his State." Thomas was incensed. "Damn him," he fumed; "I'll be even with him yet." Sherman, who was present, observed that the Virginian's poise, reputed to be impervious to shock, was shakable after all, at least when he was touched where he was tender. "He was not so imperturbable as the world supposes," the Ohioan testified years later, recalling Old Pap's reaction to the snub from his former superior and friend.

Hooker felt considerably better after Grant's revision of the attack plan, which changed his role from defensive to offensive, but the only change for Thomas was the loss of one third of his command, detached left and right to where the battle would be fought while he and his remaining four divisions stood by as spectators. Presently there was a further change, however, whereby they were given at least the chance for a ringside seat, a closer view of the action they were more or less barred from. On November 22 a rebel deserter reported that Bragg was about to evacuate his present lines. Though Grant mistrusted evidence so obtained, knowing how often those who imparted it were "loaded," this was altogether too serious to be ignored; Bragg might have plans for an all-out move against Burnside, availing himself of the railroad for a sudden descent on Knoxville, in which case Grant would be left holding the bag at Chattanooga. Moreover, the report gained credence when Buckner's division pulled out that afternoon, followed next morning by Cleburne's. Accordingly, Grant instructed Thomas to make a pretense of attacking Missionary Ridge by advancing his army, or what was left of it, about half the distance across the intervening plain. If he could do this, he would not only test the extent of the Confederate withdrawal, which might be greater than had been observed, and perhaps frighten Bragg into recalling the troops already detached; he would also secure a better location from which to demonstrate against the enemy center next day, November 24, when Sherman and Hooker — the former at last was moving into his jump-off position opposite the mouth of Chickamauga Creek — were scheduled to open their attacks against the flanks.

Thomas received his orders at 11 o'clock in the morning, and by 12.30 — so anxious were he and they for a share in the work — he had begun to maneuver his 25,000 veterans into positions from which to advance. In full view of their rivals from the Virginia and Mississippi theaters, as well as of the rebels out on the plain ahead and the tall ridge beyond, these soldiers of the Cumberland army made the most of this opportunity to refute the taunts that they had been permanently cowed by their defeat nine weeks ago. Granger's corps, with Wood in the lead and Sheridan in support, was the first to move out into the open. "It was an inspiring sight," a staff observer would recall. "Flags were flying; the quick, earnest steps of thousands beat equal time. The sharp commands of hundreds of company officers, the sound of drums, the ringing notes of the bugles, companies wheeling and countermarching and regiments getting into line, the bright sun lighting up ten thousand polished bayonets till they glistened and flashed like a flying shower of electric sparks, all looked like preparations for a peacetime pageant, rather than for the bloody work of death." Across the way, the Confederates thought so, too. They emerged from their trenches and stood on the parapets, calling to one another to come watch the Yankees pass in review. Palmer's corps followed Granger's; Johnson and Baird went through similar convolutions to get into line on the right. For the better part of an hour this continued. Then at about 1.30 the drums and bugles stepped up their tempo and changed their tone, beating and blaring the charge. That was the first the butternut watchers knew of the attack that was in midcareer before they got back into their trenches to resist it. Orchard Knob and Bushy Knob, fortified rebel outposts about in the center of the plain, were taken in a rush as the blue wave — flecked with shellbursts now, as if with foam — swept over them, engulfing those defenders who had not broken rearward in time for a getaway to the safety of the main line, back on Missionary Ridge. Promptly, or at any rate as soon as their officers could persuade them to leave off cheering and tossing their caps, the victors got to work with picks and shovels, turning the just-won intrenchments to face the other way, and there they settled down for the night, having taken their ringside seats for the fight which, now that the preliminaries were over and Sherman had his four divisions cached in their jump-off position on the left, was scheduled to begin soon after first light next morning.

A mile or more in advance of the line they had taken off from shortly after midday, Thomas and his Cumberlanders had drawn and shed the first blood after all, despite Grant's original intention to exclude them from any leading part in the accomplishment of their own deliverance. Their losses amounted to about 1100 killed and wounded, but they had inflicted nearly as many casualties as they suffered, including the prisoners they took. Perhaps by now, moreover, Grant had been disabused of his notion as to their reluctance to leave their trenches without the example of Sherman's men to inspire them. At any rate he seemed pleased: as well he might. Afterwards he told why. "The advantage was greatly on our side now," he wrote, "and if I could only have been assured that Burnside could hold out ten days longer" — this being the length of time he figured it would take him to finish whipping Bragg and then, if necessary, get reinforcements up to Knoxville — "I should have rested more easily. But we were doing the best we could for him and the cause."

Gathered about their campfires on the ridge, where they were disposed in three separate lines — one along its base, another about half-way up its steep western slope, and a third along its crest, four hundred feet above the plain — the Confederates admitted they had been surprised by the sudden conversion this afternoon of a two-corps "review" into an irresistible assault, but they still were not alarmed. Orchard Knob and Bushy Knob were merely outposts, no more integral to the defense of the main line of resistance than was the sheer bastion of Lookout Mountain, off on the distant left. What counted was Missionary Ridge itself. That was where the strength was, and the bluecoats, still beyond reach of all but the heaviest guns emplaced along the crest, would find a quite different reception awaiting them, when and if — although that seemed unlikely — they moved against it from their newly taken positions on the hilly plain below. "We feel we can kill all they send after us, notwithstanding our line is so thin that we are two yards apart," one of Breckinridge's Orphans wrote in his journal that night, looking down at the fires the Federals had kindled on the floor of the valley, as myriad as the stars they seemed to reflect. In this he was expressing the opinion of his army commander, who was convinced, as he said later, that Missionary Ridge could be "held by a line of skirmishers against any assaulting column."

A message wigwagged from Lookout after sundown, warning that a blue force seemed to be massing in the valley beyond for an uphill attack, gave Bragg no evident concern. Though the mountain was defended by only one brigade on its western flank and another on its summit, detached from Cheatham, he made no attempt to strengthen or adjust his dispositions there, apparently because he did not want to discourage the Federals, if they were indeed reckless enough to make the attempt, from breaking their heads against its rocky sheerness. Neither this new threat to his left, nor Thomas's advance that afternoon against his center, seemed to him sufficient cause for recalling either Johnson or Cleburne, who had pulled out yesterday and today. However, a message that reached him early next morning from the far right, warning that a sizable body of the enemy was crossing the Tennessee near the mouth of Chickamauga Creek, was quite another matter. He rode north at once to see for himself what this amounted to, and when he learned that what it amounted to was Sherman, whose troops he had thought were on their way to Knoxville, he reacted fast with a dispatch calling Cleburne back from Chickamauga Station. "We are heavily engaged," he told him, stressing the need for haste. "Move up rapidly to these headquarters."

There was in fact less need for haste than the southern commander knew. Sherman would not constitute an actual threat for some time now, though even he did not yet know that it would not be the rebels who would delay still further the opening of his carefully planned attack on the scantly defended northern end of Missionary Ridge, but geography, an unsuspected trick of the terrain. For the better part of the past week the red-haired Ohioan had been made nervously ill by the knowledge that he was falling behind the schedule Grant had set. "I feel as if I had a 30-pound shot in my stomach," he told a friend in the course of his muddy approach march. Today, though, all that was changed. Everything went smooth as clockwork. He had a thousand-man assault force over the river in boats by daylight, and behind them a pontoon bridge was thrown for a crossing by the main body before noon. Unopposed, except by a handful of butternut pickets who fled at their first sight of no less than four blue divisions coming at them, Sherman pushed forward onto the high ground he had examined nine days ago from the far side of the river. By late afternoon he had the position completely occupied: only to learn, to his acute dismay, that what he had taken was a detached hill, not actually even a part of Missionary Ridge, which lay beyond it, across a rocky valley. Red-faced, though he blamed the error on the inadequate map he had been given, he notified Grant of what had happened and instructed his troops to dig in for the night. They would continue — or, more properly speaking, begin — their assault on the enemy ridge at first light tomorrow, even though they had lost the element of surprise, which he and they had taken such precautions to achieve.

Seven miles away on the far right, southwest across the plain where the Cumberlanders occupied the ringside seats they had taken yesterday — "Thomas having done on the 23d what was expected of him on the 24th," Grant explained, "there was nothing for him to do this day except to strengthen his position" — a quite different kind of action was in progress, one in which the so-called "fog of war" prevailed in fact, not merely in the mind of the blue commander. Lookout had been wreathed in mist all morning and afternoon, except for tantalizing moments when the curtain would lift or part, only to descend or close again, affording the watchers little more than fleeting reassurance that the sheer bulk of the mountain was still there. Hooker's progress, if any, could not be determined by the eye, although, as Grant remarked from the command post shifted forward to Orchard Knob, "the sound of his artillery and musketry was heard incessantly." What was in progress, there beyond the gauzy screen, was what later would be called the "Battle Above the Clouds," despite objections by a correspondent that "there were no clouds to fight above, only heavy mist," and by Grant himself, who scoffed long afterwards: "The Battle of Lookout Mountain is one of the romances of the war. There was no such battle and no action even worthy to be called a battle on Lookout Mountain. It is all poetry."

Poetry it may have been, but if there were no clouds and no battle fought above them, there was at least some bleeding done, along with a great deal of hard work, in the course of this day-long skirmish in the mist. Hooker had about 12,000 troops, one division from each of the three armies on the field, with which to oppose the 1200-man brigade that stood between him and the crest of the mountain, where a second gray brigade was posted. Spread out along the east bank of Lookout Creek, with instructions to "fall back fighting over the rocks" if attacked, the Confederates did just that when the greatly superior Union mass forced a crossing near Wauhatchie and moved forward on a wide front, overlapping them on both flanks. Gun crews on the rearward heights were active at this stage of the attack, firing with precision into the blue ranks toiling upward, but this became increasingly difficult as the range decreased and it became necessary to raise the trails of the pieces higher and higher, until finally the tubes could not be depressed enough to keep them from overshooting; at which point the guns became only so much useless metal, so far as the defense of Lookout was concerned, and had to be removed to save them from being overrun. As they withdrew, the second gray brigade came down the rugged western slope to reinforce the first, and presently Stevenson sent a third brigade from the far side of the mountain. The three attempted to form a line among the rocks, but they soon found it was no use; the three blue divisions had caught the spirit of the chase and would not be denied. Supported by fire from batteries massed on Moccasin Point, just across the river, Geary's "paper collar" Easterners rounded the gray right flank and threatened to cut the defenders' line of retreat. There was a brief, hard fight near a farmhouse on a craggy bench about midway up the otherwise almost sheer north face of the mountain, and then once more the weight of numbers told. Again the Confederates fell back hastily, and this time Fighting Joe called a halt to consolidate his gains. Though he continued to probe upward, on through what was left of daylight into dusk — "I could see the whole thing," a rebel peering down from the crest was to say of the final stage of the contest; "It looked like lightning bugs on a dark night" — Hooker thought it best, except for a few patrols sent out to keep the enemy off balance, to rest his leg-weary men for tomorrow, which he expected to be as strenuous as today. He had suffered, or would suffer in the course of the three-day action, a total of 629 casualties, including 81 dead and 8 missing, but this seemed rather a bargain price for nearly half a mountain that practically everyone, blue or gray, had judged to be impregnable.

In point of fact he had won the whole mountain, though he would not know this until morning. Shortly after midnight, the Federal patrols having long since bedded down, Stevenson received instructions from Bragg to fall back across the eastern valley, in concert with Walker's division, and join in the defense of Missionary Ridge, where it was evident by now that the main Union effort would be centered. This he did, burning the single bridge over Chattanooga Creek as soon as his battered soldiers had crossed it in a darkness made profound by a total eclipse of the moon. Fighting Joe remained in full but isolated control of the "ever-lasting thunder storm" for which he had fought so hard today and was preparing to fight tomorrow, not knowing that it was entirely his already. Grant, of course, did not know this either, though in a wire he got off to Halleck, shortly after sundown, he sounded as if he did: "The fighting today progressed favorably. Sherman carried the end of Missionary Ridge, and his right is now at the tunnel, and his left at Chickamauga Creek. Troops from Lookout Valley carried the point of the mountain, and now hold the eastern slope and a point high up. Hooker reports two thousand prisoners taken, besides which a small number have fallen into our hands from Missionary Ridge."

Assuming from this, as well he might, that little remained to be accomplished around Chattanooga, Lincoln himself replied next morning with congratulations, gratitude, and a reminder: "Well done. Many thanks to all. Remember Burnside."

★ ★ ★

Little if any of the information Grant reported in his telegram to Halleck after sundown of November 24 had been true at the time he put it on the wire. Sherman not only had not "carried the end of Missionary Ridge," he had not even reached it; nor had Hooker, whose troops were still on the western, not the eastern slope of Lookout, "carried the point of the mountain." As for prisoners, Fighting Joe had inflicted fewer casualties than he suffered; the figure 2000 was a good deal closer to the total number of Confederates he encountered than it was to the number he had captured, which in fact was less than a tenth of the figure Grant passed on to Washington. However, before Lincoln's "Well done. Many thanks" arrived next morning, a part at least of what had been distorted was confirmed. The sun came up in a cloudless sky about 6.40; Lookout loomed with startling clarity, its curtain of mist dispelled. Watching from Orchard Knob, the Federal commander saw the rippling glitter of the Stars and Stripes break out on the 1200-foot peak, raised there by a patrol in proof that Geary's kid-glove Easterners had indeed "carried the point of the mountain" after all. Down on the plain, the Cumberland watchers broke into cheers at the sight, and Grant settled back, albeit impatiently, to wait for Hooker to complete his assignment, which was to proceed southeast across the intervening valley for a strike at Rossville and a drive northward up Missionary Ridge to meet Sherman driving south.

The wait, as it turned out, was a long one. Though the eastern slope of Lookout was less difficult than the western, and even afforded a winding road for the descent, the three divisions entered the valley below to find the bridge over fordless Chattanooga Creek destroyed and few materials at hand for constructing another; with the result that they were delayed some four hours in their advance on Rossville. Neither Grant nor the Cumberlanders, who knew that he did not intend to unleash them until the rebs intrenched to their front were firmly clamped between the two blue forces driving north and south along the ridge, took kindly to this evidence of Fighting Joe's ineptness, even though they had more or less anticipated it because of the blow-hard reputation he had brought with him from the East. This delay was mild in its effect, however, compared to the one on the far left, where no such failure had been expected of Grant's star general in command of his star army, whose reputation lately had become one of unfailing success and whose complaint had been that they could no longer get the Johnnies to fight them in the open.

Sherman went forward at dawn, as ordered, but found Cleburne in his path and was stopped cold. Rocked back — quite literally; for the defenders heaved boulders down on the heads of the attackers when their guns could no longer be brought to bear — he charged again and again, and again and again he was repulsed. "You may go up the hill if you like," he had rather casually instructed his brother-in-law Brigadier General Hugh Ewing, who commanded his lead division, adding: "Don't call for help until you actually need it." Ewing actually needed it about as soon as he got started, and Sherman not only supplied it, in the form of his three remaining divisions; he also threw in Howard's two, which were ordered to join him before midday. Yet nothing he could do would serve to move these six divisions over or around the one gray division in their path. About 3 o'clock, after eight hot hours of fighting, no appreciable gain, and more than 1500 casualties, including 261 captured when the Confederates made an unexpected sortie, Sherman admitted he had done all he could on this line. "Go signal Grant," he told a staff major. "The orders were that I should get as many as possible in front of me, and God knows there are enough. They've been reinforcing all day."

Those had not been his orders at the outset; nor were they now. "Attack again," Grant promptly replied, and Sherman did so, though with no better success. He was wrong, too, about enemy reinforcements. All he had had in his immediate front all day was Cleburne, whose five brigades had moved into position late the day before and organized it for defense by working most of the night, their task rendered more difficult by the eclipse of the moon, which for a time had made it necessary to work by sense of touch, including the spotting of the fourteen guns they employed today against the forty emplaced on the hill the Federals had occupied yesterday, off the nose of Missionary Ridge. Cleburne suffered a total of 222 casualties, less than one sixth the number he inflicted, and captured eight stands of colors, six of which were picked up from the ground where they had fallen in front of his line. Shortly before 4 o'clock Bragg sent him the first and only reinforcements of the day, the Orphan Brigade, detached from Bate to extend the right. The Kentuckians saw little action, since Sherman had desisted by then from his attempt to drive southward down the ridge, but one of them went up on his own for a look at what Cleburne's men had been doing all this time. "They had swept their front clean of Yankies," he wrote in his journal; "indeed, when I went up about sundown the side of the ridge in their front was strewn with dead yankies & looked like a lot of boys had been sliding down the hill side, for when a line of the enemy would be repulsed, they would start down hill & soon the whole line would be rolling down like a ball, it was so steep a hill side there."

While Cleburne and his troops were enjoying the respite they had earned, a message arrived from Hardee, directing him, as he afterwards reported, "to send to the center all the troops I could spare, as the enemy were pressing us in that quarter." Detaching two of his brigades, he accompanied them part of the way southward down the ridge to see that they made good time. "Before I had gone far, however," he added, still shocked by this development though his report was written some weeks later, "a dispatch from General Hardee reached me, with the appalling news that the enemy had pierced our center."

It was true; the Confederate center had been pierced. Bluecoats were clustered thick by now on Missionary Ridge, whooping and yelling in raucous celebration of a sudden, incredible victory scored less than three miles south of Sherman's all-day no-gain fight for Tunnel Hill, and hundreds of butternut prisoners were already on their way across the westward plain, taunted by their captors as they went: "You've been wanting to get there long enough. Now charge on Chattanooga!" Appalling as the news was, at least to gray-clad hearers, it became far more so when they learned of the manner in which it had come to pass. What one division had done against six, all morning and most of the afternoon on the far right, five divisions had not managed to do against four in resisting an attack that had lasted barely an hour from start to finish. Rephrasing the news only made it rankle more. Confronted by no worse than equal numbers in the vicinity of his own army headquarters, where he enjoyed positional advantages superior to those that enabled Cleburne's greatly inferior force to stand fast at the north end of the line, the vaunted southern fighting man had lost a soldiers' battle.

Joyous though the outcome was from the Union point of view, the slow hours leading up to it had been anything but pleasant for the overall Federal commander, who had stood by all this time on Orchard Knob and watched his carefully worked-out plans go by the board, or at any rate awry. After sending Howard's two divisions to Sherman, in futile hope that they would provide the added weight that would enable his old Army of the Tennessee to achieve the breakthrough on which those plans depended, Grant had Thomas detach Baird's division from his right and send it northward too. Thomas did so, but word came from the unhappy Sherman that he already had more troops than he could find room for on his present narrow front. So Baird was halted and put back into line where he then was, on Thomas's left. That was about 2 o'clock, and except for this minor rearrangement — Granger's two divisions now were flanked by Palmer's — the Army of the Cumberland had done nothing all day long; or all day yesterday either, for that matter. An hour later, two dispatches arrived from opposite directions. One was from Hooker, reporting that he had finally reached Rossville, where he had captured a quantity of supplies after driving the rebel outpost guards from the gap, and was sending Cruft's division north along the crest of Missionary Ridge, supported on the left and right by Geary and Osterhaus, who were deployed respectively on the western and eastern slopes. The other dispatch was from Sherman and was far less welcome, since what it said, in effect, was that he had shot his wad. Disgruntled, Grant clamped down tighter on his unlit cigar. With Fighting Joe at last where he wanted him, he had no intention of relaxing the pressure on either end of the enemy line. "Attack again," he signaled his red-haired lieutenant in reply, though with no different results, as we have seen.

All this time he had been getting increasingly restless, and when he saw what he took to be reinforcements moving northward along the ridge, he began to worry in earnest that Bragg — whose headquarters he could see plainly on the 400-foot crest, a mile and a half away, with couriers arriving and departing — was about to go over to the offensive against the stalled attackers off the north end of his line. Since Hooker was still a good three miles off and could scarcely be expected to get there before sunset, Grant figured that the quickest way to counteract the danger would be for Thomas to menace the rebel center. He did not like to order this, however, not only because it was an extremely hazardous undertaking, but also because the conditions he had insisted were necessary before the movement could be attempted had not been achieved; Bragg, unclamped, could give his full attention to any threat against his center. At last, although reluctantly, he inquired of the Virginian standing beside him: "Don't you think it's about time to advance against the rifle pits?" Instead of replying, Thomas continued to examine the enemy ridge through his binoculars, as if to show that he was not here to agree or disagree with opinions, but to execute orders. If Grant wanted him to move forward against that bristling triple line of intrenchments, in the face of all those guns frowning down from the crest, let him say so. Finally, at about 3.30, Grant did say so; whereupon Thomas at once passed the word to his corps commanders. Wood and Sheridan had their divisions in the center, with Baird supporting the former on the left and Johnson supporting the latter on the right. The signal for the attack would be the firing of six guns in quick succession, at which time the Cumberlanders, kept idle all day yesterday and up to

now today, would advance and seize the rifle pits at the base of the ridge
on the far side of the plain. At 3.40, ten minutes after Grant told Thomas
to move out, the first of the six signal guns was fired under the personal
direction of the ebullient and high-strung Gordon Granger, who stood
on the Orchard Knob parapet, lifting and lowering his right arm in
rapid sequence as he shouted: "Number One, *fire!* Number Two, *fire!*
Number Three, *fire!* Number Four, *fire!* Number Five, *fire!*"

Before the sixth gun roared the leading elements were off. "Forward, guide center, march!" sixty regimental commanders shouted, and
the 25,000 infantry in the four blue divisions began their plunge of
nearly a mile across the wooded, hilly plain. "Number Six, *fire!*" Granger cried.

At first the only reaction on the part of the defenders was a scattering of shots from the gray pickets, who fell back hastily to gain the
cover of the earthworks in their rear. Presently, though, as if recovering
from the shock of unbelief that what they saw spread out below was
real, the Confederate artillerists came alive. Bragg had 112 guns, and
most of these were trained on the mile-wide formation of bluecoats
moving toward them. "A crash like a thousand thunderclaps greeted us,"
one Federal was to remember, while a second observed that "the whole
ridge to our front had broken out like another Ætna." The effect of this
rain of projectiles, bursting over and among the close-packed ranks of
the attackers, was like that of a sudden shower on a crowd of pedestri-
ans; they quickened the pace, and those in the lead broke into a run. Well
rested from their last previous advance, just over fifty hours ago, the
men of the two center divisions caught something of the excitement of a
race, each wanting to be first to reach the objective. Then too there was
the knowledge that they were advancing in full view of their rivals on
the left and right, who had been brought here from Mississippi and Virginia to extract them from the trap that had been devised to complete
their defeat and destruction, but whose failure to carry out the required
preliminaries had resulted in the unleashing of what had plainly been regarded, up to then, as the second team. Now the roles were more or less
reversed; the second team had become the first, and those who had been
intended to be saved were being called upon to do the saving. That was
a pleasant thing to contemplate. Moreover there was the motive of revenge, a private matter strictly between them and the butternut soldiers
just ahead. "Chickamauga! Chickamauga!" the Cumberlanders were
yelling as they charged.

As they drew near the works at the base of the ridge they saw
there could be no doubt they were going to take them. Already the defenders had begun to waver, flinching from the threat of contact, and
presently, when the attackers closed to within pistol range, they broke.
"A few rushed to the rear, and with frantic eagerness began to climb the
slope," a Kansas infantryman would recall, "but nearly all, throwing

down their muskets and holding up their hands in token of surrender, leaped to our side of the intrenchments and cowered behind them, for the hail of bullets raining down from the hill was as deadly to them as to us. The first line was won."

Winning it and holding it were different things, however: as the victors soon found out. Almost at once, though they were in full control of the lower works and though the ridge was so steep that few of the guns on its crest could be brought to bear on them, the position took on the aspect of a trap. Graybacks in the second line, midway up the slope, were pouring in a murderous, plunging fire, and cannoneers were rolling shells with sputtering fuzes down the hillside to explode in the lost rifle pits below. Amid all this confusion, company officers were brandishing their sabers and shouting for the new occupants to get to work with shovels, bayonets, anything that would help to reverse the parapets and throw some dirt between themselves and the marksmen overhead; but the principal reaction was a sort of aimless milling about, combined with a good deal of ducking and dodging, and a rapidly growing realization that the only practical solution was for them to get out of this untenable position as quickly as possible, either by retreating or continuing the charge. They chose the latter course, wanting more than anything to come to grips with their tormentors. By twos and threes, then by squads and platoons as the conviction took hold, blue-clad figures began to push forward, crouching low for traction on the slope.

At first their officers called after them to stop, but they paid no attention to this, and the lieutenants and captains, affected by the spirit of the men, rushed to join them, still gesturing with their swords and yelling, superfluously and illogically, out of habit: "Follow me!" Soon even the colonels and brigadiers had caught the spirit of the advance, and presently whole regiments were surging up the ridge, aligning as best they could on the colors while calling for the bearers to climb faster.

Down at the command post on Orchard Knob, this unexpected development — plainly visible, though reduced to miniature by distance — provoked the same reaction of stunned disbelief the rebel gunners had evinced when the blue mass first began its advance across the plain. Grant, for one, saw that he might have a first-class disaster on his hands if the Confederates repulsed the Cumberlanders, then followed through with a counterattack as the demoralized bluecoats tumbled down the slope and into the valley, where no reserves had been withheld to form a straggler line on which to rally. "Thomas, who ordered those men up the ridge?" he said angrily. Thomas replied in his usual quiet way: "I don't know. *I* did not." Grant turned to Granger, whom he had just reproached sharply for spending time with the guns instead of tending to his larger duties as a corps commander. "Did you order them up, Granger?" The New Yorker denied it, emphatically but enthusiastically, for he too had caught the spirit of the charge by now.

"No; they started up without orders," he said, and he added happily: "When those fellows get started all hell can't stop them." Grant turned his attention back to the action in front, remarking as he did so that somebody was going to suffer professionally if the men who had taken the bit in their teeth were repulsed.

At first that seemed altogether likely, considering the difficulties of terrain and Bragg's reputation as a counterpuncher; but not for long. Watching the upward progress of the sixty regiments as they engaged in a gallant rivalry to see which would be first to reach the crest, a staff colonel observed that "at times their movements were in shape like the flight of migratory birds, sometimes in line, sometimes in mass, mostly in V-shaped groups, with the points toward the enemy. At these points regimental flags were flying, sometimes drooping as the bearers were shot, but never reaching the ground, for other brave hands were there to seize them." That was how it looked in small from Orchard Knob. Up close, there was the gritty sense of participation, the rasp of heavy breathing, the drum and clatter of boots on rocky ground, and always the sickening thwack of bullets entering flesh and striking bone. Phil Sheridan saw and heard it so as he stood at the base of the ridge, watching his troops in their attempt to outstrip the rivals on their left in Wood's division, and accepted a drink from a silver flask held out by a staff captain. Before he drank he lifted the flask in salute to a group of gray-clad officers he saw in front of Bragg's headquarters, directly up the slope. "Here's to you!" he called. This may have failed to attract the attention of those for whom it was intended, but it certainly did not fail in the case of a pair of gunners in a nearby rebel battery. Swinging their pieces in his direction, they returned the salute with two well-placed rounds that kicked dirt over Sheridan and the captain standing beside him. "Ah, that is ungenerous!" he replied as he brushed off his uniform; "I shall take those guns for that." First, though, he took the drink, and then he started forward, necessarily on foot because his horse had been shot from under him during the advance across the plain.

There seemed an excellent chance that he would carry out his threat, for by now the second line had been overrun, midway up the slope, and his men were driving hard for the crest beyond. They had been helped considerably in advance by the Confederate dispositions, which were faulty in several respects, probably because the natural strength of the terrain had made the defenders overconfident to the point of not believing that their preparations would be tested. For example, standing orders that the troops in the lower rifle pits were to fire no more than a couple of massed volleys when the attackers came within effective range, then fall back to the intermediate position just uphill, had not been made clear to the troops involved; with the demoralizing result that while some had attempted to hold their ground, others had seemed to flee, infecting uninformed comrades with their apparent panic. Worst of all, perhaps, the officers who laid out the upper line had erred in placing it on the geographic, rather than on the "military" crest — literally along the topmost line, that is, rather than along the highest line from which the enemy could be seen and fired on — so that many of the Federal climbers found themselves protected by defilade practically all the way to the top, and once they were there they were able to take rebel strong-points under fire from the flank, distracting the attention of the defenders from the attackers coming straight at them up the ridge. Threatened thus, the graybacks here did what those below had done already; they broke and they broke badly, despite the pleas and curses of their officers, including Bragg himself, who rode among them in a desperate, last-minute effort to persuade them to rally and drive the winded enemy troops back down the slope. "Here is your commander!" he called to them. But they either ignored him, intent as they were on getting beyond the reach of the rapid-firing bluecoats, or else they taunted him with the army catch phrase: "Here's your mule!"

When the Federals crested the ridge they saw spread out below them on the reverse slope what one of them called "the sight of our lives — men tumbling over each other in reckless confusion, hats off, some without guns, running wildly." Too blown to cheer, the victors swung their caps and gestured for the laggards to hurry forward and share the view. "My God, come see them run!" a Hoosier private shouted over his shoulder. A Kansan, writing years later, relived the excitement provoked by the tableau. This beat Bull Run, Wilson's Creek, and the opening phases of Perryville and Stones River. This beat Chickamauga. "Gray clad men rushed wildly down the hill and into the woods, tossing away knapsacks, muskets, and blankets as they ran. Batteries galloped back along the narrow, winding roads with reckless speed, and officers, frantic with rage, rushed from one panic-stricken group to another, shouting and cursing as they strove to check the headlong flight. Our men pursued the fugitives with an eagerness only equaled by their own to escape; the horses of the artillery were shot as they ran; squads of rebels were headed off and brought back as prisoners, and in ten minutes all that remained of the defiant rebel army that had so long besieged Chattanooga was captured guns, disarmed prisoners, moaning wounded, ghastly dead, and scattered, demoralized fugitives. Mission Ridge was ours."

Bragg himself had barely escaped capture, as had Breckinridge, but not their two adjutants or some 3000 other prisoners, who were taken along with 7000 abandoned small arms and 37 cannon, one third of all Bragg had. One of these last was claimed by Sheridan in person, who came running up and leaped astride one of the two guns that had fired at him a few minutes ago. Wrapping his bandy legs around the tube, he swung his hat and cheered. Harker, who commanded his third brigade, followed suit by mounting a nearby gun in a similar fashion, but scorched his seat on the hot metal and could not sit a horse for the next two weeks. In this he was less fortunate than his division commander, who either was made of sterner stuff or else had chosen a cooler piece; at any rate Sheridan stayed astride the gun and continued to cheer and swing his hat, exultant over the reversal of what had happened two months ago at Chickamauga, where he had been among those in headlong flight from fury. All round him now the men were cheering, too, having caught their breath, and Granger rode up from Orchard Knob at the height of the celebration to engage in a sort of victory dance on horseback. "I'm going to have you all court-martialed!" he shouted, laughing. "You were ordered to take the works at the foot of the hill and you've taken those on top! You have disobeyed orders, all of you, and you know that you ought to be court-martialed!"

Not that the position had been taken without cost. In fact, the cost had been about as steep as the grade up which the attack was launched: particularly to the two divisions in the center. Wood suffered 1035 casualties, as compared to a combined total of 789 for Baird and Johnson, in support on the left and right; whereas Sheridan lost 1346, a bit over twenty percent of the 6500 infantry he had had when he started forward. Moreover, there was a good deal of variation in the losses by smaller units within the larger ones, depending on the luck of the draw in their assault on different portions of the ridge. Some had cover most of the way up and therefore contributed little to the amount of blood that was shed on the slope, while others had to pass through a continuous hail of bullets and were grievously battered in the process. An Indiana regiment, for instance, started its climb with 337 effectives and lost 202 of them, or nearly sixty percent, killed and wounded in the forty-five minutes required to reach the crest. After such bleeding and exertion by the infantry, and in the absence of cavalry, which was still beyond the river because of a continuing lack of forage on the south bank, it was small wonder no true pursuit was undertaken within the brief remaining span of daylight that followed the collapse of the rebel center. Sheridan, once he had come down off his perch astride the cannon, was eager to take up the chase, but the other division commanders were not, even though they had suffered fewer casualties, and Granger declined to unleash him.

Meanwhile the Confederates made good use of the respite thus allowed them. Continuing to hold off Sherman with one hand — no difficult task, since he attempted no renewal of his attack — Cleburne prevented a widening of the breakthrough with the other, and Stewart served Hooker in much the same fashion north of Rossville. Sunset was at 4.50; Hardee rallied his and Breckinridge's fugitives on the near side of Chickamauga Creek and began a withdrawal across it under cover of darkness, one hour later. The moon rose full, drenching the fields and the lost ridge with a glistening yellow light almost bright enough to read by, if anyone had been of a mind to read. "By 9 p.m. everything was across," according to Cleburne, "except the dead and a few stragglers lingering here and there under the shadows of the trees for the purpose of being captured, faint-hearted patriots succumbing to the hardships of the war and the imagined hopelessness of the hour."

Next morning Bragg continued the withdrawal southeast into Georgia, attempting to gain the cover of Taylor's Ridge, just beyond Ringgold, and leaving a trail of charred supply dumps and broken-down wagons, as well as four more cannon, to mark the line of his retreat. He had lost, in the course of the three-day action, November 23-25, fewer than half as many killed and wounded as his adversary — 361 and 2160, as compared to 753 and 4722 in those two doleful categories — but his 4146 captured and missing, in contrast to Grant's 349, raised the Confederate total of 6667 above the Federal 5824. But that was by no means all there was to the outcome of the fighting, nor was it fitting as a yardstick by which to measure the extent of the disaster. Bragg had lost a great deal more than the scant fifteen percent of his army which these figures indicated, and a great deal more than the 41 guns his cannoneers had abandoned, even though they amounted to more than a third of all he had. Guns and men could be replaced; Chattanooga, on the other hand, was now what a northern journalist called "a gateway wrenched asunder." The road lay open into the heartland of the South, and all that stood between the bluecoats and a rapid penetration was the battered and dispirited remnant of the force they had just driven from a position its commander had deemed impregnable. And in fact he was still of that opinion, believing that all it had lacked was men determined to defend it. Unlike Lee, who at Gettysburg had said, "It's all my fault," Bragg at this stage was not inclined to shoulder even a fraction of the blame for the outcome of the contest. The burden of his official report, submitted later, was that the flaw had been in his soldiers. "No satisfactory excuse can possibly be given for the shameful conduct of the troops . . . in allowing their line to be penetrated. The position was one which ought to have been held by a line of skirmishers against any assaulting column." So he said, making no reference to the faulty dispositions or the unclear orders, both of which were his responsibility.

Not many agreed with him, however, either in his own army or in the one now in control of what he had lost. An Ohio infantryman, for example, coming forward on the morning after the battle for a walk along the northern end of Missionary Ridge, encountered the body of one of the men who had fought here under Cleburne. In the course of the recent siege he himself had learned something of privation, of the effects of hunger and exposure on the human spirit in its will to persevere against the odds, and this had given him a better understanding of the problems that had been so much a part of daily living for this dead soldier and others like him, whose own commander even now was blaming him and them, along with the bolters, for the loss of a position he and they had died in an attempt to save. Bending down for a closer look at the dead Confederate, the Ohioan afterwards told of what he saw. "He was not over fifteen years of age, and very slender in size. He was clothed in a cotton suit, and was barefooted; barefooted, [in] that cold and wet . . . November. I examined his haversack. For a day's ration there was a handful of black beans, a few pieces of sorghum, and a half dozen roasted acorns. That was an infinitely poor outfit for marching and fighting, but that Tennessee Confederate had made it answer his purpose."

Ultimately, if only in wry comment, at least one man on the Federal side agreed with Bragg as to the strength of the position, and that was Grant. Miffed by fortune's upset of his plans for Sherman's glorification, if not his own — on the first day, Thomas had played the leading role because Sherman was late in getting into position; on the second, Hooker had stolen the thunder from "above the clouds" while Sherman was attacking an undefended hill, just short of his true objective; on the third, Thomas once more occupied the limelight after Sherman was fought to a standstill by an opponent greatly his inferior in numbers — the over-all Union commander had sought to disassociate himself from a contest decided in outright violation not only of his wishes but also of his orders. "Damn the battle!" he was quoted as saying in that first fit of pique; "I had nothing to do with it." He recovered from this within a couple of hours, however, and got off a wire to Washington in which he had no reservations "in announcing a complete victory over Bragg." In time, he was even able to joke about it. Asked some years later whether he did not agree that his adversary had made a serious mistake in detaching Longstreet, he said he did, and when it was further suggested that Bragg must have considered his position impregnable, Grant agreed with that also, though his comment was accompanied by a smile and a shrewd look. "Well, it *was* impregnable," he said.

At any rate the Chattanooga gateway had been wrenched asunder, and what would come of this no man could say for certain; although some believed they knew, including members of the army now on the muddy and disconsolate retreat for Ringgold.

"Captain, this is the death knell of the Confederacy," a junior officer had remarked to his company commander as the withdrawal got under way from Missionary Ridge. "If we cannot cope with those fellows with the advantages we had on this line, there is not a line between here and the Atlantic Ocean where we can stop them."

"Hush, Lieutenant," the captain told him, slogging rearward through the darkness. "That is treason you are talking."

★ ☆ ☆

Depressed by the necessity for withdrawal and retreat, following hard upon the collapse of the Confederate center, the lieutenant overlooked the effectiveness with which Cleburne, outnumbered four or five to one, had "coped" with Sherman all day on the right. Two days later at Taylor's Ridge, as if by way of a reminder, the Arkansan repeated his performance, this time with even greater success, against Hooker and odds no worse than three to one. Moreover, this repetition of his exploit was the outcome of what had been thought to be a suicide assignment. Bragg made it to Ringgold by nightfall of November 26, fifteen miles down the railroad linking Chattanooga and Atlanta, and though so far he was more or less intact, he knew the Federals were closing on him rapidly. Encumbered as he was, and they were not, by a slow-moving wagon train hub-deep in mud, they would be certain to overtake him tomorrow unless he could do something to halt or anyhow delay them long enough to give him a new head start in the race for Dalton, another fifteen miles down the track. Accordingly, as he pressed on beyond the town and through the gap in Taylor's Ridge, he sent peremptory orders for a last-ditch stand at that point by the division guarding his rear. This was Cleburne's. It seemed hard to sacrifice good soldiers for no other purpose than to gain a little time, but Bragg believed he had no choice if he was to avoid the total destruction that would be likely to ensue if he was overtaken in his present condition, strung out on the muddy roads. "Tell General Cleburne to hold this position at all hazards," he instructed the staff officer who delivered the message, "and keep back the enemy until the artillery and transportation of the army are secure."

Though he had been told to cross in the darkness and thus avoid being overtaken by the superior blue force closing on his rear, Cleburne had stopped for the night on the west side of bridgeless East Chickamauga Creek, two miles short of the town, so his men could sleep in dry clothes before resuming the march next morning. Such concern for their welfare was characteristic of him, but it was practical as well, since he was convinced that a rear-guard action, even with a deep-running stream at their backs, would cost them fewer casualties than would lengthen the sick lists after a crossing of the waist-deep ford and a chilly halt on the east bank with no sun or exercise to warm them. Bragg's orders for a stand beyond Ringgold "at all hazards" reached him shortly before midnight, and he rode ahead to reconnoiter the position by moonlight, leaving instructions for the troops to be roused and started forward three hours later. At daybreak, having crossed the creek and filed through the streets of the Georgia hamlet, they found him waiting for them at the mouth of the narrow gorge through which the railroad plunged on its way to Atlanta. After about an hour, which he spent posting them and his two guns in accordance with a plan he had worked out while they were asleep, an enemy column emerged from the nearby eastern limits of the town, the bluecoats marching four abreast, preceded by a line of skirmishers, textbook style. Cleburne had his 4100 brush-masked graybacks hold their fire until the unsuspecting skirmishers were practically upon them, then open up with everything they had, including pistols. The head of the blasted column drew back snakelike on the writhing body, which coiled itself into attack formation and then came on again, 12,000 strong. This time there was no surprise, but the repulse was as complete. Hooker — for that was who it was, and he still had the three divisions with which he had seized Lookout Mountain three days ago — paused to take stock, then probed on the right, attacking up-hill, well south of the gap, in an attempt to outflank the defenders; only to find that they had shifted a portion of their force to meet him. Repulsed, he feinted again at the center and launched another uphill assault, this time on the left of the gap; but with the same result. Fighting Joe once more took stock, and decided to wait for his guns, which were toiling slowly eastward through the churned-up mud of the road from Chattanooga Valley, where they had been stalled until late yesterday for lack of a bridge strong enough to support them over Chattanooga Creek. By the time they arrived, the morning was gone and Cleburne had carried out his mission; Bragg's leading elements were in Dalton by then, safely beyond the craggy loom of Rocky Face Ridge, and the rest were not far behind, having been given the head start they needed. At a cost of 221 casualties — one less than he had suffered at Tunnel Hill — Cleburne had inflicted 442 by Hooker's admission. This was exactly double the number of his own, including more than a hundred prisoners he had taken along with three stands of colors, but Confederates were convinced the Federal losses were much larger than Fighting Joe admitted. A straggler from Walker's division, for example, watching the lop-sided contest from a grandstand seat on the ridge, pronounced it "the doggondest fight of the war." Down there below, he would recall years later, "the ground was piled with dead Yankees; they were piled in heaps. The scene looked unlike any battlefield I ever saw," he added. "From the foot to the top of the hill was covered with the slain, all lying on their faces. It had the appearance of the roof of a house shingled with dead Yankees."

Cleburne and his division, which he kept in position till well past noon and then withdrew unmolested, later received a joint resolution of thanks from Congress "for the victory obtained by them over superior forces of the enemy at Ringgold Gap, in the State of Georgia," but all that Hooker got from the engagement was a snub from his commander and an unceremonious return to inaction. When Grant came to write his report of the campaign, Ringgold Gap was referred to briefly as "a severe fight, in which we lost heavily in valuable officers and men," and he added an indorsement to Fighting Joe's own report that must have stung the glory-hungry general deeply: "Attention is called to that part of the report giving . . . the number of prisoners and small arms captured, which

is greater than the number really captured by the whole army." Grant
was an accomplished undercutter when he chose to be, and in Hooker's
case he did so choose, both now and down the years. For the present, he
directed him to hold his ground, "but to go no farther south at the expense of a fight." Cast once more in a supporting role, the unhappy
Easterner was told next day: "The object in remaining where you are is
to protect Sherman's flank while he is moving toward Cleveland and Loudon."

Once more the volatile redhead was the star, this time in a production entitled "The Relief of Knoxville," where Longstreet was still
hanging on and keeping Burnside under siege, despite Grant's prediction
that he would "take to the mountain passes" once the Chattanooga Federals came between him and Bragg and stood astride the rail supply line
in his rear. Sherman was altogether willing to try another turn at playing the role of savior, but he took care to have it understood that he did
not want to be left stranded in the backwater region once he had wound
up what he was being sent there to accomplish. He was utterly opposed to tying up masses of troops, least of all his own, for the purpose of
protecting a handful of civilians, many of whom he considered of doubtful loyalty anyhow, while the main stream of the war ran on to slaughter
elsewhere. "Recollect that East Tennessee is my horror," he wrote
Grant on December 1 from the near bank of the Hiwassee, while preparing to set out next day for Loudon and Knoxville. "That any military
man should send a force into East Tennessee puzzles me. Burnside is there
and must be relieved, but when relieved I want to get out, and he
should come out too."
    Burnside's men were in complete agreement; in fact, they had
been so all along. "If this is the kind of country we are fighting for," one
of them had declared on completing the southward march across the
barrens, "I am in favor of letting the rebs take their land and their niggers
and go to hell, for I wouldn't give a bit an acre for all the land I have seen
in the last four days." The trouble was that Lincoln very much wanted
them there, for precisely the reason Sherman derided: to protect the
Union-loyal citizens and relieve them of their long-borne yoke of Confederate oppression. Moreover, cooped up as they now were in Knoxville, under siege by Longstreet's two divisions plus a third that had arrived under Bushrod Johnson, the problem was not so much how to get
out as it was how to survive on meager rations. They were no longer
fighting for East Tennessee — which in point of fact they had abandoned, except for Knoxville itself and Cumberland Gap, the now inaccessible escape hatch fifty air-line miles due north — but for their lives.
    Old Peter and his soldiers were about as unhappy outside the
town — and incidentally, what with the wretched supply conditions,
about as hungry — as the Federals hemmed inside it. He had probed for

chinks in the blue defenses and, finding none, had waited for the reinforcements Bragg had said were on the way. Fewer than half of the
promised 11,000 arrived, but at least they brought him up to a strength
nearly equal to that of the force besieged. He continued to search for
weak spots, though with no better success. By November 27 — the
date of Cleburne's fight at Ringgold — coincident with the issuance of
orders for accomplishing a breakthrough at a point he had selected, a
rumor had begun to spread that Bragg had been whipped at Chattanooga. How much truth there was in this, Longstreet did not know, but
in reply next day to a suggestion from McLaws that the thing to do was
abandon the siege without further delay and return at once to Virginia,
lest they be caught between two superior Union forces, he persisted in
his belief that the best solution, if the rumor of Bragg's defeat was true,
was a quick settlement of the issue here at Knoxville. His reasons were
twofold: first because it would not do to leave a fellow commander in
the lurch, no matter how little regard he had for him personally, and second because a victory over Burnside would dispose of at least one of the
two menaces to a successful withdrawal if such a course became un-
avoidable. That is, if he stayed where he was, at least for a time, he might
draw off a portion of the blue horde rumored to be in pursuit of Bragg,
and he might also simplify his own problems, when and if the time came
for him to retire eastward over the primitive mountain roads. "It is a
great mistake to suppose that there is any safety for us in going to Virginia if General Bragg has been defeated," he told his fellow Georgian,
"for we leave him at the mercy of his victors, and with his army destroyed our own had better be also, for we will be not only destroyed,
but disgraced. There is neither safety nor honor in any other course than
the one I have chosen and ordered. . . . The assault must be made at the
time appointed, and must be made with a determination which will insure success."

The time appointed was dawn next morning, November 29, and
the point selected for assault was Fort Loudon, a bastioned earthwork
previously established by the Confederates at the tip of a long salient extended westward from the main line of intrenchments to include a hill
1000 yards beyond the limits of the town; Fort Sanders, the Federals had
renamed it, in memory of the young cavalry brigadier who had made a
successful bridge-burning raid through the region, back in June, but had
been mortally wounded two weeks ago at Campbell Station, supposedly
by a civilian sniper, while resisting the gray advance on Knoxville. Originally Longstreet had intended to use Alexander's artillery to soften up
the objective before the infantry moved in; then later he decided to stake
everything on surprise, which would be sacrificed if he employed a preliminary bombardment, and on the sheer weight of numbers massed on a
narrow front. Assigning two brigades from McLaws to the assault, with
a third in support from Jenkins — a total of about 3000 effectives, as

compared to fewer than 500 within the fort, including the crews of its twelve guns — he posted the first wave of attackers within 150 yards of the northwest corner of the works in the cold predawn darkness of the night whose end would be the signal for the jump-off. The advance was to be conducted in columns of regiments, the theory being that such a deployment in depth would give added power to the thrust and insure that there would be no wait for reinforcements in case unexpected resistance developed in the course of the attack. It was stressed that there was to be no pause for anything whatever, front or rear, and that the main thing was to keep moving. Once the position had been overrun, the surviving remnant of the garrison, if any, was to be driven eastward through the town, so that other strongpoints along the line could be taken in reverse, thus effecting a quick reduction of the whole.

Longstreet had planned carefully, with close attention to such details as had occurred to him and the specialists on his staff. But so had Burnside: as the butternut attackers discovered when they rushed forward through the dusk of that frosty Sunday morning. The first thing they struck was wire — not barbed wire; that refinement was achieved by a later generation; but telegraph wire — looped and stretched close to the ground between stakes and stumps, which not only tripped the men at the heads of the columns and sent them sprawling and cursing, but also served as an unmistakable warning to the garrison that an assault was being launched. Nor was this innovation by any means the worst of what the Confederates encountered in the course of the next hour. Continuing through and over the wire, laced in a network knee- and ankle-high, they gained the ditch to find that it was nine feet deep — not five, as they had been informed by the staffers who had done their reconnoitering with binoculars at long range — while the parapet just beyond it, slippery with half-frozen mud and a powdering of sleet, was crowded along its crest with blue defenders, ranked shoulder to shoulder and thoroughly alert, who delivered steady blasts of musketry into the packed gray mass a dozen feet below. Without scaling ladders, which no one had thought would be needed, some men tried to get up and over the wall by standing on the shoulders of their comrades, but were either hurled back or captured. One color bearer, hoisted in this fashion, was grabbed by the neck and snatched from sight, flopping like a hooked fish being landed, and though three others managed to plant their standards on the rim of the parapet, a succession of replacements was required to keep them there. All this time, two triple-shotted guns on the flank were raking the trench with a fire that dropped the dead and injured of the two assault brigades beneath the feet of the men of the third, who came sliding down the counterscarp to add to the wedged confusion. By now, with the Federals heaving lighted shells into the ditch, where they exploded with fearful effect at such close quarters, it had become appar-

ent, at least to the troops immediately concerned, that the only result of
continuing the attack — if, indeed, it could still be called that at this
stage — would be to lengthen the already considerable list of casualties.
When Longstreet, coming forward with two more brigades which he intended to throw into the uproar, learned from McLaws of the woeful
state of affairs up ahead, he rejected pleas by Jenkins and Johnson that
they be allowed to try their hand, and ordered the recall sounded. Dazed
and panicky, the survivors of the three committed brigades, or anyhow
so many of them as did not prefer surrender to the further risk of catching a bullet in the back, returned through the wire they had encountered at the outset.

Generous as ever in such matters, Burnside promptly sent out a
flag of truce and offered his old friend permission to remove his dead
and injured from the ditch. Longstreet gratefully accepted, then requested and received an extension of the truce when this turned out to be
a heavier task than he had supposed without a close-up view of the
carnage. He had suffered 813 casualties — 129 killed, 458 wounded, and
226 captured — in contrast to his adversary, who lost, out of 440 effectives in Fort Sanders at the time of the attack, a total of 8 killed and
5 wounded. Thirteen was a decidedly lucky number in this instance;
moreover, the high proportion of dead among the scant handful of
Union casualties resulted from the fact that the defenders had exposed
no more than their heads to the rattled fire of the attackers, and even
then for only so long as it took them to take aim, which was scarcely
necessary at that range and with a target of that size. Up to now, the
Federal losses for the whole campaign had been higher than those of the
besiegers, but today's losses brought the over-all totals, North and
South, respectively to 693 and 1142. What was more, these figures were
approximately final; for while the work of removing Old Peter's unfortunates was in progress he received a message informing him that
Bragg had fallen back from Chattanooga, thirty miles down the railroad
toward Atlanta, and advising him to do the same from Knoxville, either
toward Georgia or Virginia, but in any case to have Wheeler report to
Dalton as soon as possible with his three brigades. Having complied with
the instructions for the cavalry to move out, Longstreet decided to hold
his ground until he could discover whether the road to Dalton was open.
He remained in front of Knoxville until he learned from a captured dispatch, two days later, that Sherman was on the way from Loudon with
six divisions, which would give the Federals ten in all, as compared to the
Confederate three. Accordingly, on the night of December 3 he put his
trains in motion, not toward Dalton but northeast, in the direction of
Virginia, and followed shortly after dark next evening with his infantry,
unobserved. "Detached from General Lee, what a horrible failure is
Longstreet!" an eastern diarist exclaimed, forgetful of his great day at

Chickamauga and unaware that he had been sent to East Tennessee not only against his wishes but also over his protest that the expedition was tactically unwise, both from Bragg's point of view and his own.

Sherman arrived next day, riding in ahead of the relief column, which he had stopped at Maryville, eighteen miles to the south, when he learned that the Confederates had pulled back from Knoxville. Notified that the siege had been lifted, Grant proposed that Longstreet be pursued and driven across the Blue Ridge, thus to assure his removal as a hovering threat; but the redhead wanted no part of such an assignment. "A stern chase is a long one," he protested, determined to resist all efforts to shift him farther eastward from the Mississippi Valley, which he still saw as the cockpit of the war. Now that the big river had been cleared and reclaimed from source to mouth, he preferred to deal with the rebels down in Georgia, intending to complete their destruction by driving them back on the rail transportation hub eighty air-line miles across the mountains in their rear. "My troops are in excellent heart," he declared, "ready for Atlanta or anywhere." Instructed to detach two divisions to strengthen the Knoxville garrison — in case Longstreet attempted a comeback from Rogersville, where he had ended his unpursued retreat, sixty-odd miles up the Holston — Sherman had Granger proceed north from Maryville with Sheridan and Wood, while he himself returned by easy stages to Chattanooga with his own four divisions. There he found Thomas and Hooker taking a well-earned rest from their recent exertions. Now that blustery weather had arrived, the Cumberland and ex-Potomac troops were already settling down in winter camps. Similarly, Grant had transferred his headquarters back to Nashville, and presently Sherman joined him there, enjoying such relaxations as the Tennessee capital afforded outside work hours, which the two friends spent designing further troubles for the Confederacy, to be undertaken in various directions as soon as the weather cleared.

That would not be for some time, however. Meanwhile Thomas was occupying himself with the establishment of a military cemetery on Orchard Knob. The thought had occurred to him, on the day he took it, that this would make a lovely burying ground for the Union soldiers who had fallen or were still to fall in the battles hereabout, and almost before the smoke of his involuntary assault on Missionary Ridge had cleared he had a detail at work on the project. When the chaplain who was to be in charge inquired if the dead should be buried in plots assigned to the states they represented — as was being done at Gettysburg, where Lincoln had spoken a couple of weeks ago — the Virginian lowered his head in thought, then shook it decisively and made a tumbling gesture with both hands. "No, no; mix 'em up, mix 'em up," he said; "I'm tired of states rights." Increased responsibility, accompanied by a growing and reciprocal fondness for the men in the army he now led, had brought a new geniality to the stolid Rock of Chickamauga. He had even begun to tell stories on himself: as, for example, of the soldier who had come to him recently asking for a furlough. "I aint seen my old woman, General, for four months," the man explained. If he thought this could not fail in its persuasiveness he was wrong. "And I have not seen mine for two years," Thomas replied. "If a general can submit to such privation, surely a private can." Evidently the soldier had not previously considered this connection between privates and privation. At any rate he looked doubtful. "I don't know about that, General," he said. "Me and my wife aint made that way."

No doubt the Virginian's jovial mood was also due in part to the fulfillment of his vow to be "even" with his former battery commander for the insult he had received in the course of the siege that had been lifted when his Cumberlanders took the bit in their teeth and charged, "against orders," up Missionary Ridge. What was more, his satisfaction was enlarged by the knowledge that he had obtained it despite the department commander's attempt to limit his participation in the action that had finally put revenge within his reach. In that double sense, as the outcome applied to both commanders, past and present, his gratification was doubly sweet.

As for Bragg, the reconsolidation of his army behind Rocky Face Ridge — completed on November 28 with the arrival of Cleburne, who was greeted with cheers for his rebuff of Hooker at Ringgold Gap the day before — brought with it not only a sense of relief at having been delivered from destruction, but also a certain added ruefulness, a letdown following hard upon the relaxation of tension. He knew now just how narrow his escape had been and, what was worse, how unlikely he was to be so fortunate in another contest with the foe who had just flung him out of a position he had judged impregnable. Worst of all, perhaps, was the attitude of the troops, then and since. "Here's your mule!" they had hooted in response to his attempt to rally them with "Here is your commander," and he took it as a bad sign that, far from being despondent over their disgrace, many of them were grinning at the memory of their headlong break for safety. "Flicker, flicker!" they called to one another in their camps, that being their accustomed cry when they saw a man whose legs would not behave in combat. "Yaller-hammer, Alabama! Flicker, flicker, yaller-hammer!" they would shout, adding by way of reprise: "Bully for Bragg! He's hell on retreat!" Though this might be no more than their way of shrugging off embarrassment, it did not seem to him to augur well for the outcome of the next blue-gray confrontation, wherever that might be. "We hope to maintain this position," he wired Richmond the following day, "[but] should the enemy press on promptly we may have to cross the Oostenaula," another fifteen miles to the south, beyond Resaca. "My first estimate of our disaster was not too large," he continued, "and time only can restore order and morale. All possible aid should be pushed on to Resaca." And having gone so far in the way of admission, he went one step further. "I deem it due to the cause and to myself," he added, "to ask for relief from command and an investigation into the causes of the defeat."

Perhaps this last was no more than a closing flourish, such as he had employed at the end of the letter sent out after Murfreesboro, wherein he invited his lieutenants to assess his military worth. In any event, just as they had taken him at his word then, whether he meant it or not, so did Davis now. "Your dispatches of yesterday received," the adjutant general replied on the last day of November. "Your request to be relieved has been submitted to the President, who, upon your representation, directs me to notify you that you are relieved from command, which you will transfer to Lieutenant General Hardee, the officer next in rank and now present for duty."

There he had it. Or perhaps not quite; perhaps the flourish — if that was what it was — could be recalled. At any rate, if he was thus to be brought down, he would do what he could to assure that his was not a solitary departure. In sending next day, by special messenger, "a plain, unvarnished report of the operations at Chattanooga, resulting in my shameful discomfiture," he included a letter addressed to his friend the Commander in Chief, who had sustained him invariably in the past. "The disaster admits of no palliation," he wrote, "and is justly disparaging to me as a commander. I trust, however, you may find upon full investigation that the fault is not entirely mine. . . . I fear we both erred in the conclusion for me to retain command here after the clamor raised against me. The warfare has been carried on successfully, and the fruits are bitter. You must make other changes here, or our success is hopeless. . . . I can bear to be sacrificed myself, but not to see my country and my friends ruined by the vices of a few profligate men." Specifically he charged that Breckinridge had been drunk throughout the three-day battle and "totally unfit for any duty" on the retreat, while Cheatham was "equally dangerous" in that regard. As for himself, he said in closing, "I shall ever be ready to do all in my power for our common cause, but feel that some little rest will render me more efficient than I am now. Most respectfully and truly, yours, Braxton Bragg, General, &c."

Still in Dalton the following day, December 2, he tried a different tack in a second letter — still headed "Headquarters Army of Tennessee" and still signed "General, Commanding" — in which he assessed the tactical situation and made an additional suggestion: "The enemy has concentrated all his available means in front of this army, and by sheer force of numbers has triumphed over our gallant little band. No one estimates the disaster more seriously than I do, and the whole responsibility and disgrace rest on my humble head. But we can redeem the past. Let us concentrate all our available men, unite them with this gallant little army, still full of zeal and burning to redeem its lost character and prestige, and with our greatest and best leader at its head — yourself, if practicable — march the whole upon the enemy and crush him in his power and his glory. I believe it practicable, and I trust that I may be allowed to participate in the struggle which may restore to us the character, the prestige, and the country which we have just lost."

Whatever might come of this in the future, and he knew how susceptible to flattery Davis was in that respect, there was nothing for him to do now, after waiting two whole days for them to be rescinded, but carry out the instructions he had received. Painful though the parting was, at least for him — "The associations of more than two years, which bind together a commander and his trusted troops, cannot be severed without deep emotion," he remarked in the farewell address he issued that same day — he turned his duties over to Hardee, as ordered, and took his leave. In the seventeen months he had been at its head the Army of Tennessee had fought four great battles, three of which had ended in retreat though all save the last had been claimed as victories. Similarly, in the equal span of time ahead, it would fight a great many more battles that would likewise be claimed as victories although they too — once more with a single exception, comparatively as bloody as Chickamauga — would end in retreat; but not under Bragg. His tenure had ended. "I shall proceed to La Grange, Georgia, with my personal staff," he notified Richmond, "and there await further orders."

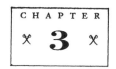
Spring Came on Forever

★ ✗ ☆

NEWS OF THE GREAT CHATTANOOGA VICTORY, which had begun on Monday and ended on Wednesday, spread throughout the North on the following day, November 26. By coincidence, in a proclamation issued eight weeks earlier at the suggestion of a lady editor, Lincoln had called upon his fellow citizens "to set apart and observe the last Thursday of November next, as a day of thanksgiving and praise to our beneficent Father who dwelleth in the Heavens." Instituted thus "in the midst of a civil war of unequaled magnitude and severity," this first national Thanksgiving was intended not only as a reminder for people to be grateful for "the blessings of fruitful fields and healthful skies," but also as an occasion for them to "implore the interposition of the Almighty Hand to heal the wounds of the nation and to restore it, as soon as may be consistent with the Divine purposes, to the full enjoyment of peace, harmony, tranquillity, and Union." Now that word of what had happened yesterday on Missionary Ridge was added to the "singular deliverances and blessings" for which the public was urged to show its gratitude today, it seemed to many that the Almighty Hand had interposed already, answering a good part of their prayers in advance, and that the end so fervently hoped for might be considerably nearer than had been supposed when the proclamation was issued in early October, not quite two weeks after the shock of Chickamauga caused those hopes to take a sudden drop. "This is truly a day of thanksgiving," Halleck wired Grant as the news of his latest triumph went out across the land and set the church bells ringing as wildly as they had rung after Donelson and Vicksburg.

Moreover, just as Thomas had taken his revenge for Chickamauga, so had Banks obtained by now at least a degree of recompense for the drubbing he had suffered in September, when he opened his campaign against coastal Texas with Franklin's botched attack on Sabine Pass. Revising his plan by reversing it, end for end, he decided to start with a landing near the Mexican border, then work his island-hopping way back east. It was true the pickings would be much slimmer at the outset, for there was little that far down the coast that was worth taking; but the objectives were unlikely to be as stoutly defended, and he would be moving toward, rather than away from, his New Orleans base of supplies, which should serve to encourage his men to fight harder and move faster, if for no other reason than to hasten their return. Accordingly, after sending Franklin's unhappy soldiers to Berwick for a renewed ascent of the Teche — an ascent that would end abruptly on November 3 at Grand Coteau, ten miles short of Opelousas, where the column was assaulted and driven back through Vermilionville to New Iberia by Richard Taylor and Tom Green, who lost 180 and inflicted 716 casualties, including the 536 fugitives they captured — he loaded aboard transports a 3500-man division, commanded by a Maine-born major general with the resounding name of Napoleon Jackson Tecumseh Dana, who set out from New Orleans on October 26, escorted by three gunboats. This time Banks went along himself, presumably to guard against snarls and hitches. At any rate there were none. On November 2 — the day before Franklin was thrown into sudden reverse at Grand Coteau — Dana put his troops ashore at Brazos Santiago, off the mouth of the Rio Grande, and though he encountered practically no resistance, the graybacks having been withdrawn to thicken the defenses in East Texas, Banks did not let this tone down the announcement of his achievement. "The flag of the Union floated over Texas today at meridian precisely," he notified Washington. "Our enterprise has been a complete success." Four days later he occupied Brownsville, just under thirty miles inland, opposite Matamoros, and sent for the puppet governor Andrew Hamilton, who had been waiting off-stage all this time and who was established there at the southernmost tip of the state and the nation, along with his gubernatorial staff of would-be cotton factors, before the month was out. Meanwhile Banks had followed up his initial success with a series of landings on Mustang and Matagorda islands, thus gaining control of Aransas Pass and Matagorda Bay. But that was all; that was as far as he got on his way back east. Galveston and the mouth of the Brazos River were too strongly held for him to attack them with Dana's present command, reduced as it was by garrison detachments, and Halleck could not be persuaded to accede to requests for reinforcements. All Banks had gained for his pains these past three months, including the drubbing at Sabine Pass, was a couple of dusty border towns and a few bedraggled miles of Texas beach, mostly barren dunes, which he described as "inclement and uncomfortable, in consequence of the sterility of the soil and the violence of the northers."

Despite the flamboyance with which they were announced — "My most sanguine expectations are more than realized," Banks had proclaimed after occupying Brownsville; "Everything is now as favorable as could be desired" — the authorities in Washington were not inclined to include these shallow coastal lodgments, amounting in fact to little more than pinpricks along one leathery flank of the Texas elephant, among those things for which the nation should be thankful on its first Thanksgiving. Hamilton governed far too small and remote an area for his claims to be taken seriously, inside or outside the state, and it seemed to Lincoln, although he later thanked Banks politically for his "successful and valuable operations," that all the general had really done was shift some 3500 of his soldiers off to the margin of the map, where they were of about as much tactical value as if their transports had gone to the bottom of the Gulf with them aboard. Halleck expressed an even dimmer view of the proceedings. "In regard to your Sabine and Rio Grande expeditions," he protested to the Massachusetts general, "no notice of your intention to make them was received here till they were actually undertaken." Old Brains was especially irked by the setback at Grand Coteau, which he saw as the result of an unwise division of force, occasioned by the unauthorized excursion down the coast. In his opinion, the Teche, the Atchafalaya, and the Red afforded the best approach to the Lone Star State, and though he understood that these streams were at present unusable even as supply routes, being practically dry at this season of the year, he wanted the entire command standing by for the early spring rise that would convert them into arteries of invasion. For this reason, as well as for the more general one that none were available, he flatly refused to send reinforcements for an attack on Galveston by the amphibious force which by now had worked its way back east to Matagorda, explaining testily that even if such an attack were successful — and even if the place did not turn out to be a trap, as it had done before — it still would be no more than a diversion from the true path of conquest.

Besides, there were nearer and larger frets, invoking more immediate concern; Knoxville, for example. "Remember Burnside," Lincoln had wired yesterday in response to Grant's announcement that victory was within reach at Chattanooga. He could breathe easier now, for while Longstreet's siege was apparently still in progress he knew that Grant, relieved of the presence of Bragg, was free to turn his attention to East Tennessee. But there was a still nearer fret, not sixty miles southwest of Washington, and though in this case the Union force was on the offensive, the Commander in Chief had learned from long experience that the strain of waiting for news of an expected success was quite as great as waiting for news of an expected failure — particularly since experience had also taught him, all too often, that anticipated triumphs had a way of turning into the worst of all defeats; Chancellorsville, for instance. Meade at last had resumed his movement southward, having taken a two-week rest from the exertion of crossing the Rappahannock, and on this Thanksgiving morning the leading elements of his army were over the Rapidan, entering the gloomy western fringe of the Wilderness in whose depths Joe Hooker had come to grief in early May, just short of seven months ago.

His decision to cross and come to grips with Lee on that forbidding ground was based in part on a growing confidence proceeding from the fact that he had whipped him rather soundly in both of their recent face-to-face encounters, first at Bristoe Station and then at Rappahannock Bridge and Kelly's Ford. Moreover, there had come to hand on November 21 a detailed intelligence report which put the enemy strength at less than 40,000 effectives, as compared to his own 84,274 on that date. Actually, Lee's total was 48,586; Meade had just under, not just over, twice as many troops as his opponent. But in any case the preponderance was encouraging, and after four days of studying the figures and the map, he distributed on November 25 a circular directing his five corps commanders to be ready to march at 6 o'clock next morning, half an hour before sunrise. Lee's two corps were strung out along the south bank of the river, one east and the other west of Clark's Mountain, their outer flanks respectively at Mine Run and Liberty Mills, some thirty miles apart; Meade's plan called for a crossing by the downstream fords, well beyond the Confederate right, and a fast march west, along the Orange Turnpike, for a blow at the rebel east flank before Lee could bring up his other corps in support. Unlike Hooker, Meade designed no feints or diversions, preferring to concentrate everything he had for the main effort. He relied entirely on speed, which would enable him to strike before his adversary had time to get set for the punch, and on the known numerical advantage, which would be far greater than two to one if he could mass and commit his fifteen infantry divisions before the rebel six achieved a concentration. All this was explained to the responsible subordinates, whose marches began on schedule from their prescribed assembly areas near Ely's and Germanna fords, well downstream from the apparently unsuspecting graybacks in their works across the way. Aside from a heavy morning fog, which screened the movement from enemy lookouts on Clark's Mountain — more evidence, it would seem, of the interposition of the Almighty Hand in favor of the Union on this Thanksgiving Day — the weather was pleasant, a bit chilly but all the more bracing for that, and the blue troops stepped out smartly along the roads and trails leading down to the various fords that had been assigned them so that a nearly simultaneous crossing could be made by the several columns. That too had been part of the design combining speed and power.

As always, there were hitches: only this time, with speed of such vital importance, they were even more exasperating than usual. What was worse, they began to crop up almost at the outset. Meade had planned with elaborate care, issuing eight-day rations to the men, for instance, to avoid the need for a slow-rolling wagon train that would take

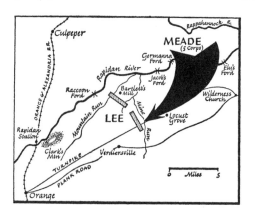

up a lot of road space and require a heavy guard; but he had neglected the human factor. In the present case, as it turned out, that factor was embodied in the person of William French, successor to Sickles as chief of the III Corps, which had been enlarged to three divisions, the same as the other four. A Maryland-born West Pointer nearing fifty, French was a tall, high-stomached man with an apoplectic look and a starchy manner, a combination that led an unadmiring staffer to remark that he resembled "one of those plethoric French colonels who are so stout, and who look so red in the face, that one would suppose someone had tied a cord tightly around their necks." So far in the war, though he had taken part in all the army's major fights except the two Bull Runs and Gettysburg, he had not distinguished himself in action. Today — and tomorrow too, for that matter, as developments would show — his performance was a good deal worse than undistinguished. Assigned to cross at Jacob's Ford, which meant that he would have the lead when the five corps turned west beyond the river, since it was the nearest of the three fords being used, he was not only late in arriving and slow in crossing, but when he found the opposite bank too steep for his battery horses to manage, he sent his artillery down to Germanna Ford and snarled the already heavy traffic there. It was dusk before he completed his crossing and called a halt close to the river, obliging those behind him to do likewise. Next morning he stepped off smartly to make up for the time lost, then promptly took the wrong fork in the road and had to countermarch. By the time he got back on the right track, the sun was past the overhead and the movement was a full day behind schedule. Red-faced and angry, for Meade was prodding him hard by now, French set out once more through the woods that screened his approach to the rebel flank, supposedly a mile away, only to run into butternut skirmishers who obliged him to call a halt and deploy his lead division. Having done so, he started forward again; but not for long. Well short of the point he had been due to reach before he encountered anything more than an outpost handful of gray pickets, the firing stepped up and he found himself involved in a full-scale engagement with what seemed to be most of the rebels in the world. Apparently Lee had made good use of the time afforded him yesterday and today by the hitches that had slowed and stalled the greatly superior mass of bluecoats closing upon him through the woods on his downstream flank.

The southern commander had indeed made use of the time so

generously allowed him. Informed by a scout on Thanksgiving Eve of the issue of eight-day rations across the way, he alerted his outposts to watch for a movement, upstream or down, and sat back to await developments. If the length of the numerical odds disturbed him, he could recall the victory he had scored against even longer odds, seven months ago, on practically this same ground. "With God's help," a young officer on his staff wrote home that night, "there shall be a Second Chancellorsville as there was a Second Manassas." Next morning, when Stuart reported the Federals crossing in force by the lower fords, Lee sent word for Hill to take up the march from beyond Clark's Mountain to join Ewell, whose corps was on the right, and shifted army headquarters the following day from Orange to Verdiersville, a dozen miles east on the plank road. He did not know yet whether Richmond or the Army of Northern Virginia was Meade's objective, but in any case he decided that his best course was to move toward him, either for an interception or for a head-on confrontation. In the absence of Ewell, who was sick, the Second Corps was under Early; Lee told him to move eastward, down the pike toward Locust Grove, and keep going until he encountered something solid. That was how it came about that French, once he recovered his sense of direction and got back on the track that afternoon, found the woods a-boil with graybacks and was obliged to engage in an unscheduled and unwanted fight, one mile short of his immediate objective. Dusk ended the brief but savage action, in which each side lost better than 500 men, and Lee had Early fall back through the darkness to a previously selected position on the far side of Mine Run, which flowed due north into the Rapidan. Hill would arrive tomorrow and extend the line southward, taking post astride the turnpike and the plank road east of Verdiersville, while Early covered the approaches to Bartlett's Mill on the far left, near the river. Anticipating with satisfaction his first purely defensive full-scale battle since Fredericksburg, just two weeks short of a full year ago, Lee instructed his men to get busy with their shovels, preparing for a repetition of that butchery.

Coming up next day through a driving rain, which made for heavy marching, the bluecoats found themselves confronted by a seven-mile line of intrenchments whose approaches had been cleared for overlapping fields of fire. They took one look at the rebel works, sited forbiddingly along a ridge on the dominant west bank of the boggy stream, and decided that for the high command to send down orders for an assault would amount to issuing death warrants for most of the troops involved. Their generals rather thought so, too, when they came forward to reconnoiter, Warren and Sedgwick on the left and right, French in the center, and Sykes and Newton in reserve. By sundown the rain had slacked and stopped, giving way to a night so cold that the water froze in the men's canteens. All next day the reconnaissance continued, and so did the spadework across the run. Meade was determined to try for a breakthrough, if one of his corps commanders would only find him a weak spot in the gray defenses. That night, when Sedgwick and Warren reported that they had found what he wanted on both flanks of the position, he issued instructions for an attack next morning. Sedgwick would open with his artillery at 7 o'clock on the right, attracting the enemy's attention in that direction, and Warren would launch an assault one hour later at the far end of the line, supported by French, who would feint at the rebel center, and by Newton, who would mass in his rear to help exploit the breakthrough. Similarly, Sykes would move up in close support of Sedgwick, whose bombardment was to be followed by an assault designed to shatter the Confederate left. With both flanks crumpled and no reserves on hand to shore them up, Lee would fall back in disarray and the blue reserves would hurry forward to complete his discomfort and destruction.

So ordered, so attempted; Uncle John opened on schedule with all his guns, while down the line the troops assigned to the assault grew tenser by the minute as the time drew near for them to go forward. Whatever the generals back at headquarters might be thinking, the men themselves, crouched in the brush and peering out across the slashings at the icy creek which they would have to cross to get within reach of the butternut infantry — dug in along the ridge to await their coming and probably smiling with anticipation as they fondled their rifles or stood by their double-shotted cannon — did not like any part of the prospect now before them. For one thing, a man even lightly hit, out there in the clearing where no stretcher bearers could get to him, would probably die in this penetrating cold. For another, they judged that their deaths would be purposeless, for they did not believe that the assault could possibly succeed. Waiting for the guns to stop their fuming, some of the soldiers passed the time by writing their names and addresses on bits of paper or chips of wood, which they fastened inside their clothes; "Killed in action, Nov. 30, 1863," a few of the gloomier or more cynical ones among them added. However, just as the artillery left off roaring and they were about to step forward into chaos, a message arrived from army headquarters: "Suspend the attack until further orders." Later they found out why. On the far left, after discovering by daylight that the rebel defenses had been greatly strengthened overnight, Warren sent word that the assault he had deemed feasible yesterday would be suicidal today. Meade rode down to see for himself, found that he agreed with this revised assessment, and canceled the attack, both left and right. Grinning, the reprieved troops discarded their improvised dogtags and thought higher than ever of Warren, who they were convinced had done the army as solid a service, in avoiding a disaster here today, as he had performed five months ago at Little Round Top or last month at Bristoe Station. What he had done, they realized, took a special kind of courage, and they were grateful not only to him but also to the commander who sustained him. Moreover, since supplies were getting low and a thaw would soften the crust of frozen mud without which no movement would be possible on the bottomless roads, Meade decided next day to withdraw the army over the same routes by which it had crossed the Rapidan, five days back, and entered this luckless woodland in the first place. So ordered, so done; the rearward movement began shortly after sunset, December 1, and continued through the night.

Glad as the departing bluecoats were to escape the wintry hug of the Wilderness, they were more fortunate than they knew. On November 30, the expected assault not having been launched against his intrenchments, Lee had been summoned to the far right by Wade Hampton, who, recovered from his Gettysburg wounds and returned to duty, had discovered an opening for a blow at the Union left, not unlike the one Hooker had received in May on his opposite flank, a few miles to the east. Looking the situation over, the southern commander liked what he saw, but decided to wait before taking advantage of it. He felt sure that Meade would attack, sooner or later, and he did not want to pass up the near certainty of another Fredericksburg, even if it meant postponing a chance for another Chancellorsville. By noon of the following day, however, with the Federals still immobile in his front, he changed his mind. "They must be attacked; they must be attacked," he muttered. Accordingly, he prepared to go over to the offensive with an all-out assault on the flank Hampton had found dangling. Sidling Early's men southward to fill the gap, Lee withdrew two of Hill's divisions from the trenches that evening and massed them south of the plank road, in the woods beyond the vulnerable enemy left, with orders to attack at dawn. Early would hold the fortified line overlooking Mine Run, while Hill drove the blue mass northward across his front and into the icy toils of the Rapidan. This time there would be no escape for Meade, as there had been for Hooker back in May, for there would be twelve solid hours of daylight for pressing the attack, not a bare two or three, as there had been when Jackson struck in the late afternoon, under circumstances otherwise much the same.

"With God's blessing," the young staffer had predicted six nights ago, "there shall be a Second Chancellorsville." But he was wrong; God's blessing was withheld. When the flankers went forward at first light they found the thickets empty, the Federals gone. Chagrined (for though he had inflicted 1653 casualties at a cost of 629 — which brought the total of his losses to 4255 since Gettysburg, as compared to Meade's 4406 — he had counted on a stunning victory, defensive or offensive), Lee ordered his cavalry after them and followed with the infantry, marching as best he could through woods the bluecoats had set afire in their wake. It was no use; Meade's head start had been substantial, and he was back across the Rapidan before he could be overtaken. In the Confederate ranks there was extreme regret at the lost opportunity, which grew in estimation, as was usual in such cases, in direct ratio to its inaccessibility. Early and Hill came under heavy criticism for having allowed the enemy to steal away unnoticed. "We miss Jackson and Longstreet terribly," the same staff officer remarked. But Lee, as always, took the blame on his own shoulders: shoulders on which he now was feeling the weight of his nearly fifty-seven years. "I am too old to command this army," he said sadly. "We should never have permitted those people to get away."

★ ★ ★

Although Davis shared the deep regret that Meade had not been punished more severely for his temporary boldness, he did not agree with Lee as to where the blame for this deliverance should rest. Conferring with the general at Orange on the eve of the brief Mine Run campaign, two weeks after his return from the roundabout western journey — it was the Commander in Chief's first visit to the Army of Northern Virginia since its departure from Richmond, nearly sixteen months before, to accomplish the suppression of Pope on the plains of Manassas — he had not failed to note the signs that Lee was aging, which indeed were unmistakable, but mainly he was impressed anew by his clear grasp of the tactical situation, his undiminished aggressiveness in the face of heavy odds, and the evident devotion of the veterans in his charge. Davis's admiration for this first of his field generals — especially by contrast with what he had observed in the course of his recent visit to the Army of Tennessee — was as strong as it had been four months ago, when he listed his reasons for refusing to accept Lee's suggestion that he be replaced as a corrective for the Gettysburg defeat. By now though, as a result of what had happened around Chattanooga the week before, he had it once again in mind to shift him to new fields. Directed to take over from Bragg, who was relieved on the day Meade began his withdrawal from the Wilderness, Hardee replied as he had done when offered the command two months ago. He appreciated "this expression of [the President's] confidence," he said, "but feeling my inability to serve the country successfully in this new sphere of duty, I respectfully decline the command if designed to be permanent." Davis then turned, as he had turned before, to Lee: with similar results. The Virginian replied that he would of course go to North Georgia, if ordered, but "I have not that confidence either in my strength or ability as would lead me of my own option to undertake the command in question."

It was Lee's opinion that Beauregard was the logical choice for the post he had vacated a year and a half ago; but Davis liked this no better than he did the notion, advanced by others, that Johnston was the best man for the job. He had small use for either candidate. Deferring action on the matter until he had had a chance to talk it over with Lee in person, he wired for him to come to Richmond as soon as possible.

Meantime the Chief Executive kept busy with affairs of state. Congress met for its fourth session on December 7, and the President's year-end message was delivered the following day.

"Gloom and unspoken despondency hang like a pall everywhere," a diarist noted on that date, adding: "Patriotism is a pretty heavy load to carry sometimes." Davis no doubt found it so on this occasion, obliged as he was to render a public account of matters better left unreviewed, since they could only thicken the gloom and add to the despondency they had provoked in the first place. In any case he made no attempt to minimize the defeats of the past fall and summer. Congress had adjourned in May; "Grave reverses befell our arms soon after your departure," he admitted at the outset. Charleston and Galveston were gleams in the prevailing murk, but they could scarcely relieve the fuliginous shadows thrown by Gettysburg and Vicksburg, along with other setbacks in that season of defeat, and the bright flame of Chickamauga had been damped by Missionary Ridge, which he confessed had been lost as the result of "misconduct by the troops." So it went, throughout the reading of the lengthy message. Gains had been slight, losses heavy. Nor did Davis hold out hope of foreign intervention, as he had done so often in the past. Diplomatically, with recognition still withheld by the great powers beyond the Atlantic, the Confederacy was about as near the end of its rope as it was financially, with $600,000,000 in paper — "more than threefold the amount required by the business of the country" — already issued by the Treasury on little better security than a vague promise, which in turn was dependent on the outcome of a war it seemed to be losing. He could only propose the forcible reduction of the volume of currency; which in itself, as a later observer remarked, amounted to "a confession of bankruptcy." The end of the contest was nowhere in sight, he told the assembled legislators, and he recommended a tightening and extension of conscription as a means of opposing the long numerical odds the Federals enjoyed. "We now know that the only reliable hope for peace is the vigor of our resistance," he declared, "while the cessation of their hostility is only to be expected from the pressure of their necessities." In closing he came back to the South's chief asset, which had won for her the sometimes grudging admiration of the world. "The patriotism of the people has proved equal to every sacrifice demanded by their country's need. We have been united as a people never were united under like circumstances before. God has blessed us with success disproportionate to our means, and under His divine favor our labors must at last be crowned with the reward due to men who have given all they possessed to the righteous defense of their inalienable rights, their homes, and their altars."

Lincoln's year-end message to the Federal Congress, which also convened on the first Monday in December, was delivered that same

Tuesday, thus affording the people of the two nations, as well as those of the world at large, another opportunity for comparing the manner and substance of what the two leaders had to say in addressing themselves to events and issues which they viewed simultaneously from opposite directions. The resultant contrast was quite as emphatic as might have been expected, given their two positions and their two natures. Not only was there the obvious difference that what were admitted on one hand as defeats were announced as victories on the other, but there was also a considerable difference in tone. While Davis, referring defiantly to "the impassable gulf which divides us," denounced the "barbarous policy" and "savage ferocity" of an adversary "hardened in crime," the northern President spoke of reconciliation and advanced suggestions for coping with certain edgy problems that would loom when bloodshed ended. He dealt only in passing with specific military triumphs, recommending the annual reports of Stanton and Halleck as "documents of great interest," and contented himself with calling attention to the vast improvement of conditions in that regard since his last State of the Union address, just one week more than a year ago today. At that time, "amid much that was cold and menacing," he reminded the legislators, "the kindest words coming from Europe were uttered in accents of pity that we were too blind to surrender a hopeless cause"; whereas now, he pointed out, "the rebel borders are pressed still further back, and by the opening of the Mississippi the country dominated by the rebellion is divided into distinct parts, with no practical communication between them." A share of the credit for this accomplishment was due to the Negro for his response to emancipation, Lincoln believed. "Of those who were slaves at the beginning of the rebellion, full one hundred thousand are now in the United States military service, about one half of which number actually bear arms in the ranks; thus giving the double advantage of taking so much labor from the insurgent cause, and supplying the places which otherwise must be filled with so many white men. So far as tested, it is difficult to say they are not as good soldiers as any."

Having said so much, and reviewed as well such divergent topics as the budget, foreign relations, immigration, the homestead law, and Indian affairs, he passed at once to the main burden of his message, contained in an appended document titled "A Proclamation of Amnesty and Reconstruction." Lately, in answer to a letter in which Zachariah Chandler, pleased by the outcome of the fall elections but alarmed by reports that the moderates were urging their views on the President during the preparation of this report on the State of the Union, had warned him to "stand firm" against such influences and pressures — "Conservatives and traitors are buried together," the Michigan senator told him; "for God's sake don't exhume their remains in your Message. They will smell worse than Lazarus did after he had been buried three days" — Lincoln had sought to calm the millionaire drygoods merchant's fears. "I am glad the elections this autumn have gone favorably," he replied, "and that I have not, by native depravity, or under evil influences, done anything bad enough to prevent the good result. I hope to 'stand fast' enough not to go backward, and yet not to go forward fast enough to wreck the country's cause." The appended document, setting forth his views on amnesty for individuals and reconstruction of the divided nation, was an example of what he meant. In essence, it provided that all Confederates — with certain specified exceptions, such as holders of public office, army generals and naval officers above the rank of lieutenant, former U.S. congressmen and judges, and anyone found guilty of mistreating prisoners of war — would receive a full executive pardon upon taking an oath of loyalty to the federal government, support of the Emancipation Proclamation, and obedience to all lawful acts in reference to slavery. Moreover, as soon as one tenth of the 1860 voters in any seceded state had taken the oath prescribed, that state would be readmitted to the Union and the enjoyment of its constitutional rights, including representation in Congress.

Reactions varied, but whether its critics thought the proclamation outrageous or sagacious, a further example of wheedling or a true gesture of magnanimity, there were the usual objections to the message as proof of Lincoln's ineptness whenever he tried to come to grips with the English language. "Its words and sentences fall in heaps, instead of flowing in a connected stream, and it is therefore difficult reading," the *Journal of Commerce* pointed out, while the Chicago *Times* was glibly scornful of the backwoods President's lack of polish. "Slipshod as have been all his literary performances," the Illinois editor complained, "this is the most slovenly of all. If they were slipshod, this is barefoot, and the feet, plainly enough, never have been shod." However, the New York *Times* found the composition "simple and yet perfectly effective," and Horace Greeley was even more admiring. He thought the proclamation "devilish good," and predicted that it would "break the back of the Rebellion," though he stopped well short of the *Tribune*'s White House correspondent's judgment that "no President's message since George Washington retired into private life has given such general satisfaction as that sent to Congress by Abraham Lincoln today."

Just how general that satisfaction might be, he did not say, but one person in emphatic disagreement was Charles Sumner, who, as he sat listening to the drone of the clerk at the joint session, favored visitors and colleagues with a demonstration of the inefficacy of caning as a corrective for infantile behavior. Watching as he "gave vent to his half-concealed anger," a journalist observed that, "during the delivery of the Message, the distinguished Senator from Massachusetts exhibited his petulance to the galleries by eccentric motions in his chair, pitching his documents and books upon the floor in ill-tempered disgust."

Sumner's disgust with this plan for reconstruction was based in part on his agreement with the New York *Herald* editor who, commenting on the proposal that ten percent of the South's voters be allowed to return the region to the Union, stated flatly that he did not believe there were "that many good men there." Besides, the Bay State senator had his own notion of the way to deal with traitors, and it was nothing at all like Lincoln's. In a recent issue of the *Atlantic Monthly* he had advocated the division of the Confederacy, as soon as it had been brought to its knees, into eleven military districts under eleven imported governors, "all receiving their authority from one source, ruling a population amounting to upward of nine millions. And this imperial domain, indefinite in extent, will also be indefinite in duration . . . with all powers, executive, legislative, and even judicial, derived from one man in Washington." Although he admitted that "in undertaking to create military governors, we reverse the policy of the Republic as solemnly declared by Jefferson, and subject the civil to the military authority," he thought such treatment no worse than was deserved by cane-swinging hotheads who had brought on the war by their pretense of secession. So far as he was concerned, though he continued to deny the right of secession, he was willing to accept it as an act of political suicide. Those eleven states were indeed out of the Union, and the victors had the right to do with them as they chose, including their resettlement with good Republican voters and the determination of when and under what conditions they were to be readmitted. Most of the members of his party agreed, foreseeing a solid Republican South.

Lincoln wanted that too, of course, but he did not believe that this was the best way to go about securing it. For one thing, such an arrangement was likely to last no longer than it took the South to get back on its feet. For another, he wanted those votes now, or at any rate in time for next year's presidential and congressional elections, not at the end of some period "indefinite in duration." Therefore he considered it "vain and profitless" to speculate on whether the rebellious states had withdrawn or could withdraw from the Union, even though this was precisely the issue on which most people thought the war was being fought. "We know that they were and we trust that they shall be in the Union," he said. "It does not greatly matter whether in the meantime they shall be considered to have been in or out."

This was a rift that would widen down the years, but for the present the Jacobins kept their objections within bounds, knowing well enough that when readmission time came round, it would be Congress that would sit in judgment on the applicants. Southward, however, the reaction was both violent and sudden. Lincoln's ruthlessness — an element of his political genius that was to receive small recognition from posthumous friends who were safe beyond his reach — had long been apparent to his foes. For example, in addition to the unkept guarantees he had given slaveholders in his inaugural address, he had declared on revoking Frémont's emancipation order that such matters "must be settled according to laws made by law-makers, and not by military proclamations," and he had classified as "simply 'dictatorship' " any government "wherein a general, or a President, may make permanent rules of property by proclamation." Thus he had written in late September of the first year of the war, exactly one year before he issued his own preliminary emancipation proclamation, which differed from Frémont's only in scope, being also military, and which showed him to be a man who would hold to principles only so long as he had more to gain than lose by them. Observing this, Confederates defined him as slippery, mendacious, and above all not to be trusted.

Certainly Davis saw him in that light, increasingly so with the passing months, and never more so than in this early-December amnesty offer. "That despot," he now called Lincoln, whose "purpose in his message and proclamation was to shut out all hope that he would *ever* treat with us, on *any* terms." Acceptance would amount to unconditional surrender, Davis asserted, and by way of showing what he meant he paraphrased the offer: "If we will break up our government, dissolve the Confederacy, disband our armies, emancipate our slaves, take an oath of allegiance binding ourselves to him and to disloyalty to our states, he proposes to pardon us and not to plunder us of anything more than the property already stolen from us.... In order to render his proposals so insulting as to secure their rejection, he joins to them a promise to support with his army one tenth of the people of any state who will attempt to set up a government over the other nine tenths, thus seeking to sow discord and suspicion among the people of the several states, and to excite them to civil war in furtherance of his ends."

Thus Davis reflected a reversed mirror-image of his adversary's offer, saying: "I do not believe that the vilest wretch would accept such terms." Without exception southern editors agreed. "We who have committed no offense need no forgiveness," they protested, quoting Benjamin Franklin's reply to a British offer of amnesty. "How impudent it is," the Richmond *Sentinel* observed of Lincoln, "to come with our brothers' blood upon his accursed hands, and ask us to accept his forgiveness! But he goes further. He makes his forgiveness dependent on terms." Congress was more vigorous in its protest. Resolutions were introduced denouncing "the truly characteristic proclamation of amnesty issued by the imbecile and unprincipled usurper who now sits enthroned upon the ruins of Constitutional liberty in Washington City," while others made it abundantly clear that the people of the Confederacy, through their elected representatives, did "hereby, solemnly and irrevocably, utterly deny, defy, spurn back, and scorn the terms of amnesty offered by Abraham Lincoln in his official proclamation." All such resolutions were tabled, however, upon the protest by one member that they "would appear to dignify a paper emanating from that wretched and detestable abortion, whose contemptible emptiness and folly will only receive the ridicule of the civilized world." It was decided, accordingly, that "the true and only treatment which that miserable and contemptible despot, Lincoln, should receive at the hands of the House is silent and unmitigated contempt."

Unmitigated this contempt might be, but silent was the one thing it was not. In fact, as various members continued to plumb and scale the various depths and heights of oratory, it grew more strident all the time. Evidently they had been touched where they were sore. And indeed, in its review of Lincoln's message, the New York *World* had warned that such would be the case. Violence was a characteristic of the revolutionary impulse, the *World* declared; "You can no more control it than a flaxen hand can fetter flame"; so that if what the President was really seeking was reconciliation — or even, as Davis claimed, division within the Confederate ranks — he could scarcely have chosen a worse approach. "If Mr Lincoln were a statesman, if he were even a man of ordinary prudence and sagacity, he would see the necessity for touching the peculiar wound of the South with as light a hand as possible." What the editor had in mind was slavery, and so did the frock-coated gentlemen in Richmond, along with much else which they believed was endangered by this war of arms and propaganda. In the course of their two-month session they gave the matter a great deal of attention, and before it was over they produced a joint resolution, issued broadcast as an "Address of Congress to the People of the Confederate States." Specifically an attack on the Lincoln administration for its policies and conduct of the war, the resolution was also an exhortation for the southern people to continue their resistance to northern force and blandishments, including the recent amnesty proclamation.

> It is absurd to pretend that a government really desirous of restoring the Union would adopt such measures as the confiscation of private property, the emancipation of slaves, the division of a sovereign state without its consent, and a proclamation that one tenth of the population of a state, and that tenth under military rule, should control the will of the remaining nine tenths. The only relation possible between the two sections under such a policy is that of conqueror and conquered, superior and dependent. Rest assured, fellow citizens, that although restoration may still be used as a war cry by the northern government, it is only to delude and betray. Fanaticism has summoned to its aid cupidity and vengeance, and nothing short of your utter subjugation, the destruction of your state governments, the overthrow of your social and political fabric, your personal and public degradation and ruin, will satisfy the demands of the North.

About midway through the lengthy document, after charging that the Federals had provoked the war and were "accountable for the blood and havoc and ruin it has caused," the legislators presented a catalogue of "atrocities too incredible for narration."

> Instead of a regular war, our resistance to the unholy efforts to crush out our national existence is treated as a rebellion, and the settled international rules between belligerents are ignored. Instead of conducting the war as betwixt two military and political organizations, it is a war against the whole population. Houses are pillaged and burned. Churches are defaced. Towns are ransacked. Clothing of women and infants is stripped from their persons. Jewelry and mementoes of the dead are stolen. Mills and implements of agriculture are destroyed. Private saltworks are broken up. The introduction of medicines is forbidden. Means of subsistence are wantonly wasted to produce beggary. Prisoners are returned with contagious diseases. . . .

The list continued, then finally broke off. "We tire of these indignities and enormities. They are too sickening for recital," the authors confessed, and passed at once to the lesson to be learned from them. "It is better to be conquered by any other nation than by the United States. It is better to be a dependency of any other power than of that. . . . We cannot afford to take steps backward. Retreat is more dangerous than advance. Behind us are inferiority and degradation. Before us is everything enticing to a patriot." As for how the war was to be won, the answer was quite simple: by perseverance.

> Moral like physical epidemics have their allotted periods, and must sooner or later be exhausted and disappear. When reason returns, our enemies will probably reflect that a people like ours, who have exhibited such capabilities and extemporized such resources, can never be subdued; that a vast expanse of territory with such a population cannot be governed as an obedient colony. Victory would not be conquest. The inextinguishable quarrel would be transmitted "from bleeding sire to son," and the struggle would be renewed between generations yet unborn. . . . There is no just reason for hopelessness or fear. Since the outbreak of the war the South has lost the nominal possession of the Mississippi River and fragments of her territory; but Federal occupation is not conquest. The fires of patriotism still burn unquenchably in the breasts of those who are subject to foreign domination. We have yet in our uninterrupted control a territory which, according to past progress, will require the enemy ten years to overrun.

In conclusion — though the words came strangely from the lips of men who, despite their nominal membership in a single national party, comprised perhaps the most fractious, factious political assembly in the western world to date — the legislators recommended "unfaltering trust," on the part of the southern people in their leaders, as the surest guide if they would tread "the path that leads to honor and peace, although it lead through tears and suffering and blood."

> Let all spirit of faction and past party differences be forgotten in the presence of our cruel foe. . . . We entreat from all a generous and hearty co-operation with the government in all branches of its administration, and with the agents, civil or military, in the performance of their duties. Moral aid has the "power of the incommunicable," and, by united efforts, by an all-comprehending and self-sacrificing patriotism, we can, with the blessing of God, avert the perils which environ us, and achieve for ourselves and children peace and freedom. Hitherto the Lord has interposed graciously to bring us victory, and in His hand there is present power to prevent this great multitude which come against us from casting us out of the possession which He has given us to inherit.

Such were the first bitter fruits of Lincoln's proclamation, offering amnesty to individuals and seeking to establish certain guidelines for the future reconstruction of the South.

★   ★   ★

Receiving on December 9 the President's instructions for him to come to Richmond, Lee supposed a decision had been reached to send him to North Georgia as Bragg's successor, despite his expressed reluctance to leave the Old Dominion and the army whose fame had grown with his own in the eighteen months since Davis placed him at its head. With Longstreet in East Tennessee, Ewell absent sick, and A. P. Hill as usual in poor health, the summons came at what seemed to him an unfortunate time, particularly since the latter two, even aside from their physical debility, had not fulfilled his expectations in their present subordinate positions. But orders were orders; he left at once. "My heart and thoughts will always be with this army," he said in a note to Stuart as he boarded at Orange a train that had him in the capital before nightfall.

He found to his relief, however, that no decision had been made regarding his transfer to the western theater. The President, in conference with his Cabinet on the matter of selecting a new leader for the army temporarily under Hardee, had merely wanted his ranking field commander there to share in the discussion. Lee's reluctance having been honored to the extent that it had removed him from consideration for the post, the advisers found it difficult to agree on a second choice. Not only were they divided among themselves; Davis withheld approval of every candidate proposed. Some were all for Beauregard, for instance, but the Commander in Chief had even less confidence in the Creole than he had in Joe Johnston, who was being recommended warmly in the press, on the floor of Congress, in letters from friends, and by Seddon.

While the Secretary admitted that he had been disappointed by his fellow Virginian's "absence of enterprise" in the recent Mississippi operations, he believed that "his military sagacity would not fail to recognize the exigencies of the time and position, and so direct all his thoughts and skill to an offensive campaign." Davis was doubtful. He rather agreed with Benjamin, who protested that during his six-month tenure as Secretary of War he had found in Johnston "tendencies to defensive strategy and a lack of knowledge of the environment." Others present inclined to the same view. On the evidence, Old Joe's talent seemed primarily for retreat: so much so, indeed, that if left to his own devices he might be expected to wind up gingerly defending Key West and complaining that he lacked transportation for a withdrawal to Cuba in the event that something threatened one of his flanks. Finally, however, at the close of a full week of discussion, Johnston was favored by a majority of those present, and the minority, though still unreconciled to his appointment, confessed that it had no one else to offer. According to Seddon, "the President, after doubt and with misgiving to the end, chose him . . . not as with exaltation on this score, but as the best on the whole to be obtained." He wired him at Meridian that same day, December 16, two weeks after Bragg had been relieved: "You will turn over the immediate command of the Army of Mississippi to Lieutenant General Polk and proceed to Dalton and assume command of the Army of Tennessee. . . . A letter of instructions will be sent to you at Dalton."

Requested to inspect the capital defenses, Lee stayed on for another five days, during which time he was lionized by the public and invited by the House of Representatives to take what was infelicitously called "a seat on the floor." After the Sunday service at Saint Paul's he was given a silent ovation as he passed down the aisle, bowing left and right to friends in the congregation, and forty-year-old Mrs Chesnut, who prided herself on her sophistication, confessed in her diary that when the general "bowed low and gave me a smile of recognition, I was ashamed of being so pleased. I blushed like a schoolgirl." A four-day extension of the visit would have allowed him to spend his first Christmas with his family since two years before the war, but he would not have it so; he was thinking of his army on the Rapidan and the men there who were far from home as this gayest of holidays drew near. For their part, while they envied, they did not resent his good fortune. In point of fact, they doubted that he would take advantage of it. "It will be more in accordance with his peculiar character," a staff major wrote from Orange to his sweetheart on December 20, "if he leaves for the army just before the great anniversary; he is so very apt to suppress or deny his personal desire when it conflicts with the performance of his duty." The young officer was right. Lee returned next day, having sacrificed a Richmond Christmas with his wife in order to be with his troops and share in their frugal celebration of what had always been for Southerners a combination of all that was best in the gladdest days of the departing year.

All was quiet in the camps along the Rapidan, but the cavalry had been kept busy in his absence — and fruitlessly busy, at that — attempting to head off or break up a raid into Southwest Virginia, deep in the army's rear, by a column of hard-riding horsemen under Averell, who had been given an independent brigade after Hooker relieved him of duty amid the fury of Chancellorsville. Regaining the safety of his own lines on the day Lee returned to Orange, Averell proudly reported that in the past two weeks his troopers had "marched, climbed, slid, and swum 355 miles," avoided superior combinations of graybacks sent to scatter or capture them, and cut the Tennessee & Virginia Railroad at Salem (just west of a hamlet called Big Lick, which twenty years later would change its name to Roanoke and grow to be a city) where three depots crammed with food and equipment on consignment to the Army of Northern Virginia were set afire. At a cost of 6 men drowned, 5 wounded, and 94 missing, he had captured some 200 of the enemy, 84 of whom he brought back with him, together with about 150 horses. This time he left no sack of coffee for his friend Fitzhugh Lee, who commanded one of the columns that failed to intercept him, but he could say, as he had said before: "Here's your visit. How do you like it?" Fitz liked it no better now than he had done in March, after Kelly's Ford. Nor did Stuart, who was presented with further evidence of the decline of the advantage he had enjoyed in the days when his superior riders were mounted on superior, well-fed horses.

Meanwhile the foot soldiers took it easy, blue and gray alike. Meade's withdrawal from Lee's formidable Mine Run front — accomplished with such skill and stealth that his opponent's resultant attitude resembled that of a greenhorn lured into the Wilderness by pranksters who left him holding the bag on a "snipe hunt" — had ended all infantry operations for the year. On both sides of the river the two armies went into winter quarters, beginning what would be a five-month rest. On the north bank, for Meade despite his crankiness was liberal in such matters, generals, colonels, majors, even captains were able to bring their wives into camp on extended visits. One witness considered their presence greatly beneficial, and not only to their husbands. "Their influence softens and humanizes much that might otherwise be harsh and repulsive," he declared. "In their company, at least, officers who should be gentlemen do not get drunk." On the other hand, a high-toned Massachusetts staff man was a good deal less enthusiastic about these army ladies. "Such a set of feminine humans I have not seen often," he wrote home. "It was Lowell's factories broken loose and gone wild." However, except on the off chance that a few orderlies got lucky, all this meant little to the enlisted men, who were obliged to depend on their own resources and limit the count of their blessings to the fact that they were not to be shot at for a while. "The troops burrowed into the earth and built their little shelters," a Federal brigadier was to recall, "and the officers and men devoted themselves to unlimited festivity, balls, horse races, cockfights, greased pigs and poles, and other games such as only soldiers can devise."

For most of the people of Richmond, women and old men and children, politicians and officeholders of high and low degree, as well as for the maimed and convalescent veterans in private homes and hospitals on the city's seven hills, this holiday season was scarcely gayer than it was for their friends and kinsmen on the Rapidan with Lee. For some few others, however, owners of plantations down the country, not yet taken over by invaders, provisions had been forwarded for laying out a meal that had at least a resemblance to the feasts of olden times. Christmas dinner at Colonel and Mrs Chesnut's, for example, included oyster soup, boiled mutton, ham, boned turkey, wild duck and partridges, plum pudding, and four kinds of wine to wash it down with. "There is life in the old land yet!" the diarist exclaimed.

Among her guests that day was John Bell Hood, the social catch of the town. Taken a few miles south of the field where he lost his leg, he had spent a month in bed on a North Georgia farm and then, because it was feared he might be captured so near the enemy lines, continued his convalescence in Atlanta for another month before coming on to Richmond in late November. With his left arm still in a sling and his right trouser leg hanging empty, his eyes deep-set in a pain-gaunted face above the full blond beard of a Wagnerian hero, the thirty-two-year-old bachelor general had the ladies fluttering around him, his hostess said, "as if it would be a luxury to pull out their handkerchiefs and have a good cry." Instead, they brought him oranges and peeled and sliced them for him, prompting another guest to remark that "the money value of friendship is easily counted now," since oranges were selling in the capital markets for five Confederate dollars each. Shortly after Chickamauga, Longstreet had recommended the Kentucky-born Texan's promotion to lieutenant general "for distinguished conduct and ability in the battle of the 20th instant." Moreover, although Hood was nearly six years younger than A. P. Hill, the present youngest officer of that rank, there was little doubt that the promotion would be confirmed; for he was now an intimate of the President's and accompanied him on carriage rides and tours of inspection, in and about the city.

Another Kentuckian was being talked about on all sides this Christmas, here and elsewhere, and did much to lift the gloom resulting from the reverses lately suffered, including his own. On November 28 word flashed across the North and South that John Morgan and six of his captains, taken with him in the course of the raid that ended near Salineville four months back, had escaped the night before from the Ohio

Penitentiary by tunneling out of their cell block and scaling the outer wall. That was all that was known for the time being, except that Buckeye posses bent on his recapture were combing the region and searching the cellars and attics of all suspected Copperheads. In mid-December, two weeks later, he turned up on the near bank of the Tennessee River, below Kingston, and soon afterwards crossed the Great Smoky Mountains to Franklin, North Carolina, well beyond reach of the searchers in his rear. The particulars of his flight were as daring as the wildest of his raids. Dressed as civilians, he and his companions had boarded a fast night express at Columbus, just outside the prison walls, and reached Cincinnati before the morning bed check showed them missing from their cells. By that time they were over the Ohio, riding south on borrowed horses — there was little in the Bluegrass that John Morgan could not have for the asking — to cross the Cumberland near Burkesville. Two of the party had been lost just outside Louisville, picked up by a Federal patrol, but the others made it all the way. Morgan himself reached Danville, Virginia, in time for Christmas dinner with his wife, who was recuperating there from a miscarriage, brought on it was said by worry about her husband and resentment of Ohio's vindictive treatment of him as a felon. Now he was with her again, and soon he would be back with the army, too. He had been summoned to Richmond, where a public reception was being planned in his honor, he was informed, "thusly [to] say to the despicable foe that in their futile efforts to degrade you before the world they have only elevated you in the estimation of all Confederate citizens, and the whole civilized world."

Anticipation of his arrival, which was scheduled for January 2, gave a lift to the spirits of the people of the capital. But for many, unable to draw on such resources as were available to the Chesnuts and their guests, the holiday itself was depressing in its contrast to the ones they had enjoyed last year and the year before, when the festivities were heightened by recent victories at Fredericksburg and Ball's Bluff. No such occasions warranted celebration now. "It is a sad, cold Christmas, and threatening snow," a government clerk recorded in his diary. "The children have a Christmas tree, but it is not burdened. Candy is held at $8 per pound." Nor did he find much evidence of merriment among his fellow townsmen when he went out for a walk that afternoon. "Occasionally an *exempt*, who has speculated, may be seen drunk. But a somber heaviness is in the countenances of men as well as in the sky above." Although, like candy, a Christmas turkey was beyond his means, "[I] do not covet one. This is no time for feasting," he declared. Presently, if only out of surfeit, Mrs Chesnut was inclined to agree. "God help my country!" she exclaimed on New Year's Day, looking back somewhat ruefully on the round of holiday parties she had given or attended. "I think we are like the sailors who break into the spirits closet when they find out the ship must sink." Reviewing her correspondence for the year now past, she came upon an early draft of a letter she had written Varina Davis during a September visit to the South Carolina plantation that furnished so many delicacies for her table. It had seemed to her then, she told the first lady, that the people were divided into two main groups, one made up of enthusiasts whose "whole duty here consists of abusing Lincoln and the Yankees, praising Jeff Davis and the army of Virginia, and wondering when this horrid war will be over," while the other included "politicians and men with no stomach for fighting, who find it easier to cuss Jeff Davis and stay at home than to go to the front with a musket. They are the kind who came out almost as soon as they went into the war, dissatisfied with the way things were managed. Joe Johnston is their polar star, the redeemer!"

Polar star and redeemer he might be to the disaffected Carolinians, as well as to the western soldiers once more in his charge, but to his superiors in Richmond he was something else again. Receiving the President's telegram of December 16, the general spent a few days putting his affairs in order, including the transfer of his present command to Polk, and then on December 22 set out by rail for North Georgia. Two days after Christmas he reached Dalton, where he took over from Hardee without further delay. Awaiting him there were the instructions promised in the wire received ten days ago in Mississippi, one set from the Commander in Chief and another from the Secretary of War, both urging an early campaign against the Federals in his front. While admitting that "the army may have been, by recent events, somewhat disheartened," Seddon believed that Johnston's presence would restore its "discipline, prestige, and confidence" in preparation for the recovery of all that had been lost. "As soon as the condition of your forces will allow," the Secretary added, "it is hoped that you will be able to assume the offensive." Davis wrote in a similar vein. Information lately received encouraged "a not unfavorable view of the material of the command," he said, and "induces me to hope that you will soon be able to commence active operations against the enemy. . . . You will not need to have it suggested that the imperative demand for prompt and vigorous action arises not only from the importance of restoring the prestige of the army, and averting the dispiriting and injurious results that must attend a season of inactivity, but also from the necessity of reoccupying the country upon the supplies of which the proper subsistence of the armies materially depends." The general on the scene could best determine "the immediate measures to be adopted in attaining this end," the President remarked, and he urged him to "communicate fully and freely with me concerning your proposed plan of action, that all the assistance and co-operation may be most advantageously afforded that it is in the power of the government to render. Trusting that your health may be preserved, and that the arduous and responsible duties you have undertaken may be success-fully accomplished, I remain very respectfully and truly yours, Jeff'n Davis."

Whereupon — in response to these conciliatory statements of confidence in the general's ability, these offers to replace past bitterness with cordiality — the old trouble rose anew, bringing with it apparent confirmation of the doubts expressed by Benjamin and others at the se-ries of high-level conferences leading to the choice of a new commander for the Army of Tennessee. Johnston had not thought he would get the post; "The temper exhibited toward me makes it very unlikely that I shall ever again occupy an important position," he told a friend in mid-September; but when he learned of his new assignment, three months later, he was delighted. This reaction lasted no longer, however, than it took him to reach Dalton and read the letters of instruction. As always, he bridled at what he considered prodding, especially from these two, who all through June had tried to persuade him to wreck his army for no purpose, so far as he could see, except as a gesture of sympathy for the garrison penned up in Vicksburg as a result of their unwisdom. Now here they were, at it again, trying to nudge him into rashness and dis-aster! His reply to Seddon was edged with irony. "The duties of military administration you point out to me shall be attended to with diligence," he said. But he added flatly: "This army is now far from being in condi-tion to 'resume the offensive.'" A similar reply went to Davis. "Your Excellency well impresses upon me the importance of recovering the territory we have lost. I feel it deeply; but difficulties appear to me in the way." These he listed in considerable detail, including a shortage of transportation and subsistence, the long numerical odds the Federals en-joyed, and the poor condition of the roads because of recent heavy rains. He might be able to resist an attack in his present position, he de-clared, but under the conditions now prevailing he could not even enter-tain the notion of delivering one. In short: "I can see no other mode of taking the offensive here than to beat the enemy when he advances, and then move forward."

There they had it — as, indeed, they had had it so often before, wherever Johnston commanded in this war. The Manassas region be-yond the Rappahannock, the York-James peninsula, the Mississippi heartland, all had been given up by him on the heels of similar protests at suggestions that he "assume the offensive" or merely stand his ground. Seddon and Davis saw their worst fears realized. If past performance was any indication of what to expect, Johnston would backpedal in response to whatever pressure the enemy brought against him in North Georgia, and this time it would be the *national* heartland that would pass into Federal possession as a result. Their inclination was to remove him be-fore that happened, but this would mean a return to the problem of finding another commander for the army, which was no more soluble now than it had been in mid-December. They had him; they would have to live with him. The result, as they continued to plead for an advance and he continued to bridle at the prodding, was increased dissatisfaction and petulance at both ends of the telegraph wires connecting Richmond and Dalton.

Whatever second thoughts his superiors might be having as to their wisdom in appointing this new commander of the Army of Tennessee, the men under him were delighted. In fact, the pleasure they had experienced on hearing of Bragg's departure was redoubled by the news that Johnston was to take his place, and according to one veteran's recollection, civilians reacted in a similar manner: "At every bivouac in the field, at every fireside in the rear, the joyous dawn of day seemed to have arisen from the night." Rations improved with the Virginian's arrival; the clothing issue was liberalized; even a system of furloughs was established. Moreover, whereas Bragg had kept to his tent between campaigns — confined there, more often than not, by dyspepsia — Johnston not only made it a point to pay frequent visits to all the camps, he also did not limit his attention to men with bars or stars on their collars. "He passed through the ranks of the common soldiers, shaking hands with every one he met," a private was to recall years later. "He restored the soldier's pride; he brought the manhood back to the private's bosom; he changed the order of roll-call, standing guard, drill, and such nonsense as that. The revolution was complete. He was loved, respected, admired; yea, almost worshipped by his troops. I do not believe there was a soldier in his army but would gladly have died for him."

This last was based in part no doubt on their knowledge that he would ask of them no dying he could spare them; that he believed, as they did, in a minimum of bloodshed, and would always sacrifice mere terrain if the price of holding it seemed to him excessive. But there was a good deal more to it than that. Veneration was deepened by affection, and the affection was returned. No matter how touchy Johnston might be in his relations with superiors, he was invariably friendly to those below him on the military ladder, considerate of their needs and never seeming to fear that this might lessen his dignity or cost him any measure of their respect. One day soon after his arrival in Dalton, for example, Cheatham brought a number of men from his division over to army headquarters in a body, accompanied by a band with which to serenade the new commander. Presently Johnston stepped hatless from his tent to thank them for the music and the visit; whereupon Cheatham performed a highly informal ceremony of introduction. "Boys," he said, affectionately patting the general's bald head two or three times as he spoke, "this is Old Joe."

✖ 2 ✖

In all seasons and all weathers, stifling heat or numbing cold, the men aboard the Federal blockaders kept their stations, stood their watches, and patrolled their designated segments of the highly irregular three thousand miles of coastline between Old Point Comfort and Matamoros. Not for them had been the thunderous runs by the frigates and gunboats under Farragut and Porter, during which the world seemed turned to flame and a man's heart pounded as if to break the confines of his ribs, or the exhilarating chases by the raiders under Semmes and Maffitt, staged hundreds of miles from the sight of land and punctuated with coaling stops in sinful foreign ports. A sailor who managed to secure a leave from one of the river fleets was sure to receive at home a hero's welcome for his share in the humbling of Vicksburg or Port Hudson, and since her sinking of the *Hatteras*, off Galveston a year ago, the *Alabama* had added an even three dozen Yankee ships and barks and schooners to her string of prizes, while the *Florida*, after her nimble sprint out of Mobile Bay, had taken just over two dozen such merchant vessels in that same span. The men on blockade duty envied blue and gray alike, not only for the stormy present but also for the future still to come. Someday perhaps, if they survived the boredom and saltpeter, there would be the question: "What did you do, Father, in the war?" Within the limitations of the truth, about the only satisfactory answer they could give — satisfactory to themselves, that is — would be: "I'd rather not talk about it."

Nor were conditions any better in that regard for the crews of ships assigned to add offensive punch to the four blockading squadrons. In contrast to 1862, when it had appeared that no salt water attack could fail, whatever the objective, the year just past had seen no fort subdued, no harbor seized, except along the scantly defended lower coast of Texas, where the year-end gains were far outweighed by the reverses suffered earlier at Galveston and Sabine Pass. If such efforts on the Gulf amounted to little, those on the Atlantic came to less. Du Pont's repulse at Charleston, and Dahlgren's protracted frustration since, had served no purpose the men could discern except to make them thankful that the brass had not seen fit to test the defenses of Wilmington or Mobile. There were dangers enough outside such places, it seemed to them, without venturing any closer: as the *Ironsides* could testify, having had her timbers shivered by the unscathed *David*. Two months later, on December 6, the monitor *Weehawken* — leader of the nine-boat iron column that had steamed into Charleston harbor back in April — met a harsher and still more ignominious fate, without an enemy in sight. Tied up to a buoy inside the bar, she had taken on an extra load of heavy ammunition which so reduced her freeboard that the ebb tide flooded an open hawse pipe and a hatch, foundering her so rapidly that she carried 31 of her crew with her on her sudden plunge to the bottom. There was small glory here for either the dead or the survivors, who were promptly transferred to other vessels to keep up the work of raising puffs of brick dust from the defiant ruin of Sumter. Morale was not helped, either, when they learned of Father Gideon's response to a request from Dahlgren — who knew something of the strain on their nerves because of the jangled state of his own — that a whiskey ration be distributed under medical supervision. Welles did not approve. He recommended that iced coffee or oatmeal mixed with water be used as a pick-me-up instead.

Boredom was the main problem, especially for the crews of the blockaders, who could not see that their day-in day-out service had much to do with fighting at all, let alone with speeding the victory which hard-war politicians and editors kept saying was just around the corner. Off Cape Fear, where the sleek gray runners steaming in from Nassau and Bermuda found cover under the unchallenged guns of Fort Fisher, a bluejacket wrote home to his mother (as the letter was paraphrased years later by a student of the era) that she could get some notion of blockade duty if she would "go to the roof on a hot summer day, talk to a half dozen degenerates, descend to the basement, drink tepid water full of iron rust, climb to the roof again, and repeat the process at intervals until she was fagged out, then go to bed with everything shut tight." Individual reactions to this monotony, which was scarcely relieved by an unbroken diet of moldy beans, stale biscuits, and sour pork, varied from fisticuffs and insubordination to homosexuality and desertion. Officers fraternized ashore with Negro women, a practice frowned on by the Navy, and mess crews specialized in the manufacture of outlaw whiskey distilled from almost any substance that would ferment in the southern heat — as in fact nearly everything would, including men. Rheumatism and scurvy kept the doctors busy, along with breakbone fever, hemorrhoids, and damage done by knuckles. These they could deal with, after their fashion, but there was no medicine for the ills of the spirit, brought on by the strain of monotony, poor food, and unhealthy living conditions, which produced much longer casualty lists than did rebel shells or torpedoes. "Give me a discharge, and let me go home," a distraught but articulate coal heaver begged his skipper after months of duty outside Charleston. "I am a poor weak, miserable, nervous, half crazy boy. . . . Everything jars upon my delicate nerves."

Inside the harbor, Beauregard was about as deep in the doldrums as were the blue-clad sailors beyond the bar. Disappointed that he had not been ordered west to resume command of the army Bragg had inherited from him, privately he was telling friends that his usefulness in the war had ended, and he predicted defeat for the Confederacy no later than spring or summer. He gave as the cause for both of these disasters "the persistent inability and obstinacy of our rulers." Primarily he meant Davis, of whom he said: "The curse of God must have been on our people when we chose him out of so many noble sons of the South, who would have carried us safely through this Revolution."

In addition to the frustration proceeding from his belief that presidential animosity, as evidenced by slights and snubs, had cost him the western command he so much wanted, the Creole's gloom was also due to the apparent failure of a new weapon he had predicted would accomplish, unassisted, the lifting of the Union blockade by the simple process of sinking the blockaders. There had arrived by rail from Mobile in mid-August, disassembled and loaded on two flatcars, a cigar-shaped metal vessel about thirty feet in length and less than four feet wide and five feet deep. Put back together and launched in Charleston harbor, she resembled the little *David*-class torpedo boats whose low silhouette made them hard for enemy lookouts to detect. Actually, though, she had been designed to carry this advantage a considerable step further, in that she was intended to travel under as well as on the water, and thus present no silhouette at all. She was, in short, the world's first submarine. Christened the *H. L. Hunley* for one of her builders, who had come from Alabama with her to instruct the Carolinians in her use, she was propeller-driven but had no engine, deriving her power from her eight-man crew, posted at cranks along her drive shaft, which they turned on orders from her coxswain-captain. Water was let into ballast tanks to lower her until she was nearly awash; then her two hatches were bolted tight from inside, and as she moved forward the skipper took her down by depressing a pair of horizontal fins, which were also used to level and raise her while in motion. To bring her all the way up, force pumps ejected the water from her tanks, decreasing her specific gravity; or in emergencies her iron keel could be jettisoned in sections by disengaging the bolts that held it on, thus causing her to bob corklike to the surface. A glass port in the forward hatch enabled the steersman to see where he was going while submerged, and interior light was supplied by candles, which also served to warn of the danger of asphyxiation by guttering when the oxygen ran low. Practice dives in Mobile Bay had demonstrated that the *Hunley* could stay down about two hours before coming up for air, and she had proved her effectiveness as an offensive weapon by torpedoing and sinking two flatboats there. Her method of attack was quite as novel as her design. Towing at the end of a 200-foot line a copper cylinder packed with ninety pounds of powder and equipped with a percussion fuze, she would dive as she approached her target, pass completely under it, then elevate a bit and drag the towline across the keel of the enemy ship until the torpdo made contact and exploded, well astern of the submarine, whose crew would be cranking hard for a getaway, still underwater, and a return to port for a new torpedo to use on the next victim. Beauregard looked the strange craft over, had her workings explained to him by Hunley, and predicted an end to the

Yankee blockade as soon as her newly volunteered crew learned to handle her well enough to launch their one-boat offensive against the U. S. Navy.

Such high hopes were often modified by sudden disappointments, and the *Hunley* was no exception to the general application of the rule. Certain drawbacks were soon as evident here as they had been at Mobile earlier: one being that she was a good deal easier to take down than she was to bring back up, particularly if something went wrong with her machinery, and something often did. She was, in fact — as might have been expected from her combination of primitive means and delicate functions — accident-prone. On August 29, two weeks after her arrival, she was moored to a steamer tied to the Fort Johnson dock, resting her "engine" between dives, when the steamer unexpectedly got underway and pulled her over on her side. Water poured in through the open hatches, front and rear, and she went down so fast that only her skipper and two nimble seamen managed to get out before she hit the bottom. This was a practical demonstration that none of the methods providing for her return to the surface by her own devices would work unless she retained enough air to lift the weight of her iron hull; a started seam or a puncture, inflicted by chance or by enemy action while she was submerged, would mean her end, or at any rate the end of the submariners locked inside her. If this had not been clear before, it certainly was now. Still, there was no difficulty in finding more volunteers to man her, and Hunley himself, as soon as she had been raised and cleared of muck and corpses, petitioned Beauregard to let him take command. He did so on September 22 and began at once a period of intensive training to familiarize his new crew with her quirks. This lasted just over three weeks. On October 15, after making a series of practice dives in the harbor, she "left the wharf at 9.25 A.M. and disappeared at 9.35. As soon as she sank," the official post-mortem continued, "air bubbles were seen to rise to the surface of the water, and from this fact it is supposed the hole at the top of the boat by which the men entered was not properly closed." That was the end of Hunley and all aboard, apparently because someone had been careless. It was also thought to be the end of the vessel that bore his name, for she was nine fathoms down. A diver found her a few days later, however, and she was hauled back up again. Beauregard was on hand when her hatch lids were removed. "The spectacle was indescribably ghastly," he later reported with a shudder of remembrance. "The unfortunate men were contorted into all sorts of horrible attitudes, some clutching candles ... others lying in the bottom tightly grappled together, and the blackened faces of all presented the expression of their despair and agony."

Despite this evidence of the grisly consequences, a third crew promptly volunteered for service under George E. Dixon, an army lieutenant who transferred from an Alabama regiment to the *Hunley* and was also a native of Mobile. Trial runs were renewed in early November, but the method of attack was not the same. Horrified by what he had seen when the unlucky boat was raised the second time, Beauregard had ordered that she was never again to function underwater, and she was equipped accordingly with a spar torpedo like the one her rival *David* had used against the *Ironsides*, ten days before she herself went into her last intentional dive. A surface vessel now like all the rest, except that she was still propelled by muscle power, she continued for the next three months to operate out of her base on Sullivan's Island, sometimes by day, sometimes by night. But conditions were never right for an attack; tide and winds conspired against her, and at times the underpowered craft was in danger of being swept out to sea because of the exhaustion of the men along her crankshaft. Finally though, in the early dusk of February 17, with a near-full moon to steer her by, a low-lying fog to screen her, and a strong-running ebb tide to increase her normal four-knot speed, Dixon maneuvered the *Hunley* out of the harbor and set a course for the Federal fleet, which lay at anchor in the wintry darkness, seven miles away.

At 8.45 the acting master of the 1200-ton screw sloop *Housatonic* — more than two hundred feet in length and mounting a total of nine guns, including an 11-inch rifle — saw what he thought at first was "a plank moving [toward us] in the water" about a hundred yards away. By the time he knew better and ordered "the chain slipped, engine backed, and all hands called to quarters" in an attempt to take evasive action and bring his guns to bear, it was too late; "The torpedo struck forward of the mizzen mast, on the starboard side, in line with the magazine." Still trembling from the shock, the big warship heeled to port and went down stern first. Five of her crew were killed or drowned, but fortunately for the others the water was shallow enough for them to save themselves by climbing the rigging, from which they were plucked by rescuers before the stricken vessel went to pieces.

There were no Confederate witnesses, for there were no Confederate survivors; the *Hunley* had made her first and last attack and had gone down with her victim, either because her hull had been cracked by the force of the explosion, only twenty feet away, or else because she was drawn into the vortex of the sinking *Housatonic*. In any case, searchers found what was left of the sloop and the submarine years later, lying side by side on the sandy bottom, just beyond the bar.

★   ★   ★

Quincy Gillmore had been about as unhappy outside Charleston as Beauregard was inside the place, although for different reasons. Six months of siege, of suffering far greater losses than he inflicted, had gained him nothing more than Morris Island, out on the rim of the harbor, and the chance to heave an occasional long-range shell into the city — a practice which his adversary had predicted would win him "a bad eminence in history." That might be, but what bothered Gillmore most was that it seemed to increase rather than lessen the resolution of the defenders. Besides, the next step was up to the navy, and Dahlgren would not take it. The result was stalemate and frustration, a sharp regret on Gillmore's part that he had come down here in the first place. He wanted to be up and doing; he wanted room for maneuver, a chance to fight an enemy he could see; none of which was available to him here. Then in mid-January a letter from the Commander in Chief relieved his claustrophobia by opening vistas to the south. He was to undertake, without delay, the conquest of Florida.

The letter was not sent through regular channels, but was delivered in person by the President's twenty-five-year-old private secretary John Hay, who arrived wearing a brand-new pair of major's leaves on the shoulders of a brand-new uniform. Moreover, the document he brought with him made it clear that he had been commissioned to play a leading role in the show about to open down the coast. If Gillmore thought it strange at first that the choice for so important a post had been based exclusively on political qualifications — for the young man had had little experience in any other line — he soon perceived, from reading the instructions, that the proposed campaign was intended to be at least as much a political as a military endeavor. "I wish the thing done in the most speedy way possible," Lincoln wrote, "so that, when done, it [will] lie within the range of the late proclamation on the subject." It was the month-old Proclamation of Amnesty and Reconstruction he meant. He already had agents at work in Louisiana and Arkansas, attempting within the framework of its provisions to establish in them the ten-percent governments he maintained would entitle them to representation in Congress, where their gratitude was expected to prove helpful to the Administration, and it had occurred to him that Florida would make a convenient addition to the list. Hay had Unionist friends there who had written to him, he informed his diary and his chief, "asking me to come down...and be their Representative." Lincoln thought it a fine idea. Useful as the young Hoosier was in his present job, he might be even more so in the House. Accordingly, after commissioning him a major and making sure that he was equipped with enough oath-blanks to accommodate the ten percent of Floridians who presumably were weary of rebellion, he gave him the letter of instructions to pass along to Gillmore and wished him success in his venture into an unfamiliar field. "Great good luck and God's blessing go with you, John," he said.

Arriving in South Carolina, Hay assured Gillmore that it was not the President's intention to disrupt his current operations against Charleston, that all he wanted was "an order directing me to go to Florida and open my books of record for the oaths, as preliminary to future proceedings." He soon found, however, that the general was not touchy on that point. Far from considering Lincoln's project an intrusion, Gillmore saw it as an indorsement and extension of a proposal he himself had made in letters to Stanton and Halleck that same week, unaware that Hay was on the way from Washington. "I have in contemplation the occupation of Florida, on the west bank of the Saint Johns River, at a very early day," he announced, requesting their approval. He had it in mind to extend his coastal holdings a hundred miles inland to the Suwannee River, which he explained would enable him: 1) "To procure an outlet for cotton, timber, lumber, turpentine, and other products"; 2) "To cut off one of the enemy's sources of commissary supplies"; 3) "To obtain recruits for my colored regiments"; and 4) — appended after receiving Lincoln's instructions, which amounted to the approval he was seeking —"To inaugurate measures for the speedy restoration of Florida to her allegiance." In addition to these four "objects and advantages," as he called them, he was also attracted to the venture by the knowledge that the Confederacy had none of its regular troops assigned to the state's defense. The only graybacks there were militia, and Gillmore believed he could walk right over them with a single veteran division from his army lying idle outside Charleston and at Hilton Head, waiting for the navy to take the step it would not take. Now that the President's letter had unleashed him, he was eager to be off, and he fretted because Hay was held up by last-minute administrative details. "There will not be an hour's delay after the major is ready," he informed Lincoln on January 21, and he added: "I have every confidence in the success of the enterprise."

It was another two weeks before the preliminaries had been attended to. Then finally, on February 6, Brigadier General Truman Seymour's division, composed of three brigades of infantry, two regiments of cavalry, and four batteries of artillery — a force of about 8000 in all, mostly Regulars, New Englanders, and Negroes — got aboard twenty transports at Hilton Head and set off down the coast, escorted by two gunboats. Next morning the flotilla steamed into the St Johns estuary and docked unopposed at Jacksonville, which had been reduced to little more than ruins by the two previous Federal occupations and deserted by all but about two dozen of its prewar families. Hay went ashore and set up shop, beginning with a line-up at the guardhouse. He explained to the captive rebels that if they took the prescribed oath they would be given certificates of loyalty and allowed to return home; otherwise they would be sent North to prison camps. "There is to be neither force nor persuasion used in this matter," he told them. "You decide for yourselves." Most signed promptly, about half making their marks, and took their leave. Hay turned next to the civilians, and though they were less eager to signify repentance for their transgressions, he succeeded in getting the signatures of a number whom he described as "men of substance and influence," presumably meaning those who still had something left to lose. Encouraged, he looked forward to lengthening the list as soon as the army extended its occupation and demonstrated that it was here to stay. Meantime he made a $500 investment in Florida real estate, partly because he knew a hard-times bargain when he saw one, but also by way of establishing residence for the political race that would follow close upon his securing the signatures of ten percent of the qualified electors.

He had reason to believe this would not take long. Gillmore and the navy had been as active in their fields of endeavor as Hay had been in his, and they had also been as successful, if not more so; at least at the outset. Steaming on past Jacksonville after debarking most of the force they had escorted down the coast, the two warships trained their guns on Picolata and Palatka, respectively thirty and fifty miles upstream, and put troops ashore to garrison them, thus establishing firm (and, as it turned out, permanent) control of a coastal region twenty to thirty miles in width and seventy miles in length, east from the St Johns River to the Atlantic and south from Fernandina, near the Georgia line, to below Saint Augustine, which had been reoccupied in late December. What was more, while the navy was consolidating these gains, Gillmore had his troops in motion westward, intent on extending the conquest inland all the way to the Suwannee, as he had said he would do when he first announced his plans.

Florida had two railroads, one running southwest from Fernandina, through Gainesville, to Cedar Key on the Gulf of Mexico, the other due west from Jacksonville to Tallahassee. He took the latter as his route of march, the Atlantic & Gulf Central, his primary objective being Lake City, about sixty miles away. Setting out on February 8, the day after his debarkation, by the following morning he had his cavalry in Baldwin, at the crossing of the two railroads and one third of the way to his goal. His infantry marched in next day, still preceded by the troopers, who pressed on ten miles down the line to Barber's and then another ten to Sanderson, only twenty miles from Lake City. But after advancing half that distance, the cavalry commander, Colonel Guy V. Henry, learned on reaching Olustee that rebel militia were massing in sizable numbers for resistance up ahead; so he turned back. It was well for him and his three small regiments that he did, if he had been counting on infantry support in case of trouble; for when he re-entered Sanderson on the 12th he found that Gillmore was withdrawing to Jacksonville, leaving Seymour to backtrack in his wake and hold Baldwin with the major part of his division while he himself returned to Hilton Head to make further arrangements he had not known were needed, until now.

He too had learned of the rebels massing at Lake City to contest a farther blue advance, and this had served to give him pause. However, his main concern was logistics: meaning supplies, primarily food and ammunition, and how to get them forward to the troops as they slogged westward across a sandy waste of stunted oaks, pine trees, and palmettos. He lacked wagons and mules to draw them, having counted on using the railroad, and though he had plenty of boxcars, captured by Henry's fast-riding troopers before they could be withdrawn beyond the Suwannee, the only locomotive he had on hand was one he had brought with him, which had promptly nullified his foresight by breaking down. So he turned back, better than halfway to his goal, not so much in fear of the gray militia up ahead — although they were reported to be numerous — as in anticipation of what would happen to his soldiers once they had eaten up the six-day rations they carried with them on their march through this barren, inland region. Before returning to Hilton Head to correct in person his miscalculation in logistics, he told Seymour to hold Baldwin at all costs, thus to cover Jacksonville in case the enemy moved against him, but otherwise to be content with consolidating rather than extending his occupation of the coastal region east of the St Johns. That was Gillmore's second miscalculation: not taking sufficiently into account the temperament of his chief subordinate, who would assume command while he himself was up the coast.

A forty-year-old Vermont-born West Pointer, Seymour had seen about as much action as any man on either side in the war, including service as an artillery captain at Sumter when the opening shots were fired. Earlier he had been brevetted twice for bravery in Mexico and the Seminole War, and he had risen about as rapidly as he could have wished in the first two years of the contest still in progress, succeeding to the command of a division in the course of the Seven Days, after which had come Second Bull Run, South Mountain, and Antietam. In all these battles, whether his job was staff or line, he had demonstrated ability; yet somehow, while earning an additional three brevets, he had missed distinction. Then had come a transfer to the Carolina coast, and there too he had performed with credit, especially in the taking of Battery Wagner, where he was severely wounded as a result of his practice of exposing himself under fire. Somehow, though, distinction still eluded him at every turn. And now there was this fruitless westward march across the barrens of North Florida, ended in midcareer by a withdrawal and followed by peremptory instructions for him to remain strictly on the defensive in the absence of a superior whose outstanding characteristic seemed to him to be an unwillingness to assume the risks that went with gain and were in fact the handholds to distinction. Gillmore left Jacksonville on February 13; Seymour managed to endure four days of inactivity in his nominal, if temporary, position as commander of the Florida expedition. Then on the fifth day he went over to the offensive.

He did this strictly on his own, ostensibly because of a report that the rebels were about to remove the rails from the Atlantic & Gulf

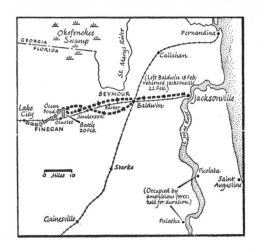

Central, which he knew would upset Gillmore's plans for a resumption of the advance to the Suwannee. It was not that he was unaware of the risks involved; he was; the question later was whether he had welcomed or ignored them. For example, garrison detachments had reduced his mobile strength to about 5500 effectives, and though he suspected that the Confederates had more troops than that around Lake City, he knew they were militia to a man and apt therefore to flinch from contact with anything that came at them in a determined manner, which was precisely what he had in mind. Moreover, he intended to make up for the possible disparity in numbers by seizing the initiative and moving with celerity once he had it. "I wish the thing done in the most speedy way possible," Lincoln had said, and Seymour demonstrated his agreement with this approach when he left Jacksonville on February 18 and cleared Baldwin before nightfall. By sundown of the following day his infantry was beyond Barber's, having covered better than thirty miles of sandy road, and his orders were for the march to be resumed at dawn. For added speed, he advanced in three columns, keeping close on the heels of the cavalry to avoid the delay of having to probe the front or shield the flanks with skirmishers detached from his three infantry brigades. All morning, February 20, he kept his soldiers on the go, slogging through Sanderson and on to Olustee without a rest halt, intent on reaching Lake City before the graybacks had time to get set for the strike. Blown, hungry, and considerably strung out, the three columns converged as they approached Ocean Pond, a swamp just beyond Olustee, around whose southern reaches the road and the railroad passed together along a narrow neck of firm ground with bogs on the left and right. It was here, barely a dozen miles from Lake City and on terrain that was scarcely fit for fighting — at any rate, not the kind of fighting he had in mind — that Seymour first encountered resistance in the form of butternut skirmishers who rose from hiding and took the heads of the three blue columns under fire, then faded back into the palmetto thickets. Recovering as best he could from the surprise, which came all the harder because he had expected to be the inflictor, not the victim, he gave orders for the pursuit to be pressed without delay. It was; but not for long. Within five minutes and two hundred yards, he found himself involved in the battle known thereafter as Olustee or Ocean Pond.

The contest lasted from shortly after noon until about 4 o'clock,

not because there was ever much doubt as to the outcome, but simply because that much time was required to make Seymour admit he'd been
whipped. In the end, it was his own men who convinced him, although
the Confederates, with four guns against his sixteen, had been highly persuasive in this regard from the start. Brigadier General Joseph Finegan,
a thirty-nine-year-old Irish-born Floridian, had about the same number
of troops as his opponent, just over or under 5500, and though they were
as green as their commander, an unblooded prewar lumberman and rail-
roader, they were by contrast rested and forewarned, having moved out
of Lake City two days ago to dig in along the near end of the swamp-
bound neck of land and there await the arrival of the bluecoats on terrain
that would cramp their style and limit their artillery advantage. As a result, the butternut militia had only to stand more or less firm and keep
shooting, whereas the attackers were obliged to try to maneuver, which
was practically impossible, hemmed in as they were on the left and right
by spongy ground and blasted from the front by masses of graybacks
who also enjoyed the protection of intrenchments. The fighting con-
sisted mainly of a series of breakdowns and disintegrations which occurred when a number of blue regiments, exposed to such obvious tactical
disadvantages, wavered and finally came apart under pressure. A New
Hampshire outfit was the first to give way, followed by another of Negro regulars who fled when their colonel was shot down, and total collapse was only forestalled by Seymour's belated permission for the rest
to withdraw. They did so in considerable haste and disorder, leaving six
of their guns behind them on the field. Early darkness ended the pursuit,
which had been delayed by another Negro regiment assigned to rear-
guard duty. Casualties totaled 1861 for the Federals, including more than
700 killed or captured, while the Confederates lost 946, with fewer than
100 dead or missing. Seymour had at last achieved distinction, but not at
all of the kind for which he yearned, since it resulted from the addition
of his name to the list of those commanders, North and South, who suffered the soundest thrashings of the war.

    Slogging rearward under cover of darkness, the whipped and bleed-
ing survivors were as bitter as they were footsore. "This moment of
grief is too sacred for anger," an officer wrote home. But that was by
no means the general reaction, which was not unlike the one displayed
on the similar withdrawal from the field of Chickamauga, five months
ago tonight. If this retreat was on a smaller scale, as far as concerned the
number of troops involved, it was at any rate much longer, and it was
harder in still other ways. Without nearly enough ambulances or wagons
to accommodate the wounded, crude litters had to be improvised, with
results that were not only painful for the men being jolted but also exhausting for the bearers. Still, they made good time: better, indeed, than
they had made on the speedy outward march. By moonrise they were
at Sanderson, ten miles from the scene of their defeat, and they passed

through Barber's before daybreak. The second of these two segments was even grimmer than the first, partly because the marchers were wearier, partly too because they lacked by then the disconcerting spur of pursuit, the rebels having halted far in the rear. Now they had time for comprehending what had happened back there at Olustee, and that had perhaps the grimmest effect of all. "Ten miles we wended or crawled along," a participant afterwards said of the small-hours trek from Sanderson to Barber's, "the wounded filling the night air with lamentations, the crippled horses neighing in pain, and the full moon kissing the cold, clammy lips of the dying." Moreover, there was no halt on the 21st at Baldwin, despite previous instructions for holding that vital crossing at all costs, and by sunup of the following morning the head of the column was in Jacksonville, which it had left four days and a hard hundred miles ago.

Gillmore's dismay, on learning of what had happened in his absence and against his orders, was increased by information that the Confederates had advanced beyond Baldwin and were intrenching a line along McGirt's Creek, midway between that place and Jacksonville. Whether this was in preparation for defense or attack he did not know, though it might well be for the latter, since they were reported to have been heavily reinforced from Georgia. In any case, the question was no longer whether he could advance to the Suwannee, as he had formerly intended, but whether he could hold the coastal strip he had seized within a week of his arrival; Beauregard had outfoxed him again, he admitted to his superiors in Washington. "The enemy have thrown so large a force into Florida," he informed Halleck on February 23, "that I judge it to be inexpedient to do more at the present time than hold the line of the Saint Johns River."

One thing he could and did do, however, and that was to relieve Seymour of the command he had abused. But this was plainly a case of locking the stable after the pony was stolen. Certainly it was no help to Hay, who was finding it much harder now to obtain signatures for his oath-blanks. In fact, many who had signed appeared to regret that they had done so; while others, as he noted in his diary, "refused to sign, on the ground that they were not repentant." It was becoming increasingly clear, with the spread of news of the recent Union defeat, that he and his chief had miscalculated the temper of the people. Florida, the least populous of the Confederate states, had furnished the smallest number of troops for the rebel armies; but that was by no means a fit basis on which to determine her zeal for the secessionist cause, which was indicated far better by the fact that she had given a larger proportion of her eligible men than had any other state. On March 3, within twelve days of the rebel victory at Olustee, Hay frankly confessed: "I am very sure that we cannot now get the President's 10th." This being so, there was little point in his remaining. Nor did he. After a side excursion to Key West

— where he went in hope of picking up a few more signatures, but found instead "a race of thieves and a degeneration of vipers" — he returned somewhat crestfallen to the capital, intending to resume his former duties if his chief would overlook the unhappy events of the past month and take him back.

He found the hostile papers in full bay, charging Lincoln with having "fooled away 2000 men in a sordid attempt to manufacture for himself three additional votes in the approaching Presidential election." Nor did Hay escape their censure as a party to the conspiracy to overawe Florida, not for any true military purpose, but merely to win himself a seat in Congress and deliver a set of committed delegates to the Republican convention. This last, they said, explained the reckless haste that had brought Seymour to defeat; for the convention would be held in June, and the hapless general had been obliged to expose his troops to slaughter in an attempt to carry out his orders to complete the intended conquest of that waste of sand in time for a new government to be formed and delegates to be chosen who would cast their votes for Lincoln's renomination. Returning at the height of the scandal aroused by the failure of his mission, Hay armed himself with extenuating documents for the confrontation with his chief. He expected at least a grilling — for there was enough unpleasant truth in the opposition's charges to make them sting far worse than the usual fabrications — but he was wrong; Lincoln assumed that the young man had done his best in a difficult situation, and did not blame him for the trouble the journalists were making. "There was no special necessity of my presenting my papers," Hay wrote in his diary that night, "as I found he thoroughly understood the state of affairs in Florida and did not seem in the least annoyed by the newspaper falsehoods about the matter."

Others received a different impression of the President's reaction to this latest in the series of attacks designed to expose him as a master of deceit, an unprincipled opportunist, a clod, a tyrant, a bawdy clown, a monster. Earlier that month a White House visitor observed that Lincoln seemed "deeply wounded" by the allegation that he had been willing to pay in blood for votes. As usual, however, even as he was ringed by critics flinging charges at his head, he could see at least one touch of humor in the situation. He told in this connection of a backwoods traveler who got caught one night in a violent storm and who floundered about in the blackness, his sense of direction lost amid blinding zigzags of lightning and deafening peals of thunder, until finally a bolt crashed directly overhead, awesome as the wrath of God, and brought him to his knees, badly frightened. By ordinary not a praying man, he kept his petition brief and to the point. "O Lord," he cried, "if it's all the same to you, give us a little more light and a little less noise!"

★ ★ ★

While Gillmore and Hay, with Seymour's manic assistance, were failing to bring Florida back into the Union under the terms of the Proclamation of Amnesty and Reconstruction, another quasi-military project which had to do with that document, and which likewise had the President's enthusiastic approval, was moving into its final preparatory stages in Virginia. Aimed at nothing so ambitious as the overnight return of the Old Dominion to its former allegiance, this second venture along those lines was an attempt to see that the people there were acquainted at first hand, rather than through the distorting columns of their local papers or the vituperative speeches of their leaders, with the terms of Lincoln's offer; in which case, it was presumed, a good many of them would be persuaded to see the wisdom of acceptance and the folly of delay. Even if the project fell a long way short of accomplishing the most that could be hoped for, it would at least create doubt and provoke division in the enemy ranks, its authors believed, at a time when the struggle was about to enter its most critical phase. Just as the Florida venture mixed war and politics, so was this Virginia expedition designed to combine a military and a propaganda effort. Lincoln had warned his adversaries that he would not leave "any available card unplayed," and this — though it would go considerably further in bloody intent, before it was over, than he had realized when he approved it — was another example of the fact that he meant exactly what he said.

Designed strictly as a cavalry operation, the project had its beginning in the mind of Judson Kilpatrick, who conceived the notion of launching a bold strike at the Confederate capital, sixty miles in Lee's rear, for the triple purpose of crippling and snarling the lines of supply and communication between the Rapidan and the James, disrupting the rebel government by jangling the nerves of the people who functioned at its center, and freeing the Union captives being held there in increasingly large numbers since the breakdown of the system of exchange. Like his purpose, his motivation was threefold: love of action, desire for acclaim, and envy. Averell having recently been applauded for his successful year-end raid into southwest Virginia, the New Jersey cavalryman planned to win far more applause by striking, not with a lone brigade, but with his whole division, and not at some remote objective on the fringes of the map, as Averell had done, but at the very solar plexus of rebellion. Such a blow would outdo all the horseback exploits that had gone before it, including the highly touted "rides" by Stuart in his heyday. Besides, Kilpatrick did not believe the hit-and-run operation would be nearly as risky, or anyhow as difficult, as it sounded. His information was that Richmond was scantly protected by inexperienced home guardsmen who would not be able to offer serious resistance to an approximately equal number of veteran troopers armed with seven-shot repeaters, not to mention the fact that his strength would be more than doubled, once he broke through the rim of the city's defenses, by the liberation and addition of some 5000 bluecoats reported to be at Libby and on Belle Isle. A more difficult problem, just now, was how to go about securing the approval he had to have before he could take off southward on the venture he was sure would bring him fame. He had little caution in his makeup, but at any rate he knew better than to propose his scheme to Pleasonton, who might hog it, or to the overcautious Meade, who would be certain to see it as harebrained and reject it in short order. Instead, he took care to communicate in private with certain persons known to be close to the highest authority of all. That was in late January, and the result was about as prompt as he expected. On February 11 a high-priority telegram clicked off the wire from Washington, addressed to the commander of the Army of the Potomac: "Unless there be strong reasons to the contrary, please send Gen. Kilpatrick to us here, for two or three days. A. Lincoln."

"Us" included Stanton, who shared with his chief a staunch, perhaps an extravagant admiration for military boldness, a quality sadly lacking in the upper echelons of the eastern theater, as they saw it, but personified by the bandy-legged general known to the army as "Kill Cavalry." The latter arrived in the capital next morning — the President's fifty-fifth birthday — and was received in private by the Secretary of War. Stanton liked the proposition even better at first hand than he had by hearsay, seeing in it, in addition to the fruits predicted by its author, the possibility of affording a real boost to morale on the home front when the news went out that Federal horsemen had clattered through the streets of Richmond, striking terror into the hearts of rebel leaders and freeing thousands of blue-clad martyrs from a durance worse than vile. Moreover, having applauded the young brigadier's conception, which was much in line with his own belief as to the manner in which this war should be fought, the Secretary passed along a suggestion from Lincoln that would give the raid an added dimension, and this was that each trooper carry with him a hundred or so copies of the recent amnesty proclamation for distribution along the way. Kilpatrick pronounced this a splendid notion, then presently, the details having been agreed on, returned to the Rapidan, encouraged and flattered by the confidence thus shown by the head of the War Department — who made it clear that he spoke as well for the Commander in Chief — in a twenty-seven-year-old subordinate, less than three years out of West Point. Hard in his wake, orders came to Culpeper directing that his division be reinforced to a strength of about 4000 for the raid he proposed and that he be given all the assistance he required, including diversionary actions by other units, foot and horse.

Meade was not happy about the project, of which he had known nothing until now. Nor was Pleasonton, who recalled the ill-fated Stoneman raid, which had been similar in purpose and conception, but which had accomplished little except "the loss to the government [of] over 7000 horses, besides the equipments and men left on the road." In short, the chief of cavalry said flatly, the expedition was "not feasible at this time." As for the proposed distribution of the President's proclamation, he suggested that this could be done better, and far cheaper, by undercover agents, and he offered "to have it freely circulated [by this method] in any section of Virginia that may be desired." But nothing came of these objections by the New Jersey cavalryman's immediate superiors. In fact, they were received in Washington as further evidence of the timidity which had crippled the eastern army from the outset. The orders were peremptory, Meade was told; Kilpatrick was to be given a free rein.

About the time of Washington's Birthday, which came ten days after Lincoln's, bales of leaflets reprinting the amnesty proclamation arrived for distribution to the raiders, who were to scatter them broadcast on the way to Richmond. There also arrived from Washington, four days later and only two days short of the jump-off date, a twenty-one-year-old colonel who came highly recommended for his "well-known gallantry, intelligence, and energy" — this last despite a wooden leg and a manner described by an admirer as "soft as a cat's." Ulric Dahlgren was his name. He was the admiral's son, but he preferred the cavalry to the navy because he believed the mounted arm would afford him more and better chances for adventure and individual accomplishment. Commissioned a captain at nineteen by Stanton himself before the war was a year old, he had served in rapid succession on the staffs of Sigel, Burnside, Hooker, and Meade, all of whom had found him useful as well as ornamental, and it had been near Boonsboro, during the pursuit of Lee after Gettysburg, that he received the wound that resulted in the amputation. Once he was able to get about on crutches he went down the coast and convalesced aboard his father's flagship outside Charleston; after which he returned to Washington, where he was jumped three ranks to colonel, reportedly the youngest in the army, and fitted for an artificial leg. While there, he learned of the preparations then in progress for the horseback strike about to be launched against the rebel capital, and he went at once to cavalry headquarters near Brandy to appeal to Pleasonton for permission to go along, despite his crippled condition. Pleasonton sent him to Kilpatrick, who not only acceded to his plea, but also gave him the all-important assignment of leading the way across the Rapidan at the head of a special 500-man detachment, with other hazardous tasks to follow in the course of the ride from that river to the James. "If successful," he wrote his father, delighted to be back in the war at all, let alone with such a daredevil role to play, "[the raid] will be the grandest thing on record; and if it fails, many of us will 'go up.' I may be captured or I may be 'tumbled over,' but it is an undertaking that if I were not in I should be ashamed to show my face again." He was especially taken with the notion that he would be riding into the very heart of the rebellion, and he added: "If we do not return, there is no better place to 'give up the ghost.' "

Jump-off was set for an hour before midnight, February 28, and proceeded without a hitch, partly because Lee was pulled off balance by Sedgwick, who had shifted his corps upstream that day, as if for a crossing in that direction, while Kilpatrick was massing his 3585 troopers under cover of the woods in rear of Ely's Ford, twenty miles downriver. At the appointed hour they splashed across, mindful of their instructions to "move with the utmost expedition possible on the shortest route past the enemy's right flank." So well did it go that by dawn the column reached Spotsylvania, fifteen miles beyond the Rapidan, unchallenged; at which point, as had been prearranged, Dahlgren and his 500 veered slightly right, while the main body continued to move straight ahead for Richmond, less than fifty miles away. The plan was for the smaller column to cross the James near Goochland, well upstream, so as to approach the rebel capital from the southwest at the same time Kilpatrick came upon it from the north, thereby causing the home-guard defenders to spread thinner and thus expose themselves to the breakthrough that would result in the clatter of Federal hoofs in the streets of their city and the release of 5000 captives from Libby and Belle Isle. Dahlgren's was the longer ride; he would have to avoid delay to arrive on schedule. Kilpatrick saw him off from Spotsylvania, wished him Godspeed as he disappeared into the misty dawn of leap-year day, then continued on his own route, south-southeast, which would bring him and his 3000 to the northern gates of Richmond, if all went as planned, at the same time the young colonel and his detached 500 came knocking at the western gates.

Speed was the watchword; Kilpatrick rode hard and fast, unopposed and apparently unpursued. This last was due in part to a second diversion, back on the Rapidan line. While Sedgwick was feinting westward, George Custer was shifting his 1500-man cavalry brigade even farther in that direction for a dash southward into Albemarle County, a movement designed to attract still more of Lee's attention away from the heavier column rounding his opposite flank. Custer, like Kilpatrick, had certain peculiarities of aspect ("This officer is one of the funniest-looking beings you ever saw," a colonel on Meade's staff wrote home, "and looks like a circus rider gone mad! He wears a huzzar jacket and tight trousers, of faded black velvet trimmed with tarnished gold lace. His head is decked with a little gray felt hat; high boots and gilt spurs complete the costume, which is enhanced by the general's coiffure, consisting in short, dry, flaxen ringlets!") but these gaudy trappings, coupled with a flamboyant personality and a reputation as a glory-hunter, did not interfere with his effectiveness when sheer courage was what was called for — as it was here, off on his own in Lee's left rear, with the task of drawing as many of Stuart's horsemen after him as possible,

away from the main effort to the east. He could scarcely have done a
better job, as it turned out. Crossing the river that same Sunday night,
some forty miles upstream from Ely's Ford, he threatened Charlottes-
ville next day and returned to the north bank of the Rapidan on Tuesday, March 1, having ridden more than a hundred miles through hostile
territory, burned three large grist mills filled with flour and grain,
and captured about fifty graybacks and 500 horses, all without the loss
of a man and only a few wounded. So well indeed had he carried out his
mission, particularly with regard to attracting the rebel cavalry's attention, that he was notified on his return, officially and in writing, of Pleasonton's "entire satisfaction . . . and gratification . . . at the prompt manner in which the duties assigned to you have been performed."

Before Custer returned to the Union lines Kilpatrick was knocking at the gates of Richmond. Across the North Anna by noon of February 29, he had paused astride the Virginia Central at Beaver Dam Station,
midway to his objective, and after setting fire to the depot and other installations, thus to discourage any pursuit by rail once Lee found out that
some 4000 blue raiders were menacing the capital in his rear, pressed on
to make camp near the South Anna by nightfall. An hour past midnight
he roused his sleeping troopers and was off again through the darkness,
undeterred by an icy rainstorm or the fact that he had received no answering signal when he sent up rockets to indicate his position to Dahlgren, whose detachment was somewhere off to the west. "No rockets
could be seen for any distance on such a night as that," an officer was to
note, recalling that the "sharp wind and sleet forced men to close their
eyes" as they rode southward, their wet clothes frozen stiff as armor.
By daylight they were over the Chickahominy near Ashland, and at 10
o'clock in the morning, having covered sixty miles of road in the past
thirty-five hours, they came jogging down the Brook Pike to within
sight of Richmond and range of its outer fortifications, five miles from
the heart of town. No sooner did they appear than they were taken under fire. Kilpatrick brought up his six guns for counterbattery work and
prepared to overrun the defenders, "believing that if they were citizen
soldiers" — by which he meant home guardsmen — "I could enter the
city." So he reported some weeks later, in the calmness of his tent. One
thing that bothered him now, though, was that the boom and clatter of
his engagement had drawn no reply from Dahlgren, who should have
arrived simultaneously on the far side of the James, there to create the
prearranged diversion, but who had either been delayed or gobbled up.
Another matter for concern was that the rebels up ahead were doing a
highly professional job of defending their position. They were in fact
part-time volunteers — government clerks, old men, and boys, considerably fewer in number than the bluecoats to their front, and serving
antiquated or worn-out guns long since replaced by new ones in Lee's
army — but they handled their pieces with such precision that Kilpatrick

began to believe that they had been reinforced by regulars. "They have too many of those damned guns!" he fumed, riding his line amid shell-bursts and withholding the order to charge until he could better determine what stood between him and the breakthrough he intended; "they keep opening new ones on us all the time."

It was strange, this sudden transformation in a hell-for-leather commander who up to now had fairly ached to put his troopers inside Richmond. He had worked all the angles to circumvent his immediate superiors, whose timidity he had seen as the main obstacle to an undertaking that simply could not fail once it got past their disapproval, and had ridden a hard sixty miles through hostile country, bristling with aggressiveness and chafing with impatience all the way. Yet now that he had come within plain view of his goal — the goal, for that matter, of every blue-clad soldier in the eastern theater — he declined to risk the last brief sprint, half a mile down the turnpike, then past or through or over "those damned guns," which were all that stood between him and the completion of the mission he had designed with his own particular talents in mind, or anyhow his notion of those talents. It was unquestionably strange, but perhaps it was not as sudden as it seemed; perhaps it had been this way all along, behind the swagger and the blustering impatience. In any case he limited his aggressiveness, here on the outskirts of his objective, to a tentative sparring match, keeping one ear cocked for some indication that Dahlgren and his daredevil 500 were knocking at the gates beyond the James. After six or seven hours of this, the rebel guns had indeed grown in numbers, along with their infantry support, as reinforcements were hustled to the threatened sector from others undisturbed along the defensive rim, and Kilpatrick finally arrived at a decision. "Feeling confident that Dahlgren had failed to cross the river, and that an attempt to enter the city at that point would but end in a bloody failure," he later reported, "I reluctantly withdrew." He fell back northeastward, recrossing the Chickahominy at Meadow Bridge to give his men and horses some badly needed sleep in the sodden fields around Mechanicsville, where Lee had opened his Seven Days offensive, just over twenty months ago.

There had been no fighting here since then, but presently there was. At 10 o'clock, unable to sleep or rest — in part because of the wet and the cold, in part because of his fret at having failed — Kilpatrick remounted his troopers and prepared to launch a night attack down the Mechanicsville road, avoiding the stoutly held pike to the west, in order to achieve a penetration that would last no longer than it took to free the prisoners and come back out again. Before he could get his weary men in line, however, he was himself attacked by rebel horsemen who came at him from the direction of Yellow Tavern, out of the darkness in his rear. Though he managed to beat off this assault, all thoughts of resuming the offensive gave way at once to the problem of survival: especially when he learned, as he soon did, that the attackers were not "citizen soldiers," which were all he had faced till now, but regulars from Wade Hampton's division, who had taken up the belated pursuit from the Rapidan line and then had narrowed the gap between him and them while he was sparring with Richmond's defenders this afternoon. His concern was no longer with the liberation of the prisoners in the city; it was rather how to keep from joining them as a prisoner himself. Once more his decision was to withdraw northeastward, and this he did, effecting a skillful disengagement to make camp at dawn near Bethesda Church, midway between the Chickahominy and the Pamunkey. Here he remained all morning, March 2, fighting off regular and irregular Confederates who were gathering in ever larger numbers all around him in the woods and swamps. He kept hoping to hear from Dahlgren, but he did not. At noon he abandoned his vigil, together with all hope of entering Richmond, and withdrew to make camp at Tunstall's Station, near McClellan's old base at White House. There at last he was joined that night by a captain and 260 men from Dahlgren's detachment. They had a gloomy tale to tell, though they did not know the even gloomier ending, which was occurring at about that same time, some dozen air-line miles to the northeast.

Despite the almost constant rain, which made for heavy going, Dahlgren had set a rapid pace after he and his picked 500 turned off from the main body at Spotsylvania before sunup, leap-year morning. Proceeding south through Fredericks Hall, where he called a midday halt to feed the horses, he crossed the South Anna late that night and rode into Goochland, thirty miles up the James from the rebel capital, as March 1 was dawning. Here he picked up a young Negro named Martin Robinson, a slave from a nearby plantation, who offered to show him a place where the bridgeless river could be forded. The colonel was in excellent spirits, for he had kept to a difficult schedule and was about to get his troopers into position for the final dash that would put them in southside Richmond before noon, just as he had promised Kilpatrick he would do. So he thought; but not for long. Arriving at the intended crossing — Jude's Ford, it was called — he found the river on the boom, swollen by the two-day rain and running too swift to be breasted; whereupon the handsome young colonel, whose manner was said to be "soft as a cat's," showed his claws. Although the guide appeared to be quite as surprised as he himself was at the condition of the ford, Dahlgren suspected treachery, and in his anger at having been thwarted — for it was clear now, if nothing else was, that he could not reach his objective either on time or from the appointed direction — ordered him hanged. This was accomplished with dispatch there by the river, one end of a picket rope being flung across a convenient limb while the other was fastened snugly about the neck of the Negro, whose protests were cut short when he left the ground. Without further delay, and almost before the suspended man had ended his comic-dreadful jig, the blue column was back in motion, trotting eastward down the north bank of the James, its commander watching intently for some sign of a ford shallow enough to be used.

Finding none he paused occasionally to set fire to a grist mill or damage a lock in the left-bank canal, which delayed him still more. It was late afternoon by the time he cleared Short Pump, eight miles from Richmond, and heard the boom of guns in the misty northeast distance. He quickened the pace, but presently he too encountered resistance, with the result that by the time he got close to the city Kilpatrick had withdrawn. So far as Dahlgren could tell, alone in the gathering dusk with rebel militia all around him, his horses sagging with fatigue and a hard rain coming down, the main body had simply vanished. His instructions in such a case — that is, once the raid was over: as it now definitely was, though not at all in the manner Kilpatrick had predicted — called for a return to the Union lines, either by way of Fredericksburg or down the York-James peninsula. He chose the former route, turning off to the north, away from Richmond and across the Chickahominy, well above Meadow Bridge. His troopers had had little sleep in the past three nights, and by now the column had split in two, some 300 of the men becoming separated from the rest in the gloom and confusion. These were the ones — 260 of them, at any rate; about forty were captured or shot from their saddles next day — who joined the main body at Tunstall's the following night. Meanwhile, Dahlgren and the remaining 200 managed to cross the Pamunkey, a few miles north of there, and continued on through the darkness to the Mattaponi, exchanging shots with roving bands of rebels all the way. This stream too they crossed, but they got only a bit farther. Approaching King and Queen Courthouse, just beyond the river, they stumbled into an ambush laid in their path by Fitz Lee's regulars, who had also arrived from the Rapidan by now. Dahlgren, riding point, decided to brazen or bluff his way through; or perhaps he recalled that he had told his father there was no better place to die. "Surrender, you damned rebels," he cried, flourishing his revolver, "or I'll shoot you!" The answering volley unhorsed him with four bullets in his body, and witnesses afterwards testified that before he struck the ground he had already given up what he had called the ghost.

Most of those with him were likewise killed or captured, a number being flushed from hiding next morning by pursuers who put bloodhounds on their trail. Kilpatrick was incensed when he heard of this unchivalrous practice from a dozen of Dahlgren's men who managed to get through to him a few days later at Yorktown, where he ended his withdrawal down the Peninsula, safe within the Union lines. He spoke, in his official report, of the colonel's death as "murder" — a curious charge for a professional to make — but he did not hesitate, in that same document, to blame the dead man for the unhappy outcome of the project he himself had planned and led. "I am satisfied that if Colonel Dahlgren had not failed in crossing the river," he declared, ". . . I should have entered the rebel capital and released our prisoners." As it was, instead of decreasing the prison population of Richmond, he had increased it by some 300 veteran troopers (his total loss was 340, but a good many of them were killed) and in addition had lost 583 horses in the course of the ride, plus another 480 too broken down to be of any further use when it was over. About the only profit he could point to was the incidental damage inflicted on various installations along the way, together with the claim that "several thousand of the President's amnesty proclamations were scattered throughout the entire country."

In point of fact, a sizable proportion of these last had been unloaded as dead weight, heaved overboard into roadside ditches when the project degenerated into a race for survival, and whatever of propaganda value was derived from the scattering of Lincoln's amnesty offer had been considerably offset by the hard-handed excesses of the blue troopers engaged in an expedition whose most lamented casualty, according to a Richmond editor, was "a boy named Martin, the property of Mr David Meems, of Goochland." Even so, the resentments stirred up in the course of the raid were mild indeed, compared to those that developed on both sides when it was over: particularly in regard to Ulric Dahlgren, whose zeal was even more in evidence after his death than it had been before he toppled from his horse near King and Queen. His body was subjected to various indignities, including the theft of his artificial leg, the clumsy removal of one of his fingers to get at a ring he was wearing, and the scavenging of other of his private possessions, such as his watch, his boots, and even his clothes. News of these atrocities created a stir of outrage in the North, but this in turn was overmatched by the furor that followed in the South upon the publication of certain papers found among his personal effects. These included the draft of an address to his command and a detailed set of instructions for what he called "a desperate undertaking." "We will cross the James River into Richmond," he had written, "destroying the bridges after us and exhorting the released prisoners to destroy and burn the hateful city; and do not allow the rebel leader Davis and his traitorous crew to escape." Thus the proposed address, though there was no evidence that it had been delivered. The instructions were more specific. "The men must keep together and well in hand," he urged, "and once in the city it must be destroyed and Jeff Davis and cabinet killed. Pioneers will go along with combustible material."

To Southerners, when these exhortations to arson and assassination were released in print, it appeared that this amounted to hoisting the black flag, and they called bitterly for emulation of the example set — conveniently forgetting, it would seem, Quantrill's previous excesses out in Kansas. One of the angriest among them was Seddon, who sent copies of the documents to Lee, stating that in his opinion their "diabolical character" required "something more than a mere informal publication in our newspapers. My own inclinations are toward the execution of at least a portion of those captured at the time.... I desire to have the benefit of your views and any suggestions you may make." Lee replied that he too was shocked by the details of this "barbarous and inhuman plot," but that execution of the captured troopers would bring retaliation, and he wanted no part of a hanging-match with the Yankees. Besides, he told the Secretary, "I do not think that reason and reflection would justify such a course. I think it better to do right, even if we suffer in so doing, than to incur the reproach of our consciences and posterity." Instead he sent the inflammatory documents across the lines to Meade, together with a note inquiring "whether the designs and instructions of Colonel Dahlgren, as set forth in these papers ... were authorized by the United States Government or by his superior officers, and also whether they have the sanction and approval of those authorities." Meade investigated the matter and replied "that neither the United States Government, myself, nor General Kilpatrick authorized, sanctioned, or approved the burning of the city of Richmond and the killing of Mr Davis and cabinet, nor any other act not required by military necessity and in accordance with the usages of war." He also included, for whatever it was worth, a letter from Kilpatrick, impugning the authenticity of the papers. "But I regret to say," Meade privately informed his wife, "Kilpatrick's reputation, and collateral evidence in my possession, rather go against this theory."

There the matter rested, so far at least as Meade and Lee were concerned. As for Lincoln, he too was willing to let it lie, if it only would, and he did not call, as he had done after the frustration of the first of his two attempts to extend the influence of his amnesty proclamation, for "more light"; there had been quite enough of that by now. Both failures were depressing for him to look back on, especially the second. The Florida expedition had been merely a fiasco, a military embarrassment, but the Kilpatrick raid was that and more, adding as it did a deeper bitterness to a fratricidal struggle which, in all conscience, was bitter enough already. It was as if Lincoln, in attempting to soothe and heal the national wounds, had reached blindly into the medicine chest and mistaken an irritant for a salve. That this had been the effect was shown in part by the reaction of newspapers North and South. Calling hotly for reprisal, the Richmond *Examiner* now saw the conflict as "a war of extermination, of indiscriminate slaughter and plunder," while the New York *Times* exulted in the damage done by the raiders in Virginia and gloated over reports brought back of "the large number of dilapidated and deserted dwellings, the ruined churches with windows out and doors ajar, the abandoned fields and workshops, the neglected plantations." As for the slave Martin Robinson, whose body had been left dangling beside unusable Jude's Ford, he had met "a fate he so richly deserved," according to the *Times*, because he had "dared to trifle with the welfare of his country."

That was what they had come to, South and North, as the war moved toward and into its fourth and bloodiest spring.

✗ 3 ✗

For Grant, the three-month span of comparative idleness that came after the storming of Missionary Ridge was nothing like the one that had followed his earlier triumph at Vicksburg. His manner then had been that of a man not only uncertain of the future, but also doubtful about the present, with time on his hands and no notion of how to use it. Lacking in effect an occupation, what he mainly had been, through that difficult time — after as well as before the New Orleans horseback accident, which had added pain without distraction and immobility without relaxation — was bored. That was by no means the case now. For one thing, there was his vast new department to be inspected, most of which he had had no chance to visit, even briefly, until the Chattanooga siege was lifted. After a well-earned Christmas rest, he went in early January to Knoxville, then up through Cumberland Gap to Barbourville, from there by way of Lexington to Louisville, and finally back down through Nashville to his starting point, with the added satisfaction of having solved a number of supply and security problems all along the route. He had always enjoyed travel, especially when it took him to new places, and what was more the trip presented many of the aspects of a triumphal tour. "All we needed was a leader," a wounded private had told him when he climbed Missionary Ridge in the wake of the men who had carried it, and that was the reaction wherever he went on his swing through East Tennessee and Central Kentucky. "*Hail to the Chief*, both words and air, greeted him at every stopping place," an associate was to recall.

Nor was this enthusiasm by any means limited to those in uniform. Called to St Louis immediately afterwards by the supposedly dangerous illness of one of his children (a false alarm, as it turned out, for the crisis was past when he arrived) he had no sooner checked into the Lindell Hotel — "U.S.Grant, Chattanooga," he signed the register — than he was besieged by admirers with invitations, including one to a banquet tendered in his honor by two hundred leading citizens, determined to outdo in lavishness the affair put on five months ago by their commercial rivals down in Memphis. This he accepted, along with a resolution of thanks from the Common Council. If he was modest in his demeanor at such functions, and brief in his response to speeches of praise, that did not mean that he enjoyed them any less. The fact was, he enjoyed them very much, comparing the treatment accorded him now with the attitude he had encountered in prewar days, a brief five years ago, when he tried his hand at selling real estate in this same city and hardscrabble farming just outside it, and failed at both so thoroughly that he had been reduced to peddling firewood in its streets. This he knew was the way of the world, but he enjoyed the drama of the contrast between then and now, especially here in his wife's home state, where the opinion once had been fairly unanimous, not only that she had married beneath her station, but also that she had saddled herself with a husband who turned out to be a failure in his chosen line of work and a ne'er-do-well in several others.

In addition to these honors done him at first hand, others came from a distance, including three that arrived in rapid order from the seat of government before the year was out. When, amid salutes and illuminations celebrating the Chattanooga triumph, news spread throughout the North that Knoxville too had been delivered, the President coupled his announcement of the victory with a recommendation that the people gather informally in their churches to pay homage to the Almighty "for this great advancement of the national cause," and he followed this next day, December 8, with a personal message to Grant, who passed it along in a general order: "Understanding that your lodgment at Chattanooga and Knoxville is now secure, I wish to tender you, and all under your command, my more than thanks — my profoundest gratitude — for the skill, courage, and perseverance with which you and they, over so great difficulties, have effected that important object. God bless you all." Congress, not to be outdone, passed before Christmas a joint resolution thanking the Illinois general and his men "for their gallantry and good conduct in the battles in which they have been engaged" and providing for "a gold medal to be struck, with suitable emblems, devices, and inscriptions, to be presented to Major General Grant . . . in the name of the people of the United States of America." In time the medal was forwarded as directed, bearing on one side a profile of the general, surrounded by a laurel wreath and a galaxy of stars, and on the other a figure of Fame holding a trumpet and a scroll inscribed with the names of his victories. The motto was "Proclaim liberty throughout the Land." Meantime a bill was offered to revive the grade of lieutenant general — previously held only by George Washington and Winfield Scott, the former briefly, the latter merely by brevet — for the purpose of assuring that Grant, for whom alone it was intended, would assume by virtue of that lofty rank the post now occupied by Halleck, who stood above him on the list of major generals. Senator James Doolittle of Wisconsin, for one, was specific in his reasons for supporting the proposal. So far in the war, he declared with an enthusiasm that avoided understatement, Grant had won 17 battles, captured 100,000 prisoners, and taken 500 pieces of artillery; "He has organized victory from the beginning, and I want him in a position where he can organize *final* victory and bring it to our armies and put an end to this rebellion."

Doolittle's colleagues wanted final victory, too, and agreed that the probable way to get it would be to apply the western formula in the East; but a majority shared two objections to the course proposed. One was that Grant was needed in the field, not behind a desk in the capital — even if the desk was that of the general-in-chief — and the other was an ingrained fear of creating a military Grand Lama who might someday develop political ambitions and use the army to further them. As a result, the bill failed to pass.

On the face of it, this seemed no great loss, since Grant by then had already offered the government his solution to the problem of how to win the war, only to have it rejected out of hand. Reverting to the proposal he had made soon after the fall of Vicksburg, he sent Charles Dana to Washington in mid-December to lay before his superiors a plan for holding the line of the Tennessee with a skeleton force while the rest of his troops steamed down the Mississippi to New Orleans, from which point they would move against Mobile and reduce it, then march through Alabama and across Georgia, living off the abundance of the Confederate heartland as they went. Meantime the Virginia army would pin Lee down by taking the offensive, and in this connection he suggested that Meade be replaced by Sherman or Baldy Smith, who could better appreciate the need for co-ordinating the eastern and the western efforts. . . . Presently Dana wired Grant that he had explained the scheme to Lincoln, Stanton, and Halleck, all three of whom had seen considerable merit in it: aside, that is, from the risk to which it would expose the weakened Union center while the bulk of the troops from there were on the way downriver. That drawback made it sound to them like something devised by McClellan; which plainly would not do. Besides, they wanted no more Chickamaugas, especially none that would be followed up by the victors, who presumably would do just that if they were given the second chance this seemed to offer. In short — except for that part of it favoring Meade's replacement by Smith, which all three chiefs applauded as an excellent idea, despite some misgivings about Baldy's "disposition and personal character" — Grant's proposal was turned down. Dana added, though, that the trio had welcomed his suggestions and had said that they would like to hear more of them, if he had any more of them in mind.

He did indeed. Still with his eye on Mobile, he then proposed a dual offensive against that place and Atlanta, the two drives to be launched simultaneously from New Orleans and Chattanooga, while the eastern army gave up its weary attempt to capture Richmond from the north and landed instead on the North Carolina coast in order to approach the rebel capital from the south, astride its lines of supply and communication. He said nothing more about replacing Meade with

Sherman — probably because he had decided he would need him to lead one of the two western columns — or with Smith, who by now had begun to exercise the talent for contention that had kept him in hot water most of his military life and would in time cause Grant, who once had seemed to think he hung the moon, to refer to him as "a clog." In his reply, which incorporated Lincoln's and Stanton's views as well as his own, Halleck did not mention Baldy either, no doubt assuming that Grant had confirmed their misgivings about the Vermonter's "disposition," but limited himself to an assessment of the strategy involved in the proposal for a double-pronged offensive, East and West. It would not do. Not only did it commit the cardinal sin of attempting two big things at once in each of the two theaters; it also required more troops than were available in either. If attempted, it would expose both Washington and Chattanooga to risks the government simply could not run, and moreover it showed the flawed conception of a commander who made enemy cities his primary objective, rather than enemy armies, as the President had lately been insisting must be done if this war was ever to be won. In Halleck's opinion, Grant would do better to concentrate on the problems at hand in Tennessee and North Georgia, and leave the large-scale thinking to those who were equipped for it. Just as Meade's objective was Lee's army, Grant's was Johnston's, and both were to keep it firmly in mind that neither Washington nor Chattanooga — nor, for that matter, East Tennessee, the region of Lincoln's acutest concern — was to be exposed to even the slightest danger while they attempted to carry out their separate missions of destroying the rebel masses in the field before them.

　　Sherman had returned by now from Knoxville. Grant informed him that the spring campaign, which would open as soon as the roads were fit for marching, would be southward against Joe Johnston and Atlanta, and every available man in both his and Thomas's armies would be needed for what promised to be the hardest fighting of the war. The redhead was all for it; but first he wanted to put an end to disruptions that had developed in the department he had left to come to Tennessee. In his absence, guerillas had taken to firing at steamboats from the banks of the big river, north and south of Vicksburg, and he did not intend to abide this outrage. "To secure the safety of the navigation of the Mississippi River," he declared, "I would slay millions. On that point I am not only insane, but mad. . . . I think I see one or two quick blows that will astonish the natives of the South and will convince them that, though to stand behind a big cottonwood and shoot at a passing boat is good sport and safe, it may still reach and kill their friends and families hundreds of miles off. For every bullet shot at a steamboat, I would shoot a thousand 30-pounder Parrotts into even helpless towns on Red, Ouachita, Yazoo, or wherever a boat can float or soldier march." To those who objected to this as war against civilians, he made the point that if rebel snipers could "fire on boats with women and children in them, we can fire and burn towns with women and children." Angry, he grew angrier by the week. Taking dinner at the home of a Union-loyal Nashville matron, for example, he turned on his hostess when she began to upbraid him for the looting his troops had done on the march to Knoxville. "Madam," he replied, "my soldiers have to subsist themselves even if the whole country must be ruined to maintain them. There are two armies here. One is in rebellion against the Union; the other is fighting for the Union. If either must starve to death, I propose it shall not be the army that is loyal." This said, he added in measured tones: "War is cruelty. There is no use trying to reform it. The crueler it is, the sooner it will be over."

His main fear just now was that the guerillas along the Lower Mississippi, emboldened by the example of the snipers, would band together in sufficient strength to attack the reduced garrisons at various river ports and thus undo much that had been accomplished, at a considerable expense of Federal blood and ingenuity, in the past year. It was Sherman's notion — a notion made more urgent by the need for reducing those garrisons still further in order to furnish additional troops for the campaign scheduled to open in North Georgia in late March or early April — to return to Mississippi between now and then, rather than keep his veteran soldiers lying idle in their winter camps, and nip this threat of renewed obstruction in the bud. As he put it in mid-December, after discussing the problem with Grant, "I think in all January and part of February I can do something in this line." He did not propose to waste his energies in running down individual snipers, which would be like trying to rid a swamp of mosquitoes by swatting them one by one, but rather to destroy the economy — the society, even, if need be — that afforded them subsistence. The way to do this, he maintained, was to wreck their production and transportation facilities so thoroughly that they would have nothing left to defend and nothing left to live on if they attempted resistance for its own sake. What was more, the situation there seemed made to order for the execution of such a project. Less than two hundred miles east of Jackson was Selma, Alabama, whose cannon foundry and other manufacturing installations Jefferson Davis had admired on his October visit, and roughly midway between them was Meridian, where three vital railroads intersected and which served as a storage and distribution center, not only for industrial products from the east, but also for grain and cattle from the fertile Black Prairie region just to the north. A rapid march by a sizable force, eastward from Vicksburg, then back again for a total distance of about five hundred miles, could be made within the two available months, he believed, and the smashing of these two major objectives, together with the widespread destruction he intended to accomplish en route, would assure a minimum of trouble for the skeleton command he would leave behind when he came back upriver to rejoin Grant for the drive on Atlanta — which Johnston, incidentally, would be much harder put to defend without the rations and guns now being sent to him from Meridian and Selma. That was what the Ohioan had had in mind when he spoke of "one or two blows that will astonish the natives."

There were, as he saw it, three main problems, each represented by an enemy commander who would have to be dealt with in launching this massive raid, first across the width of Mississippi and then beyond the Tombigbee to a point nearly halfway across Alabama. One was Polk, who had in his camps of instruction at Demopolis, between Meridian and Selma, the equivalent of two divisions with which to oppose him. Another was Johnston, who might send heavy detachments rearward by rail to catch him far from base and swamp him. The third was Forrest, who by now had attracted a considerable number of recruits to the cavalry division he was forming in North Mississippi and could be expected to investigate, in his usual slashing manner, any blue activity within reach. Discussing these problems with Grant, Sherman arrived at answers to all three. As for the first, he would employ no less than four divisions in his invasion column — two from McPherson's corps at Vicksburg and two from Hurlbut's at Memphis, which he would pick up on his way downriver — for a total of 20,000 infantry, plus about 5000 attached cavalry and artillery. That should take care of Polk, who could muster no better than half that many: unless, that is, he was reinforced by Johnston, and Grant agreed to discourage this by having Thomas menace Dalton. Forrest, the remaining concern, was to be attended to by a special force under W. Sooy Smith, recently placed at the head of all the cavalry in the Army of the Tennessee. At the same time the main body started east from Vicksburg, Smith was to set out south from West Tennessee, with instructions to occupy and defeat Forrest on the way to a link-up with Sherman at Meridian, from which point he and his troopers would take the lead on the march to Selma. His superiors saw, of course, that his more or less incidental defeat of Forrest, en route to the initial objective, was a lot to ask; but to make certain that he did not fail they arranged for him to be reinforced to a strength of 7000, roughly twice the number Forrest had in his green command. In any case, having arrived at this solution to the third of the three problems, Grant and his red-haired lieutenant parted company for a time, the latter to enjoy a Christmas leave with his family in Ohio while the former set out, shortly afterward, on the triumphal inspection tour through East Tennessee and Kentucky, followed by what turned out to be a pleasant visit to St Louis, where he was dined and toasted by civic leaders who once had looked askance at him as a poor catch for a Missouri girl.

In Memphis by mid-January, Sherman found Hurlbut busy carrying out instructions he had sent him to prepare two divisions for the trip downriver and the long march that would follow. While there, he also conferred with Smith, stressing the need for promptness and a vigorous celerity if his horsemen, with nearly twice the distance to cover from their starting point at nearby Collierville, were to reach Meridian at the same time as the foot soldiers, who would set out simultaneously from Vicksburg. Something else he stressed as well, which if neglected could bring on a far direr result than being thrown off schedule. This was what he referred to as "the nature of Forrest as a man, and of his peculiar force," a factor he first had learned to take into account at Fallen Timbers, after Shiloh, where his attempt at a pursuit had been brought to a sudden and unceremonious halt by one of the Tennessean's headlong charges, delivered in defiance not only of the odds, but also of the tactics manuals he had never read. "I explained to him," Sherman said afterwards of this conference with his chief of cavalry, "that in his route he was sure to encounter Forrest, who always attacked with a vehemence for which he must be prepared, and that, after he had repelled the first attack, he must in turn assume the most determined offensive, overwhelm him and utterly destroy his whole force." Without scoffing at the danger, Smith exhibited a confidence in the numerical advantage his superior's foresight had assured him for the impending confrontation with the so-called Wizard of the Saddle. Meantime Hurlbut completed his preparations. On the 25th he embarked with his two divisions, and Sherman followed two days later. By February 1 — the date set for Smith to begin his nearly 250-mile ride from Collierville, southeast to Okolona, then down the Mobile & Ohio to Meridian, wrecking and burning as he went — all the appointed elements of the infantry column were on hand at Vicksburg.

Sherman spent another two days making certain that all was in order for the march, which necessarily would be made without a base of supplies, and assessing the latest intelligence from spies beyond the lines. Polk by now had shifted his headquarters westward across the Tombigbee, from Demopolis to Meridian, and had posted his two divisions at Canton and Brandon, respectively under Loring and Sam French, twenty miles north and twelve miles east of Jackson, while his cavalry, under Stephen Lee, patrolled the region between the Pearl and the Big Black. Far from being alarmed by this, the northern commander was pleased to find his adversaries nearer than he had supposed; for they numbered barely half his strength, with 28 guns opposing 67 in the blue column, and the sooner he came to grips with them, the sooner they would be disposed of as a possible deterrent to his eastward progress and the destruction of everything of value in his path. Intending to move light, without tents or baggage even for corps commanders or himself, he had prescribed a minimum of equipment — "The expedition is one of celerity," he said, "and all things must tend to that"—but, even so, the twenty-day supply of such essentials as hardtack, salt, and coffee, together with ammunition and medical stores, required a 1000-wagon train. On February 3, having assured himself that all was as he had required, he passed the order that put his four divisions in motion for the Big Black River, one third of the way to Jackson, which in turn was a third of the way to Meridian, where Smith was to join him for the march on Selma, another hundred miles along the railroad he would follow all the way.

The march was in two columns, a corps in each, and so rapid that by nightfall both were over the river, trains and all, covering mile after eastward mile of ground for which they had fought in May, while headed in the opposite direction. Now as then, the weather was bright, the roads firm, and the soldiers in high spirits. They reached Edwards next day, swung past Champion Hill to end the third day's march at Bolton, and camped near Clinton the fourth night, within a dozen miles of the Mississippi capital. So far, the only resistance they had encountered was from small bands of cavalry; Lee was trying to slow their advance, and thus gain time for the two Confederate divisions to concentrate beyond the Pearl and there dispute a crossing. But Sherman saw through the design. Refusing to be delayed, he brushed the horsemen aside with his guns and kept his veterans slogging with such speed that Lee had no opportunity to destroy the pontoons of a large bridge, thrown across the river just beyond Jackson, before the Federals marched in on February 7. Twice already, in the past nine months, the torch had been put to this unfortunate town; now Sherman re-re-burned it, meantime pressing on for an uncontested crossing of the Pearl. Loring and French were in retreat by then, on opposite sides of the river — the former scuttling northward and the latter to the east, back to the places they had advanced from — having failed to get together in time to challenge the invaders at the only point where the terrain gave them a chance to prevail against the odds. Sherman kept moving. He reached Brandon the following evening — his forty-fourth birthday — and Morton on the 9th. In less than a week, he had not only covered better than half the distance between Vicksburg and Meridian; he had also scattered his opposition so effectively that now there was nothing between him and his initial objective except one badly rattled gray division, in flight from the four blue ones in its rear.

He pressed on, spurred by fear that he would be late for his rendezvous with Smith, who was due to reach Meridian tomorrow, after ten days on the road. The march was single column now, to provide a more compact defense against Lee's still-probing horsemen, and while McPherson paused for a day of destructive work on the railroad around Morton, Hurlbut made such good time that by sundown of the 12th he had passed through Decatur, northeast of Newton Station, and was less than thirty miles from Meridian. Sherman decided to wait there for McPherson, who was expected within a couple of hours. Detaching a regiment from Hurlbut's rear to serve as a guard, he and his staff unsaddled their horses in the yard of a house where an aide had arranged for supper; after which the general lay down on a bed to get some sleep. He was awakened by shouts and shots, and looked out of a window to find butternut cavalry "dashing about in a cloud of dust, firing their pistols." It developed that the colonel of the regiment detached to guard him, mistaking a front-riding group of staff officers for the head of McPherson's column, had considered himself relieved and pushed on eastward in an attempt to overtake his division before dark. When Sherman learned that this was what had happened, he sent an aide to order the regiment back on the double, while he himself prepared to retire with his companions to a corncrib for a blockhouse-style defense. Fortunately, the rebel troopers were giving their attention to some straggler wagons, never suspecting the larger prize within their reach, and before the townspeople could call it to their attention, the red-faced colonel returned on the run and drove them off, delivering the army commander from the gravest personal danger he had experienced since his near-capture at Collierville, four months ago yesterday. Presently McPherson did in fact come up, and Sherman went back to bed for a full night's sleep.

Another two days of marching brought the head of the blue column into Meridian by midafternoon of February 14. Polk had left by rail with the last of his troops that morning, retiring beyond the Tombigbee to Demopolis. After pleading in vain for reinforcements, he had concerned himself with the removal of an estimated $12,000,000 in military property, south to Mobile or east to Selma, together with the rolling stock of the three railroads; so that when Sherman marched in on Valentine's Day he found the warehouses yawning empty and the tracks deserted in all four directions. Furious at the loss, he put the blame on Smith, who should have arrived four days ago, in time to prevent the removal of the spoils, but who had neither come himself nor sent a courier to account for his departure from the schedule he had agreed to, three weeks back, in Memphis. Determined to make the most of the situation as he found it — for though the military property had been hauled away, the facilities were still there, and there was civilian property in abundance — the red-haired Ohioan gave his men a well-earned day of rest, then distributed the tools he had brought along to assure the efficient accomplishment of the object of his raid. "For five days," he subsequently reported, "10,000 men worked hard and with a will in that work of destruction, with axes, crowbars, sledges, clawbars, and with fire, and I have no hesitation in pronouncing the work as well done. Meridian, with its depots, storehouses, arsenal, hospitals, offices, hotels, and cantonments, no longer exists."

While the rest of the soldiers in the two corps were attending to the railroads — Hurlbut north and east of town, McPherson south and west, burning trestles, smashing culverts, and warping rails over bonfires fed by crossties — Sherman kept peering through the smoke for some sign of Smith and his 7000 troopers, who were to lead the march on Selma as soon as the present demolition work was finished. But there was none. "It will be a novel thing in war," he complained testily, between puffs on a cigar, "if infantry has to await the motions of cavalry."

His impatience was due in large part to the disappointing contrast between his present situation, in which the nonarrival of his cavalry left him marking time in Meridian — albeit vigorously, to a tempo set by pounding sledges and crackling flames — and the prospect that had seemed to lie before him, three weeks ago in Memphis, at the time of his conference with the commander of the mounted column. Smith not only had been eager to undertake the assignment, but had shown a ready appreciation of what was required to make it a success. He was to ride southeast to Okolona, visiting such destruction upon the inhabitants of this 100-mile swath across North Mississippi as his schedule would permit, and then turn south along the Mobile & Ohio, scourging the heart of the Black Prairie region with fire and sword, all the way to his projected link-up with the infantry, another 130 miles below, for the combined march eastward across the Tombigbee. As for the tactical danger, the cavalryman declared that the best procedure would be "to pitch into Forrest wherever I find him." He did not say this boastfully, but rather in accordance with his instructions, which advised him to do just that.

Neither a greenhorn nor a braggart, Smith was a West Pointer like his commander and fellow Ohioan, who was ten years his senior, and had risen on ability in the army to which he returned on the outbreak of war, interrupting what had promised to be (and later was) a distinguished career as a civil engineer. Graduating with Sheridan and McPherson, he had commanded a brigade at Shiloh while these other two Ohioans were still low-ranking staffers, and he led a division with such proficiency throughout the Vicksburg campaign that Grant soon afterwards made him his chief of cavalry. What was more, in the case of his present assignment, his confidence in his combat-tested ability as a leader was greatly strengthened by a look at the composition of the force he would be leading. In addition to five regiments he brought with him from Middle Tennessee, he would have at his disposal a Memphis-based division under Ben Grierson, who had ridden to fame over nearly the same route nine months before, and a veteran brigade already ordered to join him from Union City, up near the Kentucky line. Out of this total of better than 12,000 cavalry, he would select the 7000 he was to have in his hard-riding column, armed to a man with breech-loading carbines and accompanied by twenty pieces of artillery, double-teamed for speed. This would give him not only three times as many guns and twice as many troopers as were with Forrest, whose newly recruited division was all that stood between Smith and his objective, but also the largest and best-equipped body of Federal horsemen ever assembled in the western theater. It was small wonder he expressed no doubt that he could accomplish all that was asked of him at the late-January conference.

But Sherman had no sooner gone downriver than Smith learned that the 2000-man brigade from Union City, nearly one third of his intended force, was being delayed by floods and washouts all along the way. "Exceedingly chagrined," he informed the army commander that he thought it "wisest, best, and most promising" to postpone his departure until the brigade's arrival brought his column up to the strength assured him beforehand. He still felt "eager to pitch into [Forrest]," he said, "but I know that it is not your desire to 'send a boy to the mill.'" This was written on February 2, the day after he was supposed to have left Collierville and the day before Sherman left Vicksburg. As it turned out, moreover, the brigade did not reach Memphis until the 8th, and Smith found its horses so worn by their exertions that he felt obliged to give them a two-day rest. Then at last, on February 11 — one day after he was to have reached his initial objective, 230 miles away — he set out. He would "push ahead with all energy," he declared in a follow-up dispatch to Sherman, reporting that his men and their mounts were "in splendid condition" for the rigorous march. "Weather beautiful; roads getting good," he added. In a companion message to Grant, however, he sounded less ebullient. Earlier he had informed the department commander that his troopers were "well in hand, well provided with everything, and eager for the work," but now he confessed that the last-minute delay — already prolonged one day beyond the ten he was to have spent riding southward for the link-up at Meridian — had been "so long and so vexatious that I have worried myself into a state of morbid anxiety, and fear that I will be entirely too late to perform my part of the work."

Even though he was traversing, southeast of Collierville, what one of his lieutenants called a "rough, hopeless, God-forsaken" country,

despoiled by nearly two years of contention and hard-handed occupation, his spirits rose in the course of the early stages of the march,
partly because the tension of waiting had finally been relieved and
partly because his prediction that Forrest would "show fight between
the Coldwater and the Tallahatchie" was not borne out. He crossed
the former stream near Holly Springs on the 12th and the latter at
New Albany two days later — simultaneously, although he did not
know it, with Sherman's arrival in Meridian — "without firing a shot."
By now the column was badly strung out, however, and he was obliged
to call a halt while the rear elements caught up; with the result that
he did not reach Okolona until February 18. His schedule required a
march rate of about twenty-five miles a day, but in this first week he
had not averaged half that, despite the fact that he had encountered
no opposition more formidable than a "rabble of State troops" near
Pontotoc, which he brushed aside with ease, and had spent little time
on the destructive work that was so much a part of his assignment. This
last was because, so far, all he had run across that was worth destroying were a few outlying barns and gins. Now that he was astride the
M&O, however, the opportunity for such labor was considerably enlarged: so much so, indeed, that from Okolona to West Point, a distance of about thirty miles, his troopers spent more time ripping up
track and setting fires than they did in the saddle. "During two days,"
a brigade commander later wrote, "the sky was red with the flames
of burning corn and cotton."

The sky was red with more flames than these; for the blue horsemen — especially those who were off on their own, as stragglers or
outriders; "bummers," they would be called a bit later in the conflict
— did not neglect the chance to scorch the holdings of secessionists
in their path. What was more, a Federal colonel added, slaves on plantations roundabout, "driven wild with the infection, set the torch to
mansion houses, stables, cotton gins, and quarters," and "came en
masse to join our column, leaving only fire and absolute destruction
behind them." Smith, for one, was "deeply pained" to find his command
"disgraced by incendiarism of the most shocking kind. I have ordered
the first man caught in the act to be shot," he notified Grierson, "and I
have offered $500 reward for his detection." As for the Negroes, though
he had encouraged them to join him as a means of increasing the disruption of the region and decreasing its future contribution to the Confederate war effort, he now had some 3000 of them on his hands and
was finding them a severe encumbrance to his so-called "flying column," just at a time when he seemed likely to have to move his fastest.
Despite his relief that Forrest had failed to "show fight" in the early
stages of the march, it had begun to occur to him that the Tennessean
might be postponing his attack until he reached a position "where he

could concentrate a larger force, and where we would be to some extent jaded and farther from home."

By way of confirmation for these fears, a recently captured Indiana trooper managed to escape and rejoin his outfit on February 19, south of Okolona, with information that "Forrest's whole force was reported to be in the vicinity of West Point," barely a dozen miles ahead, and was "said to be 8000 or 9000 strong." Consequently when his lead elements ran into stiffer resistance next morning in that direction, Smith paused for thought. It seemed to him that his adversary, with the unexpected advantage of superior numbers, was laying a trap for him just down the line. He thought about this long and hard, and that evening his adjutant replied to a dispatch from one of his brigade commanders: "The general is very sick tonight."

His information was partly wrong, but his conclusion was entirely right. Though Forrest had a good deal less than half the number of men reported by the slippery Hoosier, he was indeed laying a trap for the blue column moving toward him down the Mobile & Ohio: a trap whose springing, incidentally, would commit his green command to its first concerted action. He had come to Mississippi in mid-November with fewer than 300 veterans from his old brigade, and two weeks later he took them northward, deep into West Tennessee, on a month-long tour of recruiting duty behind the Union lines, from which he returned by New Year's with some 3500 effectives, a sizable drove of hogs and cattle, and forty wagonloads of bacon. As here applied, the term "effectives" was questionable, however, since his recruits were mostly absentees and deserters, men who had skedaddled at least once before and could be expected to do so again at the first chance. "Forrest may cavort about that country as much as he pleases," Sherman had said when he heard what the rebel cavalryman was up to, north of Memphis. "Every conscript they now catch will cost a good man to watch." That this was a quite reasonable assertion no one knew better than the newly promoted major general who had this jumpy, unarmed mass in charge. But he depended on rigorous training and stern discipline — along with a few summary executions, if they were what was needed — to discourage the fulfillment of the Ohioan's prediction; after which would come the fighting that would knit what he now referred to as "my force of raw, undrilled, and undisciplined troops" into a cohesive unit, stamped with the aggressive personality of its leader and filled with a fierce pride in itself and him. With this in mind, he began in early January a program of unrelenting drill, mounted and dismounted, combined with a system of sharp-eyed inspections to assure compliance with his directives. This had been in progress barely a month when he received word at his headquarters, north of Panola, that Sherman was on the march from Vicksburg, 150 miles to the south, evidently intending to strike at Meridian and possibly also at Selma or Mobile. Eight days later, Smith left Collierville, 50 miles to the north, and Forrest made this second column his concern, determined to prevent a junction of the two, though even the smaller one had twice his strength and was infinitely superior in experience and equipment.

While Smith was moving southeast, from Holly Springs to Okolona, Forrest paralleled the blue march by shifting from Panola to Starkville. Outnumbered two to one, he could not risk an all-out attack in open country; nor could he lie in wait for the invaders until he knew where they were headed and what route they would take to get there. They might, for example, cross the Tombigbee east of Tupelo for a link-up with Sherman at Demopolis or Selma, leaving the graybacks crouched in a useless ambush far behind, or they might turn abruptly southwest and make for Jackson, passing in rear of the butternut column hurrying eastward. So Forrest bided his time and awaited developments, keeping his four undersized brigades spread out to counter an advance from any one of several directions. Then on February 19, when Smith began his wrecking descent of the M&O, it was plain that he intended to follow the railroad all the way to Meridian, and Forrest was free to develop a specific plan to stop him. Which he did. Sending one brigade to West Point as a bait to lure the bluecoats on, he ordered the others to take up a position three miles below, in a swampy pocket enclosed on the west and south by Sakatonchee and Oktibbeha creeks and on the east by the Tombigbee. That was the trap. The bait brigade, commanded by Colonel Jeffrey Forrest, the general's twenty-six-year-old brother, fell back next day as ordered, skirmishing lightly to draw the Federals through West Point and into the pocket prepared for their destruction. They followed cautiously, into and just beyond the town; but there they stopped, apparently for the night. Believing that they would come on again next morning, February 21, Forrest continued his preparations to receive them with a double envelopment.

He was wrong. Although there was an advance, which brought on a brief engagement, it soon became evident that this was a mere feint — a rear-guard action, designed to cover a withdrawal. Nearly two thirds of the way to his objective, Smith had given up trying to reach it; had decided, instead, to backtrack. Ahead were swamps and an enemy force reported to be larger than his own, while he was already ten full days behind schedule, still with eighty-odd miles to go and some 3000 homeless Negroes on his hands. "Under the circumstances," he afterwards declared, "I determined not to move my encumbered command into the trap set for me by the rebels."

Forrest, having gained what he called the "bulge," reacted fast. If the Yankees would not come to him, then he would go to them. And

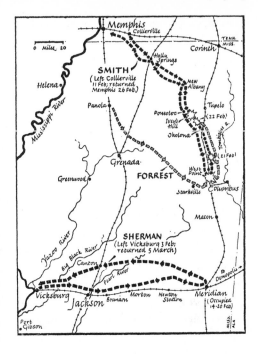

this he did, with a vengeance. Being, as he said later, "unwilling they should leave the country without a fight," he ordered his entire command to take up the pursuit of the retreating bluecoats. Moreover, the rearguard skirmish had no sooner begun than he attended to another matter of grave concern: namely, the behavior of his "raw, undrilled, and undisciplined" troopers in their reaction to being shot at, many of them for the first time. As he approached the firing line he met a panic-stricken Confederate stumbling rearward, hatless and gunless, in full flight from his first taste of combat. Forrest dismounted to intercept him, flung him face-down by the roadside, then took up a piece of brush and administered what a startled witness described as "one of the worst thrashings I have ever seen a human being get." This done, he jerked the unfortunate soldier to his feet, faced him about, and gave him a shove that sent him stumbling in the direction of the uproar he had fled from. "Now, God damn you, go back to the front and fight!" he shouted after him. "You might as well be killed there as here, for if you ever run away again you'll not get off so easy." Still raw and undrilled, but by no means undisciplined, the man rejoined his comrades on the firing line, and the story quickly spread, not only through the division — as the general no doubt intended — but also through both armies, until finally it was made the subject of a *Harper's Weekly* illustration titled "Forrest Breaking in a Conscript."

For the next two days he handled Smith in much the same fashion. After driving the rear-guard Federals through West Point, he came upon them again, three miles beyond the town, stoutly posted along a timbered ridge approachable only by a narrow causeway. His solution was to send one regiment galloping wide around the enemy flank, with orders to strike the rear, while the others dismounted to attack in front. Admittedly, this was a lot to ask of green troops, but Forrest employed a method of persuasion quite different from the one he had used a while ago on the panicked conscript. "Come on, boys!" he roared, and led the way, thus setting an example which caused one of his men to recall, years later, that "his immediate presence seemed to inspire everyone with his terrible energy, more like that of a piece of powerful steam machinery than of a human being." So led, they drove the bluecoats from the ridge, then remounted and continued the pursuit until nightfall, when their commander called a halt, midway between West Point and Okolona, in a hastily abandoned bivouac area, stocked not only with rations and forage, but also with wood for the still-burning campfires. While the graybacks bedded down and slept beside the cozy warmth provided by their foes, Smith kept his main body plodding northward and did not stop until well past midnight, within four miles of Okolona. Burdened with captured stock and runaway slaves, and weary as they were from their long march — since sunup, they had covered better than twice the distance they had managed on any one of the other nine days since they left Collierville — his men got a late start next morning. By that time Forrest, who had had his troopers up and on the go by dawn, well rested and unencumbered, had closed the ten-mile gap and was snapping again at the tail and flanks of the blue column.

Smith was learning, as Streight had learned before him, that it could be even more dangerous to run from the Tennessean than it was to stand and fight him. However, instead of turning on him with all he had, he dropped off a couple of regiments just beyond Okolona and a full brigade at Ivey's Hill, five miles farther along on the road to Pontotoc, still intent on saving his train and protecting the Negroes in his charge. After a running fight through the town, hard on the heels of the rear guard, the gray pursuers came upon the first of these two prepared positions and were brought to a halt by fire from the superior Federal weapons. At this point Forrest arrived. "Where is the enemy's whole position?" he asked Colonel Tyree Bell, whose brigade had the lead this morning. "You see it, General," Bell replied, and added: "They are preparing to charge." "Then we will charge them," Forrest said: and did. The result was a blue rout. Five guns were abandoned shortly thereafter by an artillery lieutenant who complained hotly in his report that his battery had been forced off the road and into a ditch by Union troopers who overtook him "in perfect confusion," hallooing: "Go ahead, or we'll be killed!" The chase continued to Ivey's Hill, where the defenders, allowed more time to get set, gave a considerably better account of themselves. Opening ranks to let the fugitives through, they took under well-aimed fire the two brigades advancing toward them across the prairie. At the first volley the commanders of both were shot, one in the hand, the other through the throat. The second of these was Jeffrey Forrest, and though the general reached him immediately after he fell — this youngest of his five brothers, posthumously born and sixteen years his junior, whom he had raised as a son and made into a soldier — he found him dead. He remained bent over him for a minute or two, then rose and ordered his bugler to sound the charge. The fighting that followed was savage and hand-to-hand. Within the next hour, Forrest had two horses killed under him and accounted in person for three enemy soldiers, shot or sabered.

Thus assailed, the Federals once more fell back to try another stand in a position ten miles from Pontotoc; which was also lost, along with another gun, but which at any rate ended the relentless chase that had begun two days ago, nearly fifty miles away, below West Point. "Owing to the broken down and exhausted condition of men and horses, and being almost out of ammunition," Forrest presently reported, "I was compelled to stop pursuit." Smith was unaware of this, however, and kept going even harder than before. Judging the rebel strength by Forrest's aggressiveness, he believed that Stephen Lee had arrived to join the chase, though in point of fact he now had nothing on his trial but the "rabble of state troops" he had brushed aside when he passed this way the week before, headed in the opposite direction. In Pontotoc by midnight, he resumed the march at 3 a.m. and cleared New Albany that afternoon, February 23, destroying in his rear the bridges across the Tallahatchie. All next day he kept moving, unwilling to risk another stand, and rode at last into Collierville on the 25th, having covered in five days the same distance he had required ten days to cover while going south. Not even then did he call a halt, however; he kept going all the following day, through Germantown to Memphis, there ending at last what one brigade commander described as "a weary, disheartened, almost panic-stricken flight, in the greatest disorder and confusion."

His loss in men had not been great (it amounted to 388 in all, including 155 missing, as compared to a total of 144 for his opponent — a disparity which Forrest, as the attacker, could only account for by "the fact that we kept so close to them that the enemy overshot our men") but the cost in horseflesh had been cruel. Smith returned with no more than 2200 riders who could be described as adequately mounted; the other 4800 were either on foot or astride horses no longer fit for service in the field. A corresponding loss in cavalry morale, so lately on the rise in all the Union armies, was indicated by an unhappy colonel's remark that "the expedition filled every man connected with it with a burning shame." Nor was that by any means the worst of it from the northern point of view. The worst was still to come, resulting not so much from Federal losses as from Confederate gains. Practically overnight, by this victory over twice their number — and the capture, in the process, of six guns and several stands of colors — Forrest's green recruits had acquired a considerable measure of that fierce pride which in time would enable their commander to prevail against even longer odds and for much larger stakes. Already he was preparing to go over to the offensive, beginning with a return to West Tennessee and the accomplishment there of a great deal more than the mere enlargement of his now veteran division.

Though Sherman had been doubtful of Smith's competence from the start, deeming him "too mistrustful of himself for a leader against Forrest," this took none of the sting from his censure of his fellow Ohioan for "allowing General Forrest to head him off and defeat him with an inferior force." But that was later, after he learned the gloomy particulars of the cavalry excursion, and in any case he had waited for Smith no longer than it took him to wipe the appointed meeting place off the map. By the time the frazzled horsemen returned to Memphis, Sherman had recrossed the Pearl and gone into bivouac at Canton, north of Jackson, still with no knowledge of what, if anything, had happened to the mounted column, which in fact had begun its retreat from West Point on the day he ended his five-day stay in Meridian and abandoned his proposed advance on Selma.

Not that he considered his own part in the campaign anything less than "successful in the highest degree," both on the outward march and the return, which he made along a different route, twenty-odd miles to the north, so as to avoid the grainless, cowless, hogless trail his twelve brigades of infantry had blazed while slogging eastward. "My movement to Meridian stampeded all Alabama," he informed Halleck three days later, on February 29. "Polk retreated across the Tombigbee and left me to smash things at pleasure, and I think it is well done. . . . We broke absolutely and effectually a full hundred miles of railroad . . . and made a swath of desolation fifty miles broad across the State of Mississippi which the present generation will not forget." After listing his spoils, which included "some 500 prisoners, a good many refugee families, and about ten miles of negroes," he announced that the destruction he had wrought "makes it simply impossible for the enemy to risk anything but light cavalry this side of Pearl River; consequently, I can reduce the garrisons of Memphis, Vicksburg, and Natchez to mere guards, and, in fact, it will set free 15,000 men for other duty. I could have gone on to Mobile or over to Selma," he added, "but without other concurrent operations it would have been unwise." Privately, however, in a companion letter to his wife, he confessed his regret that Smith's nonarrival had prevented him from applying what his foes were calling "the Sherman torch" to Alabama. "As it was," he chuckled, for he always enjoyed a small joke on the clergy, "I scared the bishop out of his senses."

It was Polk he meant, of course, and he was right; the bishop had indeed been frightened, not only for Meridian, Demopolis, and Selma, but also for Mobile, a greater prize than any of those others in his care. His fears for the Confederacy's only remaining Gulf port east of the Mississippi had been enlarged in late January when Farragut — who had just returned from a New York holiday, taken while the *Hartford* was being refitted in the Brooklyn Navy Yard — appeared before the place with a squadron of multigunned warships, evidently intending to launch another of his all-out attacks, not one of which had ever failed with him on hand to see that it was pressed to the required extremity. In point of fact, the admiral was only there to heighten Polk's fears for the loss of the port and to discourage him from drawing reinforcements from its garrison when Sherman began his march. There was no need to attack; he accomplished his purpose merely by his month-long presence, just outside the bay, and gained in the process much valuable information which he would put to substantial use when he came back again, not for a feint or diversion, but in earnest. As a result, when Sherman set out from Vicksburg in early February, Polk was convinced that his goal was Mobile and that what was intended was a combined assault, by land and water, designed to remove that vital port from the list of the South's assets in continuing its struggle to maintain its national existence. Outnumbered two to one, or worse, the bishop called loudly on Richmond for assistance, and Richmond passed his appeal to Johnston, the only possible source for reinforcements in a hurry. Whereupon there was staged in North Georgia a grim comedy involving a balking contest between the two commanders, blue and gray.

Johnson protested for all he was worth. In the first place, he did not believe the proposed reinforcements could reach Polk in time to head off Sherman; and what was more he was convinced that any substantial reduction of his already outnumbered force, which was being required to maintain a position that had "neither intrinsic strength nor strategic advantage," would not only expose Atlanta to capture by the blue mass in his front, but would also be likely to result in the destruction of what would remain of the army charged with its defense. This chilling presentation to the government of a choice between losing one or the other of two of its principal cities had the effect of delaying, though not of forestalling, a peremptory order requiring the immediate detachment of Hardee's corps to Polk for the purpose of covering Mobile. Received on February 16, the order began to be carried out four days later — by coincidence, on the day Sherman began his return march from Meridian — when the three divisions boarded the cars at Dalton for the long ride to Demopolis. Arriving next day they found they were unneeded; Sherman had withdrawn. Polk put them promptly back aboard the cars to rejoin Johnston, who by now was sending up distress signals of his own. His worst fears had been realized; Thomas was advancing. The Union-loyal Virginian had also received peremptory orders, and he too had delayed their execution. Instructed on February 14 to make a "formidable reconnaissance" of

Johnston's position, he took a week to get ready, then started forward from Ringgold on the eighth day, February 22, two days after Hardee departed with the divisions under Cheatham, Walker, and Cleburne. Grant's hope was that Thomas would catch his adversary off balance and thus be able to drive him back from Rocky Face Ridge and beyond Dalton, in order to "get possession of the place and hold it as a step toward a spring campaign."

With three of his seven divisions 350 roundabout miles away, Johnston was something worse than merely off balance when Thomas moved against him. Palmer's corps made the opening thrust at Tunnel Hill. Formerly occupied by Cleburne, this western spur of Rocky Face Ridge was now held only by Wheeler, whose horse artillery raised such a clatter that the bluecoats were discouraged from attacking until the following day, February 24. By then the rebel troopers had fallen back through Buzzard Roost Gap to cover the flanks of the infantry disposed along the ridge. Thomas probed the passes on the 25th, making some progress against the wide-spread defenders — especially at Dug Gap, immediately southwest of Dalton — but when Palmer launched a coordinated assault next morning he found that Hardee's three divisions, having completed their round-trip journey to Demopolis, were in position on the ridge; Cleburne, in fact, was on the flank of the flankers. Accordingly, Thomas withdrew as he had come, returning to Ringgold on the same day Sooy Smith rode back into Memphis and Sherman descended on Canton. His "formidable reconnaissance" had cost him 345 casualties and had failed in its larger purpose of seizing Dalton "as a step toward a spring campaign"; but he, like Farragut outside Mobile, had learned much that would be useful when he returned in earnest. As for Johnston, he was agreeably surprised. He had expected to be thrown into precipitate retreat; whereas his men had not only maintained the integrity of a position which he declared had "little to recommend it," but had inflicted better than twice the 167 casualties they suffered. Even more heartening than the bare tactical result was the contrast between the army's present frame of mind, here on Rocky Face Ridge, and the one that had been evidenced a dozen weeks ago on Missionary Ridge. Unquestionably its spirit had been lifted: perhaps indeed a bit too much, at least in one respect, to suit Old Joe. For in congratulating his troops on their work, he was critical of the artillery officers for having "exhibited a childish eagerness to discharge their pieces."

By now the Confederates had returned to Meridian, or at any rate to the desolation Sherman had created in its place. Speaking in Jackson on his first western visit, just over a year ago, Jefferson Davis had warned that the invaders had it in mind to handle Mississippi "without gloves," and now his words had been borne out; Meridian was an example of what the men he referred to as "worse than vandal hordes" could accomplish when their commander turned them loose with the admonition that "vigorous war . . . means universal destruction." In addition to the damage inflicted on the town itself, a total of twenty-four miles of railroad track, extending an average half dozen miles in all four directions, had been demolished, the crossties burned, the rails heated and twisted into what were known as "Sherman neckties." Beyond this circumference of utter destruction, for a distance of nearly fifty miles north and south, not a bridge or a trestle had been left unwrecked on the Mobile & Ohio. Already, in the course of their march from Jackson, the raiders had disposed of fifty-one bridges on the Southern, together with an even larger number of trestles and culverts, and they had extended their work eastward, nine miles beyond the junction, to add three more bridges and five trestles to the tally. Yet, sad as it was to survey the charred remains of what once had passed for prosperity in this nonindustrial region, sadder by far were the people of those counties through which the blue column had slogged on its way to and from the town that now was little more than a scar on the green breast of earth. They had the stunned, unbelieving look of survivors of some terrible natural disaster, such as a five-day hurricane, a tidal wave, or an earthquake: with the underlying difference that their grief had been inflicted by human design and was in fact a deliberate product of a new kind of war, quite unlike the one for which they had bargained three years ago, back in that first glad springtime of secession. It was, moreover, a war that was still in progress, and somehow that was the strangest, most distressful aspect of all. Their deprivation was incidental to the large design. They were faced with the aftermath before the finish.

Polk took no such gloomy view of the prospect. Though he could scarcely deny the all-too-evident validity of Sherman's boast of having "made a swath of desolation fifty miles broad across the State of Mississippi which the present generation will not forget," he did not agree with his adversary's further assertion that the east-central portion of the state could be written off as a factor in the conflict. "I have already taken measures to have all the roads broken up by him rebuilt," the bishop notified Richmond two days after the raiders turned back in the direction they had come from, "and shall press that work vigorously." Press it he did. Summoning to his Demopolis headquarters President Samuel Tate of the Memphis & Charleston Railroad, he put him in general charge of the restoration, with full authority to requisition both property and labor. Tate was a driver. Despite a crippling shortage of rails and spikes — not to mention the inevitable objections of planters to the impressment of such of their Negroes as had not gone off with Smith and Sherman — within twenty-six days he had the Mobile & Ohio back in operation, from Tupelo south to Mobile Bay, along with the Alabama & Mississippi, from Meridian to the Tombigbee. The Southern took longer, mainly because of administrative complications, but within another five weeks it too was open, all the way to the Pearl.

But that was later. At the time he made it, February 28, Sherman's pronouncement: "My movement cleared Mississippi at one swoop, and with the railroad thus destroyed the Confederacy cannot maintain an army save cavalry west of Tombigbee," seemed to him irrefutable. He was back in Vicksburg by then, having come on ahead of the infantry, which he left marking time in Canton, as he said afterwards, "with orders to remain till about the 3d of March" — he was still hoping Sooy Smith would turn up — "and then come into Vicksburg leisurely." Pleased by the added destruction of several miles of the Mississippi Central, north of Jackson — together with 19 locomotives, 28 cars, and 724 carwheels, which helped to ease his disappointment that Polk had managed to save the rolling stock on the other roads within his reach — he proudly announced: "Everything with my command was successful in the highest degree." That this was hardly an overstatement was evidenced by the anguished protests of his opponents and victims, soldiers and civilians, some of whom reported the damage at a larger figure than his own. Stephen Lee, for one, charged the raiders with "burning 10,000 bales of cotton and 2,000,000 bushels of corn and carrying off 8000 slaves, many mounted on stolen mules." He estimated the over-all loss at five million dollars, of which "three fourths was private property," and asked rhetorically: "Was this the warfare of the nineteenth century?" Sherman was not inclined to dispute the statistics, and he had already given his answer to Lee's question. This was indeed the warfare of the nineteenth century, at any rate as he intended to practice it, and he was not only proud of what had been accomplished by this first large-scale application of the methods that had aroused the South Carolinian's moral indignation; he was also looking forward to the time when he could apply those methods elsewhere, perhaps even in the angry young cavalryman's native state, where the provocation had begun.

First though would come Georgia; Mississippi had been something of a warm-up, a practice operation in this regard, just as perhaps Georgia in turn would be a warm-up for the Carolinas. In any case Sherman had composed at Vicksburg, by way of further preparation while waiting to set out across Mississippi, a letter to the assistant adjutant general of his army, most of whose members were in camps around Chattanooga waiting for him to return from his current excursion and lead them against Joe Johnston and Atlanta. Ostensibly addressed to Major R. M. Sawyer, the letter was in fact a warning to the civilians in his southward path, as well as a legalistic justification for military harshness, since it dealt primarily with his intention regarding "the treatment of inhabitants known or suspected to be hostile or 'secesh.' " His policy up to now, he said, had been to leave the question to local commanders of occupation forces, "but [I] am willing to give them the benefit of my acquired knowledge and experience," and though he admitted that it was "almost impossible to lay down rules" for their guidance in such matters, he proceeded to do precisely that, and more.

"In Europe, whence we derive our principles of war, as developed by their histories," he began, "wars are between kings or rulers, through hired armies, and not between peoples. These remain as it were neutral, and sell their produce to whatever army is in possession. . . . Therefore the rule was, and is, that wars are confined to the armies and should not visit the homes of families or private interests." Little or none of this applied in the present instance, however, any more than it had done in the case of the Irish insurrection against William and Mary, who dispossessed the rebels of their property, sent them forthwith into exile, and gave their lands to Scottish emigrants. The same could be done with justice here, Sherman declared, but he preferred to withhold such measures for a time, on grounds that the guilt was not entirely restricted to the guilty. "For my part," he explained, "I believe this war is the result of false political doctrine, for which we all as a people are responsible . . . and I would give all a chance to reflect and when in error to recant. . . . I am willing to bear in patience that political nonsense of slave rights, States rights, freedom of conscience, freedom of the press, and such other trash as have deluded the Southern people into war, anarchy, bloodshed, and the foulest crimes that have disgraced any time or any people." He would bear all this in patience, but only for a season; meanwhile he would have the occupation commanders "assemble the inhabitants and explain to them these plain, self-evident propositions, and tell them that it is now for them to say whether they and their children shall inherit the beautiful land which by the accident of nature had fallen to their share." After this, if they persisted in the error of their ways, would come the thunder. "If they want eternal war, well and good; we accept the issue, and will dispossess them and put our friends in their places." Moreover, the longer they delayed recanting, the sterner their fate would be. "Three years ago, by a little reflection and patience, they could have had a hundred years of peace and prosperity, but they preferred war; very well. Last year they could have saved their slaves, but now it is too late. All the powers of earth cannot return to them their slaves, any more than their dead grandfathers. Next year their lands will be taken; for in war we can take them, and rightfully, too, and in another year they may beg in vain for their lives." He warmed as he wrote, assuming the guise of an avenging angel — even the Archangel Michael — to touch on eschatology in the end. "To those who submit to the rightful law and authority, all gentleness and forbearance; but to the petulant and persistent secessionists, why, death is mercy, and the quicker he or she is disposed of the better. Satan and the rebellious saints of Heaven were allowed a continuous existence in hell merely to swell their just punishment. To such as would rebel against a Government so mild and just as ours was in peace, a punishment equal would not be unjust."

A copy went to his senator brother, with the request that it be printed for all to read, along and behind the opposing lines of battle. "It's publication would do no harm," he said, "except to turn the Richmond press against me as the prince of barbarians." Actually he was of the opinion that it would do much good, especially Southward, and he urged his adjutant to see that his views were presented to "some of the better people" of the region already occupied, with the suggestion that they pass them along to friends in whose direction he would be moving in the spring. "Read to them this letter," he wrote, "and let them use it so as to prepare them for my coming."

✗ 4 ✗

Sherman's notion of how the war could be won was definite enough, but whether it would be fought that way — with stepped-up harshness, to and through the finish — depended in no small measure on who would be directing it from the top. This was a presidential election year; the armies might have a new Commander in Chief before the advent of the victory which not even the ebullient Ohioan, in his days of highest feather, predicted would occur within the twelve-month span that lay between his return from Meridian, having demonstrated the effectiveness of his method, and the inauguration of the winner of the November contest at the polls. Moreover, the Republican convention was barely three months off, and though Lincoln had expressed a cautious willingness to stand for re-election — "A second term would be a great honor and a great labor," he had told Elihu Washburne in October, "which together, perhaps, I would not decline if tendered" — whether he would be renominated appeared doubtful. For one thing, recent tradition was against it; none of the other eight Presidents since Andrew Jackson had served beyond a single term. Besides, whatever his popularity with the people, the men who controlled the convention seemed practically unanimous in their conviction that a better candidate could be found. "Not a Senator can be named as favorable to Lincoln's renomination," the Detroit *Free Press* had reported, and the claim went uncontradicted. Nor was this opinion limited to his enemies. David Davis, who had managed his 1860 nomination, and who had been duly rewarded with a seat on the Supreme Court, declared in private: "The politicians in and out of Congress, it is believed, would put Mr Lincoln aside if they dared." Lyman Trumbull, an associate from early days and now a power in the Senate, believed however that it was not so much a question of daring as of tactics. Writing to a constituent back in Illinois, he presented the reasons behind this opposition and suggested that those who held them were merely biding their time between now and early June, when the delegates would convene in Baltimore. "The feeling for Mr Lincoln's re-election *seems* to be very general," he said, "but much of it I discover is only on the surface. You would be surprised, in talking with public men we meet here, to find how few, when you come to get at their real sentiment, are for Mr Lincoln's re-election. There is a distrust and fear that he is too undecided and inefficient to put down the rebellion. You need not be surprised if a reaction sets in before the nomination, in favor of some man supposed to possess more energy and less inclination to trust our brave boys in the hands and under the leadership of generals who have no heart in the war. The opposition to Mr L. may not show itself at all, but if it ever breaks out there will be more of it than now appears."

It broke out sooner than expected, though not from an unpredictable direction, the source of the explosion being Salmon Chase, or at any rate the men around or behind him, who saw in the adverse reaction to the overlenient Amnesty Proclamation an opportunity too fruitful to be neglected. Chase had been sobered by the Cabinet crisis of mid-December, fourteen months ago, but renewed ambition apparently caused him to forget his extreme discomfort at that time. In any case, in an attempt to influence various state conventions soon to be in session, a group of the Secretary's friends banded together and sent out in early February a "strictly private" letter afterwards known as the Pomeroy Circular. So called because it was issued over the signature of the group chairman, Senator Samuel C. Pomeroy of Kansas, a prominent Jacobin and old-line abolitionist, the document charged that "party machinery and official influence are being used to secure the perpetuation of the present Administration," asserted that "those who believe in the interests of the country and of freedom demand a change in favor of vigor and purity," and then went on to present five main points all delegates would do well to bear in mind. The first two were against Lincoln, whose re-election was not only "practically impossible" but also undesirable, since under him "the war may continue to languish" and "the cause of human liberty, and the dignity of the nation, suffer proportionately." The third point found "the 'one-term principle' absolutely essential to the certain safety of our republican institutions." The final two were devoted to Chase, who not only had "more of the qualities needed in a President during the next four years than are combined in any other candidate," but had developed, as well, "a popularity and strength ... unexpected even to his warmest admirers." Finally, each recipient was urged to "render efficient aid by exerting yourself at once to organize your section of the country" and to enter into correspondence with the undersigned chairman "for the purpose either of receiving or imparting information."

Lincoln was told of the "strictly private" circular as soon as it appeared. On February 6, Ward Lamon wrote from New York that a prominent banker there had received in his mail that morning, under the frank of an Ohio congressman, "a most scurrilous and abominable pamphlet about you, your administration, and the succession." Copies arrived from other friends on the lookout, but got no farther than Nicolay's desk; Lincoln would not read them. "I have determined to shut my eyes, so far as possible, to everything of that sort," he explained. "Mr Chase makes a good Secretary, and I shall keep him where he is. If he becomes President, all right. I hope we shall never have a worse man." He knew, of course, of the Ohioan's machinations, which were strengthened by the dispensation of some ten thousand jobs in his department, and he said of his activities as an inside critic, "I suppose he will, like the bluebottle fly, lay his eggs in every rotten spot he can find." But to some who advised that the "perfidious ingrate" be fired he replied: "I am entirely indifferent to his success or failure in these schemes, so long as he does his duty at the head of the Treasury Department." To others he maintained that "the Presidential grub" had much the same effect on the Secretary as a horsefly had on a balky plow horse; he got more work out of him when he was bit. Or perhaps it was even simpler than that. Perhaps Lincoln enjoyed watching the performance Chase gave. It was, after all, pretty much a repeat performance, and he already knew the outcome, agreeing beforehand with Welles, who predicted in his diary that the Pomeroy Circular would be "more dangerous in its recoil than its projectile." His adversaries had bided their time; now he was biding his. A Massachusetts congressman, returning from a visit to the White House at the height of this latest Chase-for-President boom, informed a colleague that Lincoln was only waiting for the Treasury chief to put himself a little more clearly in the wrong. "He thinks that Mr C. will sufficiently soon force the question. In the meantime I think he is wise in waiting till the pear is ripe."

The pear ripened over the weekend of Washington's Birthday. On Saturday, February 20, the *Constitutional Union* printed in full the text of the circular, and when it was picked up on Monday by the *National Intelligencer*, Chase could no longer pretend to be unaware of what his friends were doing in his behalf. Writing to Lincoln that same day, he declared however that he had "had no knowledge of the existence of this letter before I saw it in the *Union*." Some weeks ago, he went on, "several gentlemen" had called on him "in connection with the approaching election of Chief Magistrate," and though he had not felt that he could forbid them to work as they chose, he had "told them distinctly that I could render them no help, except what might come incidentally from the faithful discharge of public duties, for these must have my whole time"; otherwise, he knew nothing of what had been done by these gentlemen. "I have thought this explanation due to you as well as to myself," he told Lincoln. "If there is anything in my action or position which in your judgment will prejudice the public interest in my charge, I beg you to say so. I do not wish to administer the Treasury Department one day without your entire confidence. For yourself," he continued, appending a sort of amiable tailpiece to his tentative resignation, "I cherish sincere respect and esteem; and, permit me to add, affection. Differences of opinion as to administrative action have not changed these sentiments; nor have they been changed by assaults upon me by persons who profess to spread representations of your views and policy. You are not responsible for acts not your own; nor will you hold me responsible except for what I do or say myself. Great numbers now desire your re-election. Should their wishes be fulfilled by the suffrages of the people, I hope to carry with me into private life the sentiments I now cherish, whole and unimpaired."

He received next day a one-sentence reply, as inconclusive as it was brief. "Yours of yesterday in relation to the paper issued by Senator Pomeroy was duly received; and I write this note merely to say I will answer a little more fully when I can find the leisure to do so. Yours truly, A. Lincoln."

Chase out would be considerably more formidable than Chase in; Lincoln had no intention of accepting a resignation which, by splitting the party, might well lose the Republicans the election, whoever the candidate was. He did wait six full days, however, before he found "the leisure" to compose his promised answer. This may have been done primarily to allow the Ohioan plenty of time to squirm, but it also afforded others a chance to contribute to the squirmer's discomfort by heating up the griddle. When Chase spoke of "assaults upon me by persons who profess to spread representations of your views," it was the Blairs he meant: specifically, Montgomery and Frank. Back in the fall, as principal speaker at a Maryland rally, the Postmaster General had referred to the Jacobins as "co-adjutors of Presidential schemers," making it clear that he had the Treasury head in mind as the chief schemer, and since then he had been castigating his fellow Cabinet member at practically every opportunity. Even so, he was not as harsh in this regard as his brother Frank, the soldier member of the family of whom it was said, "When the Blairs go in for a fight they go in for a funeral." Soon after his corps went into winter quarters near Chattanooga, Frank Blair came to Washington as a Missouri congressman. This had required the surrender of his commission as a major general, but Lincoln had promised to take care of that. He wanted Blair to stand for Speaker of the House, a post at which so stout a fighter could be of even more use to the Administration than on the field of battle, and he agreed that if this did not work out he would restore the commission and Blair could return to his duties as a corps commander under Sherman. But the plan fell through. By the time the Missourian reached the capital in early January, Indiana's Schuyler Colfax, strongly anti-Lincoln in persuasion, had been elected Speaker. Nevertheless, since his corps was still lying idle down in Tennessee, Blair took his seat and stayed on in Washington, alert for a chance to strike at the President's enemies and his own. A chance was not long in coming. On February 5, the day the Pomeroy Circular began to go out across the land, Blair rose in the House to speak in defense of the Administration's policies on amnesty and reconstruction, opposition to which he declared had been "concocted for purposes of defeating the renomination of Mr Lincoln" in order to open the way for "rival aspirants." Everyone knew it was Chase he meant, and three weeks later, on February 27 — four days into the six allowed for squirming — he made the charge specific, along with several others. Referring to the circular, he said of the candidate favored therein: "It is a matter of surprise that a man having the instincts of a gentleman should remain in the Cabinet after the disclosure of such an intrigue against the one to whom he owes his position. [However] I suppose the President is well content that he should stay; for every hour that he remains sinks him in the contempt of every honorable mind." Beyond this, Blair asserted that "a more profligate administration of the Treasury Department never existed under any government," and that investigation would show that "the whole Mississippi Valley is rank and fetid with the frauds and corruptions of its agents . . . some of [whom] I suppose employ themselves in distributing that 'strictly private' circular which came to light the other day."

Such charges hurt badly. Damage to Chase's reputation was damage to his soul, and though he thought of himself as a scrupulous administrator of the nation's funds, he knew quite well that for political reasons he had made agents of men who could by no means be said to measure up to his own high standards. In any case — perhaps out of pity, for the punishment was heavy — Lincoln ended at least a part of the Secretary's torment, two days later, by declining his resignation. "On consideration," he declared, "I find there is really very little to say. My knowledge of Mr. Pomeroy's letter having been made *public* came to me only the day you wrote; but I had, in spite of myself, known of its *existence* several days before. I have not yet read it, and I think I shall not. I was not shocked or surprised by the appearance of the letter, because I had had knowledge of Mr. Pomeroy's committee, and of secret issues which I supposed came from it, and of secret agents who I supposed were sent out by it, for several weeks." He was saying here that if he could know so much of what was going on behind his back, Chase must have known about it too, despite his fervent denial. However that might be, Lincoln continued, "I have known just as little of these doings as my friends have allowed me to know . . . and I assure you, as you have assured me, that no assault has been made upon you by my instigation or with my countenance." Then came the close, the answer he had promised: "Whether you shall remain at the head of the Treasury Department is a question which I will not allow myself to consider from any stand-point other than my judgment of the public service, and, in that view, I do not perceive occasion for a change."

Chase was both relieved and pained: relieved to learn that he would remain at his post, which the long wait had taught him to value anew by persuading him that he was about to lose it, and pained because, as he plaintively observed, "there was no response in [the President's] letter to the sentiments of respect and esteem which mine contained." All this was rather beside the original point, however. Welles's prediction as to the "recoil" of the Pomeroy maneuver had already been borne out, its principal effect having been to rally Lincoln's friends to his support. And of these, as events had shown, there were many. By the time of his belated reply to Chase on Leap Year Day, no less than fourteen states, either by formal action of their legislatures or by delegates in convention, had gone on record in favor of a second term for the man in office. Among them were New Hampshire, where the Secretary had been born, Rhode Island, where his new son-in-law was supposedly in political control, and finally — unkindest cut — Ohio. In fact, Chase was advised by men from his home state to disentangle himself from the embarrassment into which his ambition had led him, and this he did in a letter to a Buckeye supporter, requesting that "no further consideration be given my name." He also made it clear, however, that he was only asking this from a sense of duty to the cause, which must not be endangered, even though he was still convinced that "as President I could take care of the Treasury better with the help of a Secretary than I can as Secretary without the help of a President. But our Ohio folks don't want me enough." There was the rub; there was what had given him his quietus. "I no longer have any political side," he presently was saying, "save that of my country, and there are multitudes who like me care little for men but everything for measures."

The upshot of this pose of "honorable disinterestedness," as one of the newspapers reprinting the letter called it, was a general impression that he was merely awaiting a more favorable chance to get back in the running. A member of the Pomeroy group referred to the withdrawal as "a word of declination diplomatically spoken to rouse [our] flagging spirits," and David Davis likened its author to Mr Micawber waiting for something to "turn up." Chase had dreamed too long and too grandly for those who knew him to believe that he had stopped, even though it had been demonstrated conclusively, twice over, that his dreams would not come true. "Mr Chase will subside as a presidential candidate after the nomination is made, not before," the chairman of the Republican National Committee remarked, while the New York *Herald* ventured a comparison out of nature: "The Salmon is a queer fish, very wary, often appearing to avoid the bait just before gulping it down."

· · ·

Whether Chase continued to dream and scheme made little difference now, though; Lincoln — with the Ohioan's unintentional assistance — had the nomination cinched. The election, however, was quite another matter. Despite the encouragement Republicans could draw from their successes at the polls in the past season, the outcome of the contest in November would depend even more on military than on political events of the next eight months, through spring and summer and into fall. For one thing, the fighting would be expensive both in money and blood, and the voters, as the ones who would do the paying and the bleeding, were unlikely to be satisfied with anything less than continuous victory at such prices. The past year had been highly satisfactory in this regard; Vicksburg and Missionary Ridge, even Gettysburg and Helena, were accomplishments clearly worth their cost. But the new year had started no better than the old year had ended. Sherman's destruction of Meridian could scarcely be said to offset Meade's unhappy stalemate at Mine Run or Seymour's abrupt defeat at Olustee, let alone Kilpatrick's frustration outside Richmond or the drubbing Sooy Smith had suffered at Okolona or the unprofitable demonstration Thomas had attempted against Dalton. A good part of the trouble seemed to proceed from mismanagement at the top, and the critics were likely to hold the top man responsible: especially in light of the fact that he had had a direct hand in a good proportion of these failures, all of which had been undertaken with his permission and some of which had been launched against the judgment of those below him on the military ladder. Now a reckoning time was coming, when the voters would have their say.

Congress, too, would have to face the voters: enough of it, at any rate, for defeat to cost the party now in power its comfortable majority, the loss of which would involve the surrender of committee chairmanships, the say-so in how and by whom the conflict would be pressed, easy access to much the largest pork barrel the nation had ever known, and finally the seizure and distribution of such spoils as would remain, two or three years from now, when the South was brought to its knees and placed at the disposal of the winners of the election this November. With so much at stake, it was no wonder the congressmen were jumpy at the prospect. Moreover, their nervousness was intensified by a presidential order, dated February 1, providing for the draft, on March 10, of "five hundred thousand men to serve for three years or during the war." This call for "500,000 more" — made necessary by the heavy losses in battle this past year, as well as by the pending expiration of the enlistments of those volunteers who had come forward, two and three years ago, with all the fervor Sumter and McClellan had aroused — was graphic evidence of what the campaigns about to open were expected to cost in blood and money, and as such it presented the electorate with a yardstick by which to measure the height and depth of victories and defeats. The former, then, had better be substantial if they were to count for much at the polls, and by the same token the latter had better be minor, especially if they were anything like the recent setbacks, which were so obviously the result of miscalculations at the top and for which the voters could take their revenge by the way they marked their ballots. With this danger in mind, the lawmakers had returned to considering the previously rejected bill providing for a revival of the grade of lieutenant general, which in turn would provide for a man at the top who, by a combination of professional training and proven ability in the field, could operate within a shrinking margin for error that was already too narrow for the amateur who had been in unrestricted control these past three years.

Although Congress had no power to name the officer to whom the promotion would go in the event the bill went through, it was understood that Grant was the only candidate for the honor. Besides, Lincoln would do the naming, and by now the Illinois general was as much his favorite as anyone's. Far from being resentful of what another in his place — Jefferson Davis, for example — would have considered an encroachment by the legislative branch, he welcomed the relief the bill proposed to afford him from a portion of his duties as Commander in Chief. Above all, he was prepared to welcome Grant, who had applied at Donelson, Vicksburg, and Chattanooga the victory formula Lincoln had been seeking all these years. Others had sought it, too, of course, and like him they now believed they had found it in the western commander. So many of them had done so by now, in fact, that they had provoked the only doubts he had about the general's fitness for the post. Like his friend McClernand, Lincoln was thoroughly aware that this war would produce a military hero who eventually would take up residence in the White House, and Grant's appeal in this respect had already reached the stage at which he was being wooed by prominent members of both political parties. They knew a winner when they saw one, and so did Lincoln; and that was the trouble. Involved as he was at the time in disposing of Chase, he was not anxious to promote the interests of a more formidable rival, which was precisely what he would be doing if he brought Grant to Washington as general-in-chief.

Nor was that the only drawback. There might be another even more disqualifying. "When the Presidential grub once gets in a man, it hides well," Lincoln had said of himself, and he thought this might apply as well to Grant, whose generalship would scarcely be improved by the distractive gnawing of the grub. However, when he inquired in that direction about such political aspirations, he was told the general had said in January that he not only was not a candidate for any office, but that as a soldier he believed he had no right to discuss politics at all. Pressed further, he relented so far as to add that, once the war was over, he might indeed run for mayor of Galena — so that, if elected, he could have the sidewalk put in order between his house and the railroad station. Lincoln could appreciate the humor in this (though not the unconscious irony which others would perceive a few years later, when this view of the primary use of political office would be defined as "Grantism") but he was not entirely satisfied. For one thing, that had been several weeks ago, before the would-be kingmakers had begun to fawn on Grant in earnest. Adulation might have turned his head. So Lincoln called in a friend of Grant's and asked him point-blank if the general wanted to be President. The man not only denied this; he produced a letter in which Grant said flatly that he had no political interests whatever. No doubt the statement was similar to one he made about this time in a letter to another friend, in which he declared: "My only desire will be, as it has been, to whip out rebellion in the shortest way possible, and to retain as high a position in the army afterwards as the Administration then in power may think me suitable for." Clearly, if this had been honestly said, it had not been said by a man who nurtured political ambitions. Lincoln's doubts were allayed. If Congress opened the way by passing the bill, he would see that the promotion went to the general for whom it was obviously intended.

Relief in any form would be most welcome, for the strain of frustration these past three years had brought him all too often to the verge of exhaustion and absolute despair. There was, after all, a limit to how many Fredericksburgs and Chancellorsvilles, how many Gettysburgs and Chickamaugas, even how many Olustees and Okolonas a man could survive. Mostly, though, the strain resulted from the difficulty of measuring up to private standards which he defined for a visitor whose petition he turned down, saying: "I desire to so conduct the affairs of this Administration that if, at the end, when I come to lay down the reins of power, I have lost every other friend on earth, I shall at least have one friend left, and that friend shall be deep down inside of me." Public critics he could abide or ignore, even those who called him clod or tyrant, clown or monster — "What's the harm in letting him have his fling?" he remarked of one of the worst of these; "If he did not pitch into me, he would into some poor fellow he might hurt" — but the critic lodged in his own conscience was not so easily lived with or dismissed. Some men appeared to have little trouble muffling that self-critic: not Lincoln, who saw himself "chained here in this Mecca of office-seekers," like Prometheus to his rock, a victim of his own dark-souled nature. "You flaxen men with broad faces are born with cheer, and don't know a cloud from a star," he once told a caller who fit this description; "I am of another temperament." It sometimes seemed to him, moreover, that each recovery from gloom was made at the cost of future resiliency. "Nothing touches the tired spot," he had confessed the year before, and lately he had come back to this expression. Returning from a horseback ride that had seemed to lift his spirits, he was urged by a companion to find more time for rest and relaxation. "Rest?" he said. He shook his head, as if the word was unfamiliar. "I don't know. . . . I suppose it is good for the body. But the tired part is *inside,* out of reach."

If Grant was the man who could bring this inner weariness some measure of relief, Lincoln was not only willing to call him East to try his hand; he intended to wait no longer, before he did so, than the time required by Congress to pass the necessary legislation.

★ ★ ★

Opposing the Federal war of conquest (for, rebellion or revolution, that was what it would have to come to if the North was going to win) the Confederacy was fighting for survival. This had been, and would continue to be, Davis's principal advantage over his opponent in their respective capacities as leaders of their two nations: that he did not have to persuade his people of the reality of a threat which had been only too apparent ever since the first blue-clad soldier crossed the Potomac, whereas Lincoln was obliged to invoke a danger that was primarily theoretic. In the event that the Union broke in two, democracy might or might not "perish from the earth," but there could be no doubt at all — even before Sherman created, by way of a preview, his recent "swath of desolation" across Mississippi's midriff — about what would happen to the South if its bid for independence failed. However, this was only one face of a coin whose down side bore the inscription *States Rights.* Flip the coin and the advantage passed to Lincoln.

By suspending *habeas corpus,* or by ignoring at will such writs as the courts issued, the northern President kept his left hand free to deal as harshly as he pleased with those who sought to stir up trouble in his rear. It was otherwise with Davis. Denied this resource except in such drastic instances as the insurrection two years ago in East Tennessee, he had to meet this kind of trouble with that hand fettered. Often he had claimed this disadvantage as a virtue, referring by contrast to the North as a land where citizens were imprisoned "in utter defiance of all rights guaranteed by the institutions under which they live." Now though, with the approach of the fourth spring of the war, obstruction and defeatism had swollen to such proportions that conscription could scarcely be enforced or outright traitors prosecuted, so ready were hostile judges to issue writs that kept them beyond the reach of the authorities. Davis was obliged to request of Congress that it permit him to follow procedures he had scorned. "It has been our cherished hope," he declared in a special message on February 3, "that when the great struggle in which we are engaged was past we might exhibit to the world the proud spectacle of a people . . . achieving their liberty and independence, after the bloodiest war of modern times, without a single sacrifice of civil right to military necessity. But it can no longer be doubted that the zeal with which the people sprang to arms at the beginning of the contest has, in some parts of the Confederacy, been impaired by the long continuance and magnitude of the struggle. . . . Discontent, disaffection, and disloyalty are manifested among those who, through the sacrifices of others, have enjoyed quiet and safety at home. Public meetings have been held, in some of which a treasonable design is masked by a pretense of devotion to State sovereignty, and in others is openly avowed. . . . Secret leagues and associations are being formed. In certain localities, men of no mean position do not hesitate to avow their hostility to our cause and their advocacy of peace on the terms of submission." All this was painful to admit, even in secret session, but Davis foresaw still greater problems unless the trend was checked. "Disappointment and despondency will displace the buoyant fortitude which animates [our brave soldiers] now. Desertion, already a frightful evil, will become the order of the day." He knew how sacred to his hearers the writ was, and he assured them that he would not abuse the license he was asking them to grant him. "Loyal citizens will not feel the danger, and the disloyal must be made to fear it. The very existence of extraordinary powers often renders their exercise unnecessary." In any case, he asserted in conclusion, "to temporize with disloyalty in the midst of war is but to quicken it to the growth of treason. I therefore respectfully recommend that the privilege of the writ of *habeas corpus* be suspended."

After twelve days of acrimonious debate — highlighted by an impassioned protest from the Vice President, who sent word from Georgia that if Davis was given the power he sought, "constitutional liberty will go down, never to rise again on this continent" — Congress agreed, though with profound misgivings, to a six-month suspension of the writ. However, the fight did not end there by any means. Stephens and his cohorts merely fell back to prepared positions, ranged in depth along the borders of their several sovereign states, and there continued their resistance under the banner of States Rights. "Georgians, behold your chains!" an Athens newspaper exhorted in an editorial printed alongside the newly passed regulations, which were appropriately framed in mourning borders. "Freemen of a once proud and happy country, contemplate the last act which rivets your bonds and binds you hand and foot, at the mercy of an unlimited military authority." An Alabama editor demanded the names of those congressmen "who, in secret conclave, obsequiously laid the liberties of this country at the feet of the President," so that they could be defeated if they had the gall to stand for re-election. Henry Foote, having long since warned that he "would call upon the people to rise, sword in hand, to put down the domestic tyrant who thus sought to invade their rights," proceeded to do just that. Nor was this defiance limited to words. Under the leadership of such men, Mississippi and Georgia passed flaming resolutions against the act; Louisiana presently did so, too, and North Carolina soon had a law on its books nullifying the action of the central government. Not even these modifications, crippling as they were to the purpose for which the writ had been suspended, allayed the fears of some that the rights of the states were about to be lost in "consolidation." If such a catastrophe ever came to pass, a Virginian declared, "it would be a kind boon in an overruling Providence to sweep from the earth the soil, along with the people. Better to be a wilderness of waste, than a lasting monument of lost liberty."

A wilderness of waste was what was all too likely to result from this nonrecognition of the fact that the South's whole hope for independence was held up by the bayonets of her soldiers, who in turn required the support of a strong central government if they were to be properly employed — or even, for that matter, clothed and fed — in a years-long conflict so costly in blood and money, at the stage it now had reached, that its demands could only be met by the enactment and rigid enforcement of laws which did in fact, as those who opposed them charged, involve the surrender of basic "rights" hitherto reserved to the states and the individual. Yet this was the one sacrifice the "impossiblists," who valued their rights above their chance at national independence, could not make. "Away with the idea of getting independence first, and looking after liberty afterwards," Stephens had said. "Our liberties, once lost, may be lost forever." "Why, sir," a Georgia congressman exclaimed, "this is a war for the Constitution! It is a *constitutional* war." It was also, and first, a war for survival; but the ultraconservatives, including the fire-eaters who had done so much to bring it on, had been using the weapon of States Rights too long and with too much success, when they were members of the Union, to discard it now that they had seceded. They simply would rather die than drop that cudgel, even when there was no one to use it on but their own people and nothing to strike at except the solidarity that was their one hope for victory over an adversary whose reserves of men and wealth were practically limitless. It was in this inflexibility that the bill came due for having launched a conservative revolution, and apparently it was necessarily so, even though their anomalous devotion to an untimely creed amounted to an irresistible death-wish. But that was precisely their pride. They had inherited it and they would hand it down, inviolate, to the latest generation; or they would pray God "to sweep from the earth the soil, along with the people."

No more than a casual glance at the map sufficed to show the gravity of the military situation they would not relax their civil vigilance to face. Shaded, the Federal gains of the past two years resembled the broad shadow of a bird suspended in flight above the Mississippi Valley, its head hung over Missouri, its tail spread down past New Orleans, and its wings extended from Chesapeake Bay to Texas. What shape the pres-

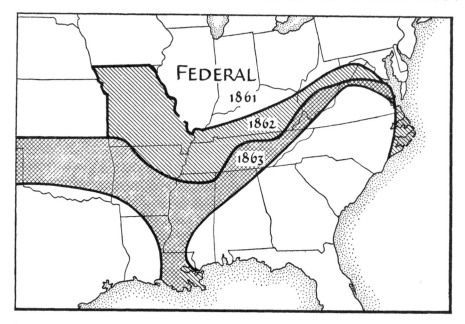

ent year would give this shadow was far from clear to those who lived in its penumbra, but they saw clearly enough that the creature who cast it could not be driven back into the land from which it had emerged; at any rate, not to stay there. R. E. Lee, after two expensive attempts to do just that, admitted as much to Davis in early February. "We are not in a condition, and never have been, in my opinion, to invade the enemy's country with a prospect of permanent benefit," he wrote, although he added that he hoped, by means of a show of force in East Tennessee or Virginia, to "alarm and embarrass him to some extent, and thus prevent his undertaking anything of magnitude against us."

Davis agreed that the South was limited by necessity to the strategic defensive. Indeed, that had been his policy from the start, pursued in the belief that Europe would intervene if the struggle could be protracted. The difference now lay in the object of such protraction. Foreign intervention was obviously never going to come, but he still hoped for intervention of another kind. In the North, a presidential election would be held in November, and he hoped for intervention by a majority of the voters, who then would have their chance to end the bloodshed by replacing Lincoln with a man who stood for peace. Peace, no matter whether it was achieved in the North or the South, in the field or at the polls, meant victory on the terms the Confederate leader had announced at the outset, saying, "All we ask is to be let alone." In the light of this possibility, the South's task was to add to the war weariness of the North; which meant, above all, that the enemy was to be allowed no more spirit-lifting triumphs — especially none like Vicksburg or Missionary Ridge, which had set all the church bells ringing beyond the Potomac and the Ohio — and that whatever was lost, under pressure of the odds, must not only be minor in value, but must also be paid for in casualties so heavy that the gain would be clearly disproportionate to the cost, particularly in the judgment of those who would be casting their ballots in November.

On the face of it — by contrast, that is, with the two preceding years, each of which had included the added burden of launching an invasion that had failed — this did not appear too difficult a task. In the past calendar year, moreover, while the Federal over-all strength was declining from 918,211 to 860,737 men, that of the Confederates increased from 446,622 to 463,181. This was not only the largest number of men the South had had under arms since the war began; it was also nearly 100,000 more than she had had two years ago, on the eve of her greatest triumphs. However, such encouragement as Davis might have derived from a comparison of these New Year's figures, showing the North-South odds reduced to less than two to one, was short-lived. One month later, Lincoln issued his call for "500,000 more."

That was better than ten times the number Lee had on the Rapidan, covering Richmond, or Johnston had around Dalton, covering Atlanta, and since the loss of either of these cities, in addition to being a strategic disaster for the South, would provide the North with a triumph that would be likely to win Lincoln the election, Davis was faced at once with the problem of how to match this call with one of his own. But the hard truth was that nothing like half that many troops — the number required if the current odds were not to be lengthened intolerably for the savage fighting that would open in the spring — could be raised under the present conscription laws, even though these had been strengthened in December by the passage of legislation that modified exemptions, put an end to the hiring of substitutes, and provided for the replacement of able-bodied men, in noncombatant jobs, with veterans who had been incapacitated by wounds or civilians who previously had been passed over for reasons of health. The bottom of the manpower barrel was not only in sight; it had been scraped practically clean to provide the army with every available male within the conscription age-range of eighteen to forty-five. One possibility, unpleasant to contemplate since it would expose the government more than ever to the charge that it was "robbing the cradle and the grave," would be to extend the range in either or both directions. Another possibility, far more fruitful, was suggested by Pat Cleburne; but it was worse than unpleasant, it was unthinkable. In early January the Irish-born former Helena lawyer prepared and read to his fellow generals in the Army of Tennessee a paper in which he examined the sinking fortunes of the Confederacy and proposed to deal simultaneously with what he conceived to be the two main problems blocking the path to independence: the manpower shortage, which was growing worse with every victory or defeat, and slavery, which he saw as a millstone the nation could no longer afford to carry in its effort to stay afloat on the sea of war. In brief, Cleburne's proposal was that the South emancipate its Negroes — thus making a virtue of necessity, since in his opinion slavery was doomed anyhow — and enlist them in its armies. This would "change the race from a dreaded weakness to a [source] of strength," he declared, and added: "We can do this more effectually than the North can now do, for we can give the Negro not only his own freedom, but that of his wife and child, and can secure it to him in his old home." Moreover, he said, such an action "would remove forever all selfish taint from our cause and place independence above every question of property. The very magnitude of the sacrifice itself, such as no nation has ever voluntarily made before, would appall our enemies . . . and fill our hearts with a pride and singleness of purpose which would clothe us with new strength in battle."

Recovering presently from the shock into which the foreign-born general's views had thrown them, the corps and division commanders were unanimous in their condemnation of the proposal, which they saw as a threat to everything they held dear. "I will not attempt to describe my feelings on being confronted by a project so startling in its character," one wrote in confidence to a friend. He labeled the paper a "monstrous proposition . . . revolting to Southern sentiment, Southern pride, and Southern honor," and predicted that "if this thing is once openly proposed to the army the total disintegration of that army will follow in a fortnight." Advised by Johnston and the others to proceed no further with the matter, Cleburne did not insist that the paper be forwarded, but another general considered it so "incendiary" in character that he took the trouble to get a copy and send it on to Richmond. There the reaction was much the same, apparently, as the one it had provoked in Dalton. Johnston received, before the month was out, a letter from the Secretary of War, expressing "the earnest conviction of the President that the dissemination or even promulgation of such opinions under the present circumstances of the Confederacy, whether in the army or among the people, can be productive only of discouragement, distraction, and dissension." The army commander was instructed to see to "the suppression, not only of the memorial itself, but likewise of all discussion and controversy respecting or growing out of it." Johnston replied that Cleburne, having observed the manner in which it was received, had already "put away his paper," and that he himself had had "no reason since to suppose that it made any impression." In point of fact, the suppression Richmond called for was so effective that nothing further was heard of the document for more than thirty years, when it finally turned up among the posthumous papers of a staff officer. One possible effect it had, however, and that was on Cleburne himself, or in any case on his career. Although Seddon had assured Johnston that "no doubt or mistrust is for a moment entertained of the patriotic intents of the gallant author of the memorial," and though the Arkansan was considered by many to be the best division commander in either army, South or North, he was never assigned any larger duties than those he had at the time he proposed to emancipate the slaves of the South and enlist them in her struggle for independence.

Davis had not been as shocked by the proposal as Seddon's letter seemed to indicate. For one thing, he agreed with the underlying premise that slavery was doomed, no matter who won or lost the war, and had said as much to his wife. What alarmed him was the reaction, the "distraction and dissension," that would follow the release of what one of its hearers had called "this monstrous proposition." Knowing, as he did, how much more violent than the generals the politicians would be in their denunciation of such views — particularly the large slaveholders among them, such as Howell Cobb, who said flatly: "If slaves will make good soldiers, our whole theory of slavery is wrong" — he foresaw that the result would be calamitous in its effect on the fortunes of the Confederacy, which would be so torn internally by any discussion of the issue that, even though the army could be doubled in size by adoption of the plan, there would be nothing left for that army to defend but discord. Even so, Davis did not completely reject the notion. He kept it — much as Lincoln had kept the Emancipation Proclamation — as an ace in the hole, to be played if all else failed.

Meantime he still was faced with the necessity for matching, at least to some degree, his adversary's call for more additional troops than there were at present in all the southern armies. Left with the alternative of extending conscription, he moved to do so in a message to Congress suggesting 1) that all industrial exemptions be abolished and 2) that the upper and lower age-range limits be raised and reduced, respectively, to fifty and seventeen. The first of these two suggestions kicked up the greater furor. Newspaper editors, who feared (groundlessly, as it turned out) that they would lose their printers if the law was strengthened to this extent, protested that freedom of the press was threatened. For others, the fear was more general. A Virginia congressman, for example, asserted that such legislation would "clothe the President with the powers of an autocrat" and invest him with "prerogatives before which those of Napoleon sink into insignificance," while Foote rose up again in his wrath to declare that "Others may vote to extend this man's power for mischief; I hold in contempt him and his whole tribe of servitors and minions." There were, however, enough of the "tribe" — or, in any case, enough of Foote's colleagues of all persuasions who saw the need for keeping the army up to a strength that would enable it to challenge the blue host that would be advancing with the spring — for the proposed measure to be adopted on February 17, the day Congress adjourned. Word went out at once to the conscription agents of the enlargement of the harvest they would be gleaning. No drawing of lots, no "wheels of fortune," such as were used in the North to select candidates for induction, were required in the South. From this time forward, it was simply the task of the agents to enroll or exempt every white male in the Confederacy between the ages of seventeen and fifty.

Davis's reaction to this granting of his request was mixed. Pleased though he was to have the measure passed, and though he himself had asked for what had been given, he was saddened by the widening of the age-range: not by the raising of the upper limit, which brought it within five years of his own age, but by the reduction of the lower limit, which seemed to him a spending of future hopes. The old and the middle-aged could be spared. The young were another matter. The South would have great need, in the years ahead, of all the talent she could muster — as much, perhaps, if she lost the war, as if she won it — yet there was no telling how much of that talent, still undeveloped at seventeen, would be destroyed and left behind, packed into shallow burial trenches on the fields of battles still unfought. It grieved him that the mill of war, as he remarked, was about to "grind the seed corn of the nation."

While the young and the old were thus being gathered in camps of instruction, where they would be converted into material fit for use in chinking what he once had called "our wall of living breasts," Davis gave his attention to strengthening and replacing the men who would lead them. The appointment in early January of George Davis of North Carolina to succeed Attorney General Watts, who had left Richmond the month before to be inaugurated as governor of Alabama, marked the first change in the Cabinet since Seddon took over the War Department, more than a year ago. Little attention was paid to this, for the post entailed few duties; but the same could not be said of two changes that followed, for they were military, and anything that involved the army was always of consuming interest. Before adjourning, Congress had authorized the President to appoint a sixth full general, thus to allow a freer hand to the commander of the Transmississippi, cut off as he was from either the direction or assistance of the central government. Davis's prompt award of the promotion to Kirby Smith, for whom of course it had been intended, was applauded by everyone, in or out of the army, except Longstreet, whose name headed the list of lieutenant generals, on which Smith's had stood second. "A soldier's honor is his all," Old Peter afterwards protested, "and of that they would rob him and degrade him in the eyes of his troops." Piqued at having thus been overleaped — and unhappy as he was anyhow, because of his late repulse at Knoxville and the disaffection that had spread through his corps in its mountainous camps around Greeneville, seventy miles to the east — his first reaction was that "the occasion seemed to demand resignation." But on second thought he decided that this "would have been unsoldierly conduct. Dispassionate judgment suggested, as the proper rounding of the soldier's life, to stay and go down with faithful comrades of long and arduous service."

Painful though the burning was in Longstreet's ample bosom, it was no more than a pinpoint gleam compared to the fires of resentment lighted by the announcement, a few days later, of the second military change. On February 22, the second anniversary of his inauguration as head of the permanent government, Davis summoned Lee to the capital for another conference. There were matters of strategy to be discussed, and something else as well. The Virginian's former post as advisor to the Commander in Chief had been vacant for more than twenty months; now Davis proposed to name Bragg as his successor. This was certain to surprise and dismay a great many people who saw the North Carolinian as the author of most of their present woes, but Davis believed that Bragg's undeniable shortcomings as a field commander — particularly his tendency to convert drawn battles into defeats by retreating, and victories into stalemates by failing to pursue — were not disqualifications for service in an advisory capacity; whereas his equally undeniable virtues, as an administrator and a strategist — his northward march into Kentucky, for example, undertaken on his own initiative at a time of deepest gloom, had reversed the whole course of the war in the western theater, and he had also proved himself (all too often, some would say) a master in the art of conducting tactical withdrawals — would be of great value to the country. Lee agreed, and the appointment was announced two days later, on February 24: "General Braxton Bragg is assigned to duty at the seat of government, and, under the direction of the President, is charged with the conduct of the military operations in the armies of the Confederacy."

Surprise and dismay, private and public, were indeed the reactions to the terrible-tempered general's elevation, coming as it did only one day short of three months since his rout at Missionary Ridge. "No doubt Bragg can give the President valuable counsel," a War Department diarist observed, but in his opinion Davis — whom he described as being "naturally a little oppugnant" — derived "a secret satisfaction in triumphing thus over popular sentiment, which just at this time is much averse to General Bragg." The sharpest attacks, as might have been expected, were launched by the editors of the Richmond *Whig* and the *Examiner*. Both employed irony in their comments, ignoring the advisory nature of Bragg's assignment by pretending to believe that Davis had given his pet general direct command over Lee and Johnston. "When a man fails in an inferior position," the *Whig* declared, "it is natural and charitable to conclude that the failure is due to the inadequacy of the task to his capabilities, and wise to give him a larger sphere for the proper exertion of his abilities." Pollard of the *Examiner* struck with a heavier hand, though his pen was no less sharp. "The judicious and opportune appointment of General Bragg to the post of commander-in-chief of the Confederate armies will be appreciated," he noted wryly, "as an illustration of that strong common sense which forms the basis of the President's character." He managed to sustain this tone for half a column, then dropped it in midsentence: "This happy announcement should enliven the confidence and enthusiasm reviving among the people like a bucket of water poured on a newly kindled grate."

Davis went his way, as he had done from the beginning. "If we succeed we shall hear nothing of these malcontents," he had told his wife three years ago in Montgomery. "If we do not, then I shall be held accountable by friends as well as foes. I will do my best." That was as much his guiding principle now as ever. He believed that Bragg would serve him and the country well in this new assignment, and so far as he was concerned the decision as to whether to use him ended there. "Opposition in any form can only disturb me inasmuch as it may endanger the public welfare," he had said. For all his aristocratic bearing and his apparent indifference to the barbs flung at him by men like Foote and Pollard, which gave rise to the persistent myth that he was deficient in feeling, he trusted the people far more than he did the politicians and journalists who catered to their weaknesses and fears, and he knew only too well the hardness of their lot in this season of lengthening death lists and spiraling inflation. Ten Confederate dollars would buy a yard of calico or a pound of coffee; bacon was $3.50 a pound, butter $4; eggs were $2 a dozen, chickens $6 a pair. Such prices made for meager living, particularly for city dwellers who had no vegetable gardens to tend or harvest. But even these were fortunate, so far at least as food was concerned, in comparison with the soldiers. The daily ration in the Army of Northern Virginia this winter was four ounces of bacon or salt pork and one pint of unbolted cornmeal, and though a private was free to scrounge what he could in his off hours, including wild onions and dandelion greens, his pay of $11 a month would not go far toward the purchase of supplements, even when they were available, which was seldom. Still, there were those who seemed to make out well enough from time to time: as a hungry infantryman, out on a greens hunt, discovered one day when he came upon a group of commissary officers enjoying an al fresco luncheon in the shade of a clump of trees. He approached the fence surrounding the grove, put his head through the palings, and gazed admiringly at the spread of food. "I say, misters," he called to the diners at last, "did any of you ever hearn tell of the battle of Chance'lorsville?"

This irrepressibility, which sustained him in adversity, this overriding sense of the ridiculous, uncramped even by the pangs of hunger, was as much a part of what made the Confederate soldier "terrible in battle" as was the high-throated yell he gave when he went into a charge or the derisive glee with which he tended to receive one, anticipating a yield of well-shod corpses. Davis counted heavily on this spirit to insure the survival of the armies and the nation through the harder times he knew would begin when the present "mud truce" ended. He was too much a military realist not to take into account the lengthening odds, but he included the imponderables in his calculations. To have done otherwise would have been to admit defeat before it came; which was not at all his way. "I cultivate hope and patience," he said, "and trust to the blunders of our enemy and the gallantry of our troops for ultimate success."

★   ★   ★

In the North, as spring drew nearer and some perspective was afforded for a backward look at the season approaching its end, there was the feeling that such minor reverses as Olustee and Okolona, disappointing though they had been at the time, were no true detractions from the significant victories scored at the outset at Rappahannock Bridge and Chattanooga. These were the pattern-setters, the more valid indications of what was to come when winter relaxed its grip and large-scale fighting was resumed. Along with this, there was also the growing belief that the nation had found in Lincoln, despite his occasional military errors, the leader it needed to see it through what remained of its fiery trial. "The President is a man of convictions," *Harper's Weekly* had declared more than a year ago, combining these two impressions. "He has certain profound persuasions and a very clear purpose. He knows what the war sprang from, and upon what ground a permanent peace can be reared. He is cautious, cool, judicial. [While] he knows that great revolutions do not go backward, he is aware that when certain great steps in their prosecution are once taken, there will be loud outcries and apprehension. But the ninth wave touches the point to which the whole sea will presently rise, although the next wave, and the next, should seem to show a falling off."

What *Harper's* had had in mind at the time was the Emancipation Proclamation, but people rereading this now could see that Missionary Ridge had been just such a ninth wave, lapping far up the military shingle, and though "the next wave, and the next," had shown a falling off, the tide would soon be at the full. Or anyhow they could believe they saw this, and they reacted accordingly. During the current interim of comparative inaction, the home-front war had taken on what would be known in the following decade as a Chautauqua aspect, a revival of the waning lyceum movement, which combined the qualities of the camp meeting and the county fair, yet added a sophistication those old-time activities had lacked. They assembled in churches, halls, and theaters to enjoy in mass the heady atmosphere of pending victory. Primarily, such gatherings were militant in tone — meaning abolitionist, for the anti-slavery element had always been the militant wing of the party now in power — with the result that those who attended could feel that they were being strengthened and uplifted at the same time they were being entertained. There was, for example, the Hutchinson family: singers who could electrify an audience with their rendition of Whittier's "Hymn of Liberty," sung to the tune of Luther's *Ein' feste Burg ist unser Gott*.

The thought might be muddled, the rhymes atrocious, but the sweetness of the singers' voice and the fervor of their delivery gave the words a power that swept the hearers along as part of the broad surge toward that same freedom for which blue-clad soldiers were giving their lives, beyond the roll of the horizon:

> *What gives the wheat-field blades of steel?*
> *What points the rebel cannon?*
> *What sets the roaring rabble's heel*
> *On the old star-spangled pennon?*
> *What breaks the oath*
> *Of the men o' the South?*
> *What whets the knife*
> *For the Union's life?*
> *Hark to the answer: Slavery!*

Or there was the Boston lecturer Wendell Phillips, who assured a New York audience of its moral superiority over a foe whose only role in life was to block the march of progress. He pictured the young man of the South, "melted in sensuality, whose face was never lighted up by a purpose since his mother looked into his cradle," and declared that for such men "War is gain. They go out of it, and they sink down." Whipped, they would return "to barrooms, to corner groceries, to chopping straw and calling it politics. [Laughter.] You might think they would go back to their professions. They never had any. You might think they would go back to the mechanic arts. They don't know how to open a jackknife. [Great merriment.] There is nowhere for them to go, unless we send them half a million of emancipated blacks to teach them how to plant cotton." His solution to the problem of how to keep the beaten South from relapsing "into a state of society more cruel than war — whose characteristics are private assassination, burning, stabbing, shooting, poisoning" — lifted the North's grim efforts to the height of a crusade: "We have not only an army to conquer. We have a state of mind to annihilate."

Phillips could always fill a hall, but the star attraction this season, all agreed, was the girl orator Anna E. Dickinson, who had begun her career on the eve of her twentieth birthday, when she lost her job at the mint in her native Philadelphia for accusing McClellan of treason at Ball's Bluff. Since then, she had come far, until now she was hailed alternately as the Joan of Arc and the Portia of the Union. Whether she spoke at the Academy of Music in her home city, at New York's Cooper Union, or at the Music Hall in Boston, the house was certain to be packed with those who came to marvel at the contrast between her virginal appearance — "her features well chiseled, her forehead and upper lip of the Greek proportion, her nostrils thin" — and the "torrent of burning, scathing, lightning eloquence," which she released in what the same reviewer called "wonderfully lengthened sentences uttered without break or pause." Hearing Anna was a dramatic experience not easily forgotten, though what you brought away with you was not so much a remembrance of what she had said as it was of the manner in which she had said it: which was how she affected Henry James, apparently, when he came to portray her, more than twenty years later, as Verena Tarrant. Her hatred of Southerners, especially Jefferson Davis, whom she compared to a hyena, was not so all-consuming that none was left for northern Democrats, who were without exception traitors to the cause of human freedom — as, indeed, were all who were not of the most radical persuasion, including such Republicans as Seward, "the Fox of the White House." She loved applause; it thrilled her, and her style became more forward as her listeners responded; so that her addresses were in a sense a form of intercourse, an exchange of emotions, back and forth across the footlights.

Quite different, but curious too in her effect on those who came to hear and see her, was another platform artist, the former slave Sojourner Truth. Tall and gaunt, utterly black, and close to eighty years of age, she made her appearances in a voluminous, floor-length, long-sleeved dress, a crocheted shawl, and the calico turban or headrag that was practically a badge of office for house servants in the South, particularly children's nurses; which was what she had been, before she won her freedom and came North. Battle Creek was now her home, and she journeyed not only through Michigan, but also through Illinois and Indiana and Ohio, including the Copperhead regions of those states, to plead for the extension of freedom to all her race, north as well as south of the Proclamation line. She spoke in a deep, musical voice, with natural grace and simple dignity, and vended as a side line, to help cover her travel expenses, photographs of herself in her speaking costume; "selling the shadow to sustain the substance," she explained. Her most valued possession, despite her illiteracy, was an autograph book containing the signatures of famous men and women she encountered along her way, one of whom would presently be the Great Emancipator himself. "For Aunty Sojourner Truth, A. Lincoln," he wrote, and she gave him one of her photographs, remarking that she sold them for her livelihood, "but this one is for you, without money and without price." She was much admired, though for the most part as an exotic, and was generally welcome wherever she went, although not always. Once in an Indiana town, for instance, when she was introduced to deliver an antislavery address to a large audience, a local Copperhead rose to repeat the rumor that she was a man, disguised in women's clothes, and to suggest that she permit a committee of ladies to examine her in private. She answered the challenge, then and there, by unfastening her dress and showing the crowd her shrunken, hound's-ear breasts. These had fed many black children, she said, but still more white children had nursed at them. By now the Copperheads — who had come to watch her, or his, exposure as a fraud — were filing out of the auditorium, a look of disgust on their faces, and Sojourner Truth shook her breasts at one of them, inquiring after him in her low contralto: "You want to suck?"

Wendell Phillips, Anna Dickinson, Sojourner Truth were only three among the many who were riding the wave of confidence that the worst was over, that the war could have but one ending now, and that it would come as soon as the South could be made to see what already was apparent in the North. Moreover, there had come with this belief a lessening of discord, not only among the people, but also in the conduct of affairs in Washington. "Never since I have been in public life has there been so little excitement in Congress," Sumner wrote on New Year's Day to a friend in England. "The way seems, at last, open. Nobody doubts the result. The assurance of the future gives calmness." This did not mean that the legislators were willing to take chances. Knowing as they did that the public's blame for any failure would be in ratio to the height of its expectations, they were in fact less willing to take chances than they had been at any time before. And it was for this reason that the bill to revive the grade of lieutenant general had itself been revived: to reduce the likelihood of military blunders at the top. "Give us, Sir, a live general!" a Michigan senator exclaimed in the course of the debate. He meant by this a man who would follow a straight path to victory, "and not let us be dragging along under influences such as have presided over the Army of the Potomac for these last many tedious and weary months; an army oscillating alternately between the Rappahannock and the Potomac, defeated today and hardly successful tomorrow, with its commanders changed almost as frequently as the moon changes its face. Sir, for one I am tired of this, and I tell [the] senators here that the country is getting weary of it."

Some proponents were in favor of naming Grant specifically in the bill, while others believed that this would be setting a dangerous precedent. Besides, Fessenden of Maine rose to ask, to whom could the promotion go if not to Grant? and then went on to point out that the honor would be greater if no name was mentioned, since to do so would be to imply that there had been a choice: "When the President says to us, as he will say unquestionably, 'I consider that General Ulysses S. Grant is the man of all others, from his great services, to be placed in this exalted position,' and when we, as we shall unquestionably, unanimously say 'Ay' to that and confirm him, have we not given him a position such as any man living or who ever lived might well be proud of, without putting his name in our bill originally and thus saying to the President, 'Sir, we cannot trust you to act on this matter unless we hint to you that we want such a man appointed'?" Lengthy and thorough the debate was, but there was never much doubt as to the outcome. Introduced on the first day of February, the measure was passed on the last, and the procedure Fessenden had outlined followed swiftly. Receiving the bill on March 1, Lincoln promptly signed it and named Grant for the honor next day. The Senate confirmed the appointment without delay, and on March 3 the general was ordered by telegraph to report at once to Washington, where he would receive his commission directly from the President.

Lincoln had been disappointed too often, over the course of the past three years, for him to allow his hopes to soar too high. He remembered McDowell and McClellan. He remembered Burnside and Hooker. Above all, he remembered Pope, who had also come East with western laurels on his brow. And there at hand, in case memory failed, was Halleck; Old Brains, too, had arrived from that direction, supposedly with a victory formula in his knapsack, and had wound up "a first-rate clerk." Still, after making all proper discounts, it seemed likely to Lincoln that now at last, in this general who had captured two rebel armies and routed a third, he had found the killer-arithmetician he had been seeking from the start.

✕ 5 ✕

Returning to Vicksburg on the last day of February, Sherman took no time out to recuperate from the rigors of the Meridian campaign, for he found there a week-old dispatch from Grant instructing him to co-operate with Banks in order to assure the success of the expedition up the Teche and the Red, which the Massachusetts general and Halleck had designed to accomplish the return of West Louisiana and East Texas to the Union, along with an estimated half million bales of hoarded cotton. Sherman himself was to rejoin Grant at Chattanooga in time to open the spring drive on Atlanta; he would therefore not participate in the Louisiana-Texas venture, save for making a short-term loan of some 10,000 troops to strengthen it; but he decided to confer in person with Banks, before he himself went back to Tennessee, on the logistical details of getting the reinforcements to him somewhere up the Red. Accordingly, he left Vicksburg that same day aboard the fast packet *Diana*, and arrived in New Orleans two days later, on March 2.

He found Banks in high spirits: not only because of the military outlook, which was considered excellent — Franklin had recovered from his early November repulse at Grand Coteau and had three divisions massed at Opelousas, ready to advance — but also because of political developments in accordance with Lincoln's reconstruction policy, whereby a Union-loyal candidate, one Michael Hahn, a native of Bavaria, had been elected governor of Louisiana by the necessary ten percent of the voters on February 22 and was to be inaugurated at New Orleans on March 5. Sherman's logistical problems were settled within two days, the arrangement being that the Vicksburg reinforcements would join Franklin at Alexandria on March 17 for the farther ascent of the Red, but Banks urged his visitor to stay over another two days for Hahn's inauguration, which he assured him would be well worth the delay. A chorus of one thousand voices, accompanied by all the bands of the army, would perform the "Anvil Chorus" in Lafayette Square, while church bells rang and cannon were fired in unison by electrical devices. Sherman declined the invitation. He had already gone on record as opposing such political procedures, and what was more, he said later, "I regarded all such ceremonies as out of place at a time when it seemed to me every hour and every minute were due to the war." His mind on destruction, not reconstruction, he reboarded the *Diana*, and three days later, on March 6, was back in Vicksburg, to which by now the destroyers of Meridian had returned, well rested from their week-long stay in Canton and the additional spoliation they had accomplished at that place.

Remaining in Vicksburg only long enough to pass on to McPherson the details of the arrangement he had made for reinforcing Banks at Alexandria on St Patrick's Day, Sherman set off upriver again the following morning, impatient to rejoin the troops he had left poised near Chattanooga, waiting alongside those under Thomas and Hooker for Grant to give the nod that would start them slogging southward, over or around Joe Johnston, into and through the heart of Georgia. "Prepare them for my coming," he had told his adjutant, in reference to the hapless civilians in his path, and now at last he was on his way. On the second day out, however, the *Diana* was hailed by a southbound packet which, to the Ohioan's surprise, turned out to have one of Grant's staff captains aboard, charged with the delivery of a highly personal letter his chief had written four days ago, on March 4, at Nashville. "Dear Sherman," it read: "The bill reviving the grade of lieutenant general in the army has become a law, and my name has been sent to the Senate for the place. I now receive orders to report to Washington immediately, in person, which indicates either a confirmation or a likelihood of confirmation. I start in the morning to comply with the order, but I shall say very distinctly on my arrival there that I shall accept no appointment which will require me to make that city my headquarters. This, however, is not what I started out to write about.... What I want is to express my thanks to you and McPherson as the men to whom, above all others, I feel indebted for whatever I have had of success. How far your advice and suggestions have been of assistance, you know. How far your execution of whatever has been given you to do entitles you to the reward I am receiving, you cannot know as well as I do. I feel all the gratitude this letter would express, giving it the most flattering construction. The word *you* I use in the plural, intending it for McPherson also," the letter concluded. "I should write to him, and will some day, but starting in the morning I do not know that I will find time just now. Your friend, U. S. Grant."

Sherman vibrated with three conflicting reactions as he read the first three sentences Grant had written: first, delight that his friend was about to be so honored: second, alarm that he had been summoned to the fleshpots of the capital: third, relief that he did not intend to stay there. However, as the boat continued to push its way slowly upriver against the booming current, the third emotion gave way in turn to the second, which came back even stronger than at first. The fact was, though he idolized his friend and superior, he had never really trusted his judgment in matters concerning his career, and though he admired his simplicity of character, seeing it in the quality that perhaps had contributed most to his success, he was forever supposing that it would get him in trouble, especially if he fell into the hands of wily men who would know how to use him for their sordid ends. "Your reputation as a general is now far above that of any man living, and partisans will maneuver for your influence," he had warned him in a letter written during the Christmas visit to Ohio, at a time when the Grant-for-President drums were beginning to rumble. He counseled him earnestly to "Preserve a plain military character and let others maneuver as they will. You will beat them not only in fame, but in doing good in the closing scenes of this war, when somebody must heal and mend up the breaches." Nowhere were the wily more in evidence than in Washington, and the more he thought about it, the more he was convinced that "Grant would not stand the intrigues of the politicians a week," even though he went there with no intention of remaining any longer than it took to get a third star tacked on each shoulder of his weathered blouse. What was more, Sherman had a mystical feeling about the Mississippi River, which he called "the great artery" of America. "I want to live out here and die here also," he wrote to another friend this week, as the *Diana* chugged upstream, "and I don't care if my grave be like De Soto's in its muddy waters." He seemed to fear that if Grant wandered far from the banks of the big river, his reaction would be like that of Antaeus when he lost contact with the earth.

Accordingly, after two days of fretting and fuming, as the boat drew near Memphis on March 10 he dashed off an answer to Grant's "more than kind and characteristic letter," thanking him in McPherson's name and his own, but protesting: "You do yourself injustice and us too much honor in assigning us so large a share of the merits which have led to your high advancement. ... At Belmont you manifested your traits, neither of us being near. At Donelson also you illustrated your character; I was not near, and General McPherson [was] in too subordinate a capacity to influence you. Until you had won Donelson, I confess I was almost cowed by the terrible array of anarchical elements that presented themselves at every point; but that victory admitted the ray of light which I have followed ever since. ... The chief characteristic in your nature is the simple faith in success you have always manifested, which I can liken to nothing else than the faith a Christian has in his Saviour. This faith gave you victory at Shiloh and Vicksburg. Also, when you have completed your best preparations, you go into battle without hesitation, as at Chattanooga; no doubts, no reserve; and I tell you that it was this that made us act with confidence. I knew wherever I was that you thought of me, and if I got in a tight place you would come — if alive. My only points of doubt were as to your knowledge of grand strategy and of books of science and history, but I confess your commonsense seems to have supplied all this."

Having disposed thus of the disclaimers and the amenities, the volatile redhead passed at once to the main burden of his letter. If Grant stayed East, Sherman almost certainly would be given full charge of the West, and yet, although personally he wanted this above all possible assignments, he was unwilling to secure it at the cost of his friend's ruin, which was what he believed would result from any such arrangement. "Do not stay in Washington," he urged him. "Halleck is better qualified than you are to stand the buffets of intrigue and policy. Come out West; take to yourself the whole Mississippi Valley. Let us make it dead sure, and I tell you the Atlantic slope and Pacific shores will follow its destiny as sure as the limbs of a tree live or die with the main trunk. We have done much; still much remains. . . . For God's sake and your country's sake, come out of Washington! I foretold to General Halleck, before he left Corinth, the inevitable result to him, and I now exhort you to come out West. Here lies the seat of the coming empire, and from the West, when our task is done, we will make short work of Charleston and Richmond and the impoverished coast of the Atlantic."

Within a week he found his warning had been too late. Arriving in Memphis next day he received on March 14 a message from Grant arranging a meeting in Nashville three days later. If Sherman took this as evidence that his chief did not intend to make his headquarters in the East, he soon learned better. In Nashville on the appointed date, invested with the rank of lieutenant general and command of all the armies of the Union, Grant informed him that the Virginia situation required personal attention; he would be returning there to stay, and Sherman would have full charge of the West. However, what with the press of visiting dignitaries, all anxious for a look at a man with three stars on each shoulder, there was so little time for a strategy conference that it was decided the two generals would travel together as far as Cincinnati on Grant's return trip east. That way, it was thought, they could talk on the cars; but the wheels made such a clatter, they finally gave up trying to shout above the racket and fell silent. In Cincinnati they checked into the Burnet House, and there at last, in a private room with a sentry at the door, they spread their maps and got to work.

"Yonder began the campaign," Sherman was to say a quarter century later, standing before the hotel on the occasion of a visit to the Ohio city. "He was to go for Lee and I was to go for Joe Johnston. That was his plan."

LIST OF MAPS

Maps drawn by George Annand, of Darien, Connecticut, from originals by the author. All are oriented north.

BIBLIOGRAPHICAL NOTE

The following bibliographical note was included with the full text of
THE CIVIL WAR: A Narrative—Fredericksburg to Meridian.

In the course of this second of three intended five-year stints, the third
of which will bring me to defeat and victory at Appomattox, my debt
has grown heavier on both sides of the line where the original material
leaves off, but most particularly on the near side of the line. Although
the *Official Records,* supplemented by various other utterances by the
participants, remain the primary source on which this narrative is based,
the hundredth anniversary has enriched the store of comment on that
contemporary evidence with biographies, studies of the conflict as a
whole, examinations of individual campaigns, and general broodings on
the minutiae—all of them, or anyhow nearly all of them, useful to the
now dwindling number of writers and readers who, surviving exposure
to the glut, continue to make that war their main historical concern. So
that, while I agree in essence with Edmund Wilson's observation that "a
day of mourning would be more appropriate," the celebration of the
Centennial has at least been of considerable use to those engaged, as I
am, in the process Robert Penn Warren has referred to as "picking the
scab of our fate."

Not that my previous obligations have not continued. They have
indeed, and they have been enlarged in the process. Kenneth P. Williams,
Douglas Southall Freeman, J. G. Randall, Lloyd Lewis, Stanley F. Horn,
Carl Sandburg, Bell I. Wiley, Bruce Catton, T. Harry Williams, Allan
Nevins, Robert S. Henry, Jay Monaghan, E. Merton Coulter, Clifford
Dowdey, Burton J. Hendrick, Margaret Leech are but a handful among
the many to whom I am indebted as guides through the labyrinth. With-
out them I not only would have missed a great many wonders along the

way, I would surely have been lost amid the intricate turnings and the uproar. Moreover, the debt continued to mount as the exploration proceeded: to Hudson Strode, for instance, for the extension of his *Jefferson Davis* at a time when the need was sore, and to Mark Mayo Boatner for his labor-saving *Civil War Dictionary.* Specific accounts of individual campaigns, lately published to expand or replace the more or less classical versions by Bigelow and others, have been of particular help through this relentless stretch of fighting. Edward J. Stackpole's *Chancellorsville,* for example, was used in conjunction with two recent biographies of the hero of that battle, Frank E. Vandiver's *Mighty Stonewall* and Lenoir Chambers' *Stonewall Jackson.* Similarly, for the Vicksburg campaign, there were Earl Schenck Miers's *The Web of Victory* and Peter F. Walker's *Vicksburg, a People at War,* plus biographies of the two commanders, *Pemberton, Defender of Vicksburg* and *Grant Moves South,* by John C. Pemberton and Bruce Catton. For Gettysburg, there were Clifford Dowdey's *Death of a Nation,* Glenn Tucker's *High Tide at Gettysburg,* and George R. Stewart's *Pickett's Charge.* For the battles around Chattanooga, there were Glenn Tucker's *Chickamauga* and Fairfax Downey's *Storming of the Gateway.* James M. Merrill's *The Rebel Shore,* Fletcher Pratt's *Civil War on Western Waters,* and Clarence E. Macartney's *Mr. Lincoln's Admirals* contributed to the naval actions, as Benjamin P. Thomas' and Harold M. Hyman's *Stanton* did to events in Washington. These too were only a few of the most recent among the many, old and new, which I hope to acknowledge in a complete bibliography at the end of the third volume, *Red River to Appomattox.* Other obligations, of a more personal nature, were carried over from the outset: to the John Simon Guggenheim Memorial Foundation, which extended my fellowship beyond the norm: to the National Park Service, whose guides helped me (as they will you) to get to know so many confusing fields: to the William Alexander Percy Memorial Library, in my home town Greenville, Mississippi, which continued its loan of the *Official Records* and other reference works: to Robert D. Loomis of Random House, who managed to keep both his temper and his enthusiasm beyond unmet deadlines: to Memphis friends, who gave me food and whiskey without demanding payment in the form of talk about the war. To all these I am grateful: and to my wife Gwyn Rainer Foote, who bore with me.

Other, less specific obligations were as heavy. The photographs of Mathew Brady, affording as they do a gritty sense of participation—of being in the presence of the uniformed and frock-coated men who fought the battles and did the thinking, such as it was—gave me as much to go on, for example, as anything mentioned above. Further afield, but no less applicable, Richmond Lattimore's translation of the *Iliad* put a Greekless author in close touch with his model. Indeed, to be complete, the list of my debts would have to be practically endless. Proust I believe has taught me more about the organization of material than even Gibbon has done, and Gibbon taught me much; Mark Twain and Faulkner would also have to be included, for they left their sign on all they touched, and in the course of this exploration of the American scene I often found that they had been there before me. In a quite different sense, I am obligated also to the governors of my native state and the adjoining states of Arkansas and Alabama for helping to lessen my sectional bias by reproducing, in their actions during several of the years that went into the writing of this volume, much that was least admirable in the position my forebears occupied when they stood up to Lincoln. I suppose, or in any case fervently hope, it is true that history never repeats itself, but I know from watching these three gentlemen that it can be terrifying in its approximations, even when the reproduction— deriving, as it does, its scale from the performers—is in miniature.

As for method, it may explain much for me to state that my favorite historian is Tacitus, who dealt mainly with high-placed scoundrels, but that the finest compliment I ever heard paid a historian was tendered by Thomas Hobbes in the foreword to his translation of *The Peloponnesian War,* in which he referred to Thucydides as "one who, though he never digress to read a Lecture, Moral or Political, upon his own Text, nor enter into men's hearts, further than the Actions themselves evidently guide him . . . filleth his Narrations with that choice of matter, and ordereth them with that Judgement, and with such perspicuity and efficacy expresseth himself that (as Plutarch saith) he maketh his Auditor a Spectator. For he setteth his Reader in the Assemblies of the People, and in their Senates, at their debating; in the Streets, at their Seditions; and in the Field, at their Battels." There indeed is something worth aiming at, however far short of attainment we fall.

—S.F.

INDEX

ABOUT THE AUTHOR

Shelby Foote was born in Greenville, Mississippi, and attended school there until he entered the University of North Carolina. During World War II he served in the European theater as a captain of field artillery. In the period after the war he wrote five novels: *Tournament, Follow Me Down, Love in a Dry Season, Shiloh,* and *Jordan County.* He was twice awarded a Guggenheim fellowship. A longtime resident of Memphis, Tennessee, he died in 2005 at the age of 88.